KU-037-703

Operation Typhoon

In October 1941 Hitler launched Operation Typhoon, the German drive to capture Moscow and knock the Soviet Union out of the war. As the last chance to escape the dire implications of a winter campaign, Hitler directed seventy-five German divisions, almost two million men and three of Germany's four panzer groups into the offensive, resulting in huge victories at Viaz'ma and Briansk – among the biggest battles of World War II. David Stahel's groundbreaking new account of Operation Typhoon captures the perspectives of both the German high command and individual soldiers, revealing that, despite success on the battlefield, the wider German war effort was in far greater trouble than is often acknowledged. Germany's hopes of final victory depended on the success of the October offensive but the autumn conditions and the stubborn resistance of the Red Army ensured that the capture of Moscow was anything but certain.

David Stahel is a lecturer at the University of New South Wales in Canberra. His previous publications include *Operation Barbarossa and Germany's Defeat in the East* (2009), *Kiev 1941* (2011) and *Nazi Policy on the Eastern Front, 1941* (2012).

Operation Typhoon

Hitler's March on Moscow, October 1941

David Stahel *(not absolutely at home in English)*

CAMBRIDGE
UNIVERSITY PRESS

CAMBRIDGE UNIVERSITY PRESS
Cambridge, New York, Melbourne, Madrid, Cape Town,
Singapore, São Paulo, Delhi, Mexico City

Cambridge University Press
The Edinburgh Building, Cambridge CB2 8RU, UK

Published in the United States of America by
Cambridge University Press, New York

www.cambridge.org
Information on this title: www.cambridge.org/9781107035126

© David Stahel 2013

This publication is in copyright. Subject to statutory exception
and to the provisions of relevant collective licensing agreements,
no reproduction of any part may take place without
the written permission of Cambridge University Press.

First published 2013

Printed by MPG Printgroup, UK

A catalogue record for this publication is available from the British Library

Library of Congress Cataloguing in Publication data

Stahel, David, 1975–
  Operation Typhoon : Hitler's march on Moscow, October 1941 / David Stahel.
    pages   cm
  Includes bibliographical references.
  ISBN 978-1-107-03512-6 (Hardback)
1. Moscow, Battle of, Moscow, Russia, 1941–1942. 2. Bock, Fedor von, 1880–
1945. 3. Germany. Heer. Heeresgruppe Mitte. 4. Moscow (Russia)–History,
Military–20th century. 5. Viaz'ma (Smolenskaia oblast', Russia)–History,
Military–20th century. 6. Briansk (Russia)–History, Military–20th century.
7. Tula (Russia)–History, Military–20th century. I. Title.
  D764.3.M6S82 2013
  940.54'2173–dc23

                                                                      2012031737

ISBN 978-1-107-03512-6 Hardback

Cambridge University Press has no responsibility for the persistence or
accuracy of URLs for external or third-party internet websites referred to
in this publication, and does not guarantee that any content on such
websites is, or will remain, accurate or appropriate.

940.544
St130

CONTENTS

ILLUSTRATIONS

MAPS

TABLES

ACKNOWLEDGEMENTS

In the summer of 1994 a forest fire swept through the former First World War battlefields on the Gallipoli peninsula in Turkey. In November and December of that year I was a first-year undergraduate who had earned a placement with the University of Istanbul planting new trees there as part of a reforestation project. In addition to large numbers of Turkish students, the project included small contingents from each of the participating First World War nations. The camp site was set up and maintained by the Turkish army and I was assigned to a large tent with thirty-seven Turkish and two German students. Our job was to work on the former battlefields clearing the burned debris, tilling the earth and planting new saplings. As I had grown up in Australia these were the first battlefields I had ever seen and they were to leave their mark. The horrors of war were an unmistakable part of the experience, but reinforced by the fact that it was all shared with former enemies.

Eighteen years later my old tent mate from Gallipoli, Jakob Graichen, and his wife Mariana Díaz have come to be among my closest friends and, as I am a teacher and historian working in Germany, they have been a source of invaluable assistance in support of my historical research. This book is dedicated to them.

As with my other works on 1941 this study has benefited from the input of a number of scholars in the field. I should like to thank Dr Alex J. Kay and Dr Jeff Rutherford who collaborated with me on another project that provided many insights into the current work as well as bringing a measure of welcome relief during long hours of research and writing. Alex and Jeff also provided much invaluable commentary on my draft manuscript for which I am most grateful. My research trips to Freiburg often coincided with visits by Dr Adrian Wettstein, whose knowledge of the Wehrmacht's structures and weaponry is, in my experience, unsurpassed. I was most grateful for his company and prompt replies to all my subsequent requests. Professor Robert Citino identified some of my manuscript's early weaknesses and helped shape improvements. His support is especially appreciated. I should also like to thank Dr Eleanor Hancock for her meticulous commentary on my manuscript. Since my first years of post-graduate study Dr Hancock has been a constant source of support and good ideas. For so many favours over the years I owe her a special degree of thanks.

On the Russian/Soviet side of my research I have been well served by a number of experts who took the time to reply to my e-mails or read sections of my draft. Dr Alexander Hill and Yan Mann read my manuscript, advised me on matters of Soviet history and helped with some referencing. Professor David Stone saved me from some glaring oversights in an early draft of my first chapter and Colonel David Glantz kindly allowed the reproduction of maps from his private collection. To all I extend my sincere gratitude.

I also wish to thank Aleks Polianichko for some Russian–English translations, Min-ku Chung for technical support and Verena Graichen for assisting with my maps. Michael Kellner and Rainer Graichen offered me the use of photographs from their grandfather and father respectively, who each served on the eastern front in 1941. I am also indebted to Chrisie Rotter, an art historian and accomplished artist in her own right, who agreed to the reproduction of an original, and carefully researched, depiction of Friedrich Barbarossa. Last, but by no means least, my thanks go to my editor Michael Watson, his assistant Chloe Howell, Karen Anderson Howes and all the staff at Cambridge University Press who have had a hand in this as well as my past books. Their assistance and professionalism have been exemplary.

GLOSSARY

BA-MA	Bundesarchiv-Militärarchiv (German Military Archive)
CSIR	Corpo di Sedizione Italiano in Russia (Italian Expeditionary Corps in Russia)
'Das Reich'	2nd SS Division
Einsatzgruppen	'action groups' of the SD and Security Police, used mainly for mass killings
Eisenbahntruppe	railroad troops
Feindbild	concept of the enemy
Generalplan Ost	General Plan East
'Grossdeutschland'	'Greater Germany' Infantry Regiment
Grosstransportraum	'large transport area'. Referring to the transport regiment responsible for bridging the gap between front-line divisions and railheads
Kampfgruppe	battle group
KTB	Kriegstagebuch (war diary)
Landser	German infantry man
Lebensraum	living space
Luftwaffe	German Air Force
LVF	Légion des Volontaires Français contre le Bolchevisme (Legion of French Volunteers Against Bolshevism)
MPT	Museumsstiftung Post und Telekommunikation (Museum Foundation Post and Telecommunications)

NCO	non-commissioned officer
NKVD	Narodnyi Komissariat Vnutrennykh Del (People's Commissariat for Internal Affairs)
OKH	Oberkommando des Heeres (High Command of the Army)
OKW	Oberkommando der Wehrmacht (High Command of the Armed Forces)
Ostheer	Eastern Army
POW	prisoner of war
Pz. Div.	Panzer Division
rasputitsa	'quagmire season'; refers to the biannual difficulties caused by heavy rains or melting snow in Russia, Belarus and Ukraine.
RSHA	Reichssicherheitshauptamt (Reich Main Security Office)
SD	Sicherheitsdienst (Security Service)
Sondermeldungen	special news bulletins
SS	Schutzstaffel (Protection Echelon)
Stavka	Soviet high command
UK	United Kingdom
USA	United States of America
USSR	Union of Soviet Socialist Republics
Vernichtungskrieg	war of annihilation
Wehrmacht	German Armed Forces

TABLES OF MILITARY RANKS AND ARMY STRUCTURES

Table of equivalent ranks

German army/ Luftwaffe	Translation used in this study	Equivalent US army rank
Officer ranks		
Generalfeldmarschall	Field Marshal	General of the Army
Generaloberst	Colonel-General	General
General	General	Lieutenant General
der Infanterie	of Infantry	
der Artillerie	of Artillery	
der Flakartillerie	of Flak Artillery	
der Flieger	of Aviation	
der Kavallerie	of Cavalry	
der Luftwaffe	of the Luftwaffe	
der Panzertruppe	of Panzer Troops	
der Pioniere	of Engineers	
Generalleutnant	Lieutenant-General	Major General
Generalmajor	Major-General	Brigadier General
Oberst	Colonel	Colonel
Oberstleutnant	Lieutenant-Colonel	Lieutenant Colonel
Major	Major	Major
Hauptmann	Captain	Captain
Oberleutnant	1st Lieutenant	1st Lieutenant
Leutnant	Lieutenant	2nd Lieutenant
Enlisted ranks		
Stabsfeldwebel	Master Sergeant	Master Sergeant
Oberfeldwebel	Technical Sergeant	Technical Sergeant
Feldwebel	Staff Sergeant	Staff Sergeant
Unterfeldwebel	Sergeant	Sergeant

(*cont.*)

German army/ Luftwaffe	Translation used in this study	Equivalent US army rank
Unteroffizier	Corporal	Corporal
Gefreiter	Private	Private 1st Class
Soldat	Private	Private 2nd Class

Source: Karl-Heinz Frieser, *The Blitzkrieg Legend. The 1940 Campaign in the West* (Annapolis, 2005) p. 355.

Structure and size of the German army

Germany army formation	English translation	Number of subordinate units	Average number of personnel[a]
Heeresgruppe	Army Group	Two or more armies	100,000 to more than a million
Armee	Army	Two or more corps	60,000–250,000
Korps	Corps	Two or more divisions	40,000–70,000
Division	Division	Two or more brigades	12,000–18,000
Brigade	Brigade	Two or more regiments	5,000–7,000
Regiment	Regiment	Two or more battalions	2,000–6,000
Bataillon	Battalion	Two or more companies	500–1,000
Kompanie	Company	Two or more platoons	100–200
Zug	Platoon		30–40

Note: [a] Wide variations of these figures occurred, especially after 1941.
Source: Author's own records.

INTRODUCTION

The launch of Operation Typhoon heralded the opening of one of the biggest German offensives of World War II. Indeed, it is surpassed in scale only by the German operations to invade France and the Low Countries in May 1940 (Case Yellow) and the Soviet Union itself in June 1941 (Operation Barbarossa). Although the fighting on the eastern front is arguably best known for Hitler's 1942 offensive to reach and conquer the oil fields of southern Russia (Case Blue), culminating in the battle for Stalingrad, Army Group South's 1942 summer offensive involved only half the number of German troops employed for Operation Typhoon. Likewise, the German summer offensive at Kursk in July 1943 saw some three-quarters of a million German troops engaged, which also falls well short of Typhoon's proportions. While the German operations to invade France and the Soviet Union were sizeably larger in scale (each involving the commitment of more than three million German troops), command in the field was split between three theatre commanders. Operation Typhoon, on the other hand, was directed by Field Marshal Fedor von Bock alone, making it the largest German field command of the war, with almost two million men taking orders from a single commander.

At the start of October 1941 Germany's war against the Soviet Union had been in progress for more than three months. They were by far the bloodiest three months of Hitler's war to date with 185,000 Germans dead[1] and many times that number of Soviet soldiers killed.[2] Hitler was desperately seeking an end to his war in the east, and to achieve this he and his generals settled on a plan for a massive new offensive in the centre of the front to seize Moscow. In order to achieve this, Army Group Centre, the largest of the three German army groups on the eastern front, was reinforced to some 1.9 million German soldiers and would engage the 1.25 million Soviet troops of the Reserve, Western and Briansk Fronts. The resulting battles at Viaz'ma and Briansk were to become some of the largest in Germany's four-year war against the Soviet Union. The new German offensive, codenamed Operation Typhoon, aimed to tear a massive hole in the centre of the Soviet front, eliminate the bulk of the Red Army before Moscow, seize control of the Soviet capital and force an end to major operations on the eastern front before the onset of winter. For this purpose the Army High Command (Oberkommando des Heeres – OKH), which directed operations on the eastern front, ordered a major reorganisation of the *Ostheer* (Eastern Army) to provide forces for the new offensive. Army Group Centre was to receive the highest concentration of panzer, motorised and infantry divisions ever assembled by Nazi Germany. In total Bock's army group took command of seventy-five divisions, which included some forty-seven infantry and fourteen panzer divisions. On 2 October, Operation Typhoon's designated start date,[3] more than 1,500 panzers and 1,000 aircraft would combine for a new blitz-style offensive that was intended to overwhelm the Soviet front and allow a rapid exploitation into the Soviet rear. Not surprisingly, engaging more than a million Soviet troops would necessitate battles of immense scale, and there could be no guarantees of the outcome. Even victory on the battlefield would by no means lead to an end of hostilities. As the Germans had seen time and again since June 1941 there was a wide gulf between operational success and strategic triumph. Operation Typhoon could not be just another extension of the German front netting another bag of Soviet prisoners; the operation had to create the conditions for a definitive victory in the east and, accordingly, the OKH concentrated everything it could spare for one vast final offensive.

If there is one aspect to Germany's war which I have sought to illuminate in my previous books,[4] it is the difficulties that were involved in the invasion of the Soviet Union. Far from waging a seamless blitzkrieg wreaking havoc on the Red Army, the German panzer groups in the conduct of their advance suffered debilitating losses, which, in the first three months of the campaign, had already undercut Germany's whole war effort. Yet the wide disparity in opposing losses between the Wehrmacht and the Red Army blinded the German command to anything but the most optimistic assessments of the war. As Germany's propaganda minister, Joseph Goebbels, noted on 3 October: 'On the opposing side there is an optimism regarding the military developments on the eastern front, which is utterly inexplicable.'[5] However, General Wilhelm Groener, who helped direct the German occupation of Ukraine in 1918, had warned against precisely such complacency when campaigning in the east. According to Groener: 'Anyone who wants to grasp the strategic nature of the eastern theatre of war must not overlook historical recollections. Beside the gate of the vast lowland between the Vistula and the Urals, which is the home of one state and one people, stands the warning figure of Napoleon, whose fate should implant in anyone who attacks Russia a sense of horror and foreboding.'[6] Historical parallels were one thing, but in the darkest days of October 1941, when Stalin confronted the prospect of losing the Soviet capital, Marshal Georgi Zhukov remained adamant that the Red Army could outdo even Alexander I in 1812 and defend Moscow against foreign seizure. Nor was Zhukov just telling Stalin what he wanted to hear. The Soviet dictator was clearly agitated and emphasised his desire for the truth in whatever form that might take. As Zhukov recounted Stalin's questioning: 'Are you sure that we will hold Moscow? I ask you about this with a pain in my soul. Tell me truthfully, as a communist.' Zhukov's answer was blunt and unequivocal, which was altogether in line with his uncompromising nature. 'We will, without fail, hold Moscow.'[7] Of course, Zhukov's assurance was by no means infallible, and Moscow continued to be confronted by a very clear and present danger, but Zhukov had one considerable advantage. As he had already learned in his defence of Leningrad, to beat the Germans he did not have to destroy an enemy force or advance his front to a distant objective; in the autumn of 1941 he needed only to prevent the Germans from obtaining their prize and thereby secure a victory by default. This was of course no straightforward task, but with the entire Moscow region rapidly transforming into a fortified military district Bock was always going to face a bloody battle, and time was not on his side in the worsening autumn conditions.

The one thing that did count overwhelmingly in Bock's favour was the professionalism of his forces. In 1941 the Wehrmacht was second to none and there was little immediate pressure which Britain could exert on Germany to help counter the blow Bock was about to deliver.[8] Yet, as Army Group Centre experienced at Minsk, Smolensk and Kiev, even successful offensives could prove remarkably costly, and none of these battles had induced the much sought-after peace dividend or capitulation from the Soviet government. Meanwhile, the longer the war lasted the more eroded the elite German panzer forces became and the more the front settled down into static positional warfare. Operation Typhoon was therefore a final effort aimed at breaking the looming danger of a stalemate and avoiding the uncertainty of a winter campaign. Capturing Moscow and ending the war in the east was always going to be a tall order, and yet, more than at any other time in 1941, the strategic situation in mid October convinced the German high command that they were set for victory against the Soviet Union. Even the Soviet government was planning for the loss of Moscow and nominated a new capital some 800 kilometres further east. Thus, for all the difficulties of the panzer groups, Hitler's new October offensive appeared to reinvigorate Germany's war in the east and, in the view of the German command, brought the *Ostheer* closer than ever to outright victory.

There can be no question that Bock's reinforced army group constituted a potent force at the beginning of October but, for all the power concentrated in the centre of the eastern front, Germany's Typhoon was on course to hit Russia's own weather storm, the so-called *rasputitsa*.[9] Throughout the summer, even periodic downpours had played havoc with German supply and transportation, forcing brief pauses in German operations. Now, however, the Germans were to encounter something entirely new. The strangling mud of the *rasputitsa* not only confronted Bock's motorised columns with an unprecedented topographical challenge, but also denied his panzer forces their much prized 'shock' and rapid manoeuvre. Yet, while the seasonal difficulties in the autumn period are the best-known impediment to Bock's autumn offensive, they were by no means the only one. Indeed, German military files make clear that the *rasputitsa* accounts for only part of the difficulties Operation Typhoon would confront and that alone it would most likely not have stopped the German offensive from maintaining its advance, albeit at a slower pace. The fact was that even after the initial battles at Viaz'ma and Briansk, Army Group Centre was still bitterly opposed by Soviet forces on the Mozhaisk line, around Kalinin and on the approaches to Tula. The road to Moscow was never open and the Red Army was never absent. Clearly, therefore, the *rasputitsa* was not the only factor which stood in the way of the German high command's plans in October 1941.

For all that Bock was able to array against the Soviet capital and for all the professionalism of his forces, on the opposing side the Soviets met the Germans with fanatical levels of determination and their trademark resilience in the face of daunting odds. The few western observers who experienced the war from within Moscow gained a sense of the totality with which the Soviet regime approached the battle. As the BBC correspondent Alexander Werth noted:

> All the military talent – discovered and tested in the first battles of the war and, in some cases, before that in the Far East – was assembled, all available reserves were thrown into battle, including some crack divisions from Central Asia and the Far East, a measure made possible by the non-aggression pact concluded with the Japanese in 1939.[10]
>
> Whatever bad memories and reservations the generals may have had, Stalin had become the indispensable unifying factor in the *patrie-en-danger* atmosphere of October–November 1941.[11]

The American journalist Henry Cassidy also took account of the historic events underway and concluded that the battle for Moscow would be hard fought. Recalling his experiences in the Soviet capital during the heady days of October 1941 Cassidy wrote: 'Every newspaper man who witnesses a momentous occasion of this kind tries to think of the one phrase which tells the full, thrilling story in a few words, the "lead" to the dispatch. While I was watching the Germans occupy Paris, I was tormented for days by such a search, even though I could send nothing. The best I could do was: "Paris fell like a lady." Now, the best I could find was: "Moscow stood up and fought like a man."'[12] Whatever one may conclude about the Soviet Union's defeats in 1941, many at the time, including numerous German officers, commented on the remarkable ability of Stalin's state to take so many losses while at the same time growing the size of the Red Army. Indeed in the two-month period from early October to early December the Soviet high command transferred enough men to the central part of the front to staff no fewer than ninety-nine new divisions.[13] As Cassidy concluded: 'The Soviet Union made its own miracles.'[14]

Others were already taking their analysis of the emerging Soviet strength to its furthest logical conclusion and predicting not only a German defeat, but in the process a new Soviet empire covering Eastern Europe. A letter by Geoffrey M. Wilson, the third secretary of the British Embassy in Moscow from 1940 to 1942, written between

30 September and 2 October 1941, set out his fears for the future with uncanny foresight:

> There is an alliance of necessity but it doesn't go much beyond that, if at all ... One of my nightmares is that if the Russian armies are eventually successful as I think they will be, they will end this war by marching to Berlin and occupying all points of Europe east. And then how are we going to get them out? ... What it all boils down to is the fact that the Russians are being led to believe that this is primarily their war and that we are quite incidental in it. Up to a point, of course, they are right, in that their sacrifices are much heavier than ours have ever been, but the fact remains that unless there is a change, there is going to be a most unholy row between us when the thing is over, and the final atmosphere of suspicion and mistrust will be far worse at the end than it was two or three years ago.[15]

Clearly the doomsday predictions of Moscow's impending fall and the end of the Soviet Union, which later also framed the events of the autumn for a generation of historians,[16] were not shared by all the participants at the time. Indeed, the view expressed by the German command at the time suggested that Soviet strength was only an illusion: it was a paper-tiger army that boasted a large number of formations with very little real value. This was the reassurance offered by the Army quartermaster-general, Major-General Eduard Wagner, in a letter he wrote on 29 September:

> At the same time they count once again, or still, numerous Russian divisions, knowing full well that they can only be rubbish and yet again replenished formations – regiments with a machine gun and untrained replacements. No wonder that we and the troops are impatiently waiting for the moment when [Army Group] Centre can go ahead, which means that everything is finished.[17]

Far from having any concerns at the Red Army's incredible resilience or the contrasting fatigue of the *Ostheer*, it was the German command's unchecked arrogance, even in the face of so much resistance, that propagated its own illusions. Lieutenant-General Friedrich Paulus, the Senior Quartermaster I at the OKH, noted after the war that by the start of the autumn of 1941 it was commonly believed that the Soviet state had been weakened 'to a fatal degree'. Not only this, Paulus concluded: 'It was felt therefore that it was still possible, with one more final effort, to achieve our 1941 objectives, albeit somewhat later than was originally envisaged.'[18] Such were the polarising extremes of the eastern campaign in the autumn of 1941 that at the same time, in the same war, well-placed figures were drawing diametrically contrasting conclusions. While the impending defeat of the Soviet Union was contemplated by some, others were already warning of a Soviet empire challenging western interests in a post-war world. Assessing events at the end of October, two of the most prominent historians of the war in the east, David Glantz and Jonathan House, drew this metaphor: 'the Wehrmacht and the Red Army resembled two punch drunk boxers, staying precariously on their feet but rapidly losing the power to hurt each other. Like prizefighters with swollen eyes, they were unable to see their opponents with sufficient clarity to judge their relative endurance.'[19] By assessing Army Group Centre's autumn offensive anew and in greater depth, I hope to penetrate the fog of distortions and gain a better insight into the state of Germany's war in October 1941.

Operation Typhoon proceeded in two phases: the first from 2 October until the end of the month and then, after a short pause while the sunken roads were left to freeze and supplies were brought up, in a subsequent offensive undertaken in the second half of November and running to 5 December. While both offensives are important, they are so for different reasons. One might conclude that the German October offensive is important for the devastating impact it had on the Red Army, while Bock's November offensive is more noteworthy for the dire ramifications it held for the Germans forces themselves. Ultimately, each offensive belongs to Army Group Centre's Operation Typhoon, but they remain separate and distinct. The October fighting included two of Germany's most important battles of World War II and, as they were utterly unprepared for what they were to encounter, the most gruelling conditions the Wehrmacht had faced so far. Such events have typically been condensed into the wider narrative of the German autumn offensive but, with Army Group Centre attacking with three panzer groups and nearly two million men, the events would seem to demand more comprehensive treatment. Indeed, it is often only by digging deeper into the records that we are able to question standard interpretations, while giving a voice to commanders and war diaries seemingly too lowly or insignificant for more superficial histories. Accordingly, this book will look at the month of October with another book to follow and take on the subsequent operations from November to early December.

As with my past books, the focus here will be on the panzer and motorised formations, which made up the cutting edge of Army Group Centre's offensive operations. My research utilises war diaries, daily orders and battle reports from the command staff at Army Group Centre as well as each of the three panzer groups, most of the available panzer corps and panzer divisions. Widespread use has also been made of wartime diaries and private correspondence among Army Group Centre's commanders and men at the front. The hope is to reflect the experience of war from both ends of the spectrum. Although I do not exclude the Soviet side of the fighting my focus is predominantly on the German experience of the war. I will start my study with a certain historical contextualisation of the Russian and Soviet theatre of war and how this has impacted centuries of military engagements prior to 1941. The attempt is to direct greater attention to the environment in which Russian wars have been fought and consider how this later departed from or reinforced the operational problems of the more technically advanced Wehrmacht.

While this study is preceded by two previous volumes dealing with German operations through Belarus and central Russia and into Ukraine, no prior knowledge of those campaigns and battles is assumed for the current study. Bock's order of battle changed significantly for the autumn offensive with the addition of Colonel-General Erich Hoepner's Panzer Group 4 (transferred from Army Group North) as well as Lieutenant-General Werner Kempf's XXXXVIII Panzer Corps[20] (transferred from Panzer Group 1). There was also an additional infantry corps and a security division (transferred from the Sixth Army and Army Group South's rear area) as well as two full panzer divisions newly deployed to the east for Operation Typhoon. In total Bock's strength rose by more than 600,000 men, which made his force nearly 50 per cent stronger than on 22 June 1941 (the first day of the war).[21] Bock now stood at the head of the largest military force Nazi Germany would ever assemble under one commander. His task, however, was equally demanding. As one of Bock's soldiers wrote shortly before the offensive began, Operation Typhoon would have to 'crack the nut' and, observing the forces assembled around him, he concluded, 'it will be some crack'.[22]

1 CONTEXTUALISING BARBAROSSA

Hunting the Bear – campaigning in the Russian theatre

While there are countless conceptual topics of relevance to our understanding of Germany's war in the east, Carl von Clausewitz's (1780–1831) interpretation of 'the country' (or countryside) as a strategic factor in the conduct of war is probably the most efficient method of linking many related problems inherent to Hitler's *Ostheer* in 1941. 'The country' is dealt with in *On War*'s Book I, 'On the Nature of War'. Clausewitz writes:

> The country – its physical features and population – is more than just the source of all armed forces proper; it is in itself an integral element among the factors at work in war – though only that part which is the actual theatre of operations or has a notable influence on it.
>
> It is possible, no doubt, to use all mobile fighting forces simultaneously; but with fortresses, rivers, mountains, inhabitants, and so forth, that cannot be done; not, in short, with the country as a whole, unless it is so small that the opening action of the war completely engulfs it …
>
> In many cases, the proportion of the means of resistance that cannot immediately be brought to bear is much higher than might at first be thought. Even when great strength had been expended on the first decision and the balance has been upset, equilibrium can be restored.[1]

It is important to remember that any discussion of these problems cannot be rendered valid or invalid based simply on any particular historical example; after all, even if Clausewitz is correct, there may well be exceptions to the rule. In other words, simply applying Clausewitz to the German experiences in 1941 is not enough to show a pattern of experience which proves or disproves the problems of the Russian theatre. Thus, in order to gain a more dependable sample, a measure of historical digression is required.

In 1632 Patriarch Filaret, the de facto ruler[2] of Muscovy,[3] started what subsequently became known as 'the Smolensk War' (1632–1634) against the Polish-Lithuanian Commonwealth. Filaret amassed a large army and in October drove it towards his objective at Smolensk. The resulting siege was long and ultimately unsuccessful, resulting in defeat for Muscovy and forcing the vanquished Russians to cede a number of towns as well as pay a substantial war indemnity. In the early seventeenth century the new Romanov dynasty, which would eventually take Russia to great-power status, was still in its infant years. The Smolensk War was its first large-scale attempt at warfare against a foreign power, but it floundered because Muscovy could neither deliver a rapid, knock-out blow nor sustain a longer campaign against the mobilised forces of King Wladyslaw IV's kingdom. According to William C. Fuller Jr, Muscovy's failure was not, however, due to the usual explanation of its backwardness and lack of modern means. On the contrary, Muscovy's military command, technology, tactics and operations were all on a par with their Polish-Lithuanian opponents. Instead, Fuller highlights what he calls 'endurance' factors as the real cause of Muscovy's defeat. This pertains to matters of logistics and transport; finance; training; and reinforcement. The east European theatre simply demanded much more from an army in the field. The increased distances meant longer campaigns, adding to monetary costs and placing extraordinary demands on the ability to sustain an army in the field. A lack of supplies in turn affected the health of the men and horses, making constant reinforcements necessary.

In the seventeenth century the vast spaces of the east had a much lower population density, all but preventing the west European practice of armies living off the land. Moreover, Muscovy's lands were not very fertile, so yields remained low. Transportation on the basic road system was largely limited to the warmer months, rendering a major military expedition in October inexpedient, especially with the addition of heavy siege guns. While Patriarch Filaret had built up a large war chest for the campaign, the absence of a standing army meant taking thousands of men out of Muscovy's economy, converting them from financial assets to financial liabilities. Muscovy's treasury therefore had to absorb massive increases in cost with less revenue. Furthermore, the costs of the army began long before the war even started because the recruits had to be gathered and trained months in advance. The reinforcement of the army was another major problem because Filaret attempted to achieve victory by an all-out effort at the beginning of the war to seize Smolensk. There was no thought given to a longer campaign and therefore no further recruitment drives, no withheld cadres for future formations, and no stocks of arms to equip additional soldiers.[4] Thus, when Wladyslaw's superior forces finally arrived at Smolensk Muscovy's army was very much on its own.

The Smolensk War was not to be the only Muscovite war in the seventeenth century that highlighted these problems of endurance,[5] but at least they resulted in a slowly evolving realisation that imported western methods of warfare, while still largely valid and useful, required significant adaptation in the east. A more pragmatic approach to Russia's strategic/military problems was undertaken by Tsar Peter I (1672–1725).[6] His victory in the Great Northern War (1700–1721) assured Russia a place among the large powers of Europe, but the war was very long and included Russian defeats as well as periods of great crisis.[7] When King Charles XII of Sweden launched his invasion of Russia from Poland in 1708 Peter quickly recognised that his forces were unequal to a direct encounter with the better-trained and more numerous Swedish army. Here for the first time Peter understood that Russia's long roads and desolate landscape not only acted to restrain the outward projection of Moscow's power, but also served in the same manner as a defensive agent. Peter therefore advocated retreat combined with a scorched-earth policy so that, in Peter's words, the Swedish 'will not find a thing anywhere'.[8] Charles reasoned that he could gain plentiful supplies by diverting his army into Ukraine for the winter before continuing his campaign in 1709. Yet the Swedish army shed men at an alarming rate as fever, dysentery, cold and hunger depleted the ranks. Charles's army did, however, survive the winter, but it was now greatly outnumbered by the Russians and subsequently defeated at the battle of Poltava in June 1709.[9]

Observing Charles's disastrous campaign Peter had had a first-hand lesson in the dangers of large-scale operations far from one's own sources of supply and replenishment. This, however, did not make solutions to such issues any easier to come by, and in Peter's new war with the Ottoman Empire (1710–1711) the same hubris that had doomed Charles XII ensnared Peter. Leading an army of just 40,000 men all the way to the distant Principality of Moldavia, Peter engaged 130,000 Turks in the Prut River Campaign. Man for man, Peter's army was much better but, vastly outnumbered and soon cut off from Russia (just as Charles had been outnumbered and cut off from Sweden), Peter was forced to accept the sultan's humiliating terms.[10] It was the same lesson from the other end of the spectrum, which at least brought into sharp contrast the problems created by the vast and inhospitable eastern theatre.

During the remainder of the eighteenth century the Russians made remarkable strides towards adapting successful warfare to the barren lands of the east. Power projection was built on an extensive network of roads leading to well-stocked and fortified towns, which helped facilitate the steady extension of Russian military assets in all directions from Moscow. If the Russian empire was attacked these strong points could be defended, forcing time-delaying sieges or leaving Russian strongholds in an invaders' rear. On the other hand, if an attacking force was too great, the Russians could adopt a more radical solution. If they resorted to Peter's scorched-earth policy, they could strip the land of both shelter and supplies, thereby denying an invader the necessary resources to sustain a long drive into the Russian interior.

To garrison its growing empire as well as provide contingents to far-off European conflicts, Russian armies had to be transported distances almost unimaginable to other European powers. During the War of the Polish Succession (1733–1738) a Russian army of 20,000 men marched first to Poland and then, in order to aid Austria against the French, continued in 1735 to Heidelberg, some 2,500 kilometres from Moscow.[11] Here the combined Austro-Russian force successfully defeated the French at the battle of Clausen. The endurance factors so evidently lacking in the Smolensk War and the Prut River Campaign had been replaced by a dynamic system of power projection. Nor was it just Russia's ability to sustain large armies over desolate territory and deliver them in fighting condition to distant battlefields. Peter I brought about many modernising reforms within the Russian army, which later tsars built upon throughout the rest of the eighteenth century.[12] In the Seven Years' War (1756–1763) Russian troops invaded East Prussia and fought with distinction even against a Prussian army that many regarded as the best in Europe at that time. They fought the Prussian King Frederick II[13] to a bloody standstill at the battle of Zorndorf (1758) and later dealt him one of the greatest defeats of his career, together with a smaller Austrian army, at the battle of Künersdorf (1759).[14] Tsarina Catherine II[15] also oversaw highly successful campaigns against the considerable numerical superiority of the Turkish Ottoman Empire in the Russo-Turkish Wars of 1768–1774 and 1787–1792.[16]

While Russian military power was in the ascendancy for much of the eighteenth century, the French revolutionary and Napoleonic wars clearly established France as the greatest military power in Europe by the early nineteenth century. Russia's efforts to resist Napoleon's dominance of the continent were crushed, together with their Austrian allies, at the battle of Austerlitz in 1805 and, after a further decisive defeat at the battle of Friedland in 1807, Tsar Alexander I signed the treaty of Tilsit, allying himself to his former French enemy. By 1812 the alliance had soured and Napoleon opted to invade Russia, believing he could quickly defeat the Russian army and then dictate to Alexander new and even more favourable terms. Both Alexander and the commander of his main army (the First Army), Field Marshal Michael Andreas Barclay de Tolly, knew that engaging Napoleon at the head of his Grande Armée offered little chance of success. Accordingly, the two resolved to undertake a series of withdrawals, drawing Napoleon into the depths of Russia, while adopting a scorched-earth policy to deny the huge French army even a basic level of sustenance. This is not to suggest that the Russian strategy at the start of the 1812 campaign was always unified, because Alexander I initially failed to appoint a single commander-in-chief governing his three armies.[17] Indeed, on 19 July 1812 Alexander I wrote to General Petr Bagration, the more impetuous commander of the Russian Second Army, of the wisdom of his retreat:

> Don't forget that we are still opposed by superior numbers at every point and for this reason we need to be cautious and not deprive ourselves of the means to carry on an effective campaign by risking all on one day. Our entire goal must be directed towards gaining time and drawing out the war as long as possible. Only by this means can we have the chance of defeating so strong an enemy who has mobilised the military resources of all Europe.[18]

Nevertheless, Alexander recognised that withdrawal was no replacement for an eventual encounter with Napoleon, and Russian strategy in the summer of 1812 was much complicated by discussions of where and when to engage the French. In the meantime the long march, harsh climate and lack of supplies soon took their toll on Napoleon's army and the ranks quickly thinned from disease, exhaustion, dehydration, malnutrition and desertion. Likewise, the lack of fodder and water, combined with the high temperatures and the constant advance, devastated the vital horse population. Napoleon's advance was not without its victories, first at Smolensk and then at Borodino, but each time the Russian army remained intact and was able to withdraw further to the east. Finally Napoleon succeeded in taking Moscow, but Alexander refused all requests for an armistice and continued to prepare for the next phase of the war. Napoleon lingered in Moscow hoping in vain that a peace deal would cement his triumph. Yet the depths of Russia afforded Alexander plenty of space to fall back and, with the autumn already well advanced, time was very much on his side. The unbeaten Napoleon faced a strategic dilemma. Retreating empty-handed looked too much like a defeat, but remaining in Moscow for the winter would almost certainly result in a real one. Finally, with no other choice, on 19 October Napoleon began retracing his steps, but the changing weather and harrying Russian attacks soon turned his retreat into a rout and his already reduced army disintegrated week by week.[19]

By December 1812 the Grande Armée that had invaded Russia only six months before had been utterly vanquished, a result that owed much more to Alexander and Barclay's strategic understanding of the eastern theatre of war than to any battlefield deed. Indeed, for the 1813 campaign a huge Russian army managed to push beyond Russia's borders without suffering the same crippling attrition associated with Napoleon's movement into the east. Having witnessed the arrival of a long Russian column in Central Europe, which had been three months on the march, one British officer noted with astonishment:

> These infantry ... and their appointments appeared as if they had not moved further than from barracks to the parade during that time. The horses and men of the cavalry bore the same freshness of appearance. Men and beasts certainly in Russia afford the most surprising material for powder service. If English battalions had marched a tenth part of the way they would have been crippled for

weeks and would scarcely have had a relic of their original equipments. Our horses would all have been foundered, and their backs too sore even for the carriage of the saddle.[20]

Explaining Russia's success against Napoleon between 1812 and 1814 is as much about the defeat of the field upon which the enemy stood as it is the defeat of the enemy army standing on the field. Clearly, 'the country', as Clausewitz framed it, was also a factor that had to be overcome.

Accounting for the outcome of these campaigns is incomprehensible without an appreciation of the strategic terrain in which the wars took place. Not only does one see the importance of endurance factors, but it would also appear evident that Clausewitz's notion of terrain, especially in these cases the Russian terrain, acted as a major factor in hindering offensive actions and, as Clausewitz termed it, 'restoring equilibrium'. In asserting the distinctive difficulties of the eastern theatre of war, one must be careful not to oversimplify the similarities that connect the wars under discussion here. The war aims, styles of command, technology, composition of armies and tactics all varied radically between the armies of Muscovy, Charles XII and Napoleon. Yet, in a broad sense, they are connected by the common strategic misconceptions they shared. The early modern Russians had first to learn this lesson, and it took much more than just their defeat in the Smolensk War,[21] but a learning curve in Russian strategic military thinking had begun; allowing for a remarkable projection of military power and at the same time bequeathing a blueprint for Russian defence. This is not to suggest that Russian and later Soviet leaders were always wise to this concept or willing to sacrifice their land for the benefit of drawing in and weakening their enemies. Militarily this may have made some sense, but politically it was disastrous. Russia's status as a great European power as well as the increasingly volatile social and political stratification throughout the nineteenth and early twentieth centuries all but removed the option of a strategic withdrawal. In the end, however, whether withdrawal was an intentional part of Russian strategy or not, Russian lands remained guarded by their size.

By the beginning of the twentieth century Russia was by no means safe from foreign invasion, and the experience of World War I only confirmed Russia's vulnerability. Yet Russia's collapse in 1917 resulted as much from internal weakness as external pressure, and the new Soviet regime, having exemplified its brutality in the subsequent civil war, eventually ensured iron-fisted control over the country. Throughout the late 1920s and 1930s there was a tremendous push towards industrialisation and modernisation of the Soviet economy. Nevertheless, when war finally came in 1941 the Red Army was reeling from a devastating military purge undertaken in the late 1930s and was caught in the midst of a service-wide restructuring. Compounding the problems, the Soviet command attempted to implement its pre-war offensive plan aimed at driving the war into German-occupied Poland. This not only failed, but also helped facilitate the encirclement of the Soviet Western Front on the main axis of the German advance. By contrast, the neighbouring Soviet South-Western Front, after a week of hard fighting, was permitted to withdraw to the Stalin Line along the Dnepr River. Here it managed to maintain effective resistance until September when it was not permitted a further withdrawal and was subsequently destroyed in the battle of Kiev.[22] By this point the German armies had pushed deep into the Soviet heartland, occupying a line extending south from Leningrad, east of Smolensk and through central Ukraine to the Perekop Isthmus at the gateway to Crimea. Achieving this line had taken more than three months of heavy fighting and, although the Germans had maintained the initiative throughout and won many large-scale battles, they had lost in the single most important respect. Neither the Wehrmacht nor the German economy could hope to sustain a long, high-intensity war across more than 2,500 kilometres of front. Operation Barbarossa had aimed for nothing less than the complete destruction of Soviet resistance in a short and decisive summer blitzkrieg. There was no thought given to a winter campaign, and no contingency plan for Barbarossa's failure. For all its substantial problems, by the end of September the Soviet Union still maintained an unbroken, active front against the Germans and was three months into its total war mobilisation. Operation Barbarossa may have been remarkably successful if one is interested only in battlefield statistics, but it was a strategic failure with disastrous implications for Nazi Germany's war effort.

In order to understand the seriousness of the German position by October 1941 a simple comparison of the opposing forces is not enough. Armies do not exist in a vacuum, and the outcome of the war, contrary to German expectations, depended far more on geostrategic and macro-economic factors than any individual battle or offensive.

The depth of resources, scale of mobilisation and size of the front rendered the Soviet Union far from collapse in October 1941. Only a long series of sustained, resource-intensive offensives, separated by temporary halts to rebuild armies and bring up supplies, could lead to outright victory on the eastern front. This was true not only of the Wehrmacht in 1941, but also of the Red Army throughout the last two years of the war. Indeed, once the Red Army was permanently on the offensive, and even with the mighty contribution of the western Allies, there was still no knock-out blow between the summer of 1943 and May 1945. Nazi Germany went down fighting to the bitter end, and there is no reason to believe that the Soviet response to the loss of Moscow, even if that had been a realisable goal, would have been any different. Indeed, the Soviets had already nominated a new capital at Kuibyshev,[23] some 800 kilometres east of Moscow, and in mid October began relocating government ministries and foreign diplomatic missions.[24] Moscow was not the key to Germany's final victory in the east; it was only the end goal of another offensive, which, like Operation Barbarossa's objectives, proved overly ambitious.

Germany's war in the east was principally directed by the Army High Command under the direction of the chief of the army general staff, Colonel-General Franz Halder. The OKH oversaw the planning and allocation of forces for Operation Barbarossa and, once the invasion was underway, assumed command for the day-to-day strategic direction of the war. The initial battles were judged great successes even though the cost in blood and materiel had been remarkably high. By the end of September there were serious doubts in the minds of some within the OKH, matched by a few of the high-ranking field commanders. It was becoming increasingly hard to see how the war could be ended in 1941, and it was clear that the German *Ostheer* was in no way prepared for a winter campaign. Yet Halder remained resolutely convinced that Soviet resistance could still be broken if only Moscow could be successfully captured in the last great German offensive of the year. Operation Typhoon, the German autumn offensive destined to begin on 2 October, was to be spearheaded by the great bulk of the *Ostheer*'s mobile divisions (panzer and motorised). The aim was to destroy the three Soviet fronts guarding Moscow and then to push on and encircle the exposed and largely defenceless Soviet capital. To achieve this, Bock's Army Group Centre was reinforced by Hoepner's Panzer Group 4 as well as additional panzer and motorised divisions from Colonel-General

1 The commander of Army Group Centre in Operation Typhoon, Field Marshal Fedor von Bock.

Ewald von Kleist's Panzer Group 1. Bock already controlled the *Ostheer*'s other two panzer groups, Colonel-General Hermann Hoth's Panzer Group 3 and Colonel-General Heinz Guderian's Panzer Group 2, giving Bock command of fourteen panzer divisions and eight and a half motorised divisions for Operation Typhoon (see Illustration 1). It was the greatest concentration of German mobile forces in World War II.

Yet after three months of fighting in the east a panzer division on paper did not equal a panzer division in strength. The two exceptions were Major-General Gustav Fehn's 5th Panzer Division and Lieutenant-General Rudolf Veiel's 2nd Panzer Division, both of which had just completed their transfer to the eastern front and had not yet seen action.[25] Between them these two divisions fielded some 450 tanks.[26] It is indicative of the losses sustained over the summer by Bock's twelve other panzer divisions that they together contained an estimated total of just 750 tanks, which when compared against their respective starting totals at the beginning of Operation Barbarossa reflects a 70 per cent drop in strength across the board.[27] The panzer groups had certainly been the driving force behind the *Ostheer*'s great encirclement battles at Minsk, Smolensk, Uman and Kiev, but, just like Napoleon's Grande Armée, their victorious advance through the Soviet Union had come at a high cost.

Soviet roads were typically of a very poor standard, which not only damaged many German vehicles but also, because of a serious absence of spare parts, rendered many repairs either short-term expedients or simply not possible at all. A further problem was the all-pervasive dust, which overwhelmed the filters of the engines, resulting initially in spiking oil consumption and ultimately causing the cylinders to seize up. Replacement engines for both trucks and tanks were in extremely short supply, and damage often resulted in the loss of the vehicle. The notion of a tank transporter was also in its infancy and, with the huge distances having to be covered by the panzers under their own power, wear and tear quickly claimed more tanks than enemy fire. Clearly, the advantages of a mechanised army proved a double-edged sword in the desolate landscape of the east, reflecting once again the enduring relevance of Clausewitz's considerations concerning 'the country' as a strategic factor in the conduct of war.

Indeed, the German faith in technology in many ways summed up the paradox of the eastern theatre. While technology certainly helped solve some of the problems faced by former invaders of Russia, it also affected 'the country' differently and thereby introduced new and unforeseen problems. The result exposed the overconfidence of the German commanders who saw all the advantages of the internal combustion engine without considering its own susceptibility to the prevailing conditions. In one illustrative example in early October, Ernst Kern, a newly arrived German recruit, shared guard duty with a veteran soldier and recorded their conversation:

> 'Have a look at the map of Russia.' [The veteran told Kern.] 'The land is immense. And how far did we advance? Not even as far as Napoleon in 1812 – our conquest is only a thin strip on the map.'

'But we have entirely different technical means and equipment than they had,' I told him. He laughed dryly. 'Well, but they are more subject to failure.'[28]

The railways were another example. At the depth that Bock's army group was operating by the end of July 1941, logistics depended on the railways for supply. The Soviet railway gauge was, however, wider than the rest of Europe, preventing German trains from simply rolling onto the Soviet network. The Germans knew this and prepared special rail-conversion teams which in theory only had to uproot the rail spikes, move the rails closer together and then hammer down the spikes again. It was therefore believed that the railways in the occupied Soviet Union could maintain contact with the army group's *Grosstransportraum* – the truck-based transport fleets bridging the railheads with the armies. Yet owing to their greater size Soviet locomotives could also carry larger loads of fuel and water and therefore travel longer distances between service stops. German locomotives, in contrast, needed more frequent stops, which posed a completely new problem for the rapid extension of the railways. While rail conversion was relatively unskilled work, the addition of locomotive sheds, turntables, sidings and water towers introduced a whole new set of requirements, which had not been foreseen and could not be improvised quickly. On average the Germans had to build one new service installation between each pair of Soviet stations and, without the requisite skilled labour or heavy construction materials, delays were inevitable.[29] The demands of the front forced every possible expedient in the construction and conversion process, resulting in a minimum standard of workmanship, which reduced the speed at which the trains could later travel. The whole process was further complicated by the Soviet scorched-earth policy, which ensured an unanticipated level of destruction to the Soviet infrastructure, necessitating even more work, and therefore delays, for the underresourced *Eisenbahntruppe* (railroad troops).[30]

At the front Bock's Army Group Centre contained almost two million men whose basic requirements could only barely be covered by the flow of supplies reaching the front. As a result there had been extremely limited stockpiling for Operation Typhoon, and German reports already before the start of the operation made clear that supporting an advance beyond the anticipated encirclement battles would not be possible.[31] Reaching Moscow was therefore being ruled out from a logistical point of view right at the beginning. Not only were the trucks and tanks impeded by 'the country' into which they advanced, but they were also restrained by the lack of fuel and ammunition. The railroads, whose job it was to supply such essentials, were themselves impeded by the vast distances and the conditions they encountered on the ground. The railways could not advance far enough, fast enough to support the demands of the campaign. Yet from Hitler at the OKW (Oberkommando der Wehrmacht – High Command of the Armed Forces) to Halder at the OKH and Bock at Army Group Centre there was no loss of enthusiasm for Operation Typhoon. The army may have been suffering from the same endurance factors that had plagued previous invaders, but to the Nazi mind the power of individual 'will' amounted to a determination to overcome all obstacles and opposing forces. Failure to do so was a reflection on the individual, not the circumstances. The requisite 'will' to carry out an order or achieve an objective was therefore accorded decisive importance.[32] Logistics had been a major problem for the *Ostheer* throughout the summer campaign, but the fact that the most immediate objectives were able to be met allowed the German high command to overlook the gravity of the problem. By ordering another large-scale offensive to the east, they merely delayed the worst of the logistical crisis, and that was all before the weather affected movement so adversely. The autumn rains did not create the supply crisis behind the eastern front; they only intensified a preordained problem, which the German command had failed to foresee.

Logistics and mobility were not the only concerns for the *Ostheer* in October 1941; endurance factors also included access to reinforcement. Clearly, Bock's panzer divisions had lost a great deal of their firepower over the preceding three months, and the addition of two full-strength panzer divisions was hardly sufficient to make good losses and drive forward on a front some 760 kilometres in length. Throughout the summer Hitler had repeatedly forbidden the reinforcement of the panzer divisions from stocks of newly produced tanks. He argued that these were to be held back for future campaigns extending, according to Hitler, 'over thousands of kilometres'.[33] Yet the greatly diminished offensive strength of Bock's panzer arm necessitated some kind of boost, and on 15 September Hitler authorised the release of sixty Czech-designed 38(t)s, 150 Mark IIIs and 96 Mark IVs.[34] This amounted to barely 300 tanks from a new production total of some 815 units (all models) turned out in the three-month period from June to August.[35] Thus, while 300 replacement tanks were certainly beneficial, this was still a distinct half-measure and could only result in an average of just twenty-five new tanks for each of Bock's panzer divisions.

Even more striking was the crippling lack of motorisation. The *Ostheer* invaded the Soviet Union with some 600,000 motor vehicles,[36] concentrated heavily within the four panzer groups. Although an exact figure for overall losses by late September is not available, Panzer Group 2 reported a loss of 30 to 40 per cent of its wheeled transport by 20 September.[37] If that figure may be extrapolated to the whole *Ostheer* then anywhere between 180,000 and 240,000 vehicles had been written off during the summer campaign and a sizeable number of those remaining might be considered functional, but in a highly provisional state of repair. To view this level of attrition in perspective, at the same time that Hitler was releasing tanks for Operation Typhoon he also authorised a consignment of replacement trucks numbering 3,500 vehicles.[38] The disparity in the figures reflects the yawning discrepancy between the *Ostheer*'s rate of loss and access to resupply. Nor was this simply attributable to Hitler's fanciful notion of withholding supply for future campaigns. The fact remains that German industrial capacity, as well as access to raw materials, was in no way equal to the staggering losses of the eastern front, not to mention the additional losses from North Africa. Across the board, from the highly technical panzer groups and air fleets to the more rudimentary infantry divisions, there was an appreciable and rapid demodernisation of the army taking place, which new supplies could ameliorate, but never rectify.

While the vehicles driving Germany's eastern blitzkrieg proved so susceptible to the prevailing conditions, the Luftwaffe introduced a new concept to warfare in Russia, one that had never been attempted before. Planes seemingly had the advantage of easily traversing the wide open spaces of the east, providing vital close arms support at the front and bombing the Soviet rear. Yet the Luftwaffe was already stretched by the war against the British, which demanded planes for North Africa, the Mediterranean, occupied France and home defence. In the early days of Operation Barbarossa, the Luftwaffe proved devastating to the Soviet air force while also harrying the Red Army in the border battles. By July, however, it was becoming increasingly difficult to support operations from airfields outside the Soviet Union, and the relocation of airfields to the east forced the Luftwaffe to operate from much more primitive and often battle-damaged bases. There was also a heavy price exacted by the unceasing combat operations. By 12 July a total of 550 German planes had been destroyed with another 336 damaged, representing about 40 per cent of all the combat-ready aircraft available on 22 June.[39] The rate of attrition was cumulative and resulted both from aerial battles against a resurgent Soviet air force and from an inability to cope with the servicing and repair of aircraft. On 21 August Field Marshal Erhard Milch, the inspector-general of the Luftwaffe, conducted a tour of airfields in the east and noted that they were littered with scores, sometimes hundreds, of damaged aircraft.[40]

The importance of military losses is, however, highly relative. For a wartime economy, endowed with investment capital, production capacity, a labour surplus and access to raw materials, losses carry much less weight. In 1941 Nazi Germany had none of these. Indeed, Germany's imperilled economic footing was one of the central reasons behind Hitler's invasion of the Soviet Union. The failure of Operation Barbarossa did not just deny Hitler his much-vaunted *Lebensraum* (living space) and its much-anticipated economic boon for Germany; it also placed a colossal new strain on an already overburdened system. Not only was Germany now committed to massive new armament expenditure and production, but these would have to be met with less domestic labour. Moreover, the pre-Barbarossa German economy had benefited from Soviet deliveries of grain, oil and precious metals, effectively circumventing Britain's blockade of the continent. Now Germany was encircled by enemies, cut off from foreign markets and still a long way from conquering Soviet oil fields or transforming a devastated Ukraine into a European breadbasket. This is not to suggest Germany's economic potential was at an end. Indeed, recent work by Adam Tooze shows there was a greater degree of rationalisation and efficiency in economic management than was previously thought, but it is wrong to assume that Albert Speer's policies as armaments minister produced an economic miracle.[41] Whatever Speer managed to achieve from 1942 onwards, with slave labour and the ruthless extortion of resources from occupied Europe, he still never came close to matching the tremendous, and ever-increasing, figures for military production within the Allied powers.[42]

Indeed Hitler had been so convinced of a German victory in the east that priority in armaments production had been shifted away from the army to the navy and air force. Accordingly, between July and December 1941 production of weapons for the army fell by 29 per cent.[43] This circumstance prompted Colonel-General Fritz Fromm, chief of the Land-Force Armaments and commander-in-chief of the Replacement Army, to remark on 16 August 1941 that the high command had to come 'out of the current cloud-cuckoo-land and down to reality'.[44] As the *Ostheer*'s operational edge was being blunted in the east and the army was taking huge casualties, the home front was tooling up to produce, among other things, enormous turbine engines and super-structures of a new high-seas fleet. With all the major powers, aside from the United States, already involved in the war against Germany, and President Franklin D. Roosevelt doing everything in his power to arm the anti-Axis alliance through Lend-Lease, the warning signs of Hitler's mistaken direction were ominous. At the same time the need for Operation Typhoon to fulfil an enormous weight of promise and deliver victory in the east had never been stronger.

Germany's material losses on the eastern front were not simply prohibitively high for Hitler's lofty operational goals, but because the war was now an attritional struggle such losses across the board could never be adequately replaced. A similar pattern of irretrievable decline affected the ranks of the field armies. By 26 September 1941 the *Ostheer* had suffered no fewer than 534,952 casualties, equalling some 15 per cent of the entire Barbarossa invasion force.[45] Fromm's Replacement Army had only 385,000 men to send as replacements,[46] leaving a 150,000-man shortfall. Not only did this leave gaps in the ranks, but from the very outset the size of the *Ostheer* was insufficient for the length and depth of the eastern front. Indeed, because Soviet Russia expands like a funnel from its western approaches, by October the *Ostheer* was holding a great deal more land with even fewer men. More worryingly still, Operation Typhoon was about to trigger a new wave of casualties, while extending the lines even further to the east. If Typhoon did not prove successful in eliminating Soviet resistance, the *Ostheer* would soon find itself confronting a winter campaign with badly depleted divisions, stretched taut across a vast front. The danger of such over-extension did not arise overnight and senior army officers who commented on the process were at the same time complicit in its realisation. Halder noted in his diary on 11 August:

Regarding the general situation, it stands out more and more clearly that we underestimated the Russian colossus, which prepared itself consciously for war with the complete unscrupulousness that is typical of totalitarian states. This statement refers just as much to organisational as to economic strengths, to traffic management, above all to pure military potential. At the start of the war we reckoned with 200 enemy divisions. Now we already count 360. These divisions are not armed and equipped in our sense, and tactically they are inadequately led in many ways. But they are there and when we destroy a dozen of them, then the Russians put another dozen in their place. The time factor favours them, as they are near to their own centres of power, while we are always moving further away from ours.

And so our troops, sprawled over an immense front line, without any depth, are subject to the incessant attacks of the enemy. These are sometimes successful, because in these enormous spaces far too many gaps must be left open.[47]

German operational success was built on speed, mobility, firepower and a strong concentration of force. Traversing great distances in the Soviet Union exacted an enormous toll on the panzer and motorised divisions, cutting mobility and reducing firepower. Thick forests and swamplands, especially north of the Pripet marshes, often cut the speed at which armoured forces could move, while periodic downpours, which transformed the ground into a morass, had the same effect. Finally, the sheer length of the front cut the ability to concentrate powerful forces into an operational 'fist'. Accordingly, as the operational edge blunted, the speed of the campaign waned and increasing sections of the front settled down into gritty positional warfare. It was here that the infantry divisions, strung out along broad areas of the front without any depth to their lines and few, if any, reserves, began to suffer heavy losses in largely unknown battles. Their lack of mobility made them particularly susceptible to enemy attacks because reinforcements could not quickly reach points of crisis in the line. The result was heavier casualties, which after each battle left even fewer men to occupy the same positions. Soldiers watched their units shrink around them or became casualties themselves. According to the chief of staff of the Fourth Army, Major-General

Günther Blumentritt, the summer defensive battles 'made very heavy demands on the troops'. He continued:

[I]n modern warfare infantry requires armoured support not only in the attack but also in the defence.

When I say our lines were thin, this is not an understatement. Divisions were assigned sectors almost twenty miles wide. Furthermore, in view of the heavy casualties already suffered in the course of the campaign, these divisions were usually under strength and tactical reserves were non-existent.[48]

By 15 September Field Marshal Günther von Kluge's Fourth Army had suffered 38,000 losses, which was by no means exceptional. In the same period, Colonel-General Adolf Strauss's Ninth Army had lost 48,000 men, while Guderian's Panzer Group 2 had lost 32,000.[49] Some companies that had started the war with 150 troops were reduced to a handful of men,[50] while numerous regiments were forced to disband a battalion in order to provide internal replacements.[51] In some divisions losses were staggering. The 137th Infantry Division, for example, suffered almost 2,000 casualties in the defensive fighting at Yel'nya between 18 August and 5 September, while the 263rd Infantry Division lost 1,200 men in a single week during the battle.[52] As one German chaplain fatalistically wrote in early September: 'Yes, many of us won't see our families any more, [and] are doomed to spend our eternal rest far from the fatherland.'[53] The heavy rate of attrition was sustainable only if the war could be ended as intended by the end of the summer. Barbarossa's failure, however, meant that the eastern army Hitler created to eliminate the Red Army was paradoxically being consumed by the struggle.

Clearly, Hitler and the Army General Staff had dramatically underestimated the Soviet Union. Not only had the technical stand and fighting prowess of the Red Army come as a complete surprise, but they had badly miscalculated the difficulties of campaigning in the eastern theatre. General of Infantry Waldemar Erfurth, who was appointed 'Commander of the Liaison Staff North' and served as the senior German adviser to the Finnish headquarters from 1941 to 1944, wrote after the war in a US Army historical study:

In the past the German General Staff had taken no interest in the history of wars in the north and east of Europe. No accounts of the wars of Russia against Swedes, Finns and Poles had ever been published in German ... The German General Staff was inclined on the whole to limit its studies to the central European region.[54]

While campaigning in Russia may have seemed to former chiefs of the Army General Staff unwarranted, excessive or even foolhardy, from the summer of 1940 Halder was confronted with precisely that prospect and yet still nothing was done. The victory of Nazi Germany was assumed from the outset, and planning for *how* that was to be achieved was undertaken at the expense of a more prudent consideration concerning *if* that could be achieved. The absence of historical studies commissioned by the general staff in the prelude to Barbarossa did not prevent other staff officers from undertaking their own investigations. Guderian claimed to have studied the campaigns of Charles XII and Napoleon,[55] while Blumentritt studied the more recent Polish–Soviet war (1919–1921). Among the most popular accounts to be studied in the prelude to Barbarossa was the memoir of General Armand de Caulaincourt, one of Napoleon's closest advisers during his Russian campaign. As Blumentritt wrote:

> All books and maps concerning Russia soon disappeared from the bookshops. I remember that Kluge's desk at his Warsaw headquarters was usually laden with such publications. In particular, Napoleon's 1812 campaign was the subject of much study. Kluge read General de Caulaincourt's account of that campaign with the greatest attention: it revealed the difficulties of fighting, and even living, in Russia.[56]

The difficulties of fighting and living in the east should have been the priority for the general staff, but, although Caulaincourt's book seems to have been widely read, little was actually learned. While not without the familiar problems of a memoir, Caulaincourt's account nevertheless makes clear that the crisis within the Grande Armée began on the road to Moscow and not just in the well-known retreat. Furthermore, Caulaincourt's account states that many of France's difficulties were rooted in what Clausewitz was at the same time learning to identify as problems of 'the country'.[57] After only four to five weeks of the campaign Caulaincourt noted:

> We were in the heart of inhabited Russia and yet, if I may be permitted the comparison, we were like a vessel without a compass in the midst of a vast ocean, knowing nothing of what was happening around us … Part of the cavalry was already worn out, the artillery and infantry were exhausted, the roads were covered with stragglers who destroyed and wasted everything … A very large number of horses had died … The rapidity of the forced

marches, the shortages of harness and spare parts, the dearth of provisions, the want of care, all had helped to kill the horses. This campaign at express speed from the Nieman [River] to Vilna, and from Vilna to Vitebsk, had, without any real result, already cost the army two lost battles and deprived it of absolutely essential provisions and supplies ... [O]ur wagons and all our transport, built for metalled roads and to accomplish ordinary distances, were in no way suitable for the roads of the country we had to traverse. The first sand we came across overwhelmed the horses ... There you have the secret and cause of our earlier disasters and of our final reverse.[58]

At the OKH Halder was planning a modern blitzkrieg and saw little value in the musings of a defeated French general from a war that had taken place 129 years before. Yet the *Ostheer* would soon be tied to many of the same roads, while the Wehrmacht's infantry divisions, which made up the great bulk of the invasion force, would likewise be entirely dependent upon the horse and cart for their supplies, munitions and heavy weapons. Not all, however, were so ignorant of the dangers. Recalling the evening before Operation Barbarossa began, Alexander Stahlberg, an officer from the 12th Panzer Division, sat with his battalion commander and compared the strategic circumstances of 1812 and 1941. Stahlberg had also read Caulaincourt's memoir and stated that the addition of motorised forces was not as decisive as many assumed. 'Panzer and motorized divisions were much faster than the infantry of 1812, but we had to be followed by infantry. Ultimately, even in 1941, the marching troops dictated our speed.'[59]

For those open to the prospect there was much of historical importance to be learned about launching a campaign into the Soviet Union. Indeed what is perhaps most striking is that the associated difficulties of 'the country' were almost as profound in 1941 as in any other period in Russia's past. Technology came with advantages and disadvantages, which the *Ostheer* had to learn the hard way. The Red Army in fact surpassed the Wehrmacht in many areas of modern weaponry,[60] and on the home front Soviet production proved more than capable of matching Germany in a costly war of attrition (see Table 1). While the *Ostheer* had struggled with the conditions in the east throughout the summer and early autumn, the fact remained that even worse was in store in terms of what 'the country' had to offer.

Table 1 *Major powers' annual military production, 1939–1945*

		1939	1940	1941	1942	1943	1944	1945[a]	Total
Germany	Aircraft	8,295	10,247	11,776	15,409	24,807	39,807	7,540	117,881
	Tanks	c. 1,300	2,200	5,200	9,200	17,300	22,100	–	57,300
	Artillery[b]	–	5,000	7,000	12,000	27,000	41,000	–	92,000
	Submarines	15	40	196	244	270	387	103	1,255
Soviet Union	Aircraft	10,382	10,565	15,735	25,436	34,900	40,300	20,900	158,218
	Tanks	2,950	2,794	6,590	24,446	24,089	28,963	15,400	105,232
	Artillery	17,348	15,300	42,300	127,000	130,000	122,400	93,000[d]	547,348
	Major naval vessels[c]	–	33	62	19	13	23	11	161
United Kingdom	Aircraft	7,940	15,049	20,094	23,672	26,263	26,461	12,070	131,549
	Tanks	969	1,399	4,841	8,611	7,476	5,000	–	28,296
	Artillery[b]	–	1,900	5,300	6,600	12,200	12,400	–	38,400
	Major naval vessels	57	148	236	239	224	188	64	1,156
United States of America	Aircraft	5,856	12,804	26,277	47,836	85,898	96,316	49,761	324,748
	Tanks	–	c. 400	4,052	24,997	29,497	17,565	11,968	88,479
	Artillery	–	c. 1,800	29,614	72,658	67,544	33,558	19,699	224,873
	Major naval vessels[c]	–	–	544	1,854	2,654	2,247	1,513	8,812
Japan	Aircraft	4,467	4,768	5,088	8,861	16,693	28,180	11,066	79,123
	Tanks	–	1,023	1,024	1,191	790	401	142	4,571
	Major naval vessels	21	30	49	68	122	248	51	589

Notes: [a] Figures for UK, USA, Japan: Jan–Apr; Germany: Jan–Aug; Soviet Union: whole year.
[b] Over 37 mm.
[c] Excludes landing craft, torpedo boats and small auxiliary vessels.
[d] Jan–Mar.
Source: Adapted from Richard Overy, 'Statistics' in I. C. B. Dear and M. R. D. Foot (eds.), *The Oxford Companion to the Second World War* (Oxford, 1995) p. 1060.

After the war Colonel-General Erhard Raus, who took part in Operation Typhoon as a major-general in the 6th Panzer Division, wrote about the special nature of the eastern theatre:

[H]e who steps for the first time on Russian soil is immediately conscious of the new, the strange, the primitive. The German soldier who crossed into Russian territory felt that he entered a different world, where he was opposed not only by the forces of the enemy but also by the forces of nature.

In 1941 the Wehrmacht did not recognize this force and was not prepared to withstand its effects. Crisis upon crisis and unnecessary suffering were the result. Only the ability of German soldiers to bear up under misfortune prevented disaster. But the German Army never recovered from the first hard blow.[61]

There are many explanations for the *Ostheer*'s poor preparation for the Barbarossa campaign,[62] but perhaps the simplest and most revealing was supplied by Field Marshal Ewald von Kleist,[63] who after the war admitted to an American at Nuremberg, 'I never read Clausewitz.' Kleist then continued: 'I don't know enough about Clausewitz to be able to tell you what his theories are. I know that the Russians must have read Clausewitz a good deal and perhaps it's too bad I didn't read it.'[64] According to one biographer, Zhukov, who commanded Soviet forces in the defence of Moscow from 10 October 1941, 'knew the military classics from Caesar to Clausewitz'.[65] Yet if German generals such as Kleist were unaware of Clausewitz's theories, it is perhaps small wonder they were also ignorant of the Russian theatre and all the perils they were to encounter there from 'the country'.

Evoking Barbarossa – twelfth-century myth and twentieth-century reality

Nestled between the Harz Mountains to the north and the Thuringian Forest to the south stands the imposing Kyffhäuser monument to Holy Roman Emperor Friedrich I (1122–1190), known by his Italian nickname 'Barbarossa' (Red Beard; see Illustration 2). The Kyffhäuser monument was built towards the end of the nineteenth century to glorify the first emperor of Germany's Second Reich, Wilhelm I. Having transcended eight hundred years of German history as a champion of foreign conquest and martial spirit, Barbarossa was the preferred symbol for the aggrandisement of Wilhelm I. The desire to associate Wilhelm I with his twelfth-century counterpart was based on more than just a desire to equate Barbarossa's strong, warlike reign with the house of Hohenzollern. There was a more peculiar rationale, built on centuries of German legend.

When Barbarossa failed to return from the Third Crusade to the Holy Lands (he drowned in a small river in Turkey) many of his subjects refused to believe that their great emperor was dead. Instead a myth spread that a spell had been cast on Barbarossa, confining him to live in the depths of a mountain – the Kyffhäuser – and that he would return again at Germany's hour of need. The legend soon became entrenched in Germanic folklore. Following the successes of Germany's wars of unification (1864–1871), Wilhelm I was seen not only as the triumphant leader of the united German kingdoms but also, to some, as the realisation of a legend, an heir to Friedrich Barbarossa's long-vacant throne. The 81 metre-high Kyffhäuser monument was built at great cost to propagate this link and remains the third-largest monument in Germany today. It depicts Barbarossa awakening on his throne while an 11-metre-high equestrian statue of Wilhelm I towers above him. The meaning was unmistakable; the legend's prophecy had been fulfilled.

Wilhelm I, who died in 1888, did not live to see the Kyffhäuser monument and only twenty-two years after its completion Germany's Second Reich was dissolved with defeat in World War I and the abolition of the Hohenzollern dynasty. The false marriage of legend and destiny was exposed and the great stone blocks atop the Kyffhäuser now tell a story of misplaced faith in historical appropriation and megalomaniac excess. Even so, Wilhelm I was not the last German leader to evoke parallels with Barbarossa and seek to equate his own deeds with those of Germany's legendary saviour.

In December 1940 with Germany already at war with a host of Allied nations led by Great Britain, Adolf Hitler committed himself to his own self-professed crusade in the east, which he codenamed Operation Barbarossa. Even more than Wilhelm I's Second Reich, Hitler's Third Reich was a heavily militarised society which extolled the virtues of the fighting man and exploited past glories for popular consumption. Now, in the largest military campaign the Third Reich would ever undertake, and indeed what remains today the largest military operation in history, Hitler evoked Barbarossa's name to crush his ideological rival in the east.

2 The Holy Roman Emperor Friedrich I (1122–1190). During his campaigns in northern Italy he acquired the sobriquet 'Barbarossa' (Red Beard).

On 22 June 1941 more than three million German soldiers, 3,505 tanks, 2,995 aircraft, 7,146 artillery pieces and more than 600,000 motor vehicles struck the Soviet Union along an enormous front 2,768 kilometres in length from the Barents Sea in the north to the Black Sea in the south. Operation Barbarossa had begun. Field Marshal Wilhelm Ritter von Leeb's Army Group North surged into the Baltic states, spearheaded by Hoepner's Panzer Group 4 and supported by Colonel-Generals Georg von Küchler's Eighteenth Army and Ernst Busch's Sixteenth Army. Deployed to Leeb's south was the largest grouping of forces on the eastern front, Bock's Army Group Centre. Tasked with encircling Soviet forces west of the Dvina and Dnepr Rivers, Bock commanded Guderian's Panzer Group 2 and Hoth's Panzer Group 3 as well as Strauss's Ninth Army and Kluge's Fourth Army. To Bock's south, thrusting into Ukraine, was Field Marshal Gerd von Rundstedt's Army Group South, consisting of Kleist's Panzer Group 1, Field Marshal Walter von Reichenau's Sixth Army, General of Infantry Carl Heinrich von Stülpnagel's Seventeenth Army and Colonel-General Eugen Ritter von Schobert's Eleventh Army.[66] In addition there were two armies from Romania, General Petre Dumitrescu's Third Army and General Nicolae Ciuperca's Fourth Army, together totalling some 325,685 men.[67] Hungary also joined the war on 27 June 1941 and sent Lieutenant-General Ferenc Szombathelyi's 'Carpathian Group', numbering some 45,000 men, into Ukraine.[68] Mussolini's fascist regime in Italy immediately pledged support for the war against the Soviet Union, but could not get General Giovanni Messe's CSIR (Italian Expeditionary Corps in Russia), numbering some 60,900 men, to the eastern front until August 1941.[69] Slovakia also joined Hitler's war in the east sending General Ferdinand Čatloš's Slovak Expeditionary Army Group with roughly 41,000 men to join Stülpnagel's Seventeenth Army.[70] The *Ostheer* also benefited from thousands of fascist and anti-communist volunteers from all over occupied Europe, who were often concentrated into special Waffen-SS units like the 5th SS Division 'Wiking'.[71] Even supposedly neutral Spain formed a division of volunteers and dispatched them to the eastern front under the command of General Agustin Muñoz Grandes.[72] Beyond the three German army groups concentrated between the Baltic and the Black Seas, German forces also operated as the junior partners of a Finnish invasion force numbering some 475,000 men and commanded by Field Marshal Carl Gustaf Emil Mannerheim.[73]

For all Hitler's talk of a pan-European crusade, in practice this was nothing more than propaganda designed to garner political support and lend legitimacy to Nazi Germany's latest war of aggression. While there would be no shortage of foreign participants in Operation Barbarossa,[74] the overwhelming bulk of the fighting would nevertheless have to be borne by the Wehrmacht. German plans were predicated on the success of their mobile divisions concentrated into the four panzer groups, the two strongest of which were allocated to Bock's Army Group Centre. Guderian's Panzer Group 2 and Hoth's Panzer Group 3 commanded more than 1,700 tanks between them[75] and constituted the operational force which posed the greatest danger to the Soviet Union. Opposed by Lieutenant-General Dmitri Pavlov's Western Front, which was heavily concentrated in the west of the Belostok Salient roughly between the joint armoured thrusts of Guderian and Hoth, Pavlov was thus half-encircled before the war had even begun (see Map 1).[76] Complicating the Western Front's predicament the Stavka (the Soviet high command) ordered Pavlov to launch immediate counterattacks to the west, which exacerbated his position by tying his forces to the front, preventing their withdrawal and facilitating their encirclement. Bock's powerful panzer groups capitalised on their favourable starting positions and in just over a week were closing an enormous

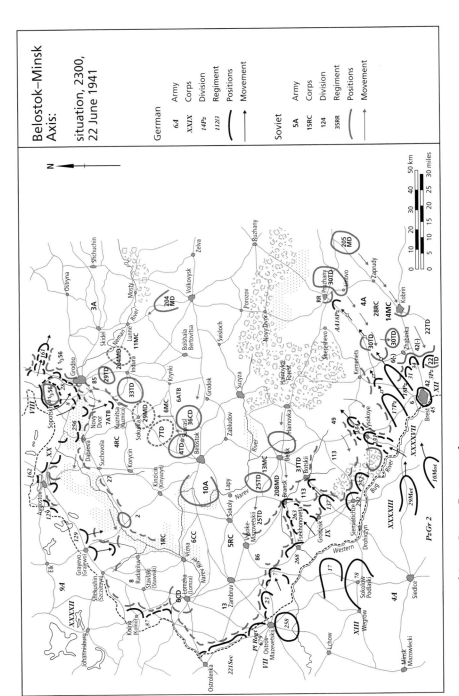

Map 1 Dispositions of Army Group Centre, 22 June 1941

pocket centred on Minsk.[77] As command and control of the Western Front collapsed, many of its constituent units were left to fend for themselves in often hopeless circumstances. While some units capitulated, many others, such as the defenders of the Brest fortress, fought on to the bitter end.[78] Already on the first day of the war Hoth's panzer group noted: 'Where the enemy appears he fights tenaciously and courageously to the death. Defectors and those seeking to surrender were not reported from any positions.'[79]

Losses on the primitive Soviet roads were also extraordinarily high and provided the clearest indication of the prohibitive cost of conducting mobile operations in the east. After only a week of operations Hoth's leading 7th Panzer Division, commanded by Major-General Hans Freiherr von Funck, reported 50 per cent losses in Mark II and III tanks, while the Mark IV tanks[80] had suffered 75 per cent losses.[81] The fact that the great majority of these losses were simply the result of wear and tear on the Soviet roads and not due to combat speaks to the tremendous 'attrition of movement' in the east. Yet combat losses were also undermining the strength of the panzer groups. On 6 July a battalion of Lieutenant-General Walter Model's 3rd Panzer Division was advancing on Zhlobin when, according to one German account, 'they received devastating fire from Russian tanks which had been cleverly concealed among houses, farmyards, and barns at the edge of the town. The Russian tanks, lying in ambush, had held their fire until the last moment.'[82] In all, twenty-two German tanks were lost, a clear indication that even at the nadir of the Red Army's fortunes in the war it was still able to deliver crippling blows.

While the fallout rate of tanks was one problem Bock's armoured forces faced, it was not the only difficulty undercutting their effectiveness. Pavlov's Western Front may have effectively disintegrated, but this still left tens of thousands of armed units now operating independently in the dense forests and marshlands of Belorussia. With ever-longer German columns stretching out across the countryside, an inevitable gap opened between the panzer spearheads and the trudging infantry, leaving the vital, but poorly armed German supply columns of the *Grosstransportraum* exposed to attack, even from small bands of men without heavy weapons. As a former officer in the 3rd Panzer Division recalled:

> During the first two days of combat, unarmoured troops and rear echelons suffered considerable losses inflicted by hostile enemy

troops cut off from their main bodies. They hid beside the march routes, opened fire by surprise, and could only be defeated in intense hand-to-hand combat. German troops had not previously experienced this type of war.[83]

Likewise, General of Infantry Gotthard Heinrici, who commanded the XXXXIII Army Corps, wrote on only the second day of the war: 'All over the large forests, in countless homesteads, sit lost soldiers who often enough shoot at us from behind.'[84] For the panzer groups the implications of an untamed rear area were immediate and profound. As they had quickly outdistanced the marching infantry divisions, a gap opened in the German area of operations through which the vulnerable motorised columns of supply trucks ran the gauntlet of marauding, bypassed Soviet units. Not surprisingly, losses spiked sharply and many vital trucks as well as their supplies were lost. An untitled memorandum sent to Army Group Centre on 3 July outlined the nature of the predicament, as well as its seriousness. The memorandum stated:

> The problem, appearing from now on in its full magnitude which must be the constant worry of all responsible departments of the army group commands ... is the daily widening of the distance between the panzer groups and the [infantry] armies.
>
> While until now this distance had relatively little effect, the early renewal of the advance by the panzer groups, with an objective more than 500 km away, will have the result that 100–200-km long stretches behind the panzer groups are more or less empty of German troops. That these extensive areas are traversed by the panzer troops almost entirely on the road means that everywhere there are still strong enemy elements roaming and a constant danger exists to the supply and communications of the panzer groups.[85]

That such dangers were not heeded soon became very evident to those charged with managing the supply apparatus. Two weeks after the memorandum was sent, the quartermaster-general's diary for the 3rd Panzer Division reported:

> The supply situation does not permit a further advance to the east. The quartermaster-general's section reported this to the general

[Model] and his staff; nevertheless the general ordered a further thrust eastward ... The supply route of the division is extremely bad and insecure, enemy elements in the forests on both sides of the highway.[86]

While losses in the vital supply columns soared from bad roads and 'partisan' attacks, as of the middle of the July the forward combat units of the two panzer groups were thrust into an even more serious crisis. Attempting to close a second giant pocket around Smolensk, the panzer and motorised divisions of Army Group Centre became critically overextended, while operating at their greatest distance from the supporting infantry armies (see Map 2). With long southern and northern flanks tying down two of Bock's five panzer corps, the remaining panzer corps were charged with encircling three Soviet armies around Smolensk as well as repelling a new wave of Soviet armies attacking from the east. Due to a lack of munitions and manpower, casualties were very high, while at the same time the encirclement was unable to be closed until more infantry support arrived towards the end of the month. In the meantime, the vital panzer and motorised divisions bore the brunt of the fighting without the ability to concentrate their strength into operational 'fists', which had proved so successful in the past. The fighting in late July and August was much more static and attritional in nature, providing a far more even playing field for the less manoeuvrable and often poorly trained rifle divisions of the Red Army. As Heid Ruehl, who served in the elite 2nd SS Division 'Das Reich', recalled:

The gunners, working like fury, finally beat off the first
Russian tank attacks, but these were then renewed in greater
strength and then our motor-cycle battalion came under heavy
pressure. We were smothered in a drum fire such as we had never
before experienced ... Because of the severe losses which it had
sustained [the] motor-cycle battalion had to be taken out of the line
and was replaced by an East Prussian engineer battalion ...
We were not the only ones on the road. Motor-cycles loaded
with wounded and other comrades, either alone or in groups, were
making their way out of the burning village, all of them completely
exhausted, dusty and sweaty. The Russian advance had rolled
over our thin infantry defensive lines and a lot of our lads did
not get out.[87]

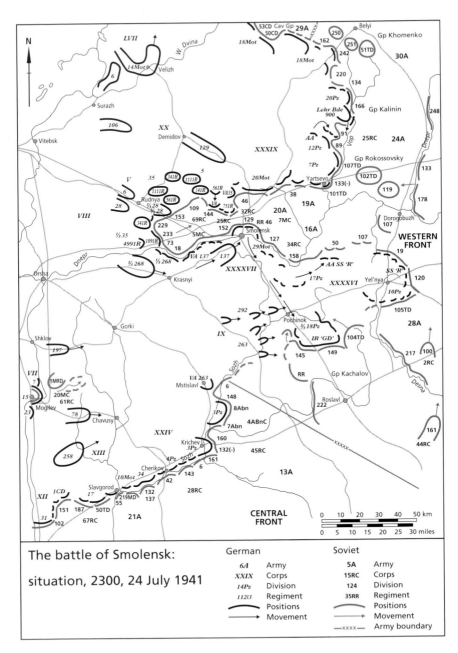

The battle of Smolensk: situation, 2300, 24 July 1941

German		Soviet	
6A	Army	5A	Army
XXIX	Corps	15RC	Corps
14Pz	Division	124	Division
1121З	Regiment	35RR	Regiment
	Positions		Positions
	Movement		Movement
			Army boundary

Map 2 Dispositions of Army Group Centre, 24 July 1941

Nor was this just a local phenomenon. There were crisis points up and down the line and Bock possessed no substantive reserves to aid beleaguered units. The German salient at Yel'nya, held by General of Panzer Troops Heinrich Freiherr von Vietinghoff's XXXXVI Panzer Corps, sent constant reports on the seriousness of its situation to Panzer Group 2. On 26 July the panzer group's war diary summarised the situation:

> At the fighting around Yel'nya the situation is especially critical. The corps has been attacked all day by strongly superior forces with panzers and artillery. The enemy achieved a breakthrough at Lipnya which has not yet been dealt with … Constant heavy artillery fire is inflicting heavy casualties on the troops. In addition there is the impact of enemy bombers. As a result of the artillery fire, the evacuation of the many wounded has so far not been possible … The corps has absolutely no reserves available. Artillery munitions have been so depleted that no shells remain for bombarding the enemy artillery. For the last few days the panzer brigade of the 10th Panzer Division has been immobilised because oil and fuel supplies are lacking. The corps can perhaps manage to hold on to its position, but only at the price of severe bloodletting.[88]

At the OKH and OKW there was consternation. Not only had the advance ground to a halt along the main strategic axis of advance, but now there was also bitter disagreement about how the campaign should be continued. Hitler had already lost faith in the OKH's direction of the war and refused their insistence for a renewed drive on Moscow. Instead Hitler prioritised offensives to clear the long and exposed flanks of Bock's army group, a move which was also calculated to assist the slower forward movement of the neighbouring northern and southern army groups.

With the elimination of the Soviet pocket at Smolensk, German propaganda trumpeted the capture of more than 300,000 Soviet POWs,[89] but the inability to close the ring effectively meant that, at a minimum, tens of thousands of Soviet troops escaped capture.[90] More importantly, while the battle of Smolensk, along with the earlier battle at Minsk, netted well over half a million POWs, such losses must be seen in the context of the Red Army's size and access to reserves. On the eve of the German invasion, the Red Army possessed a mobilisation base of some fourteen million men. By the end of June, more than five million reservists had been called up, with further mobilisations following in succession.[91] The Soviet cadre system allowed for an unheard-of rate of force generation, which completely outwitted German intelligence estimates, and disguised the real strength of the Soviet state. In July 1941 no fewer than thirteen new field armies appeared, and in August another fourteen came into service. These new reserve armies were not as well equipped or as well trained as the professional armies they replaced but, as the German mobile forces weakened, more and more of the front settled down to positional warfare, allowing the new armies time to improve both. Thus, without attempting to trivialise the scale of the Western Front's military disasters at Minsk and Smolensk, the fact remains that the Soviet Union's force-generation scheme was able to replace its losses and even dramatically expand the size of the Red Army.[92] On 22 June 1941 the Red Army numbered 5,373,000 men; by 31 August, in spite of its losses, it had grown to 6,889,000; and by 31 December 1941 the army had reached an estimated eight million men.[93]

While the Red Army was growing in size the *Ostheer* was shrinking. Although there was access to reinforcements from the German Replacement Army, these reserves were very limited and their transportation to the front could not keep pace with the rate of loss. By the start of August Army Group Centre had lost some 74,500 men, but had received only 23,000 replacements.[94] With 85 per cent of German men aged between 20 and 30 already in the Wehrmacht by the summer of 1941, and those remaining outside either ineligible for health reasons or judged too important to the war economy, the reserve manpower pool was indeed small.[95] The commander of the German Replacement Army, Colonel-General Fritz Fromm, outlined the limitations to Halder in a discussion on 20 May 1941. After deducting a share of men to act as a reserve for the Luftwaffe (90,000 men), Fromm determined that the *Ostheer* would have access to 385,000 replacements. With surprising candour Halder noted that 275,000 casualties were expected in the initial border battles, with a further 200,000 expected in September. Thus, by Halder's own figures the Replacement Army would not suffice for the demands of the campaign through to the end of September and nothing at all would remain if the war dragged on longer.[96] In the event, by the end of September, the *Ostheer* had lost even more than Halder estimated. Between 22 June and 30 September some 551,039 men were recorded as casualties,[97] a figure far exceeding the Replacement Army's capacity, plunging the *Ostheer* into a rapid and irreversible decline.

With the Red Army growing in size and the *Ostheer* decreasing, the significance of the battle of Smolensk for the *Ostheer* was less in the number of captured Soviet POWs than the extent to which the battle contributed – or failed to contribute – to the crucial objective of ending Soviet resistance. Indeed, notwithstanding the losses to the Red Army, the striking power of Hoth and Guderian's panzer groups was being decisively compromised in the summer of 1941.[98] Indeed, despite attempting to rest and refit the panzer divisions throughout the first three weeks of August, Army Group's Centre's war diary concluded on 22 August: 'The armoured units are so battle-weary and worn out that there can be no question of a mass operative mission until they have been completely replenished and repaired.'[99] Nevertheless, Bock was soon ordered back into action. His forces were split between an offensive in the north towards Velikie Luki and a major operation in the south to drive into the exposed rear of the Soviet South-Western Front. Rundstedt, Bock's counterpart in the south, privately feared the extent to which operations were now expanding as well as the time it would take to finish the campaign. In a letter to his wife on 12 August, Rundstedt wrote: 'How much longer? I have no great hope that it will be soon. The distances in Russia devour us.'[100]

The operations on Bock's flanks were conducted on a shoestring of logistics, while German progress was at least as much a commentary on Soviet weakness and inept strategic direction as German strength. Indeed, by 11 September only 34 per cent of Army Group Centre's starting total of tanks were still deemed 'combat-ready'.[101] By the end of September, the battle of Kiev in the south was, on the one hand, a major operational triumph claiming the unprecedented figure of 665,000 Soviet POWs.[102] On the other hand, however, the victory in Ukraine had not sufficed for final victory over the Soviet Union, and Army Group Centre was still opposed by a multitude of Soviet armies (see Maps 3 and 4).[103] With the summer now gone and the autumn *rasputitsa* shortly due to begin, the new German offensive to seize Moscow (Operation Typhoon) was always going to be a difficult undertaking. Yet, unlike Operation Barbarossa, Operation Typhoon was to proceed with much less motorisation. Although no exact figure exists, many tens of thousands of German vehicles had been lost during Operation Barbarossa, while the operational panzer strengths had shrunk dramatically. On 27 September Guderian's five panzer divisions (and the specialised 'panzer flame' detachment) fielded a total of 256 operational tanks,[104] which was a far cry from their combined strength of 904 tanks on 22 June 1941.[105] At the same time estimates suggest Hoth's Panzer Group 3 was down to some 280 tanks (from a starting total of 707), while Hoepner's Panzer Group 4 numbered roughly 250 tanks (from a starting total of 626).[106] Even these remaining tanks were often in a highly provisional state of repair, as Halder noted after the war: 'When the battle of Kiev ended, after ruthless demands on the already seriously worn motors, Hitler ordered the attack in the direction of Moscow, which first required that strong elements be pulled back out of Ukraine. Now it was too late. The motors were at the end of their strength.'[107] Recognising the critical weakness of the panzer divisions, Hitler, who had been withholding new production of tanks for an anticipated campaign in the Middle East, at last authorised the release of 60 Czech 38(t)s, 150 Mark IIIs and 96 Mark IVs.[108] Nevertheless, this was further supplemented by the transfer of Germany's last two panzer divisions (the 2nd and the 5th) to Hoepner's Panzer Group 4. These two divisions had spearheaded German operations in the Balkans during the invasions of Yugoslavia and Greece (April 1941), but owing to their worn-out condition at the conclusion of the campaign could not partake in Operation Barbarossa. Between them these two formations fielded some 450 tanks, raising Bock's total of panzer reinforcements to 750 tanks.

On 22 June 1941 Bock's eight panzer divisions together totalled 1,530 tanks, which was just below the total strength of his fourteen panzer divisions on 2 October. Thus Bock's panzer forces were only slightly stronger in spite of the addition of Hoepner's panzer group and four extra panzer divisions. Yet these additions are not where most of Bock's increased strength came from. Half of Bock's entire panzer forces on 2 October came from the allocation of new production and the deployment of the 2nd and 5th Panzer Divisions to the eastern front. Accordingly, after almost three and a half months of fighting on the eastern front and before the allocation of new tanks, twelve of Bock's fourteen panzer divisions contributed only half of the tanks to Operation Typhoon. Indeed, a significant percentage of these remaining tanks had moderate to serious mechanical problems, rendering them only provisionally operational. If one were to compare the numerical strengths of Bock's twelve veteran panzer divisions on 22 June and 2

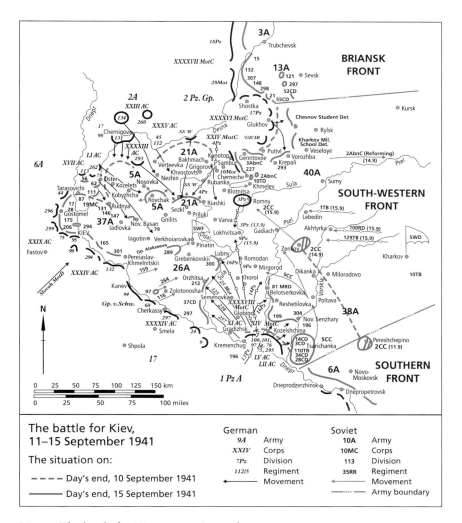

Map 3 The battle for Kiev, 11–15 September 1941

October one would record a 70 per cent drop in strength from 2,476 to 750 tanks.[109] Colonel Walter Chales de Beaulieu, the chief of staff of Panzer Group 4, noted that at the end of September 'what one referred to as a "division" was actually only a half of a division'.[110]

Clearly Bock's strength in real terms was considerably lower than the total number of divisions might suggest. Thus, while on paper the expansion of Army Group Centre's forces from 22 June to 2 October appears impressive based on the number of tanks, in truth, there were serious qualifications. Overall, Bock's panzer divisions

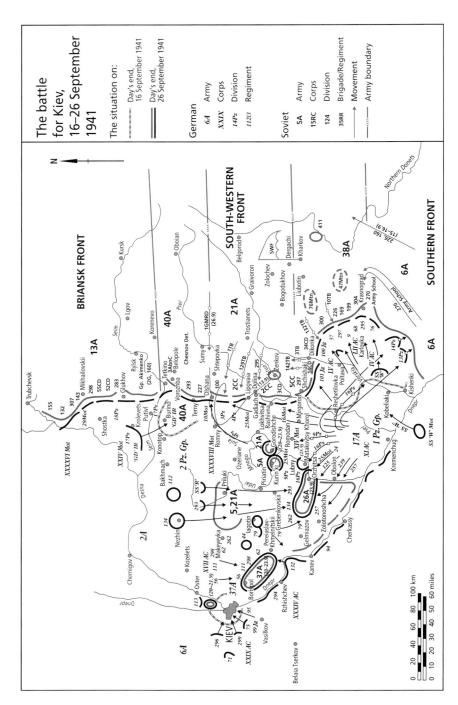

Map 4 The battle for Kiev, 16–26 September 1941

expanded from eight to fourteen, while the number of his infantry divisions grew from thirty-one to forty-seven. If one then includes all other formations, motorised infantry, cavalry and security divisions, Bock's command had increased to seventy-five and a half divisions by 2 October (see Table 2), as against a former total of forty-nine and a half divisions on 22 June. By this accounting Army Group Centre was half again as strong as it had been fourteen weeks before and numerically had risen from a starting total of 1,308,730 men to 1,929,406 men for Operation Typhoon. Yet paralleling Army Group Centre's growth in numbers was a corresponding growth in Bock's operational area. The total frontage of Army Group Centre on 22 June was 500 kilometres, but this had expanded to 760 kilometres by 2 October. Hence the one-half increase in Bock's army group was equalled by an equivalent increase in frontage, effectively eliminating the aim of achieving a greater concentration. Meanwhile, other components of Bock's command were also, like the tanks, actually in decline. Field Marshal Albrecht Kesselring, the commander of Air Fleet 2, started the war with 1,235 aircraft (all models), but by 2 October listed just 1,006 (all models).[111] Furthermore, the loss of trucks, so vital to the supply of the army group, had proved so profound that the massing of 1,500 tanks, 1,000 planes and nearly two million men could in no way be supplied by the army group's logistical apparatus, especially for an advance hundreds of kilometres in depth along a front 760 kilometres wide.

Of course, any estimation of Bock's strength is also relative to Soviet opposition. As early as July the Soviets began to prepare for a German attack on the approaches to Moscow by erecting an echeloned system of field fortifications. Colonel-General I. S. Konev's Western Front, Marshal S. M. Budenny's Reserve Front and Lieutenant-General A. I. Eremenko's Briansk Front manned the outer defensive line which ran along the Desna and Sudost Rivers to the west of Viaz'ma. Further east, there were two belts of defences separated from each other by 35 to 45 kilometres, which together were known as the Rzhev–Viaz'ma Defensive Line. Yet the most important defensive area was the Mozhaisk Defensive Line, which was anchored on four defensive regions at Volokolamsk, Mozhaisk, Maloiaroslavets and Kaluga. Altogether the Western, Reserve and Briansk Fronts commanded eleven armies in their first strategic echelon and four armies in their second. This amounted to some 1,250,000 men, 7,600 guns, 990 tanks and 667

Table 2 *Army Group Centre order of battle, 2 October 1941 (Operation Typhoon)*

Army Group Centre	Ninth Army			
Infantry Regiment 'Grossdeutschland'	161st Infantry Division			
19th Panzer Division Motorised				
'Lehrbrigade 900'				
		XXIII Army Corps		251st Infantry Division
				102nd Infantry Division
				256th Infantry Division
				206th Infantry Division
Rear Area Command (Centre)		Panzer Group 3	VI Army Corps	110th Infantry Division
707th Infantry Division				26th Infantry Division
339th Infantry Division			XXXXXI Panzer Corps	36th Motorised Infantry Div.
SS Cavalry Brigade				1st Panzer Division
				6th Infantry Division
221st Security Division			LVI Panzer Corps	14th Motorised Infantry Div.
286th Security Division				6th Panzer Division
403rd Security Division				7th Panzer Division
454th Security Division (in transfer)				129th Infantry Division
			V Army Corps	35th Infantry Division
				5th Infantry Division
				106th Infantry Division
		VIII Army Corps		28th Infantry Division
				8th Infantry Division
				87th Infantry Division
		XXVII Army Corps		255th Infantry Division
				162nd Infantry Division
				86th Infantry Division

Fourth Army	IX Army Corps		137th Infantry Division 263rd Infantry Division 183rd Infantry Division 292nd Infantry Division
	XX Army Corps		268th Infantry Division 15th Infantry Division 78th Infantry Division
	VII Army Corps		267th Infantry Division 7th Infantry Division 23rd Infantry Division 197th Infantry Division
	Panzer Group 4	LVII Panzer Corps	20th Panzer Division 3rd Motorised Infantry Div. SS 'Das Reich'
		XXXXVI Panzer Corps	5th Panzer Division 11th Panzer Division 252nd Infantry Division
		XXXX Panzer Corps	2nd Panzer Division 10th Panzer Division 258th Infantry Division
		XII Army Corps	98th Infantry Division 34th Infantry Division

Second Army 112th Infantry Division	XIII Army Corps	17th Infantry Division 260th Infantry Division
	XXXXIII Army Corps	52nd Infantry Division 131st Infantry Division
	LIII Army Corps	56th Infantry Division 31st Infantry Division 167th Infantry Division
Panzer Group 2	XXXXVII Panzer Corps	29th Motorised Infantry Div. 17th Panzer Division 18th Panzer Division
	XXIV Panzer Corps	4th Panzer Division 3rd Panzer Division 10th Motorised Infantry Div.
	XXXXVIII Panzer Corps	9th Panzer Division 25th Motorised Infantry Div. 16th Motorised Infantry Div.
	Higher Command XXXV	95th Infantry Division 296th Infantry Division
		262nd Infantry Division 293rd Infantry Division 1st Cavalry Division
	Higher Command XXXIV	45th Infantry Division 134th Infantry Division

Source: Militärgeschichtliches Forschungsamt (ed.), *Das Deutsche Reich und der Zweite Weltkrieg. Band 4. Der Angriff auf die Sowjetunion* (Stuttgart, 1983) p. 573.

aircraft. While Bock's force represented about 60 per cent of the entire *Ostheer*, the combined forces of Konev, Budenny and Eremenko accounted for only 40 per cent of the Soviet forces between the Baltic and the Black Sea.[112] In spite of being outnumbered and outgunned on the Moscow axis, across the full breadth of the eastern front the Red Army actually had more tanks than the *Ostheer* (2,715), more guns (20,580) and, in spite of its previous losses, roughly the same number of men (3.2 million).[113] In contrast to Nazi propaganda at the time, Bock's offensive was not encountering the last remnants of the Red Army, but rather a very sizeable force that in many respects was better equipped to deal with Operation Typhoon than it had been Operation Barbarossa.

On 24 September a major conference was hosted by Bock at Army Group Centre to finalise plans for the long-awaited renewal of the offensive towards Moscow. In attendance were the heads of the OKH (Halder and the commander-in-chief of the army, Field Marshal Walter von Brauchitsch), the commanders of Bock's three armies (Strauss, Kluge and Colonel-General Maximilian Freiherr von Weichs) as well as the three panzer group commanders (Hoth, Hoepner and Guderian). The assembled commanders were informed of their duties according to the OKH's plan, which had been formulated over the course of the past month. In the north, Strauss's Ninth Army together with Hoth's Panzer Group 3 were to attack from the area near Dukhovshchina and form the northern arm of the first major encirclement, closing at Viaz'ma. While Hoth's panzers would provide the striking power, Strauss's infantry would have to cover the northern wing of the whole offensive, as it had proved impossible to get Leeb's army group to extend itself any further to the east. Kluge's Fourth Army and Hoepner's Panzer Group 4 were to attack on both sides of the Roslavl–Moscow highway in the centre of Bock's front and head for Viaz'ma to close the pocket from the south. Weichs's Second Army and Guderian's Panzer Group 2 were attacking further south to break through the Soviet positions on the Desna River and co-operate in an advance to the north-east with an encirclement centred on Briansk. Reichenau's Sixth Army, attached to Army Group South, would also have to press forward in the direction of Oboian to cover as much of Bock's southern flank as possible.[114]

At the conclusion of the conference it was decided that the new offensive should begin on 2 October. Hoth had argued for 3 October, but was overruled. Guderian, on the other hand, requested and received permission for his panzer group to begin two days earlier on 30

September.[115] Guderian claimed his request was motivated by two factors. Firstly, he cited the absence of good roads in the area in which he was going to be operating and therefore the desire to make full use of the short period remaining before the autumn *rasputitsa*. The second reason he gave was his expectation of additional air support prior to the opening of the rest of Army Group Centre's offensive.[116] These factors were not, however, what convinced Bock to authorise Guderian's early start. He was concerned that Guderian was operating so far to the south that his offensive could not have any influence on the main attack for the first four or five days.[117]

In spite of the mounting difficulties posed by the eastern campaign, the German command was by and large convinced that the war against the Soviet Union could in fact be ended with one more major offensive. Successes in the north and south, sealing off Leningrad and capturing Kiev, had reinvigorated enthusiasm and raised expectations that the Soviet state was approaching collapse. Crucial in this regard were Goebbels's string of *Sondermeldungen* (special news bulletins), which openly declared the war was nearing its end. Of course the men at the front were sometimes in a better position to determine for themselves the validity of such claims and, while some expressed enthusiasm, there was also a lot of scepticism. Heinz Rahe wrote to his wife on 26 September about the upcoming offensive towards Moscow. 'I hope that in fourteen to twenty days Moscow is reached', but then noted, '– but not by us.'[118] A non-commissioned officer with the 79th Infantry Division wrote on 24 September: 'Whether there is an end to Russia this year I doubt very much. The [Soviet] military might is indeed broken, but the country is too big, and capitulation is not an option for the Russians.'[119] He then concluded with a distinct tone of war-weariness: 'Because two men can't agree on their ideas, millions of men have to bleed.'[120] In a letter to his family on 28 September Alois Scheuer summed up his experiences in the east and alluded to the many difficulties: 'What I have experienced and lived through in this quarter of a year in Russia I cannot put into words. There is much I would like to forget and never be reminded of again. I always, however, try not to lose hope and courage, but there are hours in which the loneliness and desolation are almost unbearable.'[121]

While many men at the front expressed their reservations and longed for an end to the war, Goebbels's victory propaganda was still largely successful, especially in Germany. Classified reports from the SD

(Sicherheitsdienst – the Security Service) gauging German public opinion reported on 25 September that fears of positional warfare in the east or the prospect of a winter campaign had now receded.[122] The next SD report on 29 September confirmed that more and more people were becoming convinced of a German victory before the onset of winter.[123] While acknowledging his success, Goebbels was nonetheless concerned by just how high the fever pitch of optimism had risen. Writing in his diary on 27 September Goebbels noted: 'The depression is now completely gone. At times the mood of the people goes far beyond the real possibilities. Once again one hopes that this winter the war will be over and we have very much to do in the next weeks to pull back the now extreme optimism to a normal level.'[124] Such optimism was indeed palpable and even at the front there was no shortage of those desperately wanting to believe it. Hans-Albert Giese wrote his mother on 28 September: 'In the next few days we will again march somewhat further. We look forward to it because the quicker we advance, the earlier we come home to Germany again. The news of the past few days was again really big. These Bolsheviks will not last too much longer.'[125] Another soldier, Ernst Guicking, agreed. In a letter to his wife on 29 September Guicking stated: 'Kiev is over. Now the [Army Group] Centre is due again. The great final chord will soon be played in the east. All our hopes are on the coming four weeks.'[126]

Indeed, all of Germany's hopes were pinned on the October offensive delivering the elusive final victory in the east; yet many obstacles remained. Could Army Group Centre defeat the mass of Soviet armies concentrated in defence of the capital? Could Bock's logistic apparatus sustain major operations all the way to Moscow? Could such a large city be taken by force? Would Moscow's capture result in the surrender of the Soviet government? After countless gruelling battles and hundreds of kilometres of strenuous advance, many in the *Ostheer* liked to believe that the worst of the eastern campaign was behind them. The idea of one final push to end the war; one final push to end the many deprivations and individual sufferings; one final push to secure a boundless empire of *Lebensraum*, enriching Germany for generations; or even one final push just to earn the right to return to loved ones: all of these would have been, no doubt, extremely desirable outcomes for Germany's soldiers, but were also divorced from reality. For those at the front who had been through so much, Goebbels's victory propaganda met many desperate yearnings, especially since the

alternative of continuing the war into the winter called to mind much
darker prospects. Yet, as Goebbels himself knew, his propaganda was
far from the truth. After more than three months of warfare during the
most favourable months of the year, the *Ostheer* had failed to strike
down the Soviet Union. Now, at the eleventh hour, with weakened
armies and tired men it was not just the size of the Red Army or the
vast distances remaining that should have tempered German optimism;
it was the time of the year. A Soviet pamphlet dropped to German
soldiers on 30 September stated: 'If you do not voluntarily go away
from here, you are lost. The harsh Russian winter is brewing.'[127]
Blinding snowstorms, freezing temperatures and icy winds would be
the result. Germany's typhoon was on course to collide with a Russian
winter blizzard.

The Holy Roman Emperor Friedrich Barbarossa participated in
the second crusade (1145–1149) led by his uncle Conrad III (1093–
1152) and then, as emperor, Barbarossa led numerous campaigns into
Italy. Yet in many respects Barbarossa's defining campaign was to be
his last – the third crusade to the Holy Lands which he launched in
May 1189. Although the source material relating to Barbarossa's rule
is somewhat rudimentary, the man behind the myths and legends was
unquestionably bold, at times ruthless, and driven by boundless ambi-
tion. His third crusade encompassed all of these traits and in many
respects became dependent upon his powerful force of personality to
sustain it. Having raised an enormous army, reported to have numbered
some 100,000 men with 20,000 knights, Barbarossa took the overland
route to the Holy Lands through Hungary and Constantinople and
into Anatolia. As an addendum to our discussion of 'the country',
Barbarossa's long march caused its own problems, which led to a
decline in strength even as more Christians joined the crusade during
its long march. The problems magnified once the army departed
Constantinople, being repeatedly harried and assaulted by Muslim
forces. Yet Barbarossa's presence is said to have steadied his men and
provided the army with firm direction on its hazardous journey. Not
surprisingly, therefore, Barbarossa's unexpected death (he drowned
when he fell from his horse while fording the Saleph River in full
armour) induced turmoil and doubt within his army, most of which
soon turned back towards Germany.[128]

In spite of Barbarossa's ill-fated commitment to the Third Crusade it was Hitler's own decision to style his war against the Soviet

Union as a modern-day European crusade modelled on Friedrich Barbarossa's reputation and exploits. As Hitler explained to Mile Budak, the Croatian minister stationed in Berlin, the war in the east 'is a crusade such as previously took place only against the Huns and against the Turks. This struggle must bring together and unite the European peoples.'[129] Yet Hitler's rush to parallel his own war in the east with Barbarossa's twelfth-century crusade might well have made for more symbolism than was intended or desired. Just as Friedrich Barbarossa died even before he reached the Holy Lands, Hitler's Operation Barbarossa fell well short of Moscow. Moreover, while the Christian crusaders later rallied for a fourth crusade (1202–1204), this also failed to reach the Holy Lands, just as Hitler's second attempt to take Moscow in Operation Typhoon would again fall short of its lofty expectations. In conceiving of his crusade against Bolshevism, Hitler's choice of symbolism was therefore ill conceived but, given the ultimate outcome, altogether appropriate.

2 OPERATION TYPHOON

The tempest moves east – 'the last great decisive battle of the year' (Adolf Hitler)

On the night of 1 October 1941, just hours before Operation Typhoon was due to begin, Adolf Hitler issued a proclamation that was to be read aloud to the troops of the eastern front:

> Soldiers!
>
> When I called on you to ward off the danger threatening our homeland on 22 June, you faced the greatest military power of all time. In barely three months, thanks to your bravery, my comrades, it has been possible to destroy one tank brigade after another belonging to this opponent, to eliminate countless divisions, to take uncounted prisoners, to occupy endless space … You have taken over 2,400,000 prisoners, you have destroyed or captured 17,500 tanks and over 21,000 guns, you have downed or destroyed on the ground 14,200 planes. The world has never seen anything like this![1]

While Hitler was at pains to point out the unprecedented nature of the *Ostheer*'s success, his comments also hinted at Operation Barbarossa's failure to end Soviet resistance. 'This time', he now confidently promised, everything would proceed 'according to plan' in order to deal the Soviet Union the long-awaited 'deadly blow'. With such characteristic bravado, Hitler then declared: 'Today the last great decisive battle of this year begins.'[2] Yet not everyone was convinced. Wolf Dose, a soldier in the 58th Infantry Division, wrote in his diary: 'The Führer has told us that the decisive battle in the east is beginning, a battle that will finish off the Russians – but how and where he did not say. I do not believe that the Soviet Union will capitulate.'[3] Others were more outspoken. 'The last great decisive battle of the year, *My God!* And what is the decisive result supposed to be – Moscow, Kharkov, the Volga?'[4] While throughout Germany morale had been boosted by the recent wave of *Sondermeldungen*, for those German soldiers in the forward trenches of Bock's army group – the same men who had resisted fierce Soviet attacks for the past two months – there were far fewer illusions about the difficulties of ending the war in the east. The new drive on Moscow presented daunting challenges. In the immediate prelude to Operation Typhoon Heinrich Haape recorded the activity observed on the Soviet side of the line:

> East of the Mezha, the Russians prepared a strong system of trenches, bunkers, tank-traps and barbed-wire entanglements. They laid minefields, reinforced their front-line troops, brought up supplies and gathered their strength to stand against us once more.
>
> We had to sit helplessly … and listen to stories brought back by our patrols of the rapidly developing Russian defensive system, and to read reports from our Luftwaffe spotter aircraft which saw the movement toward the front of fresh troops, guns and supply trains.[5]

Summing up the early October period another German soldier declared: 'the real hardships were about to start. The experience so far was only a prelude.'[6]

At 5:30 on the morning of 2 October Bock's offensive opened with a massed artillery bombardment followed by air and ground assaults.[7] Heinz Otto Fausten, serving in the 1st Panzer Division, wrote of 'a massive barrage of preparatory fire' before continuing: 'At around noon we crossed flattened enemy positions, our river of troops and vehicles flooding eastwards.'[8] The infantryman Helmut Pabst wrote home in a letter: '06.00. I jump on top of a dugout. There are the tanks! Giants rolling slowly towards the enemy. And the planes. One squadron after the other, unloading their bombs across the way. Army Group Centre has launched its attack.'[9] The war diary of Colonel Georg von Bismarck's 20th Panzer Division[10] labelled 2 October 'a historic day'.[11] Panzer Group 2, however, had been in action since 30 September and by the evening of 2 October Guderian had the impression that his forces had achieved a 'full breakthrough'.[12] In less than three days his subordinate XXXXVII Panzer Corps recorded capturing 3,800 POWs, destroying or capturing 17 panzers, 42 guns, 77 trucks and 300 horses.[13] To the north, Hoepner's Panzer Group 4 advanced up to 15 kilometres into Soviet positions on the first day and,[14] while the enemy it encountered was reported to be 'surprised', they nevertheless 'resisted bitterly'.[15] Hoth's Panzer Group 3 drove 20 kilometres into the Soviet lines on the first day and found enemy resistance to be less than expected.[16] The rapid advance was also attributed to the good weather, which, according to the Panzer Group 3's war diary, 'benefited all movement on the bad roads and tracks'.[17] At points where the roads did become problematic, the dry conditions allowed for simple off-road detours, avoiding serious delays.[18] The weather report for central Russia on 2 October was 'clear and sunny', providing a reminder of the opening conditions of Operation Barbarossa 103 days earlier.[19] The 5th Panzer Division's war diary labelled it simply 'offensive weather'.[20]

At Army Group Centre Bock was elated. That night he wrote in his diary: 'The army group went to the attack according to plan. We advanced so easily everywhere that doubts arose as to whether the enemy had not in fact decamped.'[21] Yet intelligence gathered from captured Soviet officers soon confirmed that no order for withdrawal had been issued and that the defending armies had been ordered to hold their positions at all costs.[22] German radio intelligence further confirmed the Red Army's dogged determination to resist and not surrender ground. Soviet intercepts read: 'Reinforcement not possible, the crossings are to be held'; 'the commander is dead I have taken over command'; 'I cannot hold any longer, destroying the radio.'[23] As Helmut Pabst observed, the German superiority at Panzer Group 3's point of main concentration was overwhelming. 'Tanks roll by, close to the gun position. A hundred have gone by already, and they're still coming on ... It looks like chaos, but it works to the minute, like clockwork. Today they want to break into the Dnieper-line, tomorrow it will be Moscow. Armoured scout cars are now joining the columns.'[24] After almost four hours watching the main grouping of Hoth's panzer group pass by, Pabst concluded: 'By now I think we've seen the last come by. It's getting quieter ... Any war film would pale by comparison. "That was really some show!" the boys are saying.'[25]

While Typhoon's opening success seemed complete, there were still some bitterly contested positions costing many German lives.

Lieutenant-General Heinrich Meyer-Bürdorf's 131st Infantry Division suffered very heavy losses on 2 October trying to clear Soviet positions opposing its front.[26] The panzer divisions also encountered difficulties with the familiar problem of inadequate bridges and, more ominously for the first day of an offensive, fuel shortages.[27] Even before the offensive had begun, fuel reserves were recognised to be worryingly small and plans were made to bring up more fuel with transport aircraft and towed gliders.[28] Yet there could be no question that Army Group Centre was making significant gains across a wide section of the eastern front, and that was the message Bock relayed to Colonel Rudolf Schmundt, the Führer's chief military adjutant at the 'Wolf's Lair' (Wolfschanze), Hitler's secluded East Prussian headquarters.[29] The news confirmed for Hitler that the war was in fact nearing its end and he was in a celebratory mood. On 3 October at the annual opening of the War Winter Relief Organisation (Kriegswinterhilfswerk) in Berlin, Hitler delivered his first national address since the opening of the war in the east. It was an auspicious occasion, allowing Hitler to recast the war in the east from a failed blitzkrieg to a seamless military operation on the verge of outright victory. Hitler stated: 'On the morning of June 22, this greatest struggle in the history of the world began. Since then, three and a half months have passed. Today I can state everything has gone according to plan.'[30]

Yet even Hitler could not hope to pass over the scale and cost of the fighting in the east, and he admitted that Germany had been caught unawares. 'However, something did deceive us', he told the German people; 'we had no idea how gigantic the preparations of this opponent against Germany and Europe had been.'[31] It was a surprisingly frank admission, probably inspired by his confidence in the defeat of the Soviet Union, which he now promised in the most direct terms. 'I say this here today because I may say today that this opponent has already broken down and will never rise again!'[32] Not only was Hitler forecasting the end to the war in the east, but he also admitted he had switched industry away from army production. 'Today, it is only a question of transport. Today, we have taken care in advance so that, in the midst of this war of materiel, I can order further production in many spheres to cease, because I know there is no opponent whom we would not be able to defeat with the existing amounts of ammunition.'[33] Hitler's speech may have reassured many of his followers, but it also reflected the depths of delusion inhibiting the German command and the credibility gap that had arisen between war propaganda and the actual situation in the east. Nevertheless, in the short term soldiers, such as Wilhelm Prüller, rejoiced at Hitler's address. Writing in his diary, Prüller noted: 'What a lift his words give us, as we crowd round the wireless set, not wanting to miss a single word! Is there a finer reward after a day of battle than to hear the Führer? Never!'[34] Erich Hager noted in his diary that after the speech: 'All sorts were really enthused. Many were drunk.'[35] Other soldiers, however, were less convinced and seemed confused by the emergent dichotomy between the public representation and personal experience of the war. Hans Jürgen Hartmann noted: 'Perhaps it is only "talk" that our enemy is broken and will never rise again. I cannot help myself – I am totally bewildered. Will the whole war still be over before winter?'[36] Certainly those with a greater over-view of events were not taken in by Hitler's confident ruse. The Italian foreign minister, Galeazzo Ciano, wrote in his diary on 3 October:

> Speech by Hitler in Berlin, which was unexpected, or almost so. First impressions are that he has tried to explain to the German people his reasons for the attack on Russia and to justify his delay in ending the war, about which he had made very definite commitments. There is no doubt that he has lost some of his vigour ... As for us, we are given no particular attention; he lumped us with the others, and this will not produce a good impression in Italy, where the wave of anti-German feeling is growing stronger and stronger.[37]

As Hitler was proclaiming that the Red Army was broken and would never rise again, Soviet forces opposing Army Group Centre fought on tenaciously even as command and control along many parts of the front began to break down.[38] Indeed at Yel'nya, the scene of so much heavy fighting from late July to early September, the German IX Army Corps, commanded by General of Infantry Hermann Geyer, was subjected to fierce Soviet counterattacks on 3 and 4 October.[39] Yet by holding doggedly to long sections of the front, the Soviet armies defending the approaches to Moscow were allowing themselves to become encircled and were thereby facilitating another Soviet disaster. Eremenko, who commanded the Briansk Front, had already unsuccessfully requested permission to withdraw his forces to new positions, while Konev, in command of the Western Front, set out for Stalin the growing danger for his forces, but likewise was not authorised to pull back.[40] By the evening of 3 October Hoth and Hoepner's panzer divisions had advanced up to 50 kilometres into the Soviet lines,[41] while in the south Guderian's spearhead 4th Panzer Division had broken into open terrain and was advancing along one of the few sealed roads in the Soviet Union. The objective was Orel, a city of 140,000 inhabitants, which lay largely undefended and at the extreme limit of the panzer division's fuel reserves. The distinguished Soviet journalist Vasily Grossman was in Orel when an alarmed colleague found him. 'The Germans are rushing straight for Orel. There are hundreds of tanks. I had a narrow escape under fire. We must leave immediately, otherwise they'll catch us here.'[42] In fact Orel was not attacked by hundreds of German tanks; rather it was taken by Arthur Wollschlaeger's 6th Company consisting of just four tanks, which alone held the city for three hours until further reinforcement began to arrive. It was a typical act of audacity, for which the German panzer forces were famous. Unsupported, Wollschlaeger's tanks simply drove into the city, securing bridges and the main railway station. As fear and astonishment gripped the local population, the 'shock' effect of Wollschlaeger's bold drive forestalled any resistance. As Wollschlaeger later recalled of his drive through the city streets: 'City life was still in full swing. When the citizens of Orel saw us, they fled into the buildings and side streets, white as ghosts.'[43]

Orel lay some 240 kilometres[44] from Guderian's starting point four days before and was captured with hardly a shot being fired. In many respects the success at Orel raised hopes that Moscow could in fact be taken in the coming days and weeks. Yet Orel was the exception, not the rule. The advance had already almost exhausted Guderian's entire stock of fuel, while the weather had remained excellent and the roads were, at least in parts, well above average for the Soviet Union. The complications of continuing major operations in the east during the Russian autumn were as yet unknown to the *Ostheer*. As a Swiss radio broadcast on 3 October noted: 'The situation this autumn is notable for what has not occurred: despite the German Wehrmacht's immense successes in Russia, no decision has come about leading to a conclusion of the campaign or a ceasefire … The Germans have lost their initial fear of the Russian winter and the vastness of Russia.'[45] As a case in point Wagner, the army quartermaster-general who was in charge of the *Ostheer*'s deeply troubled logistical apparatus, wrote in a letter on the same day (3 October): 'I think that a great success, that is to say the decisive one, will be achieved in four weeks.'[46] Perhaps the Germans had lost their fear of the Russian winter and the vastness of the Soviet Union, or maybe it had merely been supplanted by faith in Hitler's maxim: 'To the German soldier nothing is impossible!'[47] In either case Typhoon's success and easy victories were to be short-lived.

While the capture of Orel was a clear propaganda success for Bock, across other parts of the front the second day of the offensive was already revealing the worn state of the motorised divisions. After questions were raised about the sluggish mobility of Major-General Walter Krüger's 1st Panzer Division, Hoth explained that it had been deployed directly off the march from Leningrad without time to rest or refit. 'Not surprising', Halder commented and then added: 'Soon the same can also be expected from the 19th and 20th Panzer Divisions.'[48] Another problem for the German advance was the danger caused by Soviet aerial attacks, which revealed not only the increasing potency of the resurgent Soviet air force, but the frequent inability of the Luftwaffe to offer protection across wide sections of the front. As Major-General Willibald Freiherr von Langermann-Erlancamp's 4th Panzer Division thrust towards Orel, his division was repeatedly attacked. According to the divisional war diary for 3 October: 'The aerial attacks of the Russians are getting stronger. The attacks continue almost without pause, mostly 1–2 bombers with fighter cover, and are to be found along the whole route of the advance to Dmitrovsk.'[49] At the other end of Bock's front, Hoth's Panzer Group 3 was complaining of the same problem and cited one example from Lieutenant-General Walther Fischer von Weikersthal's subordinated 35th Infantry Division, which in one attack suffered fifteen dead and forty wounded.[50] Describing another attack, Albert Neuhaus wrote home to his wife on 3 October: 'Then suddenly two Russian bombers came over the road and started firing at us with their guns from 500 metres away. That happened so quickly that the usual search for cover was out of the question. Left and right things shot into the ground.'[51]

While the Soviet air force was causing problems, the aircraft of Kesselring's Air Fleet 2, covering Army Group Centre, were by no means dormant. Prior to the opening of Operation Typhoon, Kesselring had been reinforced by aircraft from Colonel-General Alexander Löhr's Air Fleet 4, assigned to Army Group South. In addition, a fresh fighter squadron was transferred to Kesselring from Western Europe along with the arrival of the Spanish Blue Squadron (Escuadrilla Azul).[52] A further two bomber squadrons were transferred to Kesselring from the newly formed Croatian Air Force Legion (Hrvatska Zrakoplovna Legija).[53] Kesselring's Air Fleet 2 was split into two corps: General of Aviation Bruno Loerzer's II Air Corps and Colonel-General Wolfram von Richthofen's VIII Air Corps. Loerzer was assigned to support Guderian's panzer group, as well as rendering some support to operations on Hoepner's right flank. Richthofen then took on the task of providing air cover for the panzer groups of Hoth and Hoepner.[54] On the first day of Operation Typhoon aircraft in Richthofen's corps averaged four sorties and some managed as many as six.[55] On the second day (3 October) a total of 984 sorties were flown throughout Kesselring's air fleet, accounting for the destruction of some 679 enemy vehicles. The next day (4 October) another 450 enemy vehicles were destroyed.[56] Yet the good flying conditions benefited both sides, and the spearheads of German panzer groups were prime targets for the Soviet air force. As Guderian noted on 5 October:

> On this day ... I gained a vivid impression of the liveliness of the Russian air force. Immediately after I had landed on Sevsk airfield, where twenty German fighters had also just come in, the Russians bombed it; this was followed by an air attack on the corps headquarters which sent the glass in the windows flying about our ears. I drove at once along the road of advance of 3rd Panzer Division. Here too we were subjected to a series of bombing attacks by small groups of from three to six Russian bombers.[57]

Attempts to ward off the Soviet attacks often led to fiercely contested dogfights, which claimed the lives of many pilots on both sides. While the Luftwaffe had started the war with a considerable qualitative advantage in training and experience, the many weeks of relentless operations had allowed surviving Soviet pilots to gain valuable experience, while every German loss reduced their net superiority. Indeed, Soviet pilots were proving capable of taking on Germany's best. On 3 October Heinrich Hoffmann, Germany's fourth-highest-ranked fighter ace with sixty-three 'victories', was shot down south of Yel'nya. The third-ranked ace, Hermann-Friedrich Joppien, had already been killed in August and the second-ranked, Heinz Bär, was recovering in hospital from wounds sustained in a crash landing. Werner Mölders, with 101 official 'victories', was the top of the table, but for propaganda reasons resulting from his success and high public profile he was withdrawn from operational flying.[58]

While the air battle over the eastern front raged, the panzer groups were rapidly enveloping major elements of three Soviet fronts in two giant pockets. In the south, Guderian's XXIV Panzer Corps, under General of Panzer Troops Leo Freiherr Geyr von Schweppenberg, thrust to the north-east to seize Orel, but Panzer Group 2 also consisted of two other panzer corps. On Guderian's southern flank, Kempf's XXXXVIII Panzer Corps was charged with maintaining contact to Army Group South as well as pushing east to cover Schweppenberg's extended right flank. On Guderian's left, General of Panzer Troops Joachim Lemelsen's XXXXVII Panzer Corps was ordered to drive due north to seize Briansk where it was hoped a large pocket could then be formed together with Weichs's Second Army. Yet while Lemelsen's lead panzer division (the 17th) was making good ground, Weichs's infantry were stalled, and the southern pocket would consequently take longer to form.[59] To the north of Weichs's Second Army was Kluge's Fourth Army together with Hoepner's Panzer Group 4. Hoepner's panzer group was numerically the strongest on the eastern front and simply smashed through the depleted ranks of the hapless Soviet Forty-Third Army. His panzer divisions then turned north-west to outflank two more Soviet armies (Twentieth and Twenty-Fourth) while heading for the rendezvous with Hoth's panzer group at Viaz'ma. On Bock's northern wing, Strauss's Ninth Army and Hoth's Panzer Group 3 were to form the left pincer for the second major pocket. Having penetrated to the Dnepr east of Kholm-Zhirkovskii and captured two bridges intact, Hoth was only 60 kilometres from Viaz'ma by the evening of 3 October (see Map 5).[60] Yet Konev desperately organised a counterattack, which succeeded in halting Hoth's progress and forcing him into a pitched battle.[61] On 4 October Lieutenant-General Franz Landgraf's 6th Panzer Division destroyed twenty-five Soviet tanks, but lost fifteen of his own. At the same time Krüger's 1st Panzer Division destroyed thirty-three Soviet tanks for an undisclosed number of German losses; however, the war diary of Panzer Group 3 noted that on 5 October: 'The counterattack of the enemy south of Kholm has unfortunately cost us heavy losses.'[62]

In spite of frantic Soviet countermeasures, the armoured rings of Bock's three panzer groups were rapidly closing, causing fear of being trapped by the oncoming Germans to spread. Witnessing the unfolding confusion, Soviet journalist Vasily Grossman noted on 4 October:

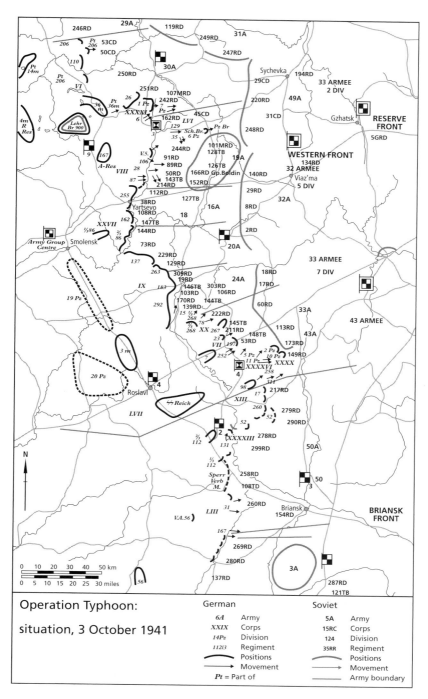

Map 5 Dispositions of Army Group Centre, 3 October 1941

> I thought I'd seen retreat, but I've never seen anything like what
> I am seeing now, and could never even imagine anything of the
> kind. Exodus! Biblical exodus! Vehicles are moving in eight lanes,
> there's the violent roaring of dozens of trucks trying simultaneously
> to tear their wheels out of the mud. Huge herds of sheep and cows
> are driven through the fields. They are followed by trains of horse-
> driven carts, there are thousands of wagons covered with coloured
> sackcloth, veneer, tin … There are also crowds of pedestrians with
> sacks, bundles, suitcases. This isn't a flood, this isn't a river, it's the
> slow movement of a flowing ocean, this flow is hundreds of metres
> wide … There are moments when I feel with complete vividness as
> if we have been transported back in time to the era of biblical
> catastrophes.[63]

It may not have been biblical, but it certainly was a catastrophe for the
Soviet Union. At the OKH the mood was one of jubilation. Indeed,
4 October was Brauchitsch's sixtieth birthday so there was a festive
breakfast with presents and in the afternoon a visit from Hitler who
joined his army commanders for tea. Hitler talked freely of sending
Guderian from Orel on to Tula, 170 kilometres to the north-east, and
then on to Moscow, a further 175 kilometres north. He also talked
of Army Group North's depleted forces renewing the offensive along
Lake Ladoga. It was a familiar pattern of rampant self-deception in
which initial successes quickly led to unrealistic overestimations of the
Ostheer's operational potential. Still, with Bock's front now moving
forward after more than two months on the defensive and the early
October weather in the east having turned unseasonably warm,[64] Hitler
and his generals were fully convinced by their own propaganda that the
war was soon to be ended. In his diary Halder noted the favourable
developments: 'Operation Typhoon is developing on a truly classic
course … The enemy is holding all parts of the front not under attack,
which bodes well for the establishment of pockets.'[65]

If Typhoon was following an altogether classic course, so too
were the operational problems now emerging. Before Guderian could
even think about driving on to Tula he first needed to address his near-
absent fuel reserves. Langermann-Erlancamp's 4th Panzer Division was
momentarily unopposed on the road to Tula, but unable to exploit its
advantage for lack of fuel.[66] On 5 October Guderian requested 500 cubic
metres of fuel be flown to an airfield near Orel, but at best Kesselring
could only manage about 70 to 100 cubic metres on 6 October.[67]

Likewise, Schweppenberg's XXIV Panzer Corps was also pleading for more fuel, which led to another demand on Kesselring's already overextended transport capacity. As Guderian acknowledged, the availability of fuel for Operation Typhoon was essential; 'the future extent of our movements was ultimately dependent on this'.[68] Nor was Panzer Group 2 the exception. Hoepner's advance on Viaz'ma was already causing problems for Vietinghoff's XXXXVI Panzer Corps because fuel shortages combined with bad roads were slowing all movement.[69] Even worse, after being halted by Soviet counterattacks on 4 October, Hoth's Panzer Group 3 could still not advance on 5 October because fuel stocks had been totally exhausted. Kesselring was again requested to fly in urgent deliveries in order to restart the attack.[70] Astonishingly, in the midst of such basic shortages and with the offensive only days old, Wagner, the army quartermaster-general, wrote in a letter on 5 October:

> Operational goals are being set that earlier would have made our hair stand on end. Eastward of Moscow! Then I estimate that the war will be mostly over, and perhaps there really will be a collapse of the [Soviet] system ... I am constantly astounded at the Führer's military judgement. He intervenes in the course of operations, one could say decisively, and up until now he has always acted correctly.[71]

Such blind devotion and professional incompetence was by no means limited to Wagner within the OKH. Indeed, given Wagner's many shortcomings and failed promises, his survival in the post of quartermaster-general only confirmed the support he, and his judgements, often enjoyed. Importantly Wagner was an enthusiast for all manner of Nazi ideals, including the power of individual 'will', which asserted the power of the spiritual over the tangible. Following this line of Nazi mythology, German troops, regardless of the supply situation, could conquer Moscow so long as they remained determined to do so. The folly of such belief should have been apparent during Operation Barbarossa, but the absence of a learning curve within the German high command doomed Operation Typhoon to repeat many of the previous mistakes.

While supply shortages constrained the German advance from behind, Soviet opposition was by no means negligible. Indeed, at points the Germans were even forced into retreat with heavy losses. On 6 October Hans Roth noted in his diary:

> Since tonight we have encountered the famous 'Moscow Proletarian Guard,' and Asians, lots of Asians, who as demonstrated by the attack, fight with utmost determination and devilish cunning. We unfortunately suffer losses, among whom are two of our best Lieutenants Forester and Kohl ... A little later those dogs attack again; we have to evacuate the position and retreat towards the hills in the northeast, all the while fighting. Only by giving it our all are we able to keep the fanatical howling horde at bay ... it looks like we'll be burying corpses![72]

Nor was this just an isolated local setback. When Langermann-Erlancamp's 4th Panzer Division attempted to advance 50 kilometres north-east of Orel to Mtsensk on 6 October it was dealt a crippling blow by an expertly managed Soviet counterstroke. In his memoir Guderian referred to the division's 'grievous casualties', but attempted to suggest that this 'was the first occasion on which the vast superiority of the Russian T-34 to our tanks became plainly apparent'.[73] In fact the superiority of the Soviet T-34 had been evident since the earliest days of the war, yet their poor tactical employment and lack of supporting arms had often negated their technical advantages. Now young Soviet commanders were learning that headlong attacks into prepared German positions were rarely successful and, as the war diary of the 4th Panzer Division noted: 'The Russian was very skilled in directing his tanks, pulling back often, only to appear again in a flanking attack. In the course of the afternoon his heavy models inflicted heavy losses.'[74]

Not only was the Soviet attack successful in forcing a German panzer division into retreat but also, even according to German sources, the Soviets did not achieve this through numerical superiority. The Germans estimated the Soviet tank force to have numbered about forty-five (all models), while the 4th Panzer Division fielded some fifty-six combat-ready tanks on the eve of the battle.[75] The Germans also advanced with a motorcycle infantry battalion, an 88mm Flak battery, a *Nebelwerfer* battalion[76] and the artillery from two battalions. Much of this also sustained losses in the ensuing engagement.[77] By the end of the day the 4th Panzer Division reported seventeen Soviet tanks destroyed for the loss of ten German, yet it was the Red Army who held the field.[78] On the following day (7 October) Langermann-Erlancamp renewed the attack, only to be beaten back again with 'heavy personnel and materiel losses'. By 9 October the 4th Panzer Division had just thirty operational tanks, and no ground had been gained.[79] The attack towards Mtsensk was again renewed, but according to the war diary of the 4th Panzer Division: 'Forward movement along the route of advance was not possible because of the superior weaponry of the Russian tanks (around twenty-five). No Russian tanks hit, unfortunately again some personnel and materiel losses (four panzers destroyed, a few damaged, one 88mm anti-aircraft gun, one 100mm cannon, one armoured half-truck,[80] one artillery observer destroyed).'[81] Clearly some units of the Red Army had learned to fight, and even outmatch, the Wehrmacht. Moreover, these successes were achieved before the winter had taken hold, which many German veterans would later blame for all their setbacks in Operation Typhoon. As Guderian himself acknowledged after witnessing part of the battle, 'They were learning.'[82]

While Soviet units were progressively adapting to German tactics, the need for a learning curve at the front was by no means limited to the Red Army. With increasing numbers of German replacements filling the gaps in the ranks, the process of adjusting to the war in the east, and its many inherent dangers, required speedy schooling within the *Ostheer*. One post-war study of small-unit actions on the eastern front concluded that several months of acclimatisation were often necessary before units could adapt and stem the high tide of casualties. The required learning curve was on occasion so large that full-strength combat units, without previous experience on the eastern front, were incapable of achieving the same tasks as those units greatly depleted by previous engagements.[83] The stubborn and unorthodox tactical approach of the Red Army often included special measures, which confounded unsuspecting *Landsers*.[84] In the first days of Operation Typhoon, advanced elements of Veiel's 2nd Panzer Division halted to engage three Soviet tanks which had been sighted 300 metres away. Round after round was fired including special armour-piecing rounds, but nothing seemed to have any effect. Only after an infantry officer worked his way round behind them was it learned that the whole advance had been halted by pock-marked and collapsing wooden tank decoys.[85] In another instance on 5 October Major-General Walter Nehring's 18th Panzer Division encountered what it referred to as 'mine dogs'.[86] These were dogs fitted with explosive devices that were triggered by a spring-loaded wooden lever that stood up from the dog's back. The dogs were trained to find food under armoured vehicles and when they crawled under a tank the lever was compressed leading to detonation.[87] Another desperate Soviet tactic was to feign death to allow unsuspecting German soldiers to pass by and then assail them from behind.[88] As Erich Kern wrote: 'Suddenly I froze – a dead Russian had moved … In a flash the "dead man" straightened up to throw the grenade ready in his hand. But our pistols were quicker.'[89]

Even more inventive was the vast system of Soviet traps discovered in heavily defended positions. In one the ground vegetation was covered by a fine webbing of wire, which was connected to a generator hidden in a bunker. When activated the net of wire charged with a deadly current. As one of the soldiers who discovered it noted, 'It was so well camouflaged that we recognized it unfortunately much too late, only after the continued accumulation of losses.'[90] In other instances the Soviets employed primitive trip-wires, which when triggered hit the victim with poisoned steel spikes. Alternatively packs of cigarettes or watches were booby-trapped with explosives and left in plain view. There was also an automatic flame-thrower that was activated by the victim stepping on a pressure panel. Other trip-wires sent mines jumping 3–4 metres into the air before exploding, and then there were the so-called devil's ditches. These were intended to be used as cover by an attacking force before exploding, sometimes for hundreds of metres, via underground detonation channels.[91] Not surprisingly, the Red Army's methods forced even hardened veterans to dread their new enemy. When Major-General Fehn, commanding the recently arrived 5th Panzer Division, told his corps commander about the nightly attacks on his command post, Vietinghoff was unmoved and simply informed his subordinate, 'such "surprises" belong to everyday experience in Russia'.[92]

Caging the Bear – Bock's encirclements at Viaz'ma and Briansk

While the three Soviet fronts opposing Bock desperately attempted to hold the line in increasingly untenable circumstances, the Stavka initially refused any withdrawals. Yet at 11:00 a.m. on 5 October, Colonel Sbytov, the Moscow district fighter commander, passed on a pilot's report of an enemy column almost 20 kilometres long, moving unopposed towards Yukhnov, a town about one-third of the way from

Typhoon's starting line to the Soviet capital (190 kilometres from Moscow). Marshal Boris Shaposhnikov, the Red Army's chief of the general staff, was informed of the report, but insisted 'there was no basis for disquiet', and a second reconnaissance plane was dispatched to confirm, or rather disprove, the sighting. When the second pilot made the same report a third pilot was sent; only when he too confirmed the presence of German troops did Shaposhnikov recognise the danger and inform Stalin. There could be no denying the seriousness of the development. Major German formations were now operating behind the Soviet line and, what is more, there was nothing between these forces and Moscow. Stalin telephoned the Moscow district staff and told them to mobilise everything they had to hold the Germans for five to seven days until reserves could be brought up.[93] The new Soviet line was to be established on the so-called Mozhaisk Defensive Line, about 110 kilometres west of Moscow and anchored on four defensive regions at Volokolamsk, Mozhaisk, Maloiaroslavets and Kaluga.[94] Stalin also belatedly authorised Konev's Western Front to conduct a withdrawal, while similar orders were also dispatched to Budenny's Reserve Front and Eremenko's Briansk Front.[95] However, as with other Soviet catastrophes, it was too little, too late. Soviet command and control was already seriously compromised, while the German panzer groups were well on their way to closing two enormous pockets. On the same day (5 October), Stalin telephoned Marshal Georgi Zhukov, the commander of the Leningrad Front, and ordered him to relinquish his command and come to Moscow.[96]

At this point an intriguing episode took place. According to Zhukov's account, when he arrived at Stalin's apartment on 7 October he found the Soviet dictator in a private discussion with L. P. Beria, the chief of the NKVD (Narodnyi Komissariat Vnutrennykh Del – People's Commissariat for Internal Affairs). Zhukov announced himself, but there was no reaction; his account then continues: 'Ignoring me, or perhaps unaware of my arrival, he [Stalin] was telling Beria to use his agencies to sound out the possibilities for making a separate peace with Germany, given the critical situation.'[97] When Stalin at last reacted to Zhukov's presence, he spoke only of the troubling new developments at the front. Later, the Soviet Union flatly denied having ever approached Nazi Germany with the intention of cutting a deal, but the idea was not without precedent. In 1918 Lenin negotiated the Treaty of Brest-Litovsk with Germany, trading 1.4 million square kilometres of land, including the Baltic states and parts of Belorussia and Ukraine, for a peace accord ensuring Russia's exit from World War I. Was Stalin now attempting a similar deal? Evidence suggests there was an attempt made to contact the Germans through Ivan Stamenov, the Bulgarian ambassador in Moscow. According to documents from the Presidential Archive in Moscow, Pavel Sudoplatov, one of Beria's most trusted agents, firstly, made contact with Stamenov in late July 1941 and posed four questions: firstly, the Soviets wanted to know why Germany had broken the non-aggression pact; secondly, they wanted to know under what conditions Germany might stop the war; thirdly, the Germans were to be asked if they would accept the Baltic states, Ukraine, Bessarabia, Bukovina and the Karelian peninsula in exchange for a deal; finally, if these territories were unacceptable what would Germany want in addition?[98] There is no record of a response and no document has come to light suggesting that any form of serious negotiations took place, yet after 22 June 1941 Hitler never wavered in his determination to avoid dealing with the Soviet Union. In his eyes the war was to end in total victory or total defeat; there would be no middle road. Whether the Soviet documents were serious attempts at opening negotiations, or purposeful attempts at providing the Germans with disinformation, as some have claimed, can probably never be ascertained for certain.[99] Certainly Stalin confronted his darkest days of the war during 1941, and it is not beyond the realm of possibility that he initiated talks with serious intentions.[100] Soviet peace feelers, however serious they may have been, came to nothing and the war was destined to be decided on the battlefield.

In early October the battlefields west of Moscow looked none too encouraging for the Red Army. When Zhukov entered Stalin's apartment on 7 October he was shown a map that reflected the extent of the disaster near Viaz'ma. As Stalin told Zhukov: 'Just like Pavlov at the beginning of the war, Konev has opened up the front to the enemy here.'[101] In fact, Stalin wanted to put Konev on trial just as he had Pavlov, but Zhukov interceded and changed the dictator's mind. Zhukov was then given the hazardous task of touring the front headquarters, establishing what needed to be done and reporting back to Stalin.[102] Zhukov's tour confirmed the Stavka's worst fears. It was clear that the great bulk of the Western and Reserve Fronts were caught in an enormous pocket centred on Viaz'ma and that the road to Moscow was completely open. Zhukov recommended to Stalin that everything possible be rushed to the Mozhaisk Defensive Line to defend the capital. With almost no regular army units available to man the new defensive positions, officer cadets, 'destroyer' battalions, people's militia (*opolchentsy*), NKVD and police units were hastily dispatched from Moscow.[103] Meanwhile, six rifle divisions, six tank brigades and ten artillery and machine-gun regiments were hurriedly dispatched from the Stavka reserve with more soon to follow. At the same time, Stalin began to draw on his Far Eastern military district (some fifty-eight divisions strong)[104] which had, until then, been largely left intact as a countermeasure and deterrent to Japanese invasion.[105] In part as a result of the intelligence confirming Japan's peaceful intentions towards the Soviet Union, provided by Richard Sorge, the Soviet spy in Japan, Stalin decided to redirect substantial numbers of troops to the threatened Moscow region.[106] In the course of October, ten Soviet divisions would be transferred to the west with more to follow.[107] On 10 October the remnants of the Reserve Front were absorbed into the Western Front and Zhukov replaced Konev as the new commanding officer.[108] The situation remained grim, but if there was any man in the Red Army who possessed the skill, determination and ruthlessness to defend Moscow it was Zhukov.

On the same day that the Soviet command shuddered over the discovery of a German column heading towards Yukhnov (5 October), the same route of advance was causing nothing but frustration for the German command. As Bock noted in his diary: 'things are a mess on the big "Roslavl–Moscow highway". Four to five columns side by side, with unauthorised Luftwaffe elements wedged in between them, clog the road on which the entire supply effort, including deliveries of fuel for the tanks, depends.'[109] By the same token, as the Soviet command trembled at the speed with which the German panzer divisions were enveloping their armies, Bock was lamenting their delay in closing the pockets. Hoth's panzer group was stalled near Kholm, while Bock noted Fehn's 5th Panzer Division, from Hoepner's panzer group, was having difficulties advancing (see Map 6). As Bock concluded, 'My main worry, getting the armoured spearheads together at Viaz'ma, remains great.'[110] While Bock fretted over what he had not yet been able to achieve, the fact remained that even without having closed the pockets Army Group Centre had accomplished a remarkable amount in the first four days of the offensive. By 6 October Bock's army group had taken 78,744 Soviet POWs and captured or destroyed 272 tanks, 541 guns, 181 anti-tank guns, 75 anti-aircraft guns and 10 planes.[111]

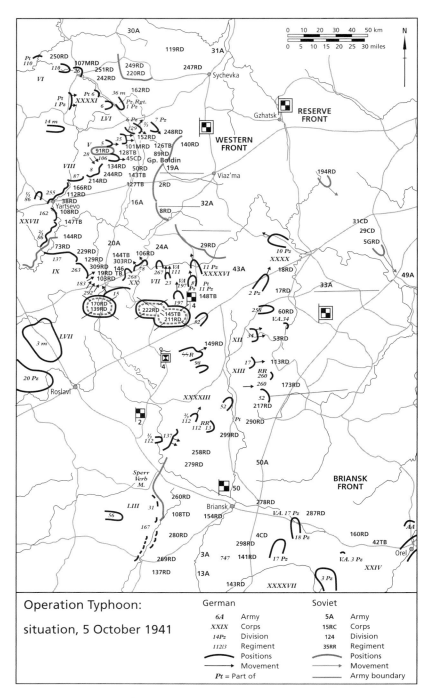

Map 6 Dispositions of Army Group Centre, 5 October 1941

Yet even in the midst of their unfolding success the German command was always prone to embittered in-fighting and on 6 October a simmering dispute between Bock and Strauss, the commander of the Ninth Army, erupted into what Bock called 'a bitter fight'. As Bock saw it, the infantry did not need to attack everywhere along the encirclement front; rather they only needed to maintain an effective perimeter, while the panzer groups enveloped the Soviet positions. Thus Bock had been critical of Strauss's attempt to order individual divisions to undertake unnecessary attacks in defensive sectors. For his part Strauss resented the interference from above as well as the removal of his only reserve (the motorised 'Lehrbrigade 900');[112] however, Bock countered that he needed to push all motorised forces up to Kholm to ensure Hoth's continued movement.[113] Things came to a head on 6 October when Bock ordered Lieutenant-General Joachim Witthöft's 86th Infantry Division to follow up in the wake of Hoth's panzers to ensure more strength on the eastern perimeter of the pocket. Strauss resisted and then claimed that the move was impossible because of the state of the roads and the supply situation leading to Kholm.[114] Their discussion became acrimonious, and afterwards Bock resolved to send Strauss a long telegram informing him of his rationale and orders:

Dear Strauss,

I regret that developments during the past ten days have led to a misunderstanding between us ... You are aware that from the very first order that I issued for this attack I have stressed orally and in writing the necessity for the infantry to follow closely the armour and support it with the greatest energy. This holds true in the case of the Viaz'ma encirclement.

I am not unaware of the extremely difficult conditions regarding supply, transportation, and communications behind your front. I do not agree, however, with your analysis that it is impossible to move your infantry. I remind you that despite adverse terrain conditions, the infantry in the other armies continue to move forward. It is imperative that we prevent the enemy from breaking out of the Viaz'ma pocket and reforming his defences to the east and northeast.

There is sound basis for my previous instructions to you. During the battles at Minsk and at Smolensk, I urged repeatedly that the armour be allowed freedom of movement as soon as possible, to prevent the enemy from regrouping his defences. This, of necessity, placed a heavy burden on the infantry, but in this campaign it affords the only chance of defeating an enemy who has traditionally used his vast, primitive terrain to his own advantage ... *This must not happen again!* ... I must enforce my will, even at the risk of endangering the friendly relations that have heretofore existed between us.[115]

On the following day (7 October) Hoth spoke with Bock and disputed Strauss's view on the impossibility of advancing infantry through to Kholm. Then there came evidence that Strauss was ignoring Bock's order to send infantry after Hoth's panzer group. That evening when Bock called Strauss and accused him of insubordination 'a lively argument developed',[116] but by this point Bock had had enough. For his iron-like resolve and at times fiery exhortations, Bock had earlier in his career been dubbed 'the Holy Fire of Küstrin'.[117] Perhaps not surprisingly, after Bock had reached the end of his tether and taken his subordinate to task, Strauss fell firmly into line.[118]

While there was open conflict with Strauss at Ninth Army, Bock also had a difference of opinion with Weichs at Second Army who felt that the more southerly pocket centred on Briansk was being closed too soon and that a deeper bite into the Soviet front should be attempted. Here Bock was much more sympathetic. In the planning stages for Operation Typhoon, Bock had himself fought a protracted, if unsuccessful, battle with the OKH for a larger encirclement, but now Bock was adamant. 'Unfortunately they [Second Army] will have to satisfy themselves with the small pocket south of Briansk.'[119] Nor was Weichs the only one of Bock's commanders having to accept a smaller than desired pocket. On 29 September Hoepner had unsuccessfully argued with Bock over the depth of the northern pocket and, while the commander of Panzer Group 4 was forced to follow orders, he remained convinced that an opportunity had been missed. In a letter home on 6 October Hoepner complained: 'Things have not been done as I have suggested, otherwise even more [Soviet POWs] would have been seized. Since the day before yesterday that was clear to me and many others.'[120] Hoepner was also being carefully watched by Kluge, his nominal superior at Fourth Army. Kluge had come to distrust panzer commanders precisely because, as he saw it, they always sought to start new battles before the old ones were completed. Thus Kluge kept Hoepner on a very short leash, leading to much friction between the two. As Hoepner

3 The commander of Panzer Group 2, Colonel-General Heinz Guderian (to the right of man with outstretched arm).

complained, 'Kluge also meddles in my affairs which always aggravates. Yesterday it came to a clash. Today I wanted to report sick ... The lower ranks don't know any more what they should do; they are always just pushed around, today there, the next day the other direction. Their hardships go unattended. Until now Kluge's interference has three times resulted in the opposite of what he had intended.'[121] Hoth also found Strauss a restrictive army commander, but he proved himself more adept at compromising where necessary and convincing his commander when he deemed it essential.

Yet if there was one man whom most of the senior command in both the OKH and at Army Group Centre had had conflict with during Operation Barbarossa it was Guderian (see Illustration 3). In early July Kluge, at that time commanding the Fourth Panzer Army to which Panzer Group 2 was subordinate, threatened to have Guderian court-martialled for insubordination.[122] Similarly, in early September Bock spoke of having Guderian relieved of his command, but was talked out of his decision.[123] Guderian was as impetuous as he was obstinate and showed himself utterly self-centred whenever a conflict arose between his own intentions and the wider needs of the army group. It is not surprising therefore that, while Hoth and Hoepner's panzer groups were still subordinate to the Ninth and Fourth Armies respectively, Guderian had proven himself an impossible subordinate and forced himself free – often by outright insubordination – of what he determined to be the constrictive ideas of infantry generals. Panzer Group 2, therefore, operated on the eastern front as an independent entity, subordinate directly to Bock at Army Group Centre. However, thanks to Goebbels's propaganda, Guderian was also the single most celebrated panzer commander in the east and a clear favourite of Hitler. In recognition of Guderian's status as an autonomous commander, on 6 October Panzer Group 2 was renamed the Second Panzer Army.[124] The same distinction was accorded to Kleist's Panzer Group 1, which was now to be known as the First Panzer Army.[125] Yet Guderian was just as belligerent as ever and, when Bock enquired about handing General of Artillery Rudolf Kaempfe's XXXV Army Corps over to Second Army and General of Infantry Alfred Waeger's XXXIV Army Corps over to Sixth Army, Guderian strongly resisted any weakening of his panzer army. As his commanding officer, Bock had learned to give Guderian a wide berth on matters of secondary importance, and the matter was resolved to Guderian's satisfaction.[126]

While opinions differed and tensions arose within Army Group Centre, one must also acknowledge the enormous pressure Bock and his commanders were under. The end of the eastern campaign had been all but promised by Hitler, and even if that lofty goal was not to be realised Army Group Centre would, at the very least, have to seize Moscow before the winter. Thus, the impending Soviet calamity on the approaches to Moscow was clearly only the beginning of what Bock and his commanders would be expected to achieve in the coming days and weeks. Progress was being made, but the margin for error was sometimes smaller than it appeared. Lieutenant-General Hans-Jürgen von Arnim's 17th Panzer Division was the spearhead of Lemelsen's XXXXVII Panzer Corps as it battled its way towards Briansk. Yet by 5 October the division had only thirty serviceable panzers left available[127] and, with long flanks requiring some armoured support, only seven tanks were on hand to continue the drive to Briansk.[128] In spite of such weakness, the ad hoc Soviet formations thrown together from whatever rear-area personnel could be found were pushed aside by the oncoming Germans. At the headquarters of Eremenko's Briansk Front, located near Briansk, there was consternation. Vasily Grossman, who had fled Orel for Briansk, was told by the staff commissar to leave the city at four o'clock in the morning on 6 October. 'He didn't bother to give us any explanation, but it wasn't necessary anyway. It was all clear, particularly after we looked at the map. Our headquarters was caught in a sack ... We were in a race. Either we had to get out of the sack first, or the Germans would tie it up while we were still inside.'[129] Eremenko himself narrowly escaped capture by remaining at his command post until German tanks were just 200 metres away.[130] That same day (6 October) Arnim's 17th Panzer Division succeeded in taking Briansk as well as its bridges across the Desna River.[131] The southern pocket was not as yet sealed, in part because the Germans had far fewer troops in the south than in the north, but with Weichs's Second Army advancing and Nehring's 18th Panzer Division arching around Briansk the pocket was loosely in place by 8 October.[132] Yet as Max Kuhnert, a soldier in Guderian's Second Panzer Army, observed, even these successful operations came at a cost. 'The Russians put up a good fight for Briansk and our casualties continued to mount. There were nearly five days of tense fighting before the ring around the town was closed completely. I felt sorry for the Russians, even when our own soldiers who had been killed were littering the advance route.'[133] If the plight of Soviet POWs could elicit the sympathies of a German soldier it bears remembering that around Briansk three entire Soviet armies (Third, Thirteenth and Fiftieth) had now been cut off.[134]

To the north, Hoth's Panzer Group 3 was at last free of Soviet counterattacks and resupplied with enough fuel for Major-General Hans Freiherr von Funck's 7th Panzer Division followed by Lieutenant-General Franz Landgraf's 6th Panzer Division to sweep south-east all the way to Viaz'ma. As one soldier from Funck's division later noted, 'We were calling the shots once again in the advance. It made a tremendous impression on us! Wherever the enemy had convinced himself he had erected an invisible barrier to hold us up, we drove over it hardly noticing. We penetrated kilometre after kilometre further eastward and soon we were well in the rear of the enemy.'[135] Hoth had cut the best hope of escape for the host of Soviet armies now trapped to the west of Viaz'ma. Moreover, just as Arnim's tanks were entering Briansk on 6 October so too were Funck's panzers appearing in the streets of Viaz'ma. Major-General K. K. Rokossovsky, who was to prove one of the Soviet Union's most outstanding generals, was in the city at the time. Suddenly the mayor rushed down into the crypt of the Viaz'ma cathedral where Rokossovsky was in talks with city officials.

'German tanks are in the city', the mayor announced. 'Who reported that?', Rokossovsky asked sceptically. 'I saw that myself from the belfry.' When Rokossovsky went to look for himself, he witnessed German tanks machine-gunning fleeing cars. Indeed Rokossovsky's own hasty exit included a narrow escape down a side street to avoid an oncoming German tank.[136] At Army Group Centre Bock rejoiced at the news from Viaz'ma and noted in his diary: 'I used this happy result to urge Panzer Group 4 to reach its own objective.'[137] Hoepner hardly needed reminding, and his spearhead led by Major-General Wolfgang Fischer's 10th Panzer Division and followed by Veiel's 2nd Panzer Division reached Viaz'ma from the south on the morning of 7 October (see Map 7).[138] The northern encirclement was closed, yet, as at Briansk, the operation to encircle the Soviet front was by no means without cost. Captain Hans von Luck, who served as part of the 7th Panzer Division's command staff, noted after the war: 'On either side of the Moscow trail tank units formed up for the attack on Viaz'ma. Against bitter resistance, the town was enveloped to the north and south, and on its eastern fringe, this pocket too was closed. Losses on both sides were heavy.'[139] The price may have been high, but trapped inside the Viaz'ma pocket were the Soviet Sixteenth, Nineteenth, Twentieth and Twenty-Fourth Armies as well as part of the Thirty-Second Army.[140] In total the twin battles of Briansk and Viaz'ma, which the Germans called the *Doppelschlacht* (double battle), trapped eight Soviet armies in part or in whole. Altogether this equalled some sixty-four rifle divisions, eleven tank brigades and fifty artillery regiments.[141] It was without question one of the Wehrmacht's most decisive achievements of World War II.

While Bock was on the verge of a success far in excess of his earlier battles at Minsk or Smolensk, his achievement had been decisively aided by the unseasonably good weather throughout the first days of October. Clear skies, dry conditions and even warm tempera-tures had allowed his armies the best possible chance to facilitate their rapid movements.[142] In Berlin Goebbels noted: 'The weather remains incredibly beautiful. Over almost the entirety of the German offensive front there is the most wonderful, cloud-free weather, which naturally can only help our operations. Maybe the God of weather, who in the past months has so often not favoured us, has seen the light and now in these deciding final days and weeks maybe does in fact stand on our side.'[143] On the following day (4 October) Hitler maintained that if the

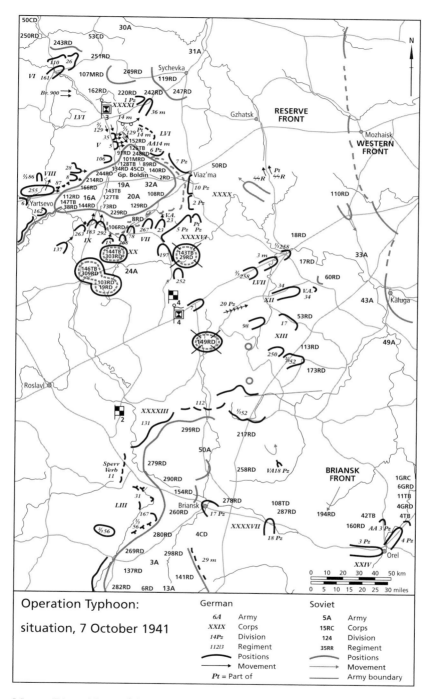

Map 7 Dispositions of Army Group Centre, 7 October 1941

weather remained halfway good for the next fourteen days the Soviet Union would be, for the most part, 'smashed'.[144] For Bock, who had feared that the diversion of Guderian's panzer group into Ukraine would not leave enough time for his attack on Moscow, the good weather buoyed his hopes. On 7 October he noted in his diary: 'If the weather holds we may be able to make up for much of what was lost through Kiev.'[145]

Yet the weather was already turning. On 6 October it turned cold during the day and the wind picked up. That evening there was rain followed by the first snow of the year.[146] As Heinrich Haape noted: 'the brief spell of fine weather was at an end. The rain again sheeted down, the temperature dropped, the rain gave way to hail, then snow. Then it rained again.'[147] By the morning of 7 October the rain had stopped, but the weather remained cold and the roads, already churned up by the volume of heavy vehicles, had transformed into the deep, clinging mud that had so often hindered the panzer groups. As Guderian noted after the first night of snow and rain: 'our vehicles could only advance at snail's pace and with great wear to the engines'.[148] For the men of Army Group Centre, the change in weather was an unnerving indication of the hardships to come. Wilhelm Prüller, who served in the 25th Motorised Infantry Division, noted in his diary: 'At night it gets really cold now and we all think it can't go on much longer. In this morass we shall soon be unable to move at all. Our baggage train couldn't even make the grade today. What will it be like in the rainy period?'[149] Indeed the psychological burden of darkening skies and biting cold, mixed with the ever-present exhaustion from months of constant marching and fighting, struck a blow to the morale of many German soldiers. Max Kuhnert, who served in the 1st Cavalry Division, recalled the sense of despair that the abrupt change in conditions brought:

> Suddenly our task in Russia seemed insurmountable, our supplies got stuck, and so did our heavy artillery, even with their heavy horses. Tanks churned their way laboriously through the mud which affected their manoeuvrability, and used more of their precious fuel than intended. The whole of Russia, so it seemed to us, was one great basin of sticky mud and we were in the middle of it.[150]

Likewise, Haape noted: 'Every man's thoughts turned in the same direction as he watched the flakes drop on the slushy roads. The first manifestations of winter! How cold and how long would the winter be? ... We watched it uneasily.'[151] Before too long even Bock was becoming nervous at what the Russian weather held in store for his army group. As Bock observed in his diary: 'The change in the weather, with its periods of snow, frost and rain, is wearing on the troops and is affecting morale. The question, "what will become of us in the winter?" is on everyone's mind.'[152] If the change in weather had an adverse affect on German morale and operations it was, for those reasons, good news for the Soviets. With the roads to Moscow effectively open, almost no credible defences to speak of and three German panzer groups between 200 and 350 kilometres from the capital, the beginning of the *rasputitsa* was a welcome occurrence. Fleeing the Briansk pocket on the night of 6–7 October as the rains started, Vasily Grossman jotted in his notebook: 'There's rain, snow, hailstones, a liquid, bottomless swamp, black pastry mixed by thousands and thousands of boots, wheels, caterpillars. And everyone is happy once again. The Germans must get stuck in our hellish autumn.'[153]

Far from curtailing their operations in light of the changing seasonal conditions, German operations at Viaz'ma and Briansk only bolstered their appetite for more victories. There was no talk of overextending the supply system or dispersing Army Group Centre's strength; after all, according to Hitler, the Soviet Union was on its knees and the fatal blow now had to be delivered. On 6 October Brauchitsch met with Hitler to present the OKH's latest directives for Bock's army group.[154] Hitler was satisfied, and the next day the commander-in-chief of the army flew to Bock's headquarters to discuss the next phase of the offensive. On Bock's northern wing, Hoth's Panzer Group 3 would be charged with making a long advance to the north-east and seizing first Rzhev and then Kalinin (today Tver).[155] As Bock recorded Brauchitsch's explanation, the move was intended 'to bring about the collapse of the enemy front facing my left wing and the right wing of Army Group North'.[156] Thus Army Group Centre was now looking to roll up the right flank of the Soviet North-Western Front – and that was to be achieved by a single panzer group after an advance over 200 kilometres to reach Kalinin. Indeed it was just as far from Viaz'ma to Kalinin as it was from Viaz'ma to Moscow, yet those two objectives were 160 kilometres apart, meaning Hoth could render little immediate aid, if required, to the drive on Moscow. Bock was also sceptical of striking towards Kalinin, but succumbed to the prevailing conviction that the Red Army was nearing its end. As he wrote in his diary on 7 October: 'I am not in total agreement with the drive to the north by Panzer Group 3. Perhaps it will be spared me, for the heavy blow inflicted today may result in the enemy, contrary to previous Russian practice, yielding opposite my front as well; some signs point to that.'[157]

While Hoth was being directed north, Hoepner's Panzer Group 4 was to immediately initiate the drive to Moscow with any forces that could be spared from the Viaz'ma encirclement front. This solution did not impress Hoepner, who was impatient to advance and unwilling to leave many of his best units engaged in a protracted struggle against the encircled Soviet armies.[158] Yet Kluge, who had unsuccessfully tried to impose his will on Guderian at the battles of Minsk and Smolensk, would brook no discussion and kept the bulk of Hoepner's panzer group firmly fixed on the Viaz'ma encirclement. Certainly Guderian had made it very clear that the elimination of pockets was the task of the infantry, not motorised divisions, and only one of the Second Panzer Army's three corps (Lemelsen's XXXXVII Panzer Corps) was committed to the Briansk pocket. Schweppenberg's XXIV Panzer Corps was given the task of pushing on to Tula and then Moscow, while Kempf's XXXXVIII Panzer Corps was directed to seize Kursk (a city of some 120,000 people)[159] before making the long 300-kilometre journey north to reinforce Schweppenberg's forces at Tula.[160] Overall, Army Group Centre's new objectives, particularly those on the flanks at Kalinin and Kursk, reflected the hubris of the German command. Any reservations, to the extent that these even existed, could not hope to compete with the tide of optimism surrounding the collapse of the whole Soviet front. Yet there were plenty of reasons for doubt. One soldier's diary for 7 October reflected the stark contradiction between the expectant hopes for an end to the war and the reality of conditions if there was none:

> We've not much petrol, and none will come for quite a while because our tankers are standing way back and it'll take them a long time to get through all the mud. Tomorrow we're to storm the town of Dmitriev, five kilometres in front of us. Everyone is saying that this is to be our last job … It would be the best thing too for all the companies are thoroughly beaten up, and many of the vehicles are already knocked out. If it really does go on though, it would be better to create a battalion out of the regiment; then it could be properly equipped with men and machines and would be ready for battle.[161]

As the German command and much of the *Ostheer* looked forward to their keenly anticipated victory, one wonders how many recalled their earlier study of Caulaincourt's 1812 campaign and the ruin that accompanied Napoleon's hubris. As Empress Elizabeth[162] wrote to her mother in the darkest days of 1812: 'The further Napoleon advances the less he should believe that any peace is possible. That is the unanimous view of the emperor and all classes of the population … each step he advances in this immense Russia brings him closer to the abyss. Let us see how he copes with the winter.'[163]

3 VIAZ'MA AND BRIANSK

Seeing which way the wind blows – Typhoon's zenith

While Bock had had his differences of opinion with his army commanders, at Army Group South Stülpnagel, the commander of the Seventeenth Army, was relieved of his command on 5 October after a clash with Rundstedt that drew in the OKH. Officially Stülpnagel departed because of sickness, but as Halder noted: 'This sickness is as a result of the pressure exerted on him because of his timid leadership.'[1] Stülpnagel's leadership was viewed as insufficiently aggressive and by early October the point was reached where Rundstedt took command of the northern wing of the Seventeenth Army out of Stülpnagel's hands in order to push it forward again.[2] Yet Stülpnagel's relief had an immediate impact on Bock's operations.

At his previous performance assessment in early 1941, Hoth had been favourably evaluated by Field Marshal Leeb, commanding Army Group North. Leeb had noted Hoth's characteristics as: 'intelligent, deliberate, good mind for operational questions, leads very well'.[3] Hoth was fluent in Russian[4] and had recent experience commanding Strauss's Ninth Army[5] during the defensive crisis on Bock's front in late August and early September. Indeed on his assessment form Leeb had written that Hoth was 'Suitable as an army commander'.[6] Thus, orders arrived from the OKH appointing Hoth as the Seventeenth Army's new commander. In spite of the fact that command of an army was viewed as a promotion, Hoth expressed a desire to remain at the head of Panzer Group 3 and Bock noted in his diary that he was 'loath to lose this

4 The new commander of Panzer Group 3, General of Panzer Troops Georg-Hans Reinhardt (appearing here with driving goggles) who replaced Colonel-General Hermann Hoth in October 1941.

outstanding armoured commander'.[7] Nevertheless, on 9 October Hoth departed for Army Group South[8] and was replaced at Panzer Group 3 by General of Panzer Troops Georg-Hans Reinhardt, who had been the commander of the XXXXI Panzer Corps (see Illustration 4). Reinhardt had himself been positively appraised at an earlier review by Kluge who determined the panzer commander to be 'very intelligent and thoroughly educated'. He also commended Reinhardt for his cool disposition in critical situations, a trait which would serve him well in the coming weeks of his new appointment.[9]

For now at least Reinhardt's new command was fortuitous. Not *eh?* only was the panzer group blocking the north-eastern escape routes of the Viaz'ma pocket, which promised a substantial role in the impending victory but also, unlike at the battle of Smolensk, there was no pressure being exerted from the east by reserve Soviet formations. On 7 October Army Group Centre noted that no Soviet formations could be observed en route to Bock's eastern front.[10] In fact, according to Luftwaffe intelligence reports, the opposite was true. On 6 October, the day before the ring was closed at Viaz'ma, pilots reported: 'From Viaz'ma towards the east the enemy was pouring out of the pincer offensive in considerable numbers.'[11] The following day (7 October) the Luftwaffe noted that a 'large number of enemy columns … had already escaped from the pincer offensive' and were 'running off in the direction of Moscow'.[12] With the enemy on the run and no identifiable reserves available, there was great confidence that Moscow's fall was inevitable. Even Heinrici, the XXXXIII Army Corps commander, whose letters and diary entries over the preceding months of Operation Barbarossa had sounded a far more demurring tone to the many triumphal declarations of impending victory, now faltered. Writing to his family on 8 October Heinrici predicted that Moscow, and in the south the Don Basin industrial area, would be in German hands before the end of the month. Yet even amidst the sweeping predictions of conquest Heinrici retained a grounded approach to the ramifications. 'It will not be easy for the Russians to replace these losses', Heinrici remarked before continuing:

> Nevertheless it is not to be assumed that the struggle with him is over. Every prisoner until now has said: And even if we are thrown back to the Urals there will not be peace between you and us. The Bolshevist cannot make peace with the National Socialist. An understanding between the two is impossible. We have indeed been hit hard, but are not beaten. We trust in the size of our country, in the enormous manpower reserves and in the help of England and America.[13]

More immediately Heinrici faced the prospect of determined Soviet breakout attempts from the Briansk pocket, which he correctly predicted would be pursued 'with the courage of the desperate'.[14] Indeed it was on 8 October that Halder first noted the pressure on Guderian's right flank (forming the encirclement ring) was becoming 'uncomfortable'.[15] That evening Kaempfe's XXXV Army Corps signalled increased enemy pressure north of Sizemka and west of Sevek.[16] The real problem for Guderian's commanders was that their lines contained gaps, which either allowed bands of Soviet soldiers to slip through or required stretching their forces to such a degree that Soviet breakout attempts might overrun their lines. There was also much confusion on both sides with local commanders seldom knowing exactly where the bulk of enemy troops were positioned. Encounter engagements were common and, irrespective of the strategic situation, Soviet forces could indeed win localised battles. On 9 October Erich

Hager wrote in his diary that his unit had stumbled on the aftermath of a recent battle in which a German tank and a whole convoy of vehicles had been 'shot to pieces'.[17] The same day (9 October) the pressure on Guderian's encirclement front increased enormously, leading to numerous crises in the German line and at least one major Soviet breakthrough. The cost to the Soviet formations was often, however, appallingly high. The main flashpoint was at Sizemka where a gap existed between Lieutenant-General Justin von Obernitz's 293rd Infantry Division and Major-General Max Fremerey's 29th Motorised Infantry Division. Obernitz was heavily attacked on his exposed right wing and pushed back first through the town of Sizemka and then further through Shilinka. Guderian desperately sought to plug the gap. He had directed Major-General Heinrich Clössner's 25th Motorised Infantry Division to fill the void (which says something about the size of the gap), but Clössner's division would only arrive later in the day, and so a nearby regiment from Lieutenant-General Friedrich-Wilhelm von Loeper's 10th Motorised Infantry Division was dispatched to do what it could. That Guderian was sufficiently worried is illustrated by the fact that he countermanded the orders of the entire XXXXVIII Panzer Corps (ordered by the OKH towards Kursk) and instructed Kempf, the commanding officer, to head 'with all available forces' to nearby Sevek. When at last Clössner's division arrived to plug the gap Guderian noted 'a violent battle raged', but concluded 'only a small number of Russians succeeded in breaking free'.[18]

This conclusion, however, was disputed by Eremenko. According to the commander of the Briansk Front, who took issue with the account presented in Guderian's memoir, the large number of German forces sent to the area around Sizemka indicates just how large the breach in the German line was. Eremenko then continued: 'He admitted that troops of the Thirteenth Army and army headquarters succeeded in crashing the line he had put up along the Seredina Buda–Sevek road. He claims, however, that only "small groups" managed to get out of the pocket. This is untrue. It was large units and whole divisions that escaped the Nazi ring.'[19] While the fighting was at its most intense around Kaempfe's XXXV Army Corps, the German forces compressing the Briansk pocket from the west (Second Army and 1st Cavalry Division) were in many places confronted by strong Soviet rear-guard actions which slowed their advance. Only in the north of the pocket did Arnim's 17th Panzer Division and Nehring's

18th Panzer Division encounter weak Soviet resistance.[20] As Bock noted on 8 October: 'Progress is slow at the Briansk pocket.'[21] Indeed Bock was deliberately excluding the Briansk pocket from official army news bulletins because it was far less secure than the larger and more tightly encircled pocket at Viaz'ma. As a result, when on 9 October the OKH released details of a second pocket at Briansk, Bock feared that the army command was promising victory in a battle that had not yet been won. As Bock noted in his diary on 9 October:

> To my regret, in the afternoon a special bulletin was issued which spoke of a second pocket at Briansk. I called Halder and told him that I had deliberately never mentioned this 'pocket' because its eastern front is more than shaky and because Guderian's weak forces are incapable of preventing some of the Russians from breaking out there … Guderian [is] scraping everything together to prevent a large-scale escape.[22]

While Guderian and Weichs struggled to cope with the pocket at Briansk, further north at the Viaz'ma pocket Strauss and Kluge enjoyed a weighty superiority. At the beginning the total size of the Viaz'ma encirclement measured roughly 75 by 35 kilometres,[23] which, given the number of Soviet armies trapped inside, provided a dense concentration of targets for the long-range artillery and Luftwaffe. The speed of the German encirclement, which was achieved only five days into Operation Typhoon, and the breakdown in Soviet forward communications probably meant that a sizeable number of Soviet formations did not immediately know just how dire their predicament had become. In any case there was no immediate attempt by the bulk of the trapped formations to escape eastwards. Twenty-four hours after the closure of the ring Panzer Group 3's war diary noted: 'Until now though it is similar to the encirclements at Minsk and Smolensk, in which the expected enemy pressure against the encirclement front is absent. The Russian remains in the pocket until he is attacked and beaten by the advancing western front.'[24] Yet this was not the whole truth: on 9 October intelligence gathered at Army Group Centre indicated that Soviet forces inside the pocket were in fact concentrating for a major breakout attempt directed towards Hoepner's panzer group in the south-east.[25] On the same day (9 October) the war diary of Fehn's 5th Panzer Division noted: 'Again and again the enemy attempts to detect "thin" sectors in the blocking front in order to break through here.'[26] While the Soviets probed to find weaknesses in Fehn's front, the attacking infantry from Strauss and Kluge's armies had little trouble finding gaps and exploiting weaknesses in the Soviet line. At Army Group Centre Bock observed on 9 October: 'The pocket at Viaz'ma is shrinking more and more. Numbers of prisoners and captured materiel growing.'[27] Similarly, Halder wrote in his diary: 'The encirclement battle at Viaz'ma continues in a downright classical manner.'[28] Yet the worst of the fighting was still to come and, as word of the German envelopment spread rapidly throughout the pocket, desperation and even panic gripped the mass of encircled Soviet men. One of them was Viktor Strazdovski who was a raw 18-year-old recruit just deployed to the front before the German offensive. He recalled that at that time the Red Army's equipment dated from World War I and even then there were not enough rifles for every man. 'We were face to face with the Germans', Strazdovski recalled, 'and we had to use these primitive weapons in real combat. We didn't feel confident.' Strazdovski then described the fear and sense of foreboding he and his comrades felt. 'When I was sent to the place where the Germans broke our defence line, you can imagine how we felt – we felt we were doomed. There were four of us, with two rifles between us, and we didn't know in which direction we would run into the Germans. The woods around us were ablaze. On the one hand we couldn't disobey our order, but on the other hand we felt doomed.'[29] Even some of the most modern Soviet weaponry was proving almost useless once caught behind German lines. Major-General Heinrich Recke's 161st Infantry Division encountered between twenty and thirty Soviet tanks which were attempting to fight, but could no longer move for want of fuel.[30]

While the pocket at Viaz'ma was sealed tighter than any of Army Group Centre's previous encirclements, it was immediately recognised that only the absolute minimum number of motorised and infantry divisions should be maintained in fixed positions. As Army Group Centre's war diary made clear: 'In the first instance the immediate release of all available strength from the [Viaz'ma] battlefield, especially motorised units, will be initiated as well as the tireless pursuit of the enemy who escaped from the encirclement to prevent, at all costs, the building of a new defensive front.'[31] Most importantly, Bock was concerned about General of Panzer Troops Adolf Kuntzen's LVII Panzer Corps, which Hoepner had held in reserve, but since 7 October was committed towards Kaluga.[32] Hoepner was chafing at the bit to attack eastwards with more strength, but Kluge's priority was clearly the maintenance of an iron ring at Viaz'ma. Nor was it just Hoepner who thought Kluge lacklustre in his pursuit of new objectives in the east. On 8 October Bock wrote in his diary: 'As it is not completely clear whether Kluge has really recognized the need for LVII Panzer Corps to begin its drive to the east immediately, I called his chief of staff and repeated that it was vital that we reach the position at Maloiaroslavets and Mozhaisk before the enemy. Haste is urgently required.'[33] Bock also wanted reconnaissance forces sent as far ahead as Moscow and emphasised the need for strong infantry forces to follow Kuntzen's panzer corps as soon as possible (see Map 8). Blumentritt, the chief of staff at Fourth Army, was in complete agreement with Bock[34] and privately shared reservations about Kluge's strategic priorities. As Blumentritt set out Fourth Army's orders: 'the panzer groups were, so far as possible, to ignore the encirclement battle which would develop in their rear at Viaz'ma and were to push on with maximum strength and all speed for Moscow'.[35] While Kluge acknowledged the need to press on eastwards, there is no question that he also harboured the frustration of missed opportunities at Minsk and Smolensk, which he viewed as less than complete victories because overambitious panzer commanders, notably Guderian, had, against his orders, sought to resume the advance too soon. Accordingly when Kluge later spoke with Bock's chief of staff at Army Group Centre, Major-General Hans von Greiffenberg, he insisted that any removal of the 2nd, 5th or 11th Panzer Divisions from the Viaz'ma encirclement was 'not possible'. Kluge also noted that the recent rains had made movement far more difficult, suggesting that the panzer divisions would serve much more purpose in their current positions. In reply Greiffenberg insisted that the pocket be compressed into extinction as soon as possible, and on 9 October Army Group Centre's war diary noted: 'All corps have the order: "Forwards, forwards, forwards!"'[36]

While Bock pressed for the earliest possible release of Hoepner's panzer forces from the encirclement front, Hitler was less concerned with the attack towards Moscow, which he considered to be a *fait accompli*, and more interested in getting Panzer Group 3 started on the long advance to the north-east to seize Rzhev and Kalinin.

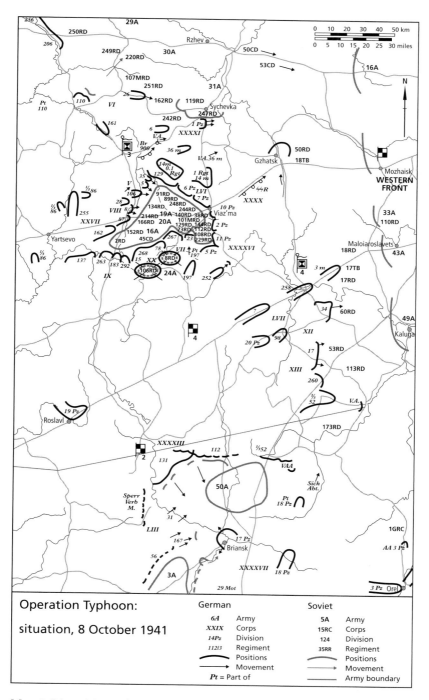

Map 8 Dispositions of Army Group Centre, 8 October 1941

Accordingly, he dispatched orders to Army Group Centre on 9 October requiring Hoepner's forces to extend themselves further north in order to provide for the early release of Reinhardt's panzer divisions. Bock was strongly against the idea, commenting that such a solution 'would take very much longer than relief by infantry, involve unnecessary lateral movements over frightful roads, and open one hole in order to plug another'.[37] Kluge was also reluctant and insisted that any such movement would not be possible for three days owing to the terrible weather and the tremendous difficulties of fuel getting to the front.[38] Indeed Army Group Centre's fuel supplies, as well as the state of the Russian roads, would now hit German operations harder than at any other time in the campaign.

One of Army Group Centre's central problems in sustaining Operation Typhoon was the inadequacy of stockpiled resources prior to the start of the campaign. The establishment of forward supply bases at Gomel, Roslavl, Smolensk and Vitebsk could feed operations only so long as stocks lasted, and fuel supplies were already running out in the first week of the offensive. Compounding the problem were the inadequacies of the railway system, the capacity of which was far too low for sustaining the number of armies that Bock now commanded. Moreover, the railways were now suffering from repeated partisan attacks which further slowed the movement of essential supplies. Already in September the quartermaster-general's Army Supply Department warned that the fuel demands of the *Ostheer*'s tanks and vehicles might prove 'insufficient to bring the eastern campaign to a conclusion in the autumn'.[39] In addition to the failings of the railways, supplies, once at the railheads, had then to be transported to the armies, but the *Grosstransportraum* – the truck-based transport fleets – could transport only about 6,500 tons of supplies, which was about half of the daily requirements of Bock's army group.[40] Clearly Army Group Centre's offensive was living on borrowed time, and to make matters even worse supplying half of Bock's day-to-day requirements necessitated good weather. Once the weather turned and the roads transformed, all movement slowed dramatically and was often brought to a standstill (see Illustration 5). As Hans Roth noted in his diary on 8 October: 'It has become lousy cold: heavy snowfall with ice storms from the north. Operations of any kind are impossible in this shitty weather.'[41] Similarly, Franz Frisch noted: 'We had problems with the early snow, and as it started to melt, the so-called roads were nothing less than a swamp.

5 As autumn rains began, the sunken Russian roads slowed Army Group Centre's drive on Moscow.

And it rained and continued to rain.' At this time Frisch was ordered to take a motorcycle and deliver a dispatch to another unit 60 kilometres away. The mud proved so thick that the motorcycle could not be ridden and he ended up pushing it nearly all the way through the mud, while the round trip lasted no less than a whole week.[42] Erhard Raus, a major-general in the 6th Panzer Division during Operation Typhoon, noted after the war: 'Even during the first stages [of the muddy season], cart and dirt roads became impassable, and major roads soon became mud-choked. Supply trucks broke through the gravel-topped roads and churned up traffic lanes until even courier service had to be carried out with tracked vehicles.'[43] A report from Lemelsen's XXXXVII Panzer Corps on 9 October noted the difficulties of movement in the prevailing conditions as well as the impact this was having on a rapid exploitation of the strategic situation: 'Movements are heavily delayed because of impassable roads. The column's speed at the moment is about 2 kilometres per hour!'[44] The same march tempo was also reported at the other end of Bock's front by Lieutenant-General Friedrich Kirchner's[45] XXXXI Panzer Corps.[46]

At Panzer Group 3 the war diary noted with relief that the good weather had held long enough for the Viaz'ma encirclement to be completed, but with the arrival of orders for the offensive towards Kalinin it was clear that the condition of the roads and absence of supplies constituted the greatest obstacle to Reinhardt's future success. As the war diary noted, 'Logistically it will be a hand-to-mouth existence; it could be that on the way the panzer group's supply breaks down.'[47] Not only were the conditions complicating movement, but the strains of the new offensive were having a predictably negative effect on the many worn-out vehicles of the panzer group. Indeed by 8 October the tonnage of supplies being moved had already dropped by 25 per cent because of lost vehicles. At the same time on the bad roads, where traction was poor, causing wheels to spin, the panzer groups' supply vehicles typically consumed double their previous quota of fuel and oil.[48] In some sectors wheeled movement became impossible. As early as 6 October in the area of Lieutenant-General Helge Auleb's 6th Infantry Division (subordinate to the XXXXI Panzer Corps) only the infantry could move forward. Wheeled vehicles and horse-drawn carts were for the most part fixed where they stood. The XXXXI Panzer Corps's war diary then continued: 'Also in the rest of the corps's area the bad road conditions reduced the freedom of movement and freedom of action so much that their influence on engagements and supplies are profound.'[49] By 8 October Panzer Group 3's war diary spoke of 'great stretches of mud', which damaged the hastily built corduroy roads (made of logs strung together) and led to long delays for all road-bound transport.[50]

While Reinhardt's panzer group faced a tall order in advancing all the way to Kalinin and then threatening the Soviet North-Western Front, Hoepner was being instructed to undertake the lion's share of the fighting on the eastern side of the Viaz'ma encirclement, advance an additional 200 kilometres through makeshift Soviet defences and then seize the Soviet capital. Yet even with the deterioration of the weather Hoepner was far from pessimistic (see Illustration 6). In a letter he wrote on 7 October the panzer commander contended 'that the clearing of the [Viaz'ma] pocket and the continued push towards Moscow can be undertaken at the same time. The surprised and weakened enemy must immediately be taken advantage of.'[51] Yet it was not just Kluge's insistence on Hoepner's panzers remaining in place near Viaz'ma that prevented a more rapid thrust on Moscow. The roads were still open to tracked vehicles, but their support demanded the accompaniment of wheeled vehicles. In addition, Hoepner's four panzer divisions near Viaz'ma were very short on fuel and one, Major-General Hans-Karl Freiherr von Esebeck's 11th Panzer Division, reported on 7 October having no fuel at all.[52] What was available to Hoepner was Kuntzen's LVII Panzer Corps, which had been held in reserve, but was now advancing eastwards. Yet Kuntzen's panzer corps consisted of just one panzer division,[53] Bismarck's 20th Panzer Division, which was one of the weakest on the eastern front. Bismarck's division had been rested in the early days of Typhoon in order to try and raise its motorised strength after the heavy losses it had sustained during its redeployment south to join Panzer Group 4. Now it was advancing in terrible conditions, which by 8 October had already cost one regiment of motorised infantry 30 per cent of its vehicles, and fuel stocks only sufficed for 50 to 80 kilometres.[54] Bismarck's panzer regiment was also shrinking fast, especially given the absence of major combat. On 9 October the 20th Panzer Division fielded fifty-five tanks (only six of which were Mark IVs), but two days later the division reported that only thirty-nine were still serviceable.[55] Hoepner may have commanded the most powerful panzer group on the eastern front, but by the second week of October, as the Russian *rasputitsa* was taking hold, only a small fraction of his tanks were heading towards Moscow.

To the south Guderian's Second Panzer Army was faring no better in the sodden conditions. On 8 October the war diary of the panzer army's quartermaster-general noted, 'The condition of the supply roads makes orderly supply impossible, individual vehicles can continue only with the help of tractors. As a result munitions and fuel at XXIV Panzer Corps are very critical.'[56] The 3rd Panzer Division's quartermaster-general noted that the situation was 'quite disastrous at Krupyshino' where hundreds of vehicles were accumulating in an impassable morass that extended for around 30 kilometres. Fuel had

6 The commander of Panzer Group 4, Colonel-General Erich Hoepner (on right).

to be flown directly to Orel,[57] but in the difficult conditions Kesselring's Air Fleet 2 with three transport groups operating Ju 52 aircraft were capable of moving only about 200 tons a day.[58] Kempf's more southerly XXXXVIII Panzer Corps was also appealing for air lifts of fuel and especially oil without which, the corps's war diary warned, 'the danger exists that in a short time a large part of the corps will not be operational'.[59] In fact the terrible weather conditions were already having the same effect. On 7 October Lieutenant-General Alfred Ritter von Hubicki's 9th Panzer Division reported 'unbelievable difficulties' and stated that because the division was travelling on country roads 'any movement is impossible'. By 10 October continued heavy snow and rainfall still rendered the roads 'completely impassable' to wheeled vehicles, forcing Hubicki to form an advanced detachment consisting solely of tracked vehicles.[60] Even Lemelsen's XXXXVII Panzer Corps, which was for the most part bound to more static positions on the Briansk encirclement, was hindered in its operations by fuel shortages.[61]

While Bock's panzer groups struggled desperately against the autumn rains, trying to capitalise on their earlier successes, the lack of understanding of these difficulties at the top of the Nazi regime was underlined by an article published by Dr Fritz Meske in the *Deutsche Allgemeine Zeitung* on 9 October:

> Weather conditions have special influence on the conduct of a war employing motorized armies in the east. However, neither our panzer divisions nor our supply columns, and least of all our infantry, are so delicate that they would have to halt an advance because of rain. We have won huge envelopment battles despite incessant rain and completely sodden roads. The weather is always the same for friend and foe alike and does not alter relative combat proportions and thus affect morale, which in any case decides battles.[62]

The morale of Bock's soldiers could hardly have been lifted by reading such absurdities and, while some might have convinced themselves it was all intended to allay fears on the home front, the more perceptive could well begin to wonder what their leaders really understood about the situation at the front. Indeed many soldiers claimed after the war to have held profound fears for what lay before them with the spectre of 1812 looming large in the back of many minds. Franz Frisch recalled: 'When the first snows fell in early October, I could only think of the fate of Napoleon.'[63] Likewise, Kurt Meissner noted, 'the big drop in temperature affected men and vehicles; we had no warm clothing and suffered accordingly ... We began to think of Napoleon's Grande Armée in the previous century.'[64] Léon Degrelle described the harmful effects of the clinging mud before concluding: 'we couldn't avoid thinking about the hundreds of thousands of men, committed to the depths of Russia, who were going to try what Napoleon had not dared to try: to maintain themselves in spite of everything in the midst of the steppes, with the enemy in front of them, the desert to their backs [and] the snow falling from the sky'.[65] Even Blumentritt, Kluge's chief of staff, looked on nervously as the difficulties mounted alongside the historical parallels. Writing of October 1941 Blumentritt noted after the war: 'And now the ghosts of the Grand Army and the memory of Napoleon's fate began to haunt our dreams … Comparisons with 1812 multiplied.'[66] If morale does in fact decide battles, as Dr Meske's article claimed, the outcome of Operation Typhoon was by no means as certain as many Nazi leaders assumed.

'The campaign in the east has been decided!' (Otto Dietrich)

In the post-war era the German generals propagated many myths to mask their own culpability for mistakes and oversights made during the war. Typically they found it convenient to blame Hitler for decisions or orders which they later claimed, on a few occasions truthfully, to have opposed. Yet one of their more commonly accepted claims was that failure to win the war in the east during 1941 resulted from the unseasonably early beginning to the inclement weather, which upset otherwise well-laid plans.[67] Apart from the fact that Operation Barbarossa was supposed to have won the war long before an autumn campaign was drawn up, the fact remains that there was nothing unusual about the onset of the Russian *rasputitsa* by mid October.[68] It was the German command, beginning with Hitler but including almost all of the army's leadership, which proved consistently impervious to any negative influence threatening to derail their plans. The triumph of the will against all odds was the central Nazi ethos, which allowed the impossible to become possible, and by 1941 the notion had been enthusiastically swallowed by almost all of the senior Wehrmacht leadership. Suddenly it appeared that the only thing that could stop the German soldier was his own lack of determination to impose himself upon his enemy and circumstances. An indomitable will to succeed, always exemplified by Hitler's own struggle to win power and 'save' Germany, was the touchstone of Nazi and, increasingly, military rationale.

With this worldview, statistical likelihood took a backseat to moral qualities, allowing the *Ostheer* to undertake operations at dangerously long odds. Driving headlong to Moscow through the Russian *rasputitsa*, capturing the Soviet capital and winning the war in the east before the onset of winter constituted one of the more remarkable examples of Nazi hubris in the regime's twelve-year existence. Yet Hitler's mind was made up and the slightest hint of doubt from a subordinate would be a commentary less on the decision itself than on the failed moral qualities of the questioner. Indeed Hitler's prophetic status cast a spell of invulnerability over many of his decisions, forestalling debate and instilling unjustified confidence in the outcome. Accordingly the long-winded strategic assessment Hitler gave in his 3 October speech, in which he promised 'this opponent has already broken down and will never rise again',[69] helped set the tone for the victory fever of Nazi propaganda. As Goebbels noted in his diary on 5 October, 'Internally the Führer's speech has worked like a wonder. All criticism, all pessimism, even all the anxiety has disappeared completely.'[70] Goebbels, of course, was one of the closest disciples of the Führer and the main propagator of the Hitler myth, which influenced his own ability to assess Hitler's often-wild hopes and assertions critically. For example, after a telephone conversation with Hitler on 7 October Goebbels noted that the dictator was 'extremely optimistic' about the situation at the front and 'only hopes that the weather remains so beautiful for a few more weeks'.[71] In fact the weather had already begun to turn, but this was no cause to halt the fanfare of victory.

On 9 October two new *Sondermeldungen* were announced 'with great ceremony', celebrating the completion of encirclements by Bock's army group. As Goebbels proudly proclaimed: 'The mood has again reached the highpoint.'[72] Yet beyond the zone of Hitler's infallibility myth, opinions were far more cautious and even hinted at doubts. Ciano, the Italian foreign minister, wrote in his diary on 9 October: 'News from the German front in Russia is more and more favourable. Will this good news be confirmed, or will we, after so many losses in men and materiel, soon be reading simply that a new front was pushed a hundred or two [hundred] kilometres farther back? This is what is really important for the course of the war.'[73] In Moscow the Soviet deputy minister of foreign affairs, Solomon Lozovsky, reacted with a display of steadfast composure to the German claim that Moscow would soon fall. 'If the Germans want to see a few hundred thousand more of their people killed,' he told a gathering of foreign journalists, 'they'll succeed in that – if in nothing else.'[74] In Britain the mood evinced confidence in the powers of resistance of their Soviet ally, emboldened by Churchill's steely praise of the Red Army. Goebbels decried the defiant tone of the British newspapers, claiming they were written as though 'they were the absolute lords of the situation'.[75] Privately Churchill harboured grave fears for his Soviet ally in 1941, but he would later maintain that it was not particularly important where the eastern front lay, even if all the way to the Ural Mountains, so long as it continued to function as a front which continually devoured German strength.[76]

While the rest of Europe watched the events in the east, Goebbels's propaganda blitz, which had showcased a pageant of military successes since the middle of September, led many Germans to believe the end of the war in the east was almost at hand. On 9 October the secret SD reports gauging German public opinion revelled: 'Much more widespread therefore is the notion that the last few victory proclamations are the beginning of a greater series of successes, which should bring the final decision in the east within reach.'[77] Understandably the German people expected that before any 'final decision' was reached more Soviet armies along the eastern front would first have to collapse and cities such as Leningrad and Moscow, which appeared stricken and scarcely defensible, would indeed have to fall. Only upon the achievement of this 'greater series of successes' would 'the final decision' be imminent. Yet the trumpets of Germany's victory fanfare were loudest at the 'Wolf's Lair', where the sense of jubilant anticipation was at its highest pitch and Hitler was impatient to celebrate his success. Hitler's tight circle of military advisers fed his mania with the head of the Wehrmacht's Operations Department, Colonel-General Alfred Jodl, proclaiming the closure of the Viaz'ma encirclement on 7 October as the most decisive day of the whole war in the east and even comparing it with Königgrätz.[78] The chief of the high command of the Wehrmacht, Field Marshal Wilhelm Keitel, asserted that the weeks of tension between Hitler and the army leadership had now been 'considerably eased' by Bock's 'crushing victory' in early October.[79] At the same time Hitler's Luftwaffe adjutant, Nicolaus von Below, stated that in the second week of October it seemed clear to everyone 'that the way to the Russian capital was free'.[80]

Accordingly when the Reich's press chief Dr Otto Dietrich, who also held the rank of an SS-*Obergruppenführer*,[81] visited Hitler on 9 October, his own exaggerated view of the strategic situation was greatly influenced by the triumphal mood he encountered. After discussions with Hitler, Dietrich stated that the dictator was convinced the Soviet Union was stricken and would never rise again. Furthermore, Dietrich later claimed that Hitler 'dictated to me word for word the statement I was to give to the press in Berlin'.[82] Yet Dietrich's claim may be viewed with some circumspection. As one American journalist – who had already observed Dietrich on numerous past occasions – noted, the

7 The Reich's press chief Dr Otto Dietrich speaking to members of the German and international press corps.

Nazi press chief possessed a strong penchant for 'daring statements and bold predictions; and revelled in superlatives'.[83] With Hitler's hubris soaring and Dietrich keen to indulge the spotlight, the stage was set for an announcement which would strike the German people and the wider world with astonishment. On 9 October Dietrich appeared grinning before the German and international press (see Illustration 7). Behind him were red velvet curtains, which were then opened to reveal a vast map of the Soviet Union. Dietrich then began to explain the strategic situation. The last remnants of the Soviet armies opposite Moscow were now caught in two steel rings that were being destroyed by the Wehrmacht. To the east, Dietrich assured his audience, was simply undefended space.[84] 'The campaign in the east has been decided by the smashing of Army Group Timoshenko', Dietrich proclaimed.[85] Neutral journalists looked on as those from Germany and the Axis nations cheered and raised their arms in the Nazi salute.[86]

The following day (10 October) the *Völkischer Beobachte*, a Nazi daily newspaper, carried banner headlines extolling the news. 'The Great Hour Has Struck!'; 'Campaign in the East Decided!'; 'The Military End of the Bolsheviks'.[87] This was mimicked in the Romanian daily *Universul*, which declared: 'The Whole Soviet Front Has Collapsed'; 'The Decision Has Been Reached'; 'The Destruction of Timoshenko's Armies Means the End of Russian Campaign'; 'Disaster for Bolshevik Armies'. Another Romanian daily, *Evenimentul*, led with the full-page headline: 'The Russian Campaign Is Over'.[88] In Italy even Mussolini, who was known for his own overwrought fantasies of martial conquest, was taken aback and viewed the latest news with reservation. As Ciano noted in his diary on 10 October: 'There have been successes [in Russia], and that is undeniable, but he [Mussolini] considers that the [recent] communiqués also bear evidence of propaganda for internal consumption.'[89] Yet Germany was not merely engaged in a propaganda exercise; there was firm belief that Soviet resistance had passed a point of no return and that Moscow would indeed soon be in German hands. In the German-administered General Government of Poland a carload of fireworks was ordered for celebrations marking the fall of Moscow, while at the same time posters were printed in Polish depicting a German soldier with a Nazi flag standing on a pile of rubble, the caption reading: 'Moscow, the Bolshevik nest in German hands'.[90] Meanwhile Berlin cinemas began advertising the forthcoming documentary, *The Germans Enter Moscow*,[91] while display windows at bookstores began stocking Russian grammar books to serve the officials and colonists of the new German eastern empire.[92] At Army Group Centre the solders were being exhorted to make the final effort towards the Soviet capital:

> Soldiers! Moscow is before you. In the course of two years of war all of the continent's capitals have bowed before you, you have marched along the streets of the best cities. Moscow remains. Force her to bow, show her the strength of your weapons, walk through her squares. Moscow means the end of the war! – Wehrmacht High Command.[93]

At the same time a special engineering squad was organised with orders, direct from Hitler, for the demolition of the Kremlin.[94] Internationally there came the first messages of congratulations from Hitler's affiliates and allies. General Francisco Franco in Spain telegrammed Hitler: 'In my name and that of the Spanish people, I send your Excellency my enthusiastic congratulations on the last and final victory of the glorious German Wehrmacht over the enemy of civilization.'[95]

While the Nazi regime was publicly announcing its victory in the east, Goebbels observed the events on 9 October with nervous trepidation. The news, he wrote, was 'almost too positive and too optimistic. When, for example, the press are given the headline: "The War Is Decided!" that surely goes too far.' At the same time Goebbels knew this would make a 'tremendous impression' both internationally and domestically, raising the stakes further and risking the prestige of the whole regime. 'I hope to God', Goebbels continued, 'that the military operations develop so that we don't suffer a psychological reverse.' Indeed the Nazi propaganda minister then revealed just how taxing the war in the east had been for him, claiming that nothing since January 1933 had gnawed at his nerves as much as the last three months.[96] Yet if Goebbels feared that events might reveal a credibility gap between the regime and the actual circumstances in the east, it was already too late to stop some of the soldiers in Bock's army group from alluding to precisely such a dichotomy. One soldier from the 6th Infantry Division noted: 'Just now we have learned that there was a *Sondermeldung* on the radio whereby the encirclement of the three remaining combat-worthy armies from Mr Timoshenko[97] ... means the final victory over the Soviet army. Hopefully someone all too eager didn't exaggerate this report.'[98] Other German soldiers immediately recognised just how wide of the mark their officials had gone and reacted with anger. Hans Roth wrote in his diary:

> On the radio we heard news of the victorious encirclement battle near Vyazma and Bryansk. The Eastern campaign has been practically decided. The remnants of the Red Army are one step away from annihilation; the Bolshevik leaders have fled from Moscow. Is the end in sight for the east? We hear this and even more over the loudspeakers; surely this will be the headline in the daily papers at home. I grab my head; how is this possible, has our leadership gone mad overnight? All of this is not true, it cannot be true; all of us here see too clearly what is going on. Do these gentlemen have blindfolds over their eyes!?![99]

Of course while many soldiers were struck by the absurdity of the official announcement there were also many who very much wanted to believe what they were hearing and willingly embraced the news. A soldier in Clössner's 25th Motorised Infantry Division rejoiced at the news, expressing only the concern that the weather remain dry enough for the 'final battles' and then, in four to six weeks, his division could be relieved of duty.[100]

By 11 October Goebbels knew he had a serious problem. 'The mood has become almost illusionary. It is not possible for the people to make a distinction between a "decision" and an "end" to the war, and one only believes that the military operations in the east are, for the most part, concluded. That is naturally by no means the case.'[101] The key, as Goebbels saw it, was to find an explanation, to tell the people how the war could carry on even after having theoretically been decided. His solution was to evoke historical parallels. 'We will refer to the example of the Prussian–Austrian war of 1866 and the German–French war of 1870–1871. Here also the decisions were reached at Königgrätz or Sedan and the wars still went on.'[102] More to the point, the newspapers dropped their talk of an impending victory and returned to reporting the events at the front. On 11 October the *Völkischer Beobachte* led with the modest headline 'Eastern Breakthrough Deepens'. On the successive days the tone remained decidedly more demure: 'Annihilation of Soviet Armies Almost Concluded' (12 October); 'The Battlefields of Viaz'ma Briansk Far Behind Front' (13 October); 'Operations in East Proceed According to Plan' (14 October).[103] Nor did the change in tone go unnoticed. Mihail Sebastian, a Romanian Jew, noted in his diary on 11 October: 'A slight, almost imperceptible lowering of the tone in today's papers. "The Hour of Collapse Is Near," said one headline in *Universul*. Yesterday the collapse was already an established fact. But the fact is that fighting is still taking place. This evening's German communiqué says that the destruction of Bryansk and Vyazma "is proceeding."'[104] Meanwhile at the front the juxtaposition of the previous day's victory announcement with the deepening hardships stirred bitter resentment. Hans Roth complained:

> Again, powerful snowstorm. All of a sudden there is a deep freeze, 7° C below zero! The roads are frozen solid. We would be able to advance if, yes if, there was any fuel! Gas and supply trucks are still far behind, somewhere stuck hopelessly sunk into the mud. About sixty per cent are somewhere stuck in the mud. That's right; this is what a victorious march forward looks like! And the muddy season has only just begun, and already after two days of rain we have these losses. All of this does not fit quite well with yesterday's victory fanfare![105]

As Blumentritt noted: 'The troops not unnaturally now resented the bombastic utterances of our propaganda.'[106] While some soldiers immediately saw through the Nazi charade, for others the arduous conditions in the days following Dietrich's speech forced them to place even more of their hopes in the regime's assurance of a rapid end to the war. As Harald Henry wrote home in a letter: 'The last days surpass everything that we have endured until now. But what helps?' Henry then expressed his one consolation, that the war would soon be over.[107] Likewise, Alfred Vilsen complained that after many months in this 'damned Russia' there was still no foreseeable way out, but he then concluded that 'trusting in our Führer in all things everything should be alright'.[108] The mood at the front thus polarised between an outright rejection and even mockery of the regime's claims, to those placing their most sincere hopes in the regime, convincing themselves that those with the full strategic overview simply knew better than the man at the front.

On the German home front the American journalist Howard K. Smith, who was living in Berlin at the time and attended Dietrich's speech, suggested that this was the breaking point for many people in their trust of the regime's reporting about the war. According to Smith, Dietrich successfully 'raised the spirits of the people to the skies', but this would shortly 'fall again down into the abyss of despair'. In the period after Dietrich's speech, German newspaper sales dropped and there was a threefold increase in people caught listening to foreign radio broadcasts, especially from London and Moscow. 'From now on', Smith declared in the aftermath of Dietrich's speech, 'a wall of distrust separated the ministry of Dr Goebbels from his people. The shepherd boy had hollered "Wolf!" too often.'[109] On 13 October the SD reports, secretly polling German public opinion, confirmed 'from all parts of the Reich' the positive effect of Dietrich's statements, which 'came as a surprise to the public and caused them to sigh with relief'. Yet even at this early stage scepticism was already plainly evident, as the report continued: 'Headlines such as "Eastern Campaign Decided – Bolshevism Militarily Defeated" have said more than the population dared to hope. It is simply incomprehensible to the people that the war against Bolshevism could have finally been decided.'[110]

A more tangible manifestation of such scepticism came in the form of a darkly humorous cartoon, which was discreetly circulated around Berlin. It pictured a German soldier standing up out of his trench and holding a sign to the enemy which read: 'Russians! You have ceased to exist! Dr Dietrich'. In the next picture the soldier is hit by a Soviet shell and is in the process of being blown apart. At the same time, down in the trench, a German officer turns to his puzzled-looking general and states: 'Stupid, these Russians, they apparently don't understand a word of German!'[111] Observing events on 12 October Goebbels determined the attitude of the population to be 'exceptionally complicated. The German people have had their hopes pulled here and there.' Yet he was in no doubt about the cause of this and candidly accepted that major blunders had been made. 'Admittedly we are to bear the greatest part of the responsibility for this. The report shows that our victory news is no longer accepted with the required attention and necessary importance because our most recent communiqués have already anticipated the final victory.'[112]

While Goebbels grappled with the propaganda mess that Hitler himself had set in motion the German dictator was still defiantly insisting that the war as a whole was approaching its end. On the night of 13–14 October Hitler told his assembled guests: 'Doubtless the time will come when I shall no longer have to concern myself with the war or the Eastern Front, for it will be only a matter of carrying out what has already been foreseen and ordered.'[113] Earlier that day (13 October) Hans Fritzsche, a top official in Goebbels's propaganda ministry, continued to pour scorn on the idea of an extension to the war. In an address to the foreign press corps Fritzsche stated: 'The military outcome of this war is decided. What remains to be done is mostly of a political nature internally and internationally.' Yet, without apparently recognising the irony involved, Fritzsche then told his assembled audience what the reality of victory in the east would mean for Germany. 'It is possible that military strains and also warlike hostilities on a small scale will endure another *eight or ten years*; this situation will not alter the will of the German government to build up and order the European continent according to German dictates.'[114] It was an assessment echoed by Hitler in private when he told his inner circle: 'The frontier police will be enough to ensure us quiet conditions necessary for the exploitation of the conquered territories. I attach no importance to a formal, juridical end to the war on the Eastern Front.'[115] If an indefinite state of small-scale warfare was the best Nazi Germany could hope for even in the widely optimistic minds of Hitler and his cronies, the proposed victory on the eastern front was hardly an occasion for great joy. However, if the war was not about to be won (for which there was overwhelming evidence), the danger to Nazi Germany extended far beyond a simple propaganda blunder.

Only three weeks into the war in the east, on 14 July 1941, Hitler issued War Directive 32a, which already at this early stage predicted victory over the Soviet Union. Accordingly, Hitler's war directive called for a substantial reduction in the size of the army and a redirection of industry towards the Luftwaffe and the navy's U-boat programme. For the army, however: 'The extension of arms and equipment and the production of new weapons, munitions and equipment will be related, with immediate effect, to the smaller forces which are contemplated for the future. Where orders have been placed for more than six months ahead all contracts beyond that period will be cancelled.'[116] By October 1941, in spite of Hitler's enduring optimism, the war in the east was clearly not at an end, but the ability of Germany's war industry to sustain the needs of the *Ostheer* almost was. Indeed in the second half of October the Wehrmacht command were still drafting plans for the imminent dissolution of one-third of the army and the transfer of hundreds of thousands of men to factories producing weapons for warfare against Britain.[117] Not only were the needs of the war in the east not being met (the fighting thus far had been sustained only by rapidly dwindling pre-invasion stockpiles), there was also the growing threat of an increasingly belligerent United States, which was shipping arms to both Britain and the Soviet Union. Mindful of the dangers, the head of the War Economy Office, General of Infantry Georg Thomas, showed Hitler a memorandum on projected American armament output between October 1941 and May 1942. According to the Wehrmacht's high command, in the coming eight months the United States would produce 4,700 combat aircraft, 2,600 armoured fighting vehicles and more than 1,600 artillery pieces. This was roughly equivalent to the annual output of Germany's war industry, and all of it could theoretically be put at the disposal of Britain or the Soviet Union.[118]

Not only did the United States' industrial potential introduce an almost insurmountable problem if Hitler could not decisively end the war in the east, in another study submitted by Thomas on 2 October the Soviet war industry was shown to be remarkably resilient to Germany's conquests. On the basis of four hypothetical scenarios, each determined by the extent of German conquests in the remainder of 1941, Thomas drew conclusions about the consequences for Soviet armament output based on the loss of raw materials and industrial areas. The conclusions were damning and warned against any immediate hopes for an economic collapse of the Soviet Union. Even in the most far-reaching scenario of German conquest (case D), which included Leningrad, Moscow and all the way to the Volga River in the south (none of which Germany would achieve in 1941), Thomas anticipated there would be 'a considerable weakening of the [Soviet] war economy, which, however, need not necessarily lead to a breakdown. This may only really be expected after the industrial areas of the Urals have been lost.'[119] Hermann Göring, head of the powerful Four-Year Plan Organisation, categorically rejected Thomas's study, labelling it 'too favourable to the Russians' and insisting that the capture of the Donets Basin would have 'decisive consequences for industry in the Urals'.[120] Events would favour Thomas's conclusions and as a result, while the German army was in decline both as a result of Hitler's industrial priorities and the ongoing losses in the east, the Allies were rapidly extending their lead in armaments production.

Even if this dire set of circumstances had been fully appreciated there were other pressures constraining the German economy and preventing a substantive response. Among the most urgent problems in October 1941 was the current rate of monetary expansion, which was threatening to overwhelm the price and wage controls adopted in the mid 1930s and plunge Germany into a new round of hyper-inflation recalling the early 1920s. A report from the Reichsbank stated: 'If one only had to reckon with a short war one could *in extremis* accept even such a short development.' Yet it was recognised that this prospect was 'improbable'[121] and when Walter Funk, the minister of economic affairs and president of the Reichsbank, went to see Hitler he was placated by gushing assurances of future wealth from the east. Two days later, on 15 October, Hitler alluded to the interim solution Nazi Germany would adopt to prop up its faltering currency and close the gap between supply and demand. 'Inflation doesn't come from the fact that more money comes into trading, but only if the individual demands more payment for the same performance. Here one must intervene. I also had to explain to [Dr Hjalmar] Schacht that the cause of the consistency of our currency is the KZ [i.e. concentration camp].'[122] Slave labour was therefore to be dramatically expanded and many prominent German industrialists were pressing the regime to make available millions of Soviet POWs for their understaffed enterprises.

On 31 October Hitler finally agreed, but the conditions and treatment of the Soviet POWs led to so many deaths that by March 1942 only 5 per cent of the 3,350,000 Red Army troops that had been captured in the war could be used as labourers.[123]

While the shortage of labourers, particularly those with skills, constituted a key bottleneck in the factories, the labour deficit also profoundly affected the mining of raw materials. Coal, for example, could be found in abundance throughout Nazi-occupied Europe, but there were nowhere near enough miners to meet German demands. At the same time, transporting the necessary tonnage of coal proved impossible due to the Europe-wide shortages of locomotives and rolling stock, much of which had been redirected for service in the vast occupied territories of the Soviet Union.[124] Oil was an even greater problem since the small production available from Romania's oil fields around Ploesti was Hitler's only natural source of supply. Production, however, was in no way sufficient to meet the needs of German industry as well as those of the army, navy and Luftwaffe. The huge demands of Operation Barbarossa could be met only by exhausting German and Romanian reserves, and even this necessitated a rapid end to hostilities. By the late autumn Germany faced a dire problem. Romanian shipments for September equalled 375,000 tonnes of oil, but these fell to 253,000 tonnes in October and to 223,000 tonnes in November. In December the tonnage dropped dramatically again to 123,000 tonnes and reached an all-time low in February 1942 with just 73,000 tonnes being delivered.[125] As the Romanian head of state, General Ion Antonescu, told the German foreign minister, Joachim von Ribbentrop, 'as for crude oil, Romania has contributed the maximum which it is in her power to contribute. She can give no more.'[126]

By mid October 1941 Germany's strategic position was anything but bright. Army Group Centre's victories did not equate to the urgently needed 'decision' Hitler believed he had secured. The political ramifications of claiming an illusory victory would prove a harmful blow to German morale, while also exposing the widening credibility gap separating Hitler's headquarters from the reality of the war. As Goebbels recognised, the regime had badly miscalculated in its representation of the war and would face increasingly difficult questions if the war could not be ended soon. That same prospect was also what troubled General Thomas, who knew better than many in the high command how badly prepared Germany was for a long war of attrition against the Allied powers. As the journalist Howard Smith noted shortly after leaving Germany at the end of 1941: 'Every fresh gain of Russian territory has meant a severe economic loss – a loss of valuable manpower from Germany's own factories.' He then concluded: 'It is often a misused statement, but it is true in the case of the Russian war, that Germany has been winning herself to death.'[127]

4 CARNAGE ON THE ROAD TO MOSCOW

Making a killing at Viaz'ma and Briansk – the pockets contract

As Hitler's Germany extolled its victory in the east, the mood at Army Group Centre was equally euphoric. The chief of the Operations Department in the Army General Staff, Colonel Adolf Heusinger, visited Army Group Centre together with Brauchitsch immediately after the closing of the pocket at Viaz'ma and wrote of the prevailing 'high spirits'. Heusinger discussed the situation with Greiffenberg, Bock's chief of staff, and Lieutenant-Colonel Henning von Tresckow, the first general-staff officer of Army Group Centre, and they agreed that 'another three weeks' were needed, 'then it will have been done'.[1] Brauchitsch was also buoyed by the success and assured Bock that 'this time it was different than at Minsk and Smolensk'.[2] According to Blumentritt:

> It is hardly surprising that Hitler, his commanders and his troops themselves now believed that the Red Army must be nearing the end of its resources both in manpower and in weapons … Great optimism prevailed in Army Group Centre, and from Field Marshal von Bock to the privates at the front we all believed and hoped that we would soon be marching through the streets of the Russian capital.[3]

Heusinger and Brauchitsch flew back to the OKH just as the rain and mud were transforming the roads and fields of the east, but for the army command an end to major operations in the east seemed at last within reach. Heusinger noted on 14 October that 'individual expeditions' to the Caucasus and Egypt would replace 'large ground operations'. More-over, Heusinger determined that in the future 'the continuation of the war will be left to the Luftwaffe and the U-boat'.[4] With such expect-ations one may assume that Dietrich's speech on 9 October came as little surprise to the men of the OKH, yet the regime's public declaration of victory angered many within the army command even though they were, for the most part, in agreement with its conclusion. Heusinger denounced what he referred to as 'this bragging and especially proph-esying' of victory, even though he maintained that the opposing Soviet forces were now largely 'untrained [men] or half-children'.[5]

Before any form of victory could hope to be proclaimed, Army Group Centre would first have to deal with its double encirclements at Viaz'ma and Briansk. Trapping such large numbers of Soviet armies may indeed have established the parameters of a great battlefield suc-cess, but that success had still to be won and the Soviet men caught in the pockets were desperate to break out at all costs. On 10 October the first major Soviet formations began battering against the German defen-sive front on the eastern side of the Viaz'ma ring (see Map 9). In many instances the German forces had had time to choose their positions and dig in, but in places the forested landscape afforded limited fields of fire, while offering Soviet forces cover from aerial attack. The first attacks began in the morning of 10 October and grew in intensity over the course of the day. Across the width of Hoepner's panzer group constant attacks had to be repelled, with the worst experienced by Vietinghoff's XXXXVI Panzer Corps, which was attacked with 'intense strength' by infantry supported by tanks and artillery. Not only were the attacks stronger than in preceding days, but they had improved in organisation and planning.[6] Above all what struck the German commanders most was the fanaticism of the Soviet soldiers who repeatedly advanced into the heaviest fire in order to break the German lines. In one sector of Veiel's 2nd Panzer Division an attack resulted in 500 Soviet dead with only 100 taken prisoner.[7] Not only did the Soviets attack against overwhelmingly superior fire, but in another sector of the front Wolfgang Horn witnessed from his observation position the 'incredible' fact that only the first wave of Soviet troops was armed. 'As the first row was mowed down', Horn explained, 'they [the second row] bent down and took the guns of those who were dead – they were destined to attack without weapons, something that was totally unfamiliar to us'.[8]

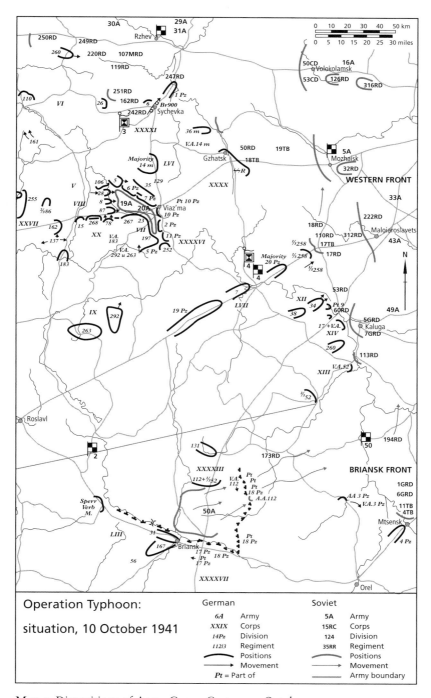

Map 9 Dispositions of Army Group Centre, 10 October 1941

While Army Group Centre's war diary noted that the pressure against Hoepner's front was 'very strong', the real area of crisis in the encirclement front on 10 October was in Major-General Heinz Hellmich's 23rd Infantry Division, which advanced into a bulging position in the south of the pocket.[9] Hellmich's division had to defend itself against what was underlined in the army group's war diary as 'very intense attacks … which in numerous places led to breakthroughs' and forced every man in the division, including non-combat elements, to take up arms. Indeed the neighbouring 267th Infantry Division had to dispatch a regiment immediately to help stem the tide of Soviet forces surging past Hellmich's broken positions, and everywhere in the rear areas troops were placed on alert.[10] On 11 October Albert Neuhaus noted from just outside the encirclement front: 'in case it should still be necessary we will be sent forward'.[11]

While Kluge and Hoepner were bearing the brunt of the Soviet break-out attempts, two panzer divisions of Reinhardt's Panzer Group 3 (6th and 7th) were still holding the line on the north of the pocket in spite of orders to begin the advance northwards towards Kalinin. Under the circumstances it was proving almost impossible for Hoepner's forces to extend themselves to relieve Reinhardt, especially since Panzer Group 3's sector was itself under constant attack from inside the pocket. Colonel Hasso-Eccard Freiherr von Manteuffel, who commanded the 6th Grenadier Regiment of the 7th Panzer Division, knew what to expect after taking part in the encirclement battles at Minsk and Smolensk. His orders to his men were simple: 'Dig in up to your necks!' When the attacks did start, the fighting was unrelenting, although the Soviet attacks were less organised than those further south. As Manteuffel explained: 'With no centralised control, the Russians massed against our positions and stormed them day and night. The enemy successfully broke through several times at night.' Initially the Soviets penetrated with small groups, but these were then followed by larger formations which exploited the gaps. 'In such cases they even penetrated battalion headquarters and artillery positions, where hand-to-hand fighting broke out.'[12] Not surprisingly, casualties in the 6th Grenadier Regiment were high, but in the 7th Grenadier Regiment the situation had been even worse. On 10 October the 7th Panzer Division's war diary described the regiment as 'perfectly beaten' after enduring almost twenty-four hours of sustained combat in which two-thirds of all the machine guns and anti-tank guns had been lost, while seventy men were killed and another eighty were wounded.[13] When the positions of the 3rd Company, which had not been overrun, were at last relieved by the arrival of tanks from the division's panzer regiment, the scene told of the desperate struggle. 'In several foxholes there were four or five dead interspersed with one or two survivors standing among the bodies of their own, rifles at the ready. Several of the machine guns were completely shot out and nobody in the company had any ammunition left ... My impression was that the soldiers of the 3rd Company had actually fought to the limit of sustainable endurance.' An officer from the 7th Regiment later explained: 'It was actually worse than Yartsevo.[14] Then the enemy attacked mainly in battalion strength. This time we had to hold back several divisions, but with motorized infantry companies spread over a 12-km sector.'[15]

As bad as things were on some points of the German line, for the great majority of the Soviet forces attempting to break out of the encirclement the situation was far more desperate. Lieutenant-General M. F. Lukin, who had been given command of the bulk of the Soviet forces inside the Viaz'ma pocket, reported his status on 10 October. 'The situation of the encircled forces has worsened sharply. There are few shells, bullets are running out, and there is no food. They eat that which the population can provide and horseflesh. Medicines and dressing materials are all used up. All tents and dwellings are overflowing with wounded.'[16] Major Ivan Shabalin was one of the soldiers trapped inside the pocket and his diary reflects the terrible uncertainty and high cost of fighting encircled. On 9 October Shabalin wrote:

> Our army is in a tragic situation: we no longer have any idea where the rear is, or where the front line is to be found – it is impossible to tell any more. And we have suffered such terrible losses. We are trying to salvage what we can, and our remaining vehicles are jam-packed with equipment; every soldier is carrying something, even strips of plywood. But all the time the ring around us closes.[17]

In fact the encirclement had been closed for two days and the ring was tightening as German forces advanced from the west. By 11 October the pocket had shrunk from an estimated 75 by 35 kilometres in size to just 20 by 20 kilometres.[18] Indeed, as the panzer groups were fighting tooth and nail on the eastern side of the pocket, further west Soviet forces offered much weaker resistance to the German infantry advancing from the west. On 10 October Bock visited Lieutenant-General Bogislav von Studnitz's 87th Infantry Division as it was pushing east of the Dnepr

River. Studnitz's men had in fact lost contact with the enemy and were simply advancing into open space. As a result Bock noted, 'those there refused to believe that there were still strong forces in the pocket and that 200,000 men had been captured already'.[19] Yet for those who saw the endless columns of Soviet POWs making their way out of the encirclement there could be no mistaking the scale of events taking place west of Viaz'ma. As Horst Lange noted in his diary on 11 October: 'This morning the prisoners from Viaz'ma came past – an incalculable succession of misery, included are very many civilians, ragged, emaciated, frozen, lacklustre, beaten. Many old men. Few intelligent faces. A stream of endless dehumanisation. No individuality … the vanquished have no more backbone.'[20] On the same day (11 October) Erich Leismeier, another soldier on the encirclement front, described the 'rich booty in material' that had fallen into German hands and his conviction that the war could not last beyond October.[21]

In many respects the experience of the battle of Viaz'ma was a contradictory one for many of the German soldiers who took part. While some records speak only of a resounding triumph, yielding untold amounts of Soviet weapons, vehicles and men, other accounts provide a far darker record in which there is little or no discussion of a victory and only a sober tale of how the fighting had all but destroyed their unit. Indeed as bad as the fighting was on 10 October it intensified on 11 October. The focal point of Soviet attacks in Hoepner's panzer group was Esebeck's 11th Panzer Division which was assaulted by masses of Soviet infantry from 2 a.m. onwards. Later, Soviet POWs revealed that three whole divisions had been thrown into the attack, which struck the front of the 111th and 110th Grenadier Regiments. Soviet losses were horrific, as men ran headlong into the concentrated fire of machine guns, mortars, artillery shells and infantry fire. Yet the panzer division's war diary makes clear that 'strong elements' managed to break through the German line, which required the deployment of the panzer regiment in order to counterattack and 'annihilate' these groups.[22] Walter Schaefer-Kehnert, an officer in the 11th Panzer Division, recalled after the war: 'I saw one of these attacks coming early in the morning. We were sitting on the top of the hills, there was fog going down to the river valley, and when the fog came up it was like a herd of vehicles and men coming up by the thousand and it made your blood freeze.' Schaefer-Kehnert ordered his men not to fire until the enemy was within range of their anti-aircraft gun and the machine guns. Only then did they open fire, cutting swaths through the Soviet ranks.[23] In testament to the dimensions of the fighting, when the attacks at last stopped it was estimated that before the 111th Grenadier Regiment alone there lay some 2,000 Soviet dead with more than 3,000 others having been taken prisoner. Not surprisingly, the same regiment was recorded to have suffered 'heavy losses' and had to be reinforced by additional units from the 252nd Infantry Division.[24] Nor was Esebeck's division the exception. Veiel's 2nd Panzer Division noted an attack on 11 October in which 800 Soviet troops were killed in one sector of its front line and 500 POWs were taken.[25] Overall Panzer Group 4 insisted that only small enemy groups succeeded in penetrating the German ring and even these, it claimed, were subsequently cleaned up by reserves behind the front.[26]

To the north, Reinhardt's Panzer Group 3 was breaking off from the encirclement front, relieved by elements of Strauss's Ninth Army. By the evening of 11 October Landgraf's 6th Panzer Division was driving to the north-east, leaving only Funck's 7th Panzer Division to continue defending against what Reinhardt described as 'strong Russian breakout attempts'.[27] Indeed the heavy casualties of the earlier battles complicated the latter ones because losses were not replaced. Platoons were dissolved and companies amalgamated to bring units up to strength, but the front did not shrink in size, meaning that units were still facing disproportionately long sectors. In one instance two platoons were directed to defend a sector three and a half kilometres wide, with the result that at least one position with forty defenders was simply overrun and all the men were killed. At the same time on another sector of the front Soviet forces ran into murderous fire, resulting in horrendous losses. One German lieutenant in the 7th Grenadier Regiment described the attack on his lines:

> The first bursts caused huge losses of people and materiel. Their attack was absolutely unbelievable. Whole columns were on the move with artillery, horse columns and lorries in between coming out of the woods behind [the village of] Shekulina. Without deviating they came directly at us. What targets they presented our forward artillery observers! They sent salvoes of artillery, without pause, one after the other into the enemy hordes. It caused a practically unbelievable destruction.[28]

Not surprisingly, on 12 October the war diary of the 7th Panzer Division described the preceding days as an 'especially large victory' while at the same time acknowledging the 'difficult fighting', which had resulted in 'gruelling losses'.[29] Even the steely Bock was moved by the reports of the fighting and the seemingly suicidal actions of Soviet commanders at Viaz'ma. Referring to the 'desperate attempts to break out', Bock noted that some enemy units advanced towards German positions in closed formation with artillery in the middle of their lines.[30]

While the fighting raged in the Viaz'ma pocket, further south the Briansk pocket was split into two by the union of Arnim's 17th Panzer Division and Major-General Wolf Trierenberg's 167th Infantry Division. Trierenberg's men had advanced east all the way to Briansk where they met with Arnim's division on 10 October. There were now pockets to the north and south of Briansk, but neither was sealed with anything approaching the strength of the German forces at Viaz'ma. Indeed the northern pocket was not even completely closed, and Nehring's 18th Panzer Division was holding the eastern perimeter with only an advanced battle group.[31] This was not just treacherous for the troops stretched dangerously thin over the front, but any attempt at lateral movement, to shift reserves between strong points, was made especially difficult by the groundless roads and roving enemy bands.[32] The area consisted of virgin forest and the defensive zone extended some 30 kilometres in length, leaving the individual strong points of the battle group at great risk. By 11 October reports were received at divisional headquarters of constant encounters with both small and large enemy groups. In the case of the latter, the battle group gave an indication of their size by stating that they had attempted to break out 'with hundreds of vehicles' leading to 'bloody' defensive battles.[33]

Yet the fact that the northern pocket was not even closed convinced Bock at Army Group Centre that 'North of Briansk the bulk of the enemy forces have probably already decamped to the east. Nevertheless, much remains to be taken there, especially in captured equipment.'[34] Yet Bock was wrong. The pocket north of Briansk still contained the bulk of the Soviet Fiftieth Army along with elements of the Third.[35] As a result, the elements of Weichs's Second Army compressing the pocket from the north (Lieutenant-General Friedrich Mieth's 112th Infantry Division and Major-General Dr Lothar Rendulic's 52nd Infantry Division) encountered stiff resistance. Ernst Guicking, an infantryman in the 52nd Infantry Division, wrote home on 10 October: 'We attack into the back of the Russian with *Sturmgeschützen* [assault guns]. Afternoon attack. The Russian is tough. Terrible forest battle, unforgettable.'[36] Bock may have misjudged where the Soviet forces north of Briansk were, but his assessment that a significant number could escape to the east proved correct. On 10 October Weichs reported that 'a strong part of the red Fiftieth Army … could not be prevented from escaping'. Moreover, Guderian informed Army Group Centre on the same day that the remainder of Nehring's panzer division was committed to containing breakouts in the southern pocket and that as a result the battle group could not be reinforced.[37]

The northern pocket at Briansk was clearly of secondary importance to the southern pocket, which Guderian knew posed a far greater threat to the rear area of his thrust on Tula if large enemy units could not be contained in the pocket. Accordingly, Guderian directed Fremerey's 29th Motorised Infantry Division, Obernitz's 293rd Infantry Division, Clössner's 25th Motorised Infantry Division, Colonel Walter Hörnlein's Infantry Regiment 'Grossdeutschland' and a regiment of Loeper's 10th Motorised Infantry Division to hold the eastern perimeter of the pocket. Guderian even sought to have Kempf's XXXXVIII Panzer Corps redirected north to reinforce the pocket because the front was so long, with constant breakthroughs and points of crisis in the line.[38] Indeed on 10 October Army Group Centre's war diary noted that Fremerey and Obernitz's divisions were under heavy attack, repelling attempts to break out, which 'in places insignificant enemy groups succeeded in doing'.[39] On the following day (11 October) the same war diary pointed further at the weaknesses of the German line by asserting: 'That individual enemy groups escape cannot however be avoided.'[40]

The Soviet forces trapped inside the pocket consisted of the Thirteenth and Third Armies and were being driven towards Guderian's Second Panzer Army by General of Infantry Karl Weisenberger's LIII Army Corps.[41] Not surprisingly the fear and desperation inside the southern Briansk pocket were spurring the Soviet troops to ever more frantic measures in order to escape the encirclement. As Eremenko, the commander of the Briansk Front who was also trapped in the southern pocket, later wrote: 'The whole Third Army was in a perilous situation. We had no fresh forces to build up an attack. It was essential that the men who had already exhausted all their strength in the previous futile assaults should regain their vigour.' With command and control largely ineffective above the regimental level, Eremenko took command of the forces in his sector and attempted to force a major breakthrough in the

German line. He sought to achieve this by overrunning one of the defensive strong points. His plan required first slipping two battalions around the German flank in order to launch an attack into the rear of the German positions and divide their defensive fire. As Eremenko's account explained:

> The time dragged. We waited with heavy hearts. Suddenly, breaking the harrowing silence, we heard heavy machine-gun and rifle fire, grenade and mortar-shell explosions, and then, to top it all, the echo of a powerful Russian "hurrah". The long-awaited assault had begun … A flare soared into the sky and the men of two regiments rose in attack chains supported by ten tanks, encouraged by the heroism of the two battalions in the enemy rear. The gunners, mortar men and machine-gunners supported the infantry and tanks with a wall of fire … The appearance of our troops in his rear, coupled with our sudden and audacious attack, stunned the enemy. Good co-ordination by all our units helped us squash his defences. The Nazis in the sector were wiped out and the route of escape from the forest lay open before us.[42]

Guderian's memoir acknowledges a major breach in the lines between the 29th and 25th Motorised Infantry Divisions on 11 October, but claimed that the 5th Machine-gun Battalion was soon able to close the gap.[43] Clearly, however, the fighting around the two Briansk pockets was less one-sided than the battles to break out of the Viaz'ma encirclement. Bock noted the contrasting situation in the two pockets on 12 October: 'Guderian is not moving forward; just like Weichs he is struggling with the Briansk pockets. The pocket at Viaz'ma has been reduced further, numbers of prisoners growing tremendously, the enemy's losses are enormous.'[44]

While Red Army soldiers were being rounded up in the tens of thousands at Viaz'ma and Briansk, the shattered Soviet front had by no means been entirely concentrated into these two distinct pockets. In fact the area around the pockets, which was predominantly wooded, provided cover for countless bands of Soviet men and their officers. Some of these were intent only on avoiding German contact, while fleeing east to rejoin Soviet lines, but others took a more aggressive stance, attacking isolated German targets, burning villages, destroying bridges and mining roads.[45] Yet the distinction between a Red Army soldier cut off behind enemy lines and a bona fide partisan soon became blurred and quickly tended towards the latter, against whom the Wehrmacht was authorised to act with the utmost severity.[46] The transformation in how the Soviet enemy was depicted can be seen in the war diary of Kuntzen's LVII Panzer Corps, which on 10 October spoke only of 'Russians' operating on both sides of their advance route, but just two days later the same problem was said to result from 'increased partisan activity'.[47] The distinction was an important one. Partisans themselves were to be shot out of hand, particularly as the parallel extermination of the Soviet Jews was repeatedly framed as indistinguishable from the anti-partisan campaign. Indeed at a special anti-partisan conference in September hosted by the commander of Army Group Centre's rear area, General of Infantry Max von Schenckendorff, the maxim, 'Where there's a Jew there's a partisan, and where there's a partisan there's a Jew', predominated.[48]

With cut-off Soviet troops being equated with partisans and partisans with Jews, the terminology used added to the delegitimisation of resistance, while simultaneously legitimating murder. Nor were such actions confined to the rear areas and spared the regular troops at the front. On 10 October an order by Reichenau, the commander of the Sixth Army, fused what he referred to as the 'Jew–Bolshevik system' with the 'bestialities inflicted on the German and related peoples'. As a result, Reichenau instructed his men 'the soldier must have full under-standing of the need for the harsh but just punishment of Jewish sub-humanity'. He then inextricably related the harsh measures advocated for the Jews to the extermination campaign being fought against the partisans. 'The battle against the enemy behind the front is still not being taken seriously enough. Insidious, cruel *partisans* and degenerate women are still being taken as prisoners of war; snipers and tramps, half-uniformed or in civilian clothes, are being handled like decent soldiers and taken away to the detention camps.'[49] The implication that partisans could be 'half-uniformed' reflects the lack of distinction that Reichenau's order now insisted upon. Nor was this just a reflection of Reichenau's well-known Nazi sympathies.[50] Two days after the order was issued on 12 October Rundstedt, the commander of Army Group South, declared himself 'completely in agreement' with the order and distributed it further.[51] Word of the order quickly spread and when the OKH reviewed a copy it decided to pass it on to all army groups and armies in the east, requesting them 'to issue appropriate instructions along the same lines'.[52]

In the forward areas of Army Group Centre a foretaste of what was to become one of the most dangerous regions of 'partisan' activity over the winter of 1941/1942 was clearly emerging in the first half of October 1941 (see Illustration 8).[53] As Hoepner's panzer group concentrated on securing the perimeter of the encircled Soviet forces at Viaz'ma, Vietinghoff's XXXXVI Panzer Corps recorded in its war diary: 'The breakthrough [of the Soviet front] took place too quickly to really clear the area. Everywhere, particularly in the forests, remain enemy elements left behind.'[54] Nor was this an inconsequential problem. On 5 October the war diary of Fehn's 5th Panzer Division included a rebuke of the lower orders within the rear area after an attack educed a 'mood of panic' (*Panikstimmung*) within the ranks. It referred to the men 'wildly shooting into the air' and suggested that this resulted from green troops who were 'not well established' in the conditions of the east.[55] Nearby, Veiel's 2nd Panzer Division noted being engaged in what it described as a 'partisan battle' in which five of its men were

8 A German shot dead from behind. During the autumn of 1941 Soviet partisan attacks markedly increased in the rear areas of Army Group Centre.

killed and nine were wounded. As the war diary noted, retribution was swift: 'Civil population stood united with the partisans. Fifty Russians shot down.'[56] Beyond the large number of Red Army troops still at large behind the German lines, Reinhardt's Panzer Group 3 made it clear that given the inability to guard the vast numbers of captured Soviet POWs adequately 'a further growth of the partisan nuisance is not to be avoided'.[57] On 10 and 11 October the quartermaster's war diary at Guderian's Second Panzer Army noted that the 'very strained' supply situation was as much due to the 'impossibility' of the sodden roads as the 'constant enemy breakthroughs of the supply roads'.[58]

Individual German accounts also noted the increased insecurity in the surrounding areas and immediately began referring to the cut-off Soviet soldiers by the more sinister designation 'partisan'. Infantryman Horst Lange wrote in his diary on 12 October: 'The whole area is full of dispersed Russians, who continue their partisan operations.'[59] In part the doggedness of Soviet resistance may be traced to Stalin's Order Number 270 of 16 August 1941, which declared those who surrendered or deserted traitors and then stated 'the families of whom are subject to arrest'.[60] Peter von der Osten-Sacken noted that over the autumn of 1941 partisan activity became more and more apparent. 'Trains were derailed, supply columns attacked and munitions depots blown up. Dispatch riders and truck drivers were shot from behind and often weak staging posts were attacked with all Germans killed. The embitterment was great on both sides and not infrequently it came to barbarity.'[61] Yet not all attacks behind the German front in 1941 were simply the result of cut-off Soviet soldiers, and estimates suggest there may have been upwards of 65,000 people throughout the occupied Soviet Union already in underground organisations or operating as partisans during 1941.[62] The eagerness of German anti-partisan operations to employ exemplary violence by targeting civilian areas deemed 'suspect' is represented by the fact that Army Group Centre alone recorded killing around 80,000 'partisans' for the loss of some 3,284 men between July 1941 and May 1942.[63] In one of the most infamous examples Major-General Gustav Freiherr von Mauchen-Heim genannt von Bechtoldsheim's 707th Infantry Division reported taking 10,940 prisoners in anti-partisan operations in just four weeks starting on 11 October. Of these prisoners 10,431 were subsequently shot, although only 90 rifles were found.[64] As Osten-Sacken noted: 'Prisoners were not taken. Whoever was identified as a partisan had to be expected to be shot. That went also for the civilian population when they offered shelter to the partisans.'[65] The ruthlessness of German anti-partisan measures as well as the poor quality of training and leadership within the partisan movement in 1941 accounted for its decline over the winter of 1941–1942. By January 1942 the movement contained only an estimated 30,000 combatants, but this was its nadir and from the spring of 1942 the widespread disillusionment with the new German occupation as well as the perceived improvement in the Soviet war effort helped transform the movement into an increasingly robust and potent military force.[66]

Forward on the flanks – Bock's willful overextension

While the Soviet armies that were to have defended Moscow were being rapidly broken up and destroyed inside the German pockets, German intelligence believed the road to Moscow was open with only special units of the NKVD and People's Militias remaining available to defend the capital.[67] Even Soviet sources indicate that there were only around 90,000 troops available to stem the German tide.[68] Yet the charge to Moscow was not as straightforward as a simple comparison of the opposing forces. Bock faced a number of profound problems. To begin with, the mass of encircled Soviet armies were trapped but not yet defeated. This bought Zhukov, now in charge of defending Moscow, time to build up and reorganise his defences, while at the same time inflicting in places serious losses on the motorised formations deployed to the encirclement front. The time lost was also a serious factor given the rapid deterioration of the weather, which, with more and more rain and none of the summer heat to dry the ground, increased the number of regions where bottomless conditions halted all movement. By the second week of October the roads in Bock's extensive operational area varied between passable, sometimes with the addition of drainage ditches or felled trees strung together to form corduroy roads, and those already sunk into the mire, along which only tracked vehicles or tractors could pass. Another complication was that forces freed from the encirclement front (particularly Panzer Group 3) were being sent to distant objectives on the flanks and not directly towards Moscow. Indeed of the eight panzer corps in Army Group Centre only two (Kuntzen's LVII Panzer Corps and Schweppenberg's XXIV Panzer Corps) were attempting to advance towards Moscow, and then with only mixed success.

On 9 October Kuntzen's corps reported that the shortage of trucks and fuel made the advance 'hardly possible'.[69] Nevertheless the corps was ordered to push forward anyway and soon discovered that the Soviets were employing a new tactic, which proved a remarkably economical as well as effective form of defence. Under the prevailing conditions the panzer spearheads were almost exclusively bound to the roads as cross-country advances were all but impossible to supply. As a result the Germans could not bring their superior numbers to bear, and Soviet resistance often had to be met head on without the option of rapid flanking attacks. As Kuntzen's war diary noted, this allowed small Soviet battle groups with infantry, artillery and a few tanks to delay or even hold the German advance.[70] What is more, the Soviet T-34 tank, already superior in speed, armour and armament, now revealed itself to be far better adapted to the conditions, with wider tracks allowing it to traverse with relative ease the no man's land of sodden fields. As the LVII Panzer Corps discovered, 'the infantry possess no weapon which can effectively combat the heavily armoured tanks'.[71] Even more of a threat than the T-34 was the enormous Soviet KV-1 tank, which was practically invulnerable to all but the German 88mm anti-aircraft gun. One German soldier inspecting a captured KV-1 counted no less than thirty-five hits in the turret from German 37mm and 50mm anti-tank guns. The hulk showed signs of an estimated forty further hits forcing the soldier to conclude: 'It must have overrun several German anti-tank guns.'[72] In spite of the difficulties, Kuntzen's panzer corps relentlessly fought its way forward and on 11 October captured the town of Medyn 140 kilometres from Moscow. Yet Soviet resistance escalated with each renewal of the advance, resulting in a proportional rise in German casualties. On 13 October Lieutenant-General Curt Jahn's 3rd Motorised Infantry Division committed three battalions to the attack with each losing more than 100 men in the course of the day's fighting, while the panzer regiment of Bismarck's 20th Panzer Division was noted on the same day to have lost all its company commanders.[73] By the following day (14 October) Bismarck's division was reduced to just thirty-seven operational tanks.[74]

To the south Schweppenberg's XXIV Panzer Corps had been unsuccessfully attempting to take Mtsensk (50 kilometres north-east of Orel) since 6 October. Repeated attacks by Langermann-Erlancamp's 4th Panzer Division had been repulsed with heavy losses. Here again the Red Army was employing new tactics, which involved a frontal attack by infantry to engage and 'hold' the German front, while Soviet tanks

manoeuvred around the flank and attacked from the rear. As Guderian
noted: 'Descriptions of the quality and, above all, of the new tactical
handling of the Russian tanks were very worrying. Our defensive weapons
available at the period were only successful against the T-34 when the
conditions were unusually favourable.'[75] The condition of the German
battle group formed to assault Mtsensk on 10 October was anything but
hopeful. Its commander, Colonel Heinrich Eberbach, recorded: 'the forces
were exhausted, had suffered setbacks, were wearing wet uniforms and
were chilled through and through'. He also noted a near-total absence of
hand grenades and ammunition for the machine guns, while the enemy, he
claimed, were numerically superior and entrenched in defensive positions.[76]

The mood was so depressed that Guderian recalled: 'For the first
time during this exacting campaign Colonel Eberbach gave the impression
of being exhausted, and the exhaustion that was now noticeable was less
physical than spiritual. It was indeed startling to see how deeply our
best officers had been affected by the latest battles.'[77] On 10 October
Eberbach's battle group managed to outflank the Soviet defensive positions and fight their way into Mtsensk; by the following day the town was
completely in German hands.[78] Yet Schweppenberg's corps was still 120
kilometres short of its objective at Tula, while Langermann-Erlancamp's
4th Panzer Division fielded just forty operational tanks on 12 October.[79]
Moreover, only a trickle of supplies was reaching the forward positions,
and the Second Panzer Army's quartermaster anticipated no major
improvement until the ground froze and hardened.[80] For months men
like Colonel Eberbach had been struggling tirelessly to achieve their objectives, often under the most difficult of circumstances, only to receive new
orders and new objectives. The breaking of morale was less a commentary
on the difficulties of seizing Mtsensk than on the endlessness of the German
campaign in the east and constant need to achieve more with less.

As the difficulties of maintaining offensive operations mounted,
the problems were scarcely appreciated within the high command,
which was still beset by the euphoria of Typhoon's early success.
Contrasting this with the depressed mood within his panzer army
Guderian wrote: 'What a contrast to the high spirits in evidence at the
OKH and at Army Group Centre! Here was a radical difference of
attitude which as time went on grew wider until it could scarcely be
bridged.' Guderian even characterised his superiors within the army as
'drunk with the scent of victory'.[81] At Army Group Centre there was
recognition of the new Soviet tactic of heavily defending the roads and

settlements leading to Moscow at the expense of maintaining a broad front.[82] Yet the degree of difficulty this entailed for the German advance as well as the much more even playing field it afforded Zhukov's limited resources were entirely lost on Bock. There would now be heavy fighting on the narrow 'road fronts', but Bock, mindful of the bad roads, limited supplies and even worse weather to come, was advocating light forces to maintain the advance's movement and speed. In a conversation with Halder on 11 October the commander of Army Group Centre spoke of the coming operation to encircle Moscow and stated: 'It can as a result only be done simply and as "colonial-like" as possible. The enemy situation will allow this.'[83] Here Bock was fundamentally wrong. While Kuntzen and Schweppenberg made some progress in the second week of October, their forces were clearly inadequate to crack the Moscow defensive perimeter, let alone encircle the Soviet capital. From another point of view, however, Bock was also correct. As Army Group Centre's bulk wallowed in the mud and struggled to maintain itself in the absence of supplies, a general advance could not be conducted and certainly not rapidly. Moving up large numbers of heavy formations equipped for protracted battle would take much more time, and this was precisely what Zhukov needed.

While the drive on Moscow was underresourced even against the meagre Soviet forces at hand, the German high command was adamant that objectives on the distant flanks could be undertaken simultaneously with the encirclement of Moscow. In the south Guderian had wanted to divert Kempf's XXXXVIII Panzer Corps to shore up his position at the Briansk pocket, but this contravened the orders of the OKH, which directed it to maintain contact with Army Group South and strike east towards Kursk. In the prevailing conditions neither set of orders mattered much. The area of the XXXXVIII Panzer Corps was one of the worst affected by the autumn rains, and the corps war diary noted on 12 October: 'The divisions are all completely fixed [by the mud].'[84] In the rear area, hundreds of vehicles were stuck and left stranded in the vast bottomless plains of sunken mire.[85] As one soldier observed: 'The mud is extraordinarily sticky because the soil is permeated with oily residues. ... The water does not flow, it stagnates; the dirt clings to the feet of man and beast.'[86] It also buried vehicles up to their axles, which not only compromised Kempf's supply, but also exposed his corps to devastating losses in the event of a Soviet counterattack. This is precisely what took place on 12 October, reflecting the importance of maintaining manoeuvrability in both the offensive and the defensive, while also underlining the greater mobility of the Red Army in the unwieldy conditions. Hubicki's 9th Panzer Division bore the brunt of the attack, which broke through the front and penetrated into the rear area north of the village of Amon. The division's war diary noted: 'countless vehicles destroyed and individual German soldiers remaining killed'. In the aftermath of the attack rallying the many dispersed groups of men and organising them to a command post could be achieved only by the air-dropping of leaflets.[87] Hubicki was able to rebuild his front, but his division was still more than 80 kilometres from Kursk, which under the circumstances was going to take an enormous effort to reach.

While Kempf's panzer corps was attempting to take Kursk with just one panzer division (supported by two divisions of motorised infantry), at the other end of Bock's front Reinhardt's Panzer Group 3 was being diverted to seize Kalinin. Kirchner's XXXXI Panzer Corps had taken no part in the encirclement at Viaz'ma, initially providing flank support to General of Panzer Troops Ferdinand Schaal's LVI Panzer Corps and then receiving orders to strike north-east towards Kalinin. Spearheading the XXXXI Panzer Corps was Krüger's 1st Panzer Division, which endured rolling enemy air attacks in the early days of the campaign[88] and then conducted a major battle with the Soviet 107th Motorised Rifle Division on 6 October. In this action sixty Soviet tanks were destroyed for an unknown number of German losses,[89] but two days before the battle on 4 October Krüger was already down to just forty operational panzers.[90] Air attacks again proved costly on 8 October,[91] and Colonel Hans Röttiger, the chief of staff of the XXXXI Panzer Corps, claimed that Soviet aerial attacks 'surpassed everything so far experienced in Russia'.[92]

Of more concern to Krüger were the changing weather and deteriorating road conditions. Here the wooded country of Bock's northern flank provided an interim solution. As Siegfried Knappe reported: 'The only way we could move vehicles was to corduroy the roads with small tree trunks laid side by side to provide a solid surface … Such roads were difficult footing for the horses, and the vehicles jolted over them, but at least we could transport supplies and ammunition.'[93] With Soviet resistance lacklustre and mobility better than on other stretches of the front, Kirchner's corps began its long march to the north-east. On 10 October the town of Sychevka, 70 kilometres north of Viaz'ma, was captured along with 1,200 POWs, twenty wagons of rolling stock and four halls full of airplane parts and motors.[94] Yet Kalinin was another 150 kilometres (linear distance) north-east of Sychevka, and Colonel Röttiger, at the XXXXI Panzer Corps, was clear about the difficulties that posed: 'The inadequate stockpiling of supplies ... bore bitter fruit at that time. The available supplies were in no way sufficient for such a far-reaching operation.' Even getting as far as Sychevka, Röttiger noted, proved exceedingly taxing for the supply columns, which 'suffered great losses' and thus considerably decreased the net tonnage transported.

Yet it was not just the bad roads and condition of the vehicles that hampered the flow of supplies; the main supply depot for Panzer Group 3 was itself sometimes devoid of essential stocks, and the trucks waited for days for the next shipment to arrive.[95] Reinhardt knew that every contingency would need to be exhausted in order to bridge the gap in logistics and reach his distant objective. Accordingly Reinhardt issued a special order on 11 October which required Panzer Group 3 to undertake radical measures:

> The difficulties of panzer troops' vehicle conditions and fuel supply are known to the higher command. Without consideration of these [factors] the operation must be brought to an end even if the set objectives [ending at Kalinin] can only be reached with some of the units and the vehicles must be driven to the limit of their capabilities. Every contingency must be exhausted in order to offset the low fuel supplies and, in spite of the condition of the vehicles, ensure that battle-worthy elements are able to carry out the mission ... Panzer, motorised infantry, engineering and communication troops are to be divided up and grouped so that units with capable vehicles can be set up and separated from the less useful. It must be understood that only brigades or reinforced regiments will remain of the divisions.[96]

Cannibalising whole divisions to form rapid battle groups suggests that Reinhardt was anticipating an end to major operations, while also falling into line with Bock's belief that lighter forces would suffice to exploit the collapse of the Soviet front. The folly of such thinking would become apparent in the week ahead. For now, however, Kirchner's XXXXI Panzer Corps prepared for the next stage of its advance, while Schaal's LVI Panzer Corps began releasing the first of its two panzer divisions (Landgraf's 6th Panzer Division) from the Viaz'ma pocket.

Kirchner's plan of attack was simple: Krüger's 1st Panzer Division would operate in the centre, driving the attack forward with Colonel Walther Krause's motorised infantry regiment 'Lehrbrigade 900' in reserve. Auleb's 6th Infantry Division would screen the corps's long left flank to the west, while Lieutenant-General Otto Ottenbacher's 36th Motorised Infantry Division was to advance on the right with its front facing east to guard against Soviet counterattacks. Lacking the motorisation of the other divisions, Auleb's 6th Infantry Division had to strain every effort to maintain the pace. As one doctor from the division later wrote:

> The weather deteriorated. It became colder and snowed the whole day. But the snow did not remain for long. It was churned into the black earth, into which our vehicles sank deeper and deeper. The troops hauled and pushed the wheels of the transports; the gallant little panje horses sweated and strained; at times we had to take a brief ten-minute rest from sheer exhaustion; then back to the transport, our legs in the black mud up to our knees. Anything to keep the wheels moving. To make up for lost time, and in a desperate race against the weather that we knew would worsen, we marched the night through and reached the area north of Sychevka on 11 October.[97]

For the motorised divisions Reinhardt's order meant drastic measures. To save fuel, vehicles not deemed absolutely necessary for combat were left behind and had their remaining fuel siphoned out.[98] On 11 October Zubtsov, 40 kilometres north of Sychevka, was captured. Yet in testament to the insatiable demands of the higher command on the same day, with Kirchner still well short of Kalinin, Bock informed Reinhardt that, once Kalinin had been reached, 'the armoured group will probably receive orders to continue its advance to Torzhok', which was another 60 kilometres to the north-west. Additionally, Bock informed Reinhardt that he would probably also have to reconnoitre north of Kalinin in the direction of Rameshki, more than 50 kilometres due north.[99] It was the same kind of delusional planning, making limitless demands on the men, that the German generals would later accuse Hitler of having done, to the ruin of their supposedly well-crafted operations. Moreover, as Röttiger noted, even if the fuel and forces could be found for this operation, the sizeable Soviet forces currently fleeing the newly emerging German pocket would probably overrun them.[100] Indeed if one heeds Reinhardt's warning and keeps in mind that Krüger's force consisted of only a brigade, or even a reinforced regiment, defending such vast spaces against enemy breakthroughs was almost certainly impossible, especially given the examples of the pockets further south.

On 12 October Krüger's 1st Panzer Division took Staritsa, 45 kilometres north-east of Zubtsov (see Map 10). On the same day the distance that had opened up between the leading elements of Panzer Group 3 and Strauss's Ninth Army convinced Bock to subordinate Reinhardt directly to Army Group Centre.[101] This came as welcome news to the panzer commanders who had long resented taking orders from, as they saw it, infantry-minded generals. Yet of even greater significance on 12 October was the capture of some 500 Soviet trucks, although the war diary did not record how many were still operational.[102] Either way any intact captured truck was at least a vital source of spare parts and sometimes additional fuel. Indeed such unofficial acquisitions were vital to the ongoing mobility of the whole *Ostheer* and were keenly sought by all formations. As Gottlob Bidermann noted: 'The troops had become masters at fending for themselves … the company attempted to make captured trucks usable. From the vast quantities of captured enemy materiel left behind by the retreating enemy … our troops were able to assemble a large quantity of serviceable vehicles. The company commander brought in an entire fuel truck, which greatly augmented our inventory of "black", or unofficial, fuel supplies.'[103]

The XXXXI Panzer Corps was also afforded the air support of Richthofen's VIII Air Corps, which, in addition to providing air cover and attacking enemy positions, also provided real-time intelligence by dropping handwritten reports from scout planes. On 12 October Krüger's division received one such report which read: 'Road to Kalinin clogged with fleeing enemy columns, no more organised resistance!'[104] Krüger decided to continue his advance into the night of 12–13 October, yet this resulted in the remarkable circumstance that German tanks and motorised infantry were advancing through the middle of fleeing Soviet troops. Heinz Otto Fausten, who took part in the march, recalled: 'We dashed on, through scenes of total disorder. Red Army commanders swore at us from their vehicles, believing that we were Russians fleeing from the front. Enemy vehicles cut into our column, joined us for a while and then, realising our identity swerved off again. It was all quite incredible.'[105] The operations officer at of the 1st Panzer Division, Lieutenant-Colonel Walther Wenck, who, rather uncharacteristically for a German staff officer, was renowned for his wry humour, reported back to the

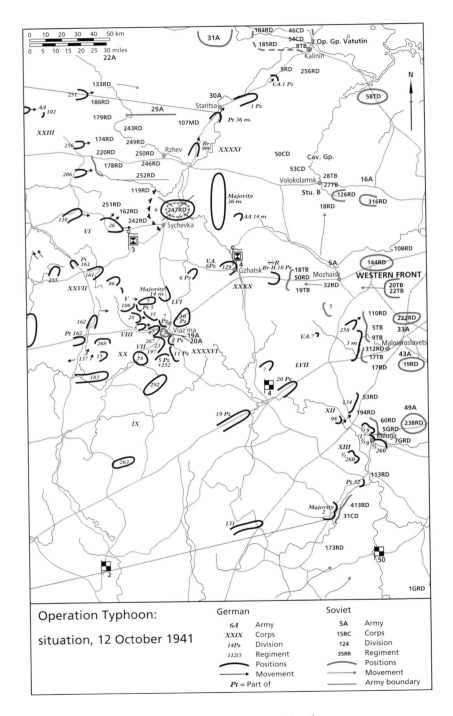

Map 10 Dispositions of Army Group Centre, 12 October 1941

corps: 'Russian units, although not included in our march tables, are attempting continuously to share our road space, and thus are partly responsible for the delay of our advance on Kalinin. Please advise what to do?' The message was returned: 'As usual, 1st Panzer Division has priority along the route of advance. Reinforce traffic control!!'[106] On the same night Major Carl Wagener, the operations officer at Panzer Group 3, recorded a routine question to the leading panzer company, 'Who is driving point?' The answer came back: 'Ivan'.[107]

While some of the men made light of their situation the fact remained that Krüger's advanced group had long since outstretched the flanking protection of Auleb's and Ottenbacher's divisions and were dangerously extending themselves deep into enemy territory. Moreover, the men were tired and cold from the almost continuous marches. Helmut Pabst, who took part in the advance to Kalinin, wrote home in a letter:

> The going's good on the frozen roads of this country of hills crowed with villages. But fifty-five kilometres is a lot. It took us from eight in the morning till two a.m. next day. And then we didn't find billets. The few houses in our rest area had been allocated long before. But the boys wormed themselves into the overcrowded rooms, determined to get warm even if it meant standing.[108]

Indeed the now freezing nightly temperatures introduced new problems into the march. The war diary of Panzer Group 3 noted as early as 10 October that tank motors had to be left idling during the night in order to prevent them from freezing. This, however, exacerbated the fuel shortage.[109]

For all the difficulties on the long march Krüger's 1st Panzer Division rolled into the city of Kalinin in the early morning of 13 October having advanced more than 70 kilometres from Staritsa and roughly 150 kilometres from Sychevka. As at Orel ten days before the streetcars were still running and the local population stood stunned at the sudden sight of German tanks arriving in their streets. However, the surreal spectacle did not last long and there was soon fierce street-fighting in which the civilian population took an active part.[110] As with Mogilev in July, Dnepropetrovsk in August and Leningrad in September, the Germans would again find that reaching a city was only the first step in capturing it. What is more, only the vanguard of Krüger's division was available for the costly urban fighting underway, with the rest of his division strung out over the 150 kilometres of the advance route.[111] To further complicate matters, Bock had since decided to order Reinhardt to continue the advance on to Torzhok.[112] The overextension of Panzer Group 3, so costly in the fighting at Smolensk, was again proceeding apace.

In the second week of October Army Group Centre was well placed for a triumphant operational victory, inflicting serious damage on the Red Army and advancing its line a significant distance towards Moscow. Strategically, however, their operational success was wildly overestimated, and the same problems and oversights that had undercut Operation Barbarossa were now resurfacing to confound Operation Typhoon. Yet failure to grasp strategic realities was not an exclusively German phenomenon. The Soviet leadership had completely misjudged German strategic intentions, while disastrously overestimating the strengths of the Western, Reserve and Briansk Fronts. The Stavka's strategic deployments had also placed their field armies too close to the border, raising the danger of encirclement. Screening the front with light forces while holding back larger formations to identify and counterattack German penetrations would have prevented, or at least greatly limited, the size of the pockets.

Yet while both sides were guilty of misreading or ignoring certain strategic realities, the Soviet Union had a far better understanding of the war in one fundamental respect. From the first days of the conflict the Soviets acknowledged and planned for a long and costly struggle. In October 1941 the idea of liberating all Soviet territory, to say nothing of conquering Nazi Germany, appeared a distant hope even for the most committed communist. As a result, while Hitler continued to drastically underestimate the economic implications of fighting the war in the east, the Soviet Union was already three months into its 'total war' mobilisation, producing armaments in quantity. Indeed, even amidst the crisis months of 1941 when the Soviet Union was losing vast tracts of land and desperately having to relocate a large part of its heavy industry, Stalin's factories were still outproducing Nazi Germany in many of the key indexes of weapons. In October 1941 the Soviets produced some 500 new tanks,[113] while in the same month Germany, with far fewer constraints, managed only 387.[114] Not only were Soviet tanks of superior quality, but as more factories were converted to war production and others were reassembled after relocation the production figures rose accordingly. By March 1942 Soviet factories were turning out 1,000 new tanks a month[115] and that figure continued to rise over the course of the year. By contrast German production in March 1942 had actually dropped to just 336 tanks (see Illustration 9 and Table 3, which

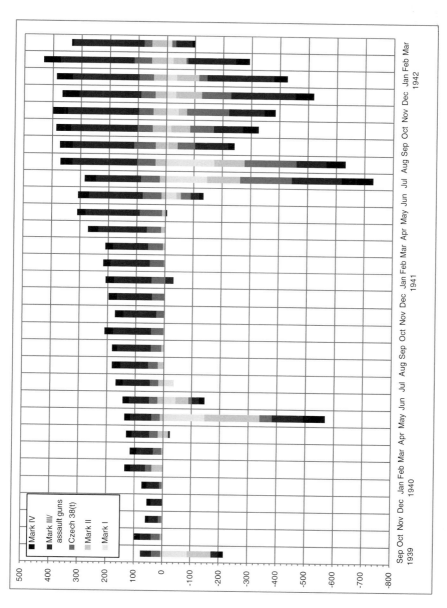

9 German tank production and combat losses, September 1939 to March 1942.

Table 3 *German tank production and combat losses, September 1939 to March 1942*

		Production						Combat losses					
		Mark I	Mark II^a	Czech 38(t)	Mark III^b	Mark IV	Total	Mark I	Mark II^a	Czech 38(t)	Mark III^b	Mark IV	Total
1939	Sep	5		31	40		76	−89	−83		−26	−19	−217
	Oct	8		30	40	20	98						0
	Nov	2		11	35	11	59						0
	Dec				42	14	56						0
1940	Jan		2	10	42	20	74						0
	Feb		38	24	52	20	134						0
	Mar		4	31	57	24	116						0
	Apr		19	30	61	20	130	−5	−13		−6		−24
	May		12	30	75	20	137	−145	−194	−43	−110	−77	−569
	Jun		20	30	70	23	143	−43	−46	−11	−25	−20	−145
	Jul		18	30	96	26	170	−36					−36
	Aug		20	35	97	30	182	−3					−3
	Sep		10	35	120	17	182						0
	Oct		2	44	135	30	211						0
	Nov			27	117	30	174						0
	Dec			44	123	30	197						0
1941	Jan			45	132	31	208		−2		−30		−32
	Feb		3	50	138	26	217						0
	Mar		7	53	122	28	210						0
	Apr		15	49	171	36	271						0
	May		12	78	191	29	310				−5	−1	−6
	Jun		15	65	189	38	307	−39	−16	−33	−30	−16	−134

Jul	21	65	161	38	285	−146	−117	−182	−175	−111	−731
Aug	36	64	229	44	373	−171	−106	−183	−104	−70	−634
Sep	37	76	216	46	375	−8	−32	−62	−116	−23	−241
Oct	48	53	235	51	387	−18	−65	−85	−102	−55	−325
Nov	45	50	252	52	399	−42	−30	−149	−126	−38	−385
Dec	39	50	217	61	367	−33	−92	−102	−227	−65	−519
1942 Jan	45	50	235	57	387	−37	−76	−31	−234	−48	−426
Feb	53	61	261	58	433	−22	−46	−8	−167	−49	−292
Mar	53	28	247	8	336	−16	−3	−12	−57	−10	−98

Notes: The figures reported here do not include losses due to technical reasons, i.e. non-serviceable tanks.

[a] Including flamethrower and anti-aircraft tanks.

[b] Including assault guns.

Source: Adapted from Rolf-Dieter Müller, 'Beginnings of a Reorganization of the War Economy at the Turn of 1941/1942' in Militärgeschichtliches Forschungsamt (ed.), *Germany and the Second World War. Volume V/I. Organization and Mobilization of the German Sphere of Power* (Oxford, 2000) p. 728.

Communique: "The annihilation is proceeding according to schedule."

10 The Red Army's resistance to the German invasion was also celebrated outside the Soviet Union. Already in August 1941 the American cartoonist Dr Seuss (Theodor Geisel) was drawing attention to the difficulty of Hitler's undertaking in the east.

represent the data in different ways) and the 1942 total was some 15,000 tanks *fewer* than the Soviet Union (24,446 Soviet to 9,200 German).[116]

While Stalin was building his war economy on a firm footing, the Soviet public was also being steeled against any thought of defeat. Unlike German propaganda, which led its people to believe the war would be won within weeks, Soviet propaganda, while promising an ultimate victory, was careful in 1941 to establish the 'total' nature of the conflict and instill the idea that there was no alternative to continued resistance. In this way the disasters at the front mattered less because, against an enemy waging a war of annihilation, there was no alternative but to continue the struggle. Accordingly, German atrocities were a central theme of Soviet propaganda, with posters such as 'Death to the Child Murderers', featuring a dead girl with a pair of bloody, swastika-emblazoned boots walking away. Other posters were clearly aimed at the soldiers of the Red Army, with slogans such as 'Shoot the Murderers of Our Wives and Children', 'Soldier, Save Me from Slavery' and 'Warrior of the Red Army Save Us' (for an example of American pro-Soviet propaganda, see Illustration 10). At the same time the people were exhorted to fight on and given the impression that victory was inevitable. V. Koretskii's poster showed a mass of armed civilians with

the simple slogan 'Our Strength Is Incalculable'. Meanwhile the immediate crisis at the front could hardly be ignored with posters demanding:
'Defend Our Capital', 'We've Fought, We're Fighting, and We'll Fight
on'[117] and 'We Will Defend Mother Moscow'.[118]

While Soviet propaganda fired the struggle to new heights, it
certainly was not always based on truth. Solomon Lozovsky, the Soviet
deputy minister of foreign affairs, stated on 6 October that Germany had
sustained three and a half million dead in the war so far.[119] The next day,
as the Germans closed their encirclement at Viaz'ma, Lozovsky rather
awkwardly insisted: 'The farther east the Germans push, the nearer they
will get to the grave of Nazi Germany.'[120] It hardly seemed the most logical
comment, but, on the other hand, the overextension of Army Group
Centre had worked to the Soviet Union's advantage in the summer and,
with Bock now attempting to advance on a front aiming at Torzhok in the
north, Moscow in the centre and Kursk in the south – some 600 kilometres
in width – the success of Operation Typhoon was anything but assured.

While Bock spread his resources thin, Zhukov concentrated on
defending the Mozhaisk Defensive Line located about 110 kilometres
west of Moscow and anchored on the four main approaches to the
city at Volokolamsk, Mozhaisk, Maloiaroslavets and Kaluga. On
10 October Zhukov took charge of what was left of the Western
Front, reinforced by officer cadets, people's militia, NKVD and police
units from Moscow. Yet Zhukov still only commanded a force of
about, 90,000 men on 13 October, and thus the Stavka merged the
Moscow Reserve Front into the Western Front, providing the nucleus of
the new Fifth, Sixteenth, Forty-Third and Forty-Ninth Armies.[121] Yet in
mid October these were armies only in name and as Zhukov explained:

> These forces were far from adequate for a continuous line of
> defense, so we decided to cover the main routes first of all –
> Volokolamsk, Istrin, Mozhaisk, Maloiaroslavets, Podol'sk-Kaluga.
> The basic artillery and antitank resources were also being
> concentrated along these approaches … Extensive field-engineering
> work was under way to the rear of the first echelon troops in order
> to develop the defense in depth. Antitank obstacles were placed
> along all axes of advance threatened by tanks. Reserves were being
> pulled up to the main approaches.[122]

As early as 5 October Stalin had ordered that reserves from the North-
Western Front and South-Western Front be transferred to Moscow;

these were in addition to reinforcements en route from the Soviet Far East.[123] While Zhukov concentrated on defending the immediate approaches to Moscow on 12 October, he sent his newly appointed deputy Konev, the former head of the Western Front, to deal with the German breakthrough towards Kalinin. Konev took with him three rifle divisions and a tank brigade, while he was reinforced by another tank brigade and four more divisions arriving from the North-Western Front.[124] On 17 October Konev's forces were reorganised and regrouped to incorporate the newly allocated Twenty-Second, Twenty-Ninth and Thirtieth Armies. On the same day (17 October) his command was redesignated the Kalinin Front.[125]

In Moscow Stalin was hopeful that Zhukov would hold the Germans in front of Moscow as he had at Leningrad, but memories of the disaster at Kiev forewarned the Soviet dictator against expecting too much even from his best generals. Accordingly, Stalin hoped for the best and planned for the worst. A special committee was formed to 'prepare to take the industrial enterprises of Moscow and the Moscow area out of commission'. On 9 October they identified 1,119 enterprises for total destruction (with explosives) or damage (by fire). On 12 October it was determined that a new defensive line on the immediate approaches to the city should be built within twenty days. To achieve this no fewer than a quarter of a million people, mostly women, were forcibly mobilised from the city and sent out to dig anti-tank ditches and construct bunkers (see Illustration 11).[126] It was hard physical work and at times also dangerous, as Olga Sapozh-nikova recalled: 'We were taken some kilometers out of Moscow. There was a very large crowd of us, and we were told to dig trenches … On the very first day we were machine-gunned by a Fritz who swooped right down on us. Eleven of the girls were killed, and four wounded.'[127] On 14 October Stalin ordered the evacuation of four of Moscow's most prestigious theatres (the Lenin State Theatre, the Maxim Gorky Moscow Artistic Academic Theatre, the Little Academic Theatre and the Vakhtangov Theatre), and these were soon followed by Moscow University and all foreign embassies.[128] The Soviet capital was becoming less and less a functioning city and more a defensive bulwark in the long Soviet front. What is more, the true extent of the Soviet front's collapse was only now being acknowledged. As the British ambassador to the Soviet Union, Stafford Cripps, observed after a military briefing on 11 October: 'It was a

11 As the Germans approached Moscow, Soviet civilians, predominantly women, were sent out to dig anti-tank ditches.

depressing picture ... the position of Moscow is extremely dangerous at the moment.'[129] Even more alarmingly, the United States military attaché in Moscow reported on 10 October that it seemed 'the end of Russian resistance is not far away'.[130]

5 BOCK'S FINAL TRIUMPH

'We shall all die out here' – the battle of Viaz'ma

On 3 November 1812 Viaz'ma gave its name to another battle against another would-be conqueror of Russia, Napoleon Bonaparte. On that occasion it was the Russian forces that were attempting to cut off a part of the French army as it retreated towards Smolensk. The attempt was unsuccessful, but the Russians liberated Viaz'ma in the process and, for the first time in the war, the battle resulted in much heavier losses for the French.[1] Viaz'ma was therefore a historic signpost, known to Russians as one of the hallowed battlegrounds on which the country's freedom from foreign rule was won. The disaster unfolding at Viaz'ma 129 years later could not have offered a starker contrast and has been accepted as nothing short of a calamity for the Soviet Union. Yet that view was later contested by Zhukov in his post-war memoir. While the collapse of the Soviet front and subsequent encirclement represented an undeniable failure of the Soviet command, the refusal of the trapped armies to capitulate, even in the face of overwhelming odds, played an important role in stemming Hitler's drive on Moscow. As Zhukov explained:

> Thanks to the persistence and staunchness of our troops who fought in the encirclement near Viaz'ma, we had gained time invaluable for strengthening the Mozhaisk defence line. And so it was not in vain that the surrounded troops laid down their lives and shed their blood. Their heroic deeds, their enormous contribution to the defence of Moscow, still remains to be put into writing.[2]

Indeed the fanatical Soviet resistance within the Viaz'ma pocket did more than just buy Zhukov time. Although any comparative German/ Soviet loss ratio reflects a hopeless imbalance in favour of Bock's forces, the fact remains that German losses were heaviest among Hoepner's panzer divisions, cutting their operational strength for the later offensive towards Moscow. As one German nurse serving behind Army Group Centre in October 1941 noted:

> There were so many casualties there that we had to put the wounded in improvised beds in the aisles. In the battle of Viaz'ma our panzers had achieved the incredible … but at what price? I toiled in those days like a machine, as did everyone, the work was endless. Nevertheless, so many wounded died that we could have saved if only they had been brought to us sooner! They had to wait for help for far too long in the mud, the wounds festered or gangrene had spread through the body so that the surgeon could only amputate. It was terrible, so terrible that I have no words to describe these scenes.[3]

By 12 October Bock was euphoric at the news coming back from Viaz'ma and remarked in his diary that 'the enemy's losses are enormous'.[4] Yet the German command was not asking itself at what price such victories were being won, and it was only at the encirclement front that German officers saw how their units were battered, bloodied and even at times wiped out during the defensive battles. After heavy fighting in the area of Esebeck's 11th Panzer Division on 11 October, the battle continued on 12 October with a renewed attack by fresh waves of Soviet troops. To the German defenders, who had already counted thousands of enemy dead before their lines, the renewed Soviet attacks, taking place over fields already strewn with bodies, were psychologically as well as physically exhausting. If ammunition ran out, the machine gun jammed or enemy fire pinned them down, the massed assault waves could not be halted. Yet Soviet attacks sometimes simply overwhelmed the German defensive fire, despite all barrels blazing. It was horrendously expensive, but periodically successful. During the early hours of 12 October Esebeck's front was broken and the Soviet attack proceeded right up to the divisional command post before the arrival of the panzer regiment drove back the attackers 'with enormous losses'.[5] Father Ernst Tewes, a Catholic priest with the 11th Panzer Division, noted that another counterattack by the infantry to clear the German positions 'had resulted in a horrendous bloodbath on the Russian side. Terrible. Again there were Russian women in uniform, beyond those even children. All dead.'[6] The division also captured some 2,000 Soviet POWs during the course of the night,[7] but another report noted 'individual groups escaped to the east'.[8]

Fehn's 5th Panzer Division was also heavily attacked on 12 and 13 October, repeating the disturbingly familiar scenes of carnage. After the battle it was estimated that in front of the positions of just two companies some 2,000 Soviet troops lay dead.[9] The idea of attempting to break through a well-defended position with massed human assaults had been increasingly discredited since the middle of the nineteenth century. By 1941 the contest between men and steel had long since been decided in favour of the latter, but repeated Soviet attempts to prevail with massed assaults testify to the gross inadequacy of Soviet officer training.[10] Yet Soviet tactics at Viaz'ma were also hamstrung by the absence of supporting arms, combined with the pressure to break out, as soon as possible, from the rapidly closing noose. Indeed for many Soviet commanders determined not to surrender there were few credible alternatives to charging the German lines with every man they could muster. Even for the battle-hardened German veterans of the eastern front, confronting such massed wave assaults proved a harrowing ordeal, and thinly defended sections of the front were indeed threatened with being overrun.

Esebeck's and Fehn's panzer divisions belonged to Vietinghoff's XXXXVI Panzer Corps which by 13 October had taken 34,150 POWs and captured or destroyed 139 guns, 38 anti-tank guns, 4 tanks and 800 trucks.[11] From these figures the corps determined that it must have been attacked by an entire Soviet army.[12] Operating further north was Veiel's 2nd Panzer Division, which also found itself under attack from overwhelming Soviet strength. An account by H. E. Braun, an anti-tank gunner, offers a vivid insight into what the men of Veiel's divisions endured. As night fell, Braun recalled that a hue of red illuminated the sky to the west as remote villages burned and distant battles rumbled. Occasionally a sharp detonation was audible, and as darkness descended Braun and his comrades could hear that movement and the sound of engines was picking up beyond their lines. 'The tension was unbearable', Braun recalled shortly before flares were fired into the night sky. These revealed at first hundreds and then thousands of Soviet troops, together with Cossack cavalry and columns of trucks advancing

on the thinly held German front. 'Blood froze', Braun recalled, but the
defensive fire started cutting swaths through the Soviet ranks. Throughout the night, the attacks ebbed and flowed. Braun recalled that 'several
times the attacking Russians were shot to pieces directly before the
positions'. The latter waves of Soviet soldiers built mounds from their
own dead to provide cover, while groups of others crawled up among
the dead and wounded to launch sudden rushes at the German lines.
Burning trucks illuminated parts of the battlefield until the first light of
dawn arrived and the attacks finally ceased. Braun believed the fighting
was over until the enemy, resembling 'the head of a hydra, with ever
new earth-brown forms', launched a new attack driven forward by 'a
sea of Red Army soldiers'. As Braun observed:

> Like a storm flood the [enemy] flow began to trickle over the
> embankments into the ditches. Then small breaches were torn aside
> until finally the unstoppable wave flooded into the hinterland.
> Brave [German] infantrymen and in places even antitank teams
> with guns were trampled into the ground by the mass of humanity
> driven by the certainty of death to seek an escape to the east.[13]

Some strong points in the German front held out as defensive 'islands'
firing in all directions. To the rear Braun explained: 'Now came the time
for the logistics men and the staffs ... Cooks fought, weapons in hand,
from their kitchens and rear-area drivers fought for their naked lives.'
Yet into the breach surged the Soviet forces. 'Russian lorries raced by at
full speed, completely full of soldiers.' In defensive battles the panzer
divisions employed their panzer regiment as a kind of fire brigade – a
mobile reserve rushed to plug holes in the line. Veiel now committed his
3rd Panzer Regiment into the mêlée, and the tanks arrived firing both
their main armament and machine guns. 'They fired without aiming
straight into the masses', Braun observed, 'hitting Red Army men who
had broken through and their own men.' With the commitment of
tanks, the attack was broken up and driven back.[14] On paper it was
another victorious battle, but it came at a heavy price to Veiel's division
and it was not their first or even their last engagement at Viaz'ma.

   While Hoepner's Panzer Group 4 undertook the lion's share
of the work on the eastern and southern side of the encirclement, by
12 October there was only one panzer division left from Reinhardt's
Panzer Group 3. Funck's 7th Panzer Division was holding a narrow

section on the northern flank of the pocket just west of Viaz'ma. Here too there were violent engagements requiring the commitment of the 25th Panzer Regiment. Reinhardt also commanded the V Army Corps, under General of Infantry Richard Ruoff, which covered Funck's right flank and extended to the north-west. Essentially Reinhardt's forces acted as the anvil while General of Artillery Walter Heitz's VIII Army Corps, belonging to Strauss's Ninth Army, acted as the hammer and drove the Soviets into Reinhardt's prepared positions. Strategically it was a textbook operation and Reinhardt looked forward to a rapid conclusion of the battle so he could concentrate his attention on the fighting at Kalinin. At the tactical level, however, crushing whole Soviet armies was anything but straightforward and the costs, while light by comparison, could still be shattering to the already weakened divisions involved. Erich Krause, a soldier in Weikersthal's 35th Infantry Division (one of three divisions in Ruoff's corps), kept a diary of his experiences at the battle of Viaz'ma.[15] As was the case with almost all German infantry divisions, Krause's unit marched to the battlefield, arriving at their positions on the encirclement front on 12 October. As Krause noted in his diary: 'We are still not getting any rest though we have spent seven weeks fighting and can hardly move our sore, bleeding feet. They demand too much of us soldiers.' Nevertheless, having taken up positions about 16 kilometres from Viaz'ma, Krause's unit dug in and waited. Shortly before midnight there was some isolated shooting, then, Krause noted, 'all hell was let loose'. Following an almost identical pattern to Braun's account, Krause wrote that the battle raged for most of the night before a lull at 5 a.m.; this was followed an hour later by an attack renewed 'with fresh vigour'. This time Soviet tanks led the way and Krause's battalion started to break and run:

> All the swearing of the officers and NCOs availed nothing.
> Everybody ran away from the Russian tanks. At times we
> succeeded in rallying the men and making a stand, but all the same
> there was a whole stream of them now taking to their heels. Our
> killed and wounded, and our guns and other materiel we
> abandoned on the field. A shocking picture that I should never
> forget as long as I live … I thank the Lord for delivering me out of
> the jaws of death.

As Krause concluded: 'The Russians strained every effort to break through, which they succeeded in doing in the end.'[16] Not surprisingly,

Funck's mobile reserve (the 25th Panzer Regiment) was kept busy trying to restore breaches in the line.

A letter from Karl Fuchs, a tank commander in Funck's division, reflected a far greater confidence in the fighting at Viaz'ma, suggesting that the immense strain of defending static positions was not always shared within the panzer regiment.[17] Fuchs wrote to his father on 12 October:

> You must have heard the special announcements about Viaz'ma. Yes, you can find me here. I almost think that this battle is the last flickering moment of a once powerful Russia. For days now the enemy has tried to break out of our iron encirclement, but their efforts have been in vain. Whenever there is a hot spot, we appear like ghosts and engage the enemy in battle. Yesterday must have been our company's proudest day in this campaign. The alarm sounded and our tanks moved out! Russian tanks reinforced with support troops wanted to break out of our ring … Once the fog lifted from the valley, we really let them have it with every barrel. Tanks, antiaircraft guns and trucks and the infantry fired on everything in sight. Once the main body of our company arrived, our comrades destroyed their remaining forces … You can see that we are prepared at all times to beat the enemy wherever he may appear![18]

Yet as the battle reached its final climax Funck's panzers could not be everywhere at once and the infantry continued to suffer heavily. The 7th Grenadier Regiment was attacked on the morning of 14 October and reported: 'Heavy Russian tanks have broken through the main combat line at 3rd Battalion … The tanks cannot be beaten by our weaponry … The men have no ammunition left and are being run down by Russian tanks.'[19] Indeed some 700 men from Funck's panzer division were lost in the defensive fighting at the Viaz'ma pocket. In one company of 140 men, 105 were killed or wounded.[20] The heavy fighting also caused losses within the 25th Panzer Regiment, and by 15 October the tone of Karl Fuchs's letters was striking a markedly different chord. The death of his good friend Roland caused Fuchs to ask: 'Why did he have to give his life now, with the end practically in sight?'[21]

By 13 October the Viaz'ma pocket was being broken up into a number of smaller pockets as the advancing infantry from the west began meeting Hoepner and Reinhardt's panzer troops.[22] This largely ended the major battles around the area of Viaz'ma, although it would remain highly dangerous country for individual German units for weeks to come. Even rear-area units were not safe, because there had been no way to effectively seal off and comb every square metre of the pocket, meaning that, while some Soviet units fought their way out, others, knowingly or not, simply slipped through the German cordon. On 11 October the central radio exchange for Hoepner's panzer group was heavily attacked in spite of being well to the rear in a supposedly secure location. In addition to significant material damage, four officers, twelve NCOs (non-commissioned officers) and forty-four men were killed or wounded.[23] In another attack a German unit of unknown size was annihilated when a Soviet force ambushed it as it marched into a gully.[24] The war diary of Vietinghoff's XXXXVI Panzer Corps noted on 13 October: 'The clearing of the section of the pocket south-west of Viaz'ma is taking more time than the corps had anticipated. Again and again appear enemy splinter groups, which, with energetic leadership, conduct dogged resistance. There are also difficulties with the terrain, which could not be made readily apparent from the maps.'[25] Walter Neuser wrote to his parents on 15 October about the extent of the security problems in his area: 'The forests are still full of Russians so that unintentionally remaining behind usually results in death. Daily reports about attacks.'[26]

As the fighting finally abated before the defensive lines of the panzer divisions, the scenes from the battlefield told the terrible story of Viaz'ma's human toll. Walter Schaefer-Kehnert, an officer in Esebeck's 11th Panzer Division, recalled seeing Russian girls walking around the battlefield: 'I will never forget them – in trousers and dressed like soldiers, and they got in a cart, with a horse, and had a barrel of water and then went around giving water to the dying Russian soldiers lying on that field ... They were lying there by the thousand like the battlefield of old history'.[27] Albert Neuhaus noted in a letter on 14 October that the brown uniforms of the Soviet soldiers covered the ground 'like dead rabbits'.[28] Fifteen-year-old Maria Denisova lived in a village in the area of the Viaz'ma pocket and lost both parents during the fighting. Her father was shot as a suspected partisan and her mother was killed when a hand grenade was thrown into the cellar in which she was taking refuge. When the fighting finally ended and Maria emerged into the open she recalled the scene:

> There were so many dead bodies all over the place. We walked on them as if it was a floor covered with bodies. They were next to each other and on top on each other. Some didn't have legs, heads or other parts. We had to walk on them since there was no other place to step. Everything was covered with them: the entire river and the riverbank. It's awful to remember! The river was red with blood as if there was only blood flowing there.[29]

Marching past one of the battlefields from the pocket Horst Lange wrote in his diary on 15 October: 'Hills of dead Russians, snowed over, sometimes with horrendous wounds.' Lange then told of seeing more dead Russians on the road and described how they were driven over by German vehicles until they were completely flat.[30] After surveying the battlefields of the pocket where Panzer Group 3 had fought, Karl Fuchs wrote home in a letter on 15 October: 'I will never forget my impression of this destruction.'[31] Richthofen, commanding the VIII Air Corps, gained perhaps the most striking impression of the sheer volume of the killing at Viaz'ma when he flew over the pocket. 'There are horrific scenes of destruction in the places where the Red Army soldiers have made unsuccessful attempts to break out. The Russians have suffered a total bloodbath. Piles of bodies, heaps of abandoned equipment and guns are strewn everywhere.'[32]

Yet the grotesque scenes of death and destruction were not just on the Soviet side, and many German troops lost comrades during the course of the fighting. While this evoked silent grief and mourning in most, it stirred hatred in others. Karl Fuchs, for example, remained bitter about the loss of his friend Roland and sought retribution: 'We tie down our helmets and think of revenge, revenge for our dead comrades.'[33] Indeed, as the German mopping-up operations began, the ruthlessness and bloodshed which had typified the fighting itself carried over into the clearing operations. The fact that the remaining Soviet units had not surrendered led many German commanders to condemn them immediately as partisans to be shot on sight. So-called clearing operations were often horribly murderous affairs. In a post-war interview Wolfgang Horn, a soldier who served in a panzer division at Viaz'ma, recalled discovering a group of unarmed Soviet soldiers cowering behind a destroyed vehicle. Horn approached them and ordered them in Russian to raise their hands, but the frightened men huddled together covering their heads with their hands and arms. Unmoved, Horn then explained: 'When they don't surrender we shoot them. It was natural for us to do so ... They are cowards – they didn't deserve any better anyhow.'[34]

On 14 October Bock pronounced that the battle of Viaz'ma was over.[35] Blumentritt, who oversaw the fighting from the headquarters of the Fourth Army, described it as a 'textbook battle' and suggested, 'we might well look back on our past achievements with pride, and forward with confidence'.[36] Yet as was so often the case among German general staff officers, Blumentritt's enthusiasm for Army Group Centre's achievement at Viaz'ma fell well short of an appropriate strategic contextualisation. Battles do not exist in a vacuum and cannot be judged simply on the index of losses for and against. As Clausewitz recognised, a battle is only one element of a larger process, a means to an end that must be weighted and considered within the context of the ultimate objective. Viaz'ma was an undisputed operational victory, surpassed in scale only by the battle of Kiev in September; however, strategic success depended on Viaz'ma bringing about the collapse of Soviet resistance or, at the very least, the fall of Moscow. These were the real objectives of Bock's army group in Operation Typhoon. Sweeping battlefield victories and large new tracts of captured enemy territory were the familiar signposts of German operations in 1941, but they had not been able to force an end to the war. Now, with economic pressures biting and winter looming, for which the *Ostheer* was utterly unprepared, Bock had to deliver the knock-out blow in the east. His failure to do so need not ameliorate the scale of the Soviet debacle at Viaz'ma, nor detract from Bock's handling of the battle. Viaz'ma was, as one historian called it, 'a perfect "Cannae"'.[37] However, Soviet losses in the battle, as alarming as these undoubtedly were, did not prevent Zhukov from rebuilding his front and conducting a fighting defence of Moscow. German losses, by contrast, while far lower, were hardly insignificant and must be considered in the full light of German strategic objectives as well as the consequences for failure in that regard. The battle of Viaz'ma was without question another sweeping operational success for Germany, yet the implications of that success were not equal to the hopes, and indeed desperate requirements, of the *Ostheer*.

Whatever Viaz'ma may have failed to achieve, the statistics of what Army Group Centre did accomplish speak for themselves. On 2 October some 1.25 million Soviet troops were deployed on the approaches to Moscow in three Soviet fronts. Not even two weeks later, on the day Bock pronounced the battle of Viaz'ma to be over (14 October), Army Group Centre had taken 508,919 Soviet POWs and captured or destroyed 876 tanks, 2,891 guns, 465 anti-tank guns, 355 anti-aircraft guns and 46 planes.[38] These totals stem mainly from the fighting around Viaz'ma, but also included Soviet losses from the smaller and still active pockets north-east and south of Briansk. Even though the fighting at Viaz'ma was officially declared to be over, large numbers of Soviet POWs were still being rounded up and registered. On 15 October, only a day after Bock's declared victory at Viaz'ma, Army Group Centre raised its total POW count by another 50,000 men to 558,825 Soviet captives. At the same time almost 200 more Soviet tanks were determined to have been destroyed or captured, along with 844 more guns and dozens more anti-tank and anti-aircraft guns.[39] As impressive as these figures were, at the same time, they had an unnerving effect on the German rank and file who found it difficult to comprehend the sheer scale of the Red Army. Hans von Luck, an officer in the 7th Panzer Division, wrote: 'After mopping up of the Viaz'ma pocket, we asked ourselves how Stalin kept producing new divisions … And whence came the thousands of tanks and guns?'[40] On the Soviet side, however, there was no mystery and certainly no sense that the armies lost at Viaz'ma were somehow expendable or easily replaced. Indeed, for many there was incredulity that yet another disaster, and on such a grand scale, could befall Soviet forces. Viktor Strazdovski noted: 'What happened there [at Viaz'ma] is like a mincing machine, when people are sent to a sure death, unarmed to fight a well-trained army.'[41]

There can be no question that Viaz'ma was an unmitigated disaster for the Red Army, yet the German ring was by no means hermetically sealed, and tens of thousands of Soviet troops managed to escape the encirclement and flee back to Soviet lines. Yakov Pinus wrote in a letter to a friend: 'When we got to Viaz'ma (I was with a small group from our regiment) we were surrounded again. It took me two weeks to work my way out. I covered nearly two hundred miles behind the German lines, and on 19 October I got out to Dorokhovo. As I learned later, few of our boys managed to get out.'[42] Abram Gordon's 5th (Frunze) Division was reduced to just 2,000 men when the order came to break out to the east. After their next battle they were reduced to just 300 men. In the course of the fighting a number of German captives had been taken who, unable to be effectively guarded, were promptly murdered. Gordon's group continued to flee east, but again ran into German forces near Yukhnov and, without ammunition, was captured. After surviving the German screening process, which attempted to identify Jews and commissars, Gordon, along with another officer, managed to escape from their makeshift prison in a slaughterhouse and finally reached Soviet lines on 16 December. Nor was this the end of his ordeal. Gordon and his co-escapee, Lieutenant Smirnov, were then sent to an NKVD special detachment in Moscow for interrogation. Gordon was released for continued service in the army, but Smirnov was sent to a camp where he subsequently died.[43]

Interrogation for Soviet soldiers returning from periods behind German lines was not only typical; in many cases it was the least that could be expected. Soviet counterespionage (in 1943 formed into an agency known as SMERSH – Death to Spies) interrogated, tortured, imprisoned and executed all those suspected of collusion with the Germans, and any soldier not having died at the front defending his position was cause for mistrust. Even Jewish soldiers who made their way back to Soviet lines were still viewed with suspicion. One recalled being asked: 'How could you, a Jew, save yourself from the hands of the Germans? What assignment did the [German] officer give you?' Another Jewish soldier who successfully fled the Viaz'ma pocket was subsequently sentenced to five years in the Gulag by the NKVD.[44] Perhaps it was a justified fear of both the German and Soviet systems that drove a small number of Soviet soldiers to live on secretly in the forests around Viaz'ma. Even as late as the spring of 1942 Maria Denisova told of spotting the occasional soldier. 'We were scared of them,' she recalled; 'they were so ugly with their long beards … I don't know how they survived or what they ate.'[45] The conditions for those who remained in the forests near Viaz'ma, either by choice as partisans or as an alternative to captivity, made survival during the first winter of the war very difficult.[46] For the Soviet soldiers encircled near Viaz'ma the best chance for survival was to run the gauntlet of German forces and then present a convincing case at their NKVD interrogation. Indeed some 85,000 men found their way back to Soviet lines from the Viaz'ma pocket, and many of these rejoined the Red Army soon afterwards.[47]

On the night of 12–13 October Lieutenant-General M. F. Lukin, who had been given command of the bulk of the Soviet forces inside the Viaz'ma pocket, forced a breakout with the remnants of two divisions. Lukin had astutely chosen a sector of swampy terrain in which German armour could not manoeuvre. The breakout was successful, with some of his men eventually making their way back to the Soviet defensive line near Mozhaisk and Kaluga, but Lukin himself was badly wounded in the attempt and captured by German forces.[48] The commanders of the Soviet Twentieth and Thirty-Second Armies, Major-General A. N. Ershakov and Major-General S. V. Vishnevsky, were also captured, while the commander of the Twenty-Fourth Army, Major-General K. I. Rakutin, was killed in the fighting.[49] The loss of so many army commanders in the battle of Viaz'ma testifies to the calamity befalling the Red Army in the first half of October. This is further underscored by that fact that more Soviet armies were being destroyed in the battle of Briansk and even further afield by Army Group South in what the Germans referred to as the battle on the Sea of Azov.[50]

While the area around Viaz'ma was soon being dotted with the mass graves of fallen Soviet soldiers, they were never far from the countless individual graves dug for German soldiers. Indeed Army Group Centre's losses in only the first half of October numbered no less than 48,000 men. These came on top of the 229,000 men lost up until 1 October, leading to a total of 277,000 men by 16 October 1941. At the same time Bock had received just 151,000 replacements, and the reserves of the Replacement Army had all but been exhausted, meaning that the shortages in the combat units could not be made good.[51] Clearly Operation Typhoon's success was coming at great cost to Army Group Centre. Alone in the fighting to recapture the strongly contested town of Yel'nya, Geyer's IX Army Corps sustained some 5,000 casualties between 2 and 8 October.[52] Meanwhile, with so many fugitive Soviet soldiers caught behind enemy lines, Hans Roth summed up the ever-present danger of operations to all elements of command. 'It is typical for this campaign that soldiers from all branches take on infantry duties as needed. There are no designated headquarters anymore. The higher ranks are no longer giving orders from secure locations. Now, everyone, officer or secretary, carries a weapon at all times, and uses it.'[53] From sudden sniper attacks and brief firefights to full-scale battles lasting hours, fighting for many units within Army Group Centre was a daily occurrence, demanding a constant state of alert and bringing ever more casualties. One German priest wrote in autumn 1941:

> Today I buried some more of my former parishioners, *Gebirgsjäger* [mountain troops], who have died in this frightful land. Three more letters to write to add to the total of all those which I have written

already in this war. The deleted names of the fallen are now more numerous in my pocket diary than the names of the living. My parish is bleeding to death on the plains of this country. We shall all die out here.[54]

Such feelings of impending doom were by no means extreme or exceptional. The troops at the front were repeatedly watching their comrades die or sustain awful wounds, leading many to wonder if and when their turn would come. Siegfried Knappe recalled: 'To the combat soldier, life became an endless series of hard physical work, raw courage, occasional laughter, and a terrible sense of living out a merciless fate that would inevitably culminate in his death or mangling.'[55] Similarly, Gottlob Bidermann wrote after the death of a comrade:

> The thoughts of those gathered nearby remained deeply personal, and one could not escape feeling an intense pity for our brother in the grey tunic who had been struck; yet with these thoughts each man turned to concentrate upon himself, about how he could be the next to fall, the next to meet his destiny in Russia. We became at times possessed by these thoughts, as helpless against them as against the death that had quickly enveloped our brother soldier. Thus began the realization that we were being consumed by this foreign land.[56]

Another German soldier wrote home in despair:

> What will become of me? ... I am tormented by the thought that I'll get killed. Many are the German graves I've seen and many Germans lie still unburied. How terrible it all is! ... We are suffering great losses. I fixed up my trench and lined it up with straw. I would very much like to ask the others if they ever saw someone who had dug his own grave. I can't bear these gruesome thoughts anymore, so help me God![57]

Not surprisingly the German public was being torn between the official reports claiming the absolute dominance of the German army and the private letters from relatives and friends, which often fuelled a far darker picture and circulated in German society as rumours and gossip. On 16 October Goebbels released a new *Sondermeldung* reporting that Bock's army group had taken 560,000 Soviet POWs and that 4,133 guns had been captured or destroyed.[58] Yet after being bombarded for the previous month with repeated *Sondermeldungen* claiming persistent German victories, the question of how high German losses really were was a matter of some speculation and concern. As one letter sent to the eastern front complained: 'They didn't say a word about this either over the radio or in the newspapers. That's why we don't believe anything anymore. The losses are always on the other side.'[59] Another letter sent to a German soldier in the east complained about the same problem: 'You wrote us a lot that we did not know before … How are we actually to know what is really going on? You don't find such things in the newspapers or in the newsreels. Everything goes smoothly there. Unfortunately the unvarnished truth looks somewhat different.'[60]

Ingeborg Ochsenknecht, a nurse working behind the eastern front, told her father after hearing about the *Ostheer*'s victories on the radio: 'I only know one thing, that the people in the radio are not telling the truth. We hear a completely different story about the progress of the war from the wounded.' Her father then replied: 'True enough. They lie to us; they think we are stupid.'[61] Yet the young Wehrmacht recruits now reaching the eastern front from their training barracks expressed relief that they had not missed the fighting and displayed all the confidence of Goebbels's propaganda. As Hans von Luck noted: 'The young ones had first to get used to the hard conditions. At home, all they had heard about was the "tremendous forward drive" and that "Russia would be defeated in the near future."'[62] Another group of raw recruits on their way to the front received their first instruction on the rigours of warfare in the east from the returning soldiers they met. 'We watched transports of wounded soldiers coming back; one pulled up next to us and we talked to some of the comrades. What they told us about the icy battle conditions and the hammering they had received from the Red Army toned down much of our arrogance.'[63]

In Nazi Germany feelings of superiority over the Soviet Union usually proceeded in tandem with one's proximity to the eastern front. It is not surprising therefore that Hitler, along with his senior generals in the OKW and OKH, consistently demanded much more than the *Ostheer* could deliver. At the same time, in distant North Africa, General of Panzer Troops Erwin Rommel noted on 12 October in a letter to his wife: 'Wonderful news from Russia. After the conclusion of the great battles, we can expect the advance east to go fast and thus remove all possibility of the enemy creating any significant new forces.'[64] Yet by mid October nothing in the midst of Russia's *rasputitsa* was moving quickly and, if distance alone can explain Rommel's overblown assessment, Bock's own optimism is harder to understand. The commander of Army Group Centre failed to heed any warnings and drove his armies relentlessly on, determined to seize the victory he felt sure he had won. At the highest levels any misgivings were dismissed and doubters were shunned. The battle of Viaz'ma had cleared the approaches to Moscow and, with Kluge and Hoepner now free to vigorously reinforce the drive east, the meagre remnants of Zhukov's ramshackle Western Front, backed only by communist youth brigades and hastily raised workers' battalions, would soon be crushed.

On the Soviet side the situation was indeed grim, but the battle of Viaz'ma soon took on a very different meaning. In much the same way that the rout of the British and Allied forces at Dunkirk in May–June 1940 rapidly transformed itself (thanks in part to Churchill's rhetoric) into a heroic escape, the Soviets likewise interpreted a victory out of a defeat. At Dunkirk the British lost a battle in order to save an army, while at Viaz'ma the Soviets lost multiple armies to save their capital. Here the end justified the means and, however much mismanagement and incompetence the Soviet commanders demonstrated on the battlefield, the Wehrmacht ultimately failed to take Moscow in 1941, just as their victory at Dunkirk had routed, but not destroyed, the British army in 1940. As Zhukov later explained, it was in the bitter days *after* the encirclement of Viaz'ma that precious time was won to prepare the defences of Moscow:

> In mid October it was essential to gain time to prepare our defences. If we assess the actions of the 16th, 19th, 20th, 24th and 32nd Armies and the Boldin Group encircled west of Viaz'ma in light of this, their heroic fighting deserves special tribute. Thanks to the steadfastness of our troops in the Vyazma area, the foe's main forces were held up for some extremely critical days. We won precious time to organize our defense along the Mozhaisk line.[65]

Viaz'ma, the great German offensive victory, or Viaz'ma, the first bulwark of Moscow's defensive success, may all be a matter of perspective, but at the end of the day Operation Typhoon was not just about the battle of Viaz'ma. The German high command was aiming for much more wide-ranging objectives, which, in mid October, were still a long way from being achieved. In this sense it must be again kept in mind that battles are not ends in themselves; they take their meaning from the strategic and political circumstances they elicit. Contrary to some past depictions of Operation Typhoon, in mid October 1941 the Wehrmacht was not at the precipice of victory, Moscow was not about to fall and the Soviet Union's ability to go on waging war extended far beyond the weakened forces positioned around Moscow. The battle of Viaz'ma was over, but Hitler's drive on Moscow had only cleared its first hurdle.

'I have lived through hell' – the battle of Briansk

While the encirclement at Viaz'ma was without doubt Army Group Centre's pre-eminent battle on the road to Moscow, further south the parallel battle of Briansk was in some respects an even tougher nut to crack. While the pocket at Viaz'ma was a comparatively tight encirclement, Briansk was soon split into two pockets extending over a vast area and pressurised by a much lower density of German troops. Bock's intelligence on the size of the two pockets north and south of Briansk was also rudimentary. On 11 October Army Group Centre's war diary reported that the pocket north of Briansk was 'as good as ended'.[66] Yet the following day (12 October) Nehring's 18th Panzer Division still reported defensive battles to fend off Soviet breakthrough attempts. The situation had worsened by 13 October with the 18th Panzer Division's war diary reporting:

> The situation during the night is always especially critical when the enemy, with numerical superiority, storms a position. Our own security measures are simply overrun and then, in small groups, [the enemy] breaks out to the east. A change of this fact is, as a result of the weak forces available, simply not possible. Accordingly, besides the very high bloody losses of the enemy our own heavy losses are not to be avoided.[67]

Fighting to extinguish the pocket south of Briansk, Lemelsen's XXXXVII Panzer Corps was experiencing similar difficulties. Not only were there insufficient forces at hand, but the terrain was so thickly wooded that the heavier weapons of the panzer corps could not be deployed where needed, and aerial intelligence produced meagre results. Poor infrastructure and bad weather further hampered German attempts to concentrate their forces against what was described as a 'superior' enemy.[68] Acknowledging the difficulties near Briansk, Bock wrote in his diary: 'As a result of the fighting [around Briansk] and the awful road conditions, Guderian has not been able to continue to the northeast – a success for the Russians, whose stubbornness paid off.'[69] It was this kind of the success that Soviet commanders later chose to remember amid the chaos and staggering losses of early October.

While on 14 October Bock was declaring the battle of Viaz'ma over,[70] the fighting around Briansk was still approaching its zenith. On 13 October Eremenko, the commander of the encircled Briansk Front, was directing operations in the Borshchevo area when he was seriously wounded by a German aerial attack. Flown out of the pocket in a small Po-2 aircraft, Eremenko was later visited in hospital by Stalin and questioned about the situation at the front. 'I replied briefly that the troops had been assaulting the enemy ring for eight days and had finally broken through.'[71] Indeed German records reported that 'combat-worthy elements of the enemy managed to break through' Fremerey's 29th Motorised Infantry Division on 13 October. Yet with all of Lemelsen's panzer corps fully committed to the long encirclement front, reserves to deal with the breakthrough had to be sought elsewhere. Schweppenberg's XXIV Panzer Corps had been making slow progress north of Orel in the direction of Tula, but now received orders to dispatch a force to intercept the enemy.[72] German reports as to the size of the Soviet force varied from two whole divisions to a force of just 600 to 1,000 men.[73] Whatever the case, the German command was sufficiently concerned to redirect forces from Schweppenberg's lagging attack to deal with the problem. As Guderian observed in regard to the stubborn Soviet resistance in the second week of October: 'The prospect of rapid, decisive victories was fading in consequence.'[74]

In the northern pocket Nehring's 18th Panzer Division was again in the thick of the fighting. On the night of 13–14 October Soviet forces broke through its lines and managed to maintain a 2-kilometre breach in the German line until German tanks arrived just before noon to close it. At the same time Hörnlein's nearby Infantry Regiment 'Grossdeutschland' was subjected to fierce breakthrough attempts by a greatly superior enemy force (belonging to the former Soviet Fiftieth Army). German reports speak of Soviet bayonet charges, which, in the wooded terrain, succeeded in reaching German lines, instigating bitter hand-to-hand fighting. On this day alone Hörnlein's regiment lost five company commanders including some of their revered Knight's Cross recipients, but his men also took between 3,000 and 4,000 Soviet POWs (including elements of the Fiftieth Army's command staff).[75] The following day Nehring's 18th Panzer Division reported 'daily thousands of prisoners brought in', while in one place 159 Soviet guns were captured.[76] To the south between 9 and 14 October Lemelsen's XXXXVII Panzer Corps had taken some 23,000 Soviet POWs[77] and by 19 October that figure had risen to 61,544.[78]

The battle of Briansk had all the hallmarks of another German victory, but again the cost was proving high, while time was ticking away from the long-overdue drive on Moscow. As Bock noted in his diary on 15 October:

> The fighting at the Briansk pockets is quite unpredictable; today, for example, a German regiment of [Lieutenant-General Conrad von Cochenhausen's] 134th [Infantry] Division was surrounded on all sides in the southernmost pocket ... Guderian informed me that because of the stubborn enemy resistance the advance by his army to the northwest will not be possible until the Briansk pocket is eliminated and his forces have regrouped. This will take some days.[79]

Meanwhile on the encirclement fronts the men of Weichs's Second Army and Guderian's Second Panzer Army were enduring some of the bitterest fighting they had experienced in the whole eastern campaign. Ernst Guicking of the 52nd Infantry Division wrote home to his wife on 16 October: 'Ten days' fighting as we have not yet experienced it. And ten days of deprivation. But always forward.'[80] In another letter home written on 16 October Will Thomas, who himself would soon die in Russia, wrote: 'Where should I start to explain? Actually I can say nothing. My heart is still so full of all the horrors and difficulties of the last days and hours.' Yet later in the letter Thomas alluded to some of the strains of the fighting he had endured. 'Again and again comrades fall left and right, so that I often believed I was left alone in the field.'[81] Similarly Harald Henry wrote home on 17 October about the psychological torments he had endured during the fighting near Briansk:

> To no avail, if one believed every time one had survived the worst. There always comes more. Since I last wrote you I have lived through hell ... That I survived 15 October, the most terrible day of

my life, seems a wonder. How sick my whole body is, but I will certainly not be allowed into the hospital … I am too miserable to write more. Later I will tell of these days, what can be said. I wish everything would end. What have we been through! Oh God![82]

For the German soldiers who endured the battle of Briansk, once the immediate terror of the fighting had passed they were then confronted by the ghastly sights of fresh battlefields littered with dead. Ernst Guicking wrote to his wife on 15 October: 'Combing the forests. Past a destroyed Russian baggage train. Terrible sight. Shredded horses and men. Dead gun molls. A destroyed battery. 300 dead Russians. Unimaginable. This was the revenge of the Regiment "Grossdeutschland" for their two fallen Knight's Cross holders.'[83] On the same day (15 October) Major Shabalin, a Soviet officer trapped in another part of the Briansk pocket, despaired at his predicament and the state of his command. Writing by the light of a bonfire Shabalin wrote: 'The Germans are everywhere – incessant gunfire, mortar and machine-gun exchanges. I wandered around, seeing heaps of dead bodies and the most unspeakable horrors – ghastly evidence of the enemy's bombardment. Hungry and unable to sleep, I took a bottle of alcohol and went into the forest. I fear our total destruction is imminent … Our military strength has simply dissolved around us.'[84] Natalia Peshkova, a Soviet doctor trapped in the Briansk pocket, reported that her group moved east navigating by the sun and completely oblivious to the location of German or Soviet forces.[85] On 17 October the northernmost pocket in the battle of Briansk was finally eliminated after one last desperate battle.[86] Guicking recorded in a letter how the Russians had been corralled into a narrow space and had then tried to break through the German lines. The aftermath revolted him, but at the same time numbed his sensitivity to such mass killing. 'We stumble around between fallen Russians. It is true horror … endless dead. Many women among them. No battlefield could look worse. Over the past ten days we have got used to it. We have got used to this horror … Great is our success, but also bitter and painful are our losses. Such dear and brave comrades lie here in the Russian soil.'[87]

Indeed Guderian's Second Panzer Army had lost more than 2,000 men in only the first ten days of October and another 2,300 by 20 October, bringing his total casualties since 22 June 1941 to 45,643 men.[88] As Guderian observed in his memoir: 'if the figures for the total

casualties since the start of the campaign were examined it was a grave
and tragic total. The troops had received a number of replacements, but
although these were keen and eager men they as yet lacked the combat
experience and toughness of the older men.'[89] Yet the fighting at
Briansk did not simply constitute routine losses for the forces involved.
The war diary of the 18th Panzer Division noted casualties during the
battle were 'comparatively high',[90] while Army Group Centre's war
diary labelled it an 'embittered, costly battle for both sides'.[91] It was
only on 18 October that Bock could declare the pocket south of Briansk
'finished' and at last order Guderian to concentrate all his efforts on
resuming his advance to Tula.[92]

    If one accepts the Soviet viewpoint that the Red Army's stub-
born resistance in the double encirclements at Viaz'ma and Briansk
contributed decisively to the successful defence of Moscow,[93] then
Briansk, despite involving far fewer men, may well have been the more
significant triumph for Zhukov. Over a considerably larger area than the
battle of Viaz'ma the remnants of the Briansk Front delayed Guderian
and Weichs from 6 to 18 October, buying the Red Army precious time to
build and man the new defensive lines. Yet however much the Soviet
strategic position may have benefited from the prolonged fighting at
Viaz'ma and Briansk, nothing should disguise the fact that the double
encirclements were, in the first analysis, a calamity for the Soviet state.
No less than seven Soviet armies were destroyed, with others badly
mauled by the fighting. Of the ninety-five Soviet divisions which made
up the Western, Reserve and Briansk Fronts on 2 October, sixty-four
were subsequently destroyed in the fighting. Additionally, eleven of
fifteen tank brigades and fifty of sixty-two attached artillery regiments
were lost. At the start of Operation Typhoon the three Soviet fronts
together commanded some 1.25 million men; an estimated 85,000 Red
Army troops successfully fought their way out of the pocket at Viaz'ma
and another 23,000 made it back to Soviet lines from the Briansk
encirclements. The retreating Soviet Twenty-Second, Twenty-Ninth
and Thirty-Third Armies, as well as Group Ermakov, together accounted
for a further 98,000 men. All told, the total number of escapees probably
amounted to about 250,000 men, leaving some one million who were
either killed or captured.[94] Bock stated on 19 October that the twin
battles at Viaz'ma and Briansk constituted 'the greatest feat of arms of
the campaign!'[95] A German *Sondermeldung* announcing the results
of the two battles was issued on 18 October,[96] while the total number

of Soviet prisoners captured at Viaz'ma and Briansk was determined to be 673,098 POWs,[97] leaving a rough figure of some 325,000 men who might be said to have been killed or wounded during the course of the fighting. By any standard of losses in warfare for the period in question this was an extraordinary total, which again underlines the unique place the Nazi–Soviet war holds in military history. Yet, for all the death and suffering on the battlefields leading to Moscow, an even greater human tragedy was about to play out in the German rear areas as hundreds of thousands of Soviet soldiers found themselves at the mercy of the Wehrmacht and Germany's rear-area security organs (see Illustration 12).

A conversation recorded by British intelligence at Trent Park in August 1944 between Lieutenant-General Georg Neuffer and Colonel Hans Reimann, both veteran commanders from the eastern front in 1941, gave a candid insight into the treatment of Soviet POWs after capture.[98] Neuffer began:

> That transporting of the Russians to the rear from Viaz'ma was a ghastly business!
>
> [Reimann:] It was gruesome. I was present when they were being transported from Korosten to just outside Lovo. They were driven like cattle from the trucks to the drinking troughs and bludgeoned to keep their ranks. There were troughs at the stations; they rushed to them and drank like beasts; after that they were given just a bit of something to eat. Then they were again driven onto the wagons, there were sixty or seventy men in one cattle truck! Each time the train halted ten of them were taken out dead; they had suffocated for lack of oxygen …
>
> [Neuffer:] … Just to see that column of [POWs] after the twin battle of Viaz'ma–Briansk, when the [POWs] were taken to the rear on foot, far beyond Smolensk. I often travelled along that route – the ditches by the side of the roads were full of shot Russians. Cars had driven into them; it was really ghastly![99]

Similarly Josef Deck, an artilleryman with the 17th Panzer Division, noted the misery of the Soviet POWs taken near Briansk. 'We passed endless columns of prisoners, starving, exhausted, dying men – some falling before the wheels of our cars into the snow, others, dull and apathetic, in rotting clothes, collapsing as they marched.'[100] During an inspection tour of the front on 20 October, Bock noted having witnessed tens of thousands of Soviet POWs on the road. 'Dead-tired

12 Soviet prisoners of war taken in the aftermath of the October battles.

and half-starved, these unfortunate people stagger along. Many have fallen dead or collapsed from exhaustion on the road.'[101] An Italian medical officer observed one Soviet prisoner transport and noted how it was 'managed' by the German guards:

> There they were: an endless, brownish column of defeated, defenceless and humiliated soldiers, pushed along and beaten by a handful of Germans … They tried to press against one another for warmth against the cold. Red marks on their bodies testified to the blows inflicted on them by their guards … Some [of the Soviet POWs were] very young. Some middle-aged – all of them ran to

avoid the sticks of the German guards which fell without
discrimination. At times there were gaps in the ranks, but these
were soon filled by prisoners pushing from behind. The procession
passed for a good ten minutes and still there was no sign of the end.
There must have been thousands of men ...

A few faces expressed hate, most expressed nothing but fear –
vile, degrading fear. Many of the prisoners were limping. Some
advanced by hopping awkwardly, like big birds. Many were
keeping up with the group only because they were helped along by
their comrades. The worst beating was taken by those who
threatened to delay the march of the column ...

At last we saw the rear of the column. Here the wounded, the
sick, the weak and the exhausted were struggling on, supported and
sometimes carried by their comrades, kicked and beaten by the
guards, dragging their feet on the asphalt road, staggering under the
blows, their eyes wild with the fear of death.[102]

Not surprisingly the roads which carried the prisoner transports were
littered with bodies. Those unable to keep up with the column were
simply shot and left unburied.[103] Soviet women observing the passing
columns wept openly; many searched for the faces of loved ones, but
any attempt to help the men by throwing bread to the column provoked
angry responses from the German guards.[104]

Once at the POW camps, the combination of disease, cold
and hunger depleted the ranks at an astonishing rate. Countless
thousands of Soviet POWs were dying each week by the end of
October and the mortality rate would remain high throughout the
winter until a total of almost two million former Red Army soldiers
were dead by February 1942.[105] Konrad Jarausch, who worked in
one of the POW camps, wrote home on 15 October that his camp
held 7,000 POWs and was already grossly overburdened without the
capacity to feed the prisoners or treat the many wounded. As he was
concluding his letter, a further 2,000 POWs were arriving escorted
by only four German guards. 'Things are absolutely chaotic',[106]
Jarausch concluded. In another letter a week later (on 23 October)
Jarausch noted that the camp population had swelled to 11,000
POWs and two days after that (25 October) to 20,000. One of the
Soviet inmates summed up the experience in straightforward terms;
'This is hell', he told Jarausch.[107] Such horrendous conditions were
by no means the exception, driving many men to the most desperate

acts including cannibalism. One account from October 1941 by Léon Degrelle, a Belgian volunteer in the Waffen-SS, noted:

> During a station stopover one night, we were awakened by terrible cries. We hurried to open the doors of a car full of prisoners: Asiatics, as hungry as piranhas, fought each other while snatching pieces of meat. That prized meat was human flesh! The prisoners were fighting over the remains of a dead Mongol, who has been cut apart with pieces of tin from cans of food. Certain prisoners had felt cheated by being left out of the distribution, which resulted in the brawl. Gnawed bones had been tossed outside through the bars. They were scattered, bloody, alongside the railway car on the muddy ground.[108]

While the future well-being of the more than 650,000 Soviet POWs was clearly hanging in the balance, their fate was not what concerned Bock and his fellow officers at Army Group Centre. In the immediate aftermath of the battle of Viaz'ma, the army group's commanders were in a confident mood and keen to exploit their victories and seize control of the Soviet capital, the capture of which they believed was all but assured. On 13 October Bock received approval from Heusinger at the OKH (Halder was recovering after falling from a horse and dislocating his right arm)[109] to trust the investment of Moscow almost solely to Kluge's Fourth Army.[110] There was little sense that this would pose serious problems after the Soviet front had been so utterly shattered. As the chief of staff of the Fourth Army, Blumentritt, later wrote: 'All that lay between us and the capital was the so-called Moscow Defensive Position. We had no reason to believe that this would prove a particularly difficult nut to crack.'[111] Nor was this just the view of the army. Richthofen, the celebrated Luftwaffe commander of the VIII Air Corps, wrote in his diary on 11 October: 'The Russians can be finished off militarily, if everybody makes an all out effort.'[112] The Reich's press chief, Otto Dietrich, was again keen to emphasise the importance of German victories before Moscow,[113] but Goebbels, who received detailed daily military briefings, was far more alert to the ominous state of affairs on Bock's front. Writing in his diary on 13 October Goebbels noted: 'The roads have become bottomless as a result of the bad weather. It is almost completely impossible for the motorised troops to advance. Only the advance of the marching troops is possible. This is to say that our offensive operations are not proceeding with the annihilating thrusts that we had actually promised after the first victories.'[114]

Whatever Goebbels may have privately believed about the progress of the campaign his victory propaganda was still sounding a triumphant tune, and many in Germany as well as in the east were convinced the end must finally be at hand. Heinrich Witt wrote in a letter on 14 October: 'Everywhere one hears the same astonishment, that the fighting should be over by 18 October. That could be true when one thinks just how incredibly much is deployed here.'[115] On the following day (15 October) Heinz Heppermann stated: 'And the reports signify yes, the annihilation [of the Soviet Union] is imminent!'[116] Ludwig Bumke wrote on 18 October that he and his comrades still believed Hitler's speech from 3 October[117] in which he stated that the Soviets would be finished before the onset of winter. Ironically Bumke believed he even had proof of this fact because 'the request of the battalion for winter clothes has been rejected'.[118]

Yet Goebbels's fears for the future of the campaign proved well founded and, despite the battlefield victories, the buoyed hopes and bombastic claims of German propaganda were soon to be re-examined. For many within the *Ostheer*, the middle of October began a new and rapid expansion of the emerging credibility gap between official reports and the day-to-day reality of the war. The unmistakable claims of Dietrich and the Nazi news outlets, heralding an end to the war in the east, now had to be proven, and the scepticism of those soldiers who questioned official reports grew accordingly. Writing to his family on 17 October Adolf B noted:

> The last *Sondermeldungen* sounded exceedingly joyous: Odessa taken, Petersburg and Moscow invested, everywhere the Red Army struck by annihilating blows and similar additional victory news! One may think the war in the east could soon be over … At the moment it is minus seven degrees and outside the snow is twenty centimetres deep. Vehicles can hardly drive anymore; the country roads are muddy to such an extent that one gets stuck everywhere.[119]

Clearly the infamous Russian *rasputitsa* was taking hold and bogging down movement, just as it had in past wars. That this constituted a major problem to mobile operation was nothing new, but neither Hitler, the OKH nor the generals at Army Group Centre took any serious account of the seasonal difficulties involved. Operations were simply to plough right through the autumn mud. The German generals themselves were in fact at least as much a factor in Typhoon's failure as the much famed 'General Mud' and later 'General Winter', which after the war German veterans liked to credit with saving the Soviet Union in 1941.[120] As one former officer in the OKH noted after the war: 'That it is cold in Russia at this time belongs to the ABC of an eastern campaign.'[121] As early as 7 October Hans Roth noted in his diary:

> The weather is changing: an icy northern wind whips over the vast plains. Slowly but surely the cold is seeping through the thin cloth of our shabby coats. Our hands are numb and stiff. Olchana lies in shambles, there is not a single room to be found far and wide that could offer us some warmth. And slowly, a premonition comes over me: it is gradually becoming clear even to the most incorrigible optimist that the hardest part is still before us; the second merciless enemy is advancing – the Russian winter.[122]

By Roth's estimation the steadfast confidence of the army command seemingly surpassed even the most incorrigible optimist, but Roth was certainly not alone in fearing the worst with the onset of winter conditions. On the same day that the first snow was recorded (7 October) Wilhelm Prüller confided in his diary: 'Tonight we had the first real Russian snowstorm. The snow didn't stay on the ground, but the wind whistled through every nook and cranny of our hut, and we expected the straw roof to take off at any moment. A nice foretaste of the coming winter. That can be a real mess!'[123] Others felt already resigned to their fate and held out little hope for the future. The diary of Pastor Sebacher stated on 7 October: 'I gave up hope of getting out of Russia this winter. Once the country is snowbound there will be no salvation' (see Illustration 13).[124]

Part of the problem confronting the Germans was their utter incomprehension of how to cope with the conditions they were encountering, and in many cases the learning curve was a deadly one. Russian peasants typically slept in large one-room huts on top of oversized clay stoves providing warmth, but these could also prove fatal when overheated. The primitive stoves easily caught fire when incorrectly managed and many huts, overcrowded with exhausted German soldiers, burned to the ground. On the night of 6–7 October the house in which the command staff of Panzer Group 3 was billeted burned to the ground as the result of an overheated stove. The lack of overcrowding on this occasion meant no one was hurt, but many subsequent fires would prove deadly.[125] The army issued a special pamphlet to the troops

13 After the dust and heat of the summer, in October 1941 the vehicles of Army Group Centre were frequently exposed to temperatures below freezing.

trying to provide practical tips for managing while ill equipped in the cold weather. It advised that an extra pair of army socks could be cut to provide holes for the thumb and index finger allowing the discharge of a weapon. As one soldier commented bitterly: 'Someone was obviously not aware that our boots have been almost worn to scrap and that our socks were little more than rags, already with so many holes in them that we would have no difficulty in finding enough to poke all five fingers through.'[126] Recognising their deficiencies in winter tactics and survival techniques, the OKH sought help from Finland, and a winter warfare school was later established in Kankaapää, Finland.[127] Yet in October 1941 survival against the cold was an improvised affair in which the men of Bock's army group largely had to fend for themselves, and superiors condoned any behaviour which benefited their troops.

Throughout the summer of 1941 the men of Army Group Centre had been encouraged to requisition foodstuffs to ease the demand on the fragile logistics system. This, at times, resulted in lavish bounties, which went far beyond the minimum needs of the troops and contributed to the impoverishment of the people. In fact countless Soviet peasants starved over the coming winter because their meagre holdings of livestock and grain had been stolen in the preceding summer and autumn.[128] As Hans von Luck stated, sometimes 'there was nothing to "requisition" in order to improve the diet of the troops'.[129] Luck admitted, however, 'we helped ourselves as far as we could', without apparently giving a thought to what the people would then be left to eat. Yet in October 1941 as the temperature dropped many Russian homes were also raided for winter clothing. As Luck's account continued, he recounted how the army 'requisitioned warm Russian sheepskins to give to our motorcyclists and grenadiers'.[130] Again nothing was written about what the Russian civilians were left to wear. Not only were peasant homes plundered for winter clothing, but so too were the columns of Soviet POWs who lost boots, coats and anything of value. One account spoke of a prisoner transport in which the first thirty to forty men were almost naked and had to press together for warmth during the march.[131] Max Landowski reported that even a Russian deserter was treated no differently: 'When he arrived, our lads started to take his clothes away. One took his hat, the next took his boots, another needed his coat, and in the end the bloke stood there stripped to his underpants.' He was subsequently shot because, as Landowski commented, 'The Russian couldn't have walked like that, he would have frozen to death.'[132] Dead Soviet soldiers were also a source of supply. Gottlob Bidermann wrote that he and his comrades insulated their bunker with overcoats, 'stripped from the enemy dead in front of our positions. The Soviet army dead provided us with thick, brown flannel gloves as well.'[133] Another soldier, Max Kuhnert, dressed almost entirely in Russian clothing with a thick quilted coat and fur cap, which he thought made him look 'odd', but kept him warm.[134] Yet Kuhnert's appearance could easily prove fatal as, despite the addition of German military insignia, one former officer noted in a post-war study, 'the wearers were often mistaken for enemy and fired upon by friendly troops'.[135]

While Bock's troops did their best to provide for themselves, there were almost two million men in Army Group Centre on 2 October (and over a million more in the remainder of the *Ostheer*), and there was simply no way of adequately equipping them all in time for winter. The army command had prioritised fuel and armament shipments over bulky winter clothing. The idea was to end the war in the east in one final all-out effort, and no resource was to be spared in the pursuit of that goal. Requests for winter clothing were not only refused, but, according to Guderian, the subordinate armies also 'were instructed not to make further unnecessary requests of this type'.[136] The idea that precious transport capacity be reserved for winter clothing was seen within the high command almost as an admission of defeat and a resignation that a winter campaign had become unavoidable. The result was a steadfast refusal to acknowledge the scale of the problem or do anything substantive about it. As Guderian observed, the consequences would be seen in the suffering of the men. 'Preparations made for the winter were utterly inadequate. For weeks we had been requesting anti-freeze for the water-coolers of our engines; we saw as little of this as we did of winter clothing for the troops. This lack of warm clothes was, in the difficult months ahead, to prove the greatest problem and cause the greatest suffering to our soldiers.'[137] Not only did the German high command refuse to take steps which actively assisted their troops, they even took steps which worsened their plight. At Riga, thousands of Jewish labourers were employed, some directly under Army Group North's command, tailoring millions of captured sheepskins into articles of clothing for the troops. They produced ear-protectors, fur caps, waistcoats and more. This, however, did not save them. At the end of November 1941 the entire workforce were shot 'in accordance with the Führer's orders' when the Riga ghetto was liquidated.[138]

While Jewish lives were worth nothing in the eyes of the German occupiers, the value of non-Jewish Soviet citizens was scarcely better, and the needs of the German forces always came first. As the temperature dropped, German soldiers found they could no longer sleep outside as they had for much of the summer. Suddenly the peasant huts, which most German soldiers had previously avoided for fear of lice, bugs or vermin, became welcome refuges from the cold. The problem was that there was seldom enough room for all the German troops, so the occupant families were simply cast out of their own homes. Henry Metelmann wrote of how his unit acquired shelter in the autumn of 1941:

> Our orders were to occupy one cottage per crew, and to throw the peasants out. When we entered 'ours', a woman and her three young children were sitting around the table by the window, obviously having just finished a meal. She was clearly frightened of us, and I could see that her hands were shaking, while the kids stayed in their seats and looked at us with large, non-understanding eyes. Our Sergeant came straight to the point: 'Raus!' [Out!] and pointed to the door. When the mother started to remonstrate and her children to cry, he repeated 'Raus!', opened the door and waved

his hand towards the outside in a manner which could not be mistaken anywhere … Outside it was bitterly cold … I watched them through the small window standing by their bundles in the snow, looking helplessly in all directions, not knowing what to do … When I looked back a little later, they were gone; I did not want to think about it anymore.[139]

Metelmann may have expressed unease about the practice, but there were many German soldiers for whom the bitter cold and extreme fatigue extinguished any sensitivity towards the people they rendered homeless. Other soldiers felt no compassion at the best of times and expressed an outright hatred for the Slavic peoples, whom they denounced as backwards or even dangerous enemies. Accordingly, after having stolen their food and later their clothing, many German soldiers felt no compunction about taking their homes too. Wilhelm Prüller's diary relates the heartlessness of the expulsion process:

> You should see the act the civilians put on when we make it clear to them that we intend to use their sties to sleep in. A weeping and yelling begins, as if their throats were being cut, until we chuck them out. Whether young or old, man or wife, they stand in their rags and tatters on the doorstep and can't be persuaded to go … When we finally threaten them at pistol point, they disappear.[140]

No doubt many Soviet peasants could well guess at the fate that awaited them and their families without shelter during the colder months of the year. Yet antagonising the Germans was a risky proposition, which as Hans Becker described could result in far worse than the loss of a house. 'An angry word or sign of resentment might lead to a man being hunted out of his home or denounced as a partisan. In the latter case he would either be shot out of hand or locked up to meet, more probably sooner than later, a revoltingly cruel death.' Becker also noted how short-sighted the practice was from a military perspective. 'As far as I could judge, men were practically forced to join these guerrillas – by the German army![141] Their hovels were occupied by soldiers who ordered their unwilling hosts around to suit their own convenience.'[142] In one instance, two officers from Major-General Wilhelm Ritter von Thoma's 20th Panzer Division,[143] who were being hosted in a peasant's house, proceeded to get drunk. After a time one man told the other, 'I can't stand the sight of these peasants' faces!' He then abruptly shot the father of the family dead, causing his wife 'to scream and howl' while hiding in the corner with their three young children. Soon the men grew tired of the wailing and shot the woman followed, in interludes, by each of the children.[144] It was a stark indication of the value of Russian lives and, while many German soldiers did not condone such purposefully murderous acts, at the same time, few expressed any reservation about simply expelling civilians from their homes – an action which often resulted in the same outcome. As Max Kuhnert explained: 'Whether people were still in the houses or not made no difference, this was war.'[145] But it was not just war; it was a war of annihilation (*Vernichtungskrieg*).[146]

6   EXPLOITING THE BREACH

Into the Bear's cave – Bock's drive on Moscow

While the battle at Viaz'ma was an undeniable success for Bock, his real objective in Operation Typhoon was to strike down Soviet power by taking Moscow. To the German command, this had now come tantalisingly close to fruition. The defending forces of the Red Army had been largely destroyed at Viaz'ma, and the remaining distance to the Soviet capital was less than the distances previously covered by earlier offensives at Minsk and Smolensk. Moscow's fall seemed almost preordained, but events on the ground suggested a far more troubling forecast of the next stage of the German offensive.

In the defensive battles on the eastern edge of the Viaz'ma pocket, the motorised forces of General of Panzer Troops Georg Stumme's XXXX Panzer Corps and Vietinghoff's XXXXVI Panzer Corps had played largely static roles. Under strict instructions from Kluge at Fourth Army, Hoepner had to maintain a tight perimeter, which aimed at preventing large-scale breakouts, but also prevented Panzer Group 4 from sending more forces in the direction of Moscow. Hoepner fumed at Kluge's short-sightedness[1] in spite of the fact that even his heavy concentrations of motorised forces at Viaz'ma had trouble containing the trapped Soviet armies. Irrespective of such difficulties, Hoepner later complained: 'The speed of the thrust to Moscow was reduced by the mistakes of the higher command.'[2] Hoepner could only send Kuntzen's LVII Panzer Corps towards Kaluga on 7 October and *Obergruppenführer* Paul Hausser's 'Das Reich' (belonging to

Stumme's XXXX Panzer Corps) towards Gzhatsk. Kuntzen's panzer corps initially consisted of only one panzer division (the 20th)[3] and this was down to just thirty-nine serviceable tanks by 11 October.[4] Hausser's 'Das Reich' suffered even more heavily. In a flanking attack by Soviet tanks on 10 October the division suffered 500 losses,[5] while on 14 October Hausser himself was seriously wounded by a grenade splinter (losing his right eye).[6] The sodden ground also plagued the attack, with the 20th Panzer Division's war diary describing the smaller roads leading off the highway as 'catastrophic' and reporting the loss of many vehicles.[7] On 14 October the Fourth Army reported to Army Group Centre that 'movement by motorised vehicles off the roads is impossible'.[8] At the same time it reported that 'Das Reich' had to continue its attack 'on foot' because the vehicles could no longer move forwards.[9] Although temperatures now dropped below freezing most nights, they rose again during the day preventing the ground from hardening. As Wilhelm Prüller wrote on 13 October: 'Snow and rain alternate the whole time and the ground flatly refuses to harden up. It only freezes at night, when it's cold, but at 7.00 in the morning it thaws again.'[10]

On 14 October, with the battle of Viaz'ma at last concluded, Vietinghoff's XXXXVI Panzer Corps was at last permitted to resume the drive east. Following in the wake of 'Das Reich', Esebeck's 11th Panzer Division (Vietinghoff's spearhead) passed first through Gzhatsk (which had been captured in heavy fighting on 9 October)[11] and then continued to the north-east. Yet progress was noted to be 'very slow' on roads that were described as 'almost impassable'.[12] Numerous streams crisscrossed the advance route and, despite the best efforts of the engineers to reinforce the many small bridges, most of them collapsed. Other bridges remained intact, but promptly sank into the morass under the weight of a tank. In the conditions attempting any kind of forward or flanking reconnaissance was deemed 'pointless'[13] and maps of the area were judged 'unreliable', so the divisional command had little idea of what they might come across.[14] Not surprisingly, even with no reports of enemy resistance, on 15 October Esebeck's division managed 'only around 25 km'.[15] Even with such a limited advance, the loss of traction on the roads forced an inordinate consumption of fuel for the distance travelled. With supplies of fuel already limited, on 16 October Esebeck took the drastic step of leaving behind parts of his panzer regiment to create fuel reserves for the leading *Kampfgruppe* (battle group).[16]

Already two days earlier, on 14 October, Vietinghoff's XXXXVI Panzer Corps had ordered its constituent divisions not to advance with any unnecessary or unreliable vehicles,[17] meaning Esebeck's motorised spearhead was rapidly weakening even without enemy contact.

Advancing to the south of Esebeck's 11th Panzer Division on a roughly parallel course was Veiel's 2nd Panzer Division, which was numerically one of the most powerful on the eastern front at that time. Yet its many tanks necessitated more fuel, and by 17 October Veiel's reserves were exhausted and his advance halted until more supplies could reach the front on 19 October.[18] Of course the Red Army was even worse off and interrogations of enemy troops captured by Veiel's men revealed just how desperate the Soviet state was for recruits. The POWs were all from Kazakhstan and had arrived on the Moscow front just three days before. They had had barely two months of training and their regiment was only partially armed. Yet this did not mean they should be underestimated. On the same day the POWs were captured (17 October) Veiel's division lost seven tanks in one attack.[19] While Veiel's advance stalled, Esebeck's *Kampfgruppe* attempted to press on. The temperature, however, during 17 and 18 October became noticeably warmer and the mud, which had somewhat coagulated in the colder climate, now thinned into a watery quagmire.[20] Heavy rainfall on 18 and 19 October across the whole of Army Group Centre's front added to the problem and virtually paralysed all movement for wheeled vehicles.[21] As one soldier noted: 'The rain just wouldn't stop, it poured and kept on pouring, the mud became a mire, deeper and deeper.'[22] The war diary of Vietinghoff's panzer corps recorded the extent to which the many related difficulties now endangered its planned envelopment of Moscow:

> The corps has serious concerns about the achievement [of its orders] because after careful study of the maps the fact becomes clear that for this operation there is only one single road available. The corps will be forced to advance with three divisions on this one road, which from experience and the time of year will be bad. As a result the corps will not be able to adequately utilise its striking power, but will always only be able to commit weak spearheads. Furthermore, the supply convoys will move only with great difficulty.[23]

As if to prove the point it was observed that Esebeck's 11th Panzer Division was summoning all its resources to move forward with just one battalion but, as the corps concluded, the attack could not succeed 'because its strength is too weak'.[24] Another officer noted that, whereas the normal length of a panzer division was around forty kilometres, by the middle of October his division was spread over some 300 kilometres.[25]

Stumme's XXXX Panzer Corps contained only one panzer division (the 10th), which had been largely tied up in the fighting near Viaz'ma, but a reinforced *Kampfgruppe* had been dispatched east to support the advance of 'Das Reich'. On 14 October the remainder of the division departed Viaz'ma for the east where Hausser's 'Das Reich' was engaged in bitter fighting to break the Mozhaisk Defensive Line, which centred on the four fortified towns of Volokolamsk in the north to Mozhaisk and Maloiaroslavets, and down to Kaluga. While many in the German high command believed the back of Soviet resistance had been broken, Hausser's division, attacking east towards Mozhaisk, encountered an elaborate system of defences, which, aided by the autumn rains and the stubborn resistance of the Viaz'ma pocket, the Soviets had been able to erect in record time. A report by *Obersturm-führer*[26] Günther Heysing tells of what the soldiers of 'Das Reich' encountered: 'built-in rows of electrically ignited flamethrowers, all sorts of tank obstacles, boggy streams, minefields, wire-entanglements, bunker systems, steep slopes and concealed forest positions'. In addition, Heysing stated that the Soviet troops defended their line with 'concentrated defensive fire from artillery, flak, anti-tank guns, mortars, rockets and machine guns'.[27] It was on this day (14 October) that Hausser, commanding 'Das Reich', was wounded and replaced by *Oberführer*[28] Wilhelm Bittrich. At the time elements of Fischer's 10th Panzer Division were engaging Soviet positions a few kilometres further north on the former battleground of Borodino. It was here that the Russian army met Napoleon on 7 September 1812 and fought one of the bloodiest battles of the entire Napoleonic era.[29] Fischer's panzer division confronted Colonel Viktor Polosukhin's 32nd Rifle Division, reinforced by three tank brigades and the cadets from a Moscow military college. At the Borodino military museum under 'Purpose of Visit' Polosukhin had written, 'I have come to defend the battlefield.'[30] Colonel Chales de Beaulieu, the chief of staff at Panzer Group 4, noted: 'It looked as if Napoleon's costly victory in 1812 was once more to be replayed.'[31] Indeed Fischer's panzer forces attacked the Shevardino Redoubt, just as Napoleon had 129 years before.[32] In two days of fighting on 16 and 17 October, Fischer's division suffered 280 wounded and an undisclosed number of dead.[33] As Hoepner observed with some measure of incredulity: 'The Russians no longer have a recognisable army so should not have the capacity to conduct a successful defence here. Yet the formations opposing us – [from] the Siberian 32nd Rifle Brigade – have proved remarkably effective.'[34] There was even one local reverse in which Fischer's men were driven back by Polosukhin's cadets, but after five days of standing their ground in front of Mozhaisk and at grievous cost, which included 80 per cent losses among the 4,000 young cadets, Mozhaisk fell on 18 October.[35] Stumme's XXXX Panzer Corps had breached Zhukov's defences, but not in time to outrun the worsening Russian *rasputitsa*. As Lieutenant Heysing reported on the same day (18 October), 'the Russian autumn rains have set in and are depriving the German soldiers of the victory they have already won. It is pouring day and night. It rains and snows alternately without letup. The ground is soaking up the moisture with a sponge and the German attack is stuck knee-deep in the mire.'[36] In addition to the condition of the roads, the condition of the men also necessitated a pause. A report from 'Das Reich' to the SS headquarters in Berlin noted 'a rest of several days, where possible in warm and heated billets, is essential for the success of any new attack'.[37]

While the panzer divisions of Vietinghoff's and Stumme's corps first had to complete the fighting at the Viaz'ma pocket, Kuntzen's LVII Panzer Corps was never committed to the encirclement and therefore commenced its drive east far sooner. Nevertheless Thoma's 20th Panzer Division, which constituted Kuntzen's spearhead, made such slow progress on the sodden roads that it was no faster in reaching the Mozhaisk Defensive Line than Fischer's 10th Panzer Division, which fought for days at Viaz'ma. Indeed, as a reflection of the difficult road conditions, the most significant initial success in the exploitation of the collapsed Soviet front was not achieved by Hoepner's motorised divisions, but rather by Kluge's and Weichs's marching infantry divisions. General of Infantry Hans-Gustav Felber's XIII Army Corps (belonging to Weichs's Second Army) and General of Infantry Walter Schroth's XII Army Corps (belonging to Kluge's Fourth Army) together reached the southern tip of the Mozhaisk Defensive Line at Kaluga on 10 October. With such sizeable German forces so deep behind Soviet defences, and almost no time for Zhukov to organise replacements or establish new positions, Kaluga fell on 12 October.[38] When the lead elements of Thoma's 20th

Panzer Division did at last engage the Mozhaisk Defensive Line on 16 October the division retained only thirty-four serviceable panzers (and only four of these were Mark IVs).[39] Kuntzen's second panzer division, Lieutenant-General Otto von Knobelsdorff's 19th Panzer Division, attacked the defences outside Maloiaroslavets and suffered accordingly. On 16 October Knobelsdorff's division lost twelve tanks in the fighting[40] and on the following day (17 October) another eighteen, a total of thirty tanks destroyed in just two days.[41] Maloiaroslavets fell shortly thereafter, but as Bock noted on 17 October: 'Enemy resistance is especially stubborn in front of the Fourth Army.'[42]

As Knobelsdorff was struggling to take Maloiaroslavets, Lieutenant-General Erich Schroeck's 98th Infantry Division was fighting for the nearby town of Detschino, which finally fell on 19 October. As one of Schroeck's battalion commanders (Lieutenant-Colonel von Bose) observed: 'Not a lot can be demanded of us anymore ... Battle strength of the battalion is around 190 men. In the attack on Detschino the battalion lost almost one hundred men, forty-eight of these dead. In twenty-four hours five company commanders were lost.'[43] Undoubtedly Zhukov's Western Front was lacking in many areas, but it proved that it was still capable of tenacious resistance and that Moscow was defended by much more than just the fabled General Mud. Indeed, after receiving a report from Kuntzen's LVII Panzer Corps, Army Group Centre's war diary noted: 'In the opinion of the corps the last battles for the enemy positions were the hardest of the entire eastern campaign because the enemy is especially tough and defends from pre-war concrete bunkers.'[44] Bock also acknowledged that Kuntzen's corps was in an 'especially difficult position' and did not possess enough infantry, but there was little he could offer until the bulk of Kluge's infantry divisions arrived from the battlefields around Viaz'ma.[45] Kluge did what he could. He had ordered all heavy artillery to be left behind and only light vehicles were to accompany the march, but in what were described as 'catastrophic road conditions' Kluge noted that not even twenty kilometres a day could be covered.[46]

While the panzer corps of Vietinghoff, Stumme and Kuntzen pushed forward with all the vigour and élan that were the hallmark of their past success, by mid October the offensive was far too slow to break through and encircle the Soviet positions. The blitz tactics, which had so utterly shattered the Soviet front in early October when conditions were dry and the panzer forces more tightly concentrated, were now impossible (see Map 11). In place of a lightning assault Hoepner's panzer group engaged in a grinding frontal push, which quickly drained resources that Army Group Centre's overstretched supply system could not replace. Furthermore, in abandoning much of their heavy equipment in order to keep the advance moving, German commanders were forsaking much of the firepower necessary to break the concrete bunkers and entrenched fortifications of the new Soviet lines. Above all, the Red Army had not melted away as the German command had expected. The Fourth Army (with Hoepner's subordinate Panzer Group 4) was still pressing forward, but it was largely unsupported on the flanks as Guderian's Second Panzer Army was still far to the south and Reinhardt's Panzer Group 3 was tied up at Kalinin with Strauss's Ninth Army rushing north to support it or mopping up at Viaz'ma.[47] The expectation was that Zhukov's meagre forces would simply be swept aside and Kluge and Hoepner would soon arrive at the Soviet capital.

Planning for the siege of Moscow was in fact already underway, and Hitler was adamant that the city not be occupied by German troops. According to Heusinger at the OKH, the city was expected to be 'to a large extent mined' and was 'too dangerous for the troops', which no doubt reflected the German occupation of Kiev at the end of September, where numerous prominent buildings were destroyed by bombs after the Germans had occupied them.[48] Brauchitsch proposed a 45-kilometre exclusion zone from the centre of the city, but Bock rejected this out of hand as it would require too many troops and allow the Soviets too much freedom of movement. Consequently Bock insisted on a much closer encirclement.[49] Yet, as with the example of Leningrad, the implications of encircling a major urban area containing millions of civilians did not register any concerns within Army Group Centre. Indeed the army group's war diary dutifully noted that: 'all measures were to be taken that make the lives of the population and the encircled troops unbearable'.[50]

While the German leadership focused on the coming siege of Moscow, there is no indication that Hitler, the OKH or Bock recognised that Army Group Centre might struggle to get that far. On 15 October British radio was already comparing Bock's offensive to a car stuck in the mud – the motor was running, the wheels were turning, but it was not moving forward.[51] Publicly Goebbels rejected such propaganda as simply wishful thinking, but in private he too seemed to accept the

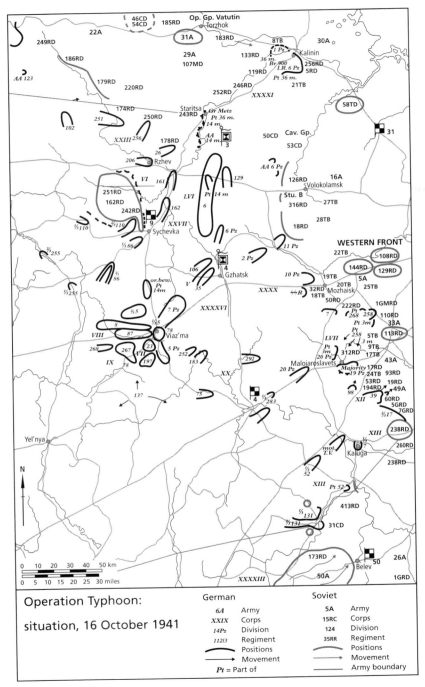

Operation Typhoon: situation, 16 October 1941

German		Soviet	
6A	Army	5A	Army
XXIX	Corps	15RC	Corps
14Pz	Division	124	Division
11213	Regiment	35RR	Regiment
Positions		Positions	
Movement		Movement	
Pt = Part of		Army boundary	

Map 11 Dispositions of Army Group Centre, 16 October 1941

comparison. When Dietrich, the Reich's press chief, called on Goebbels after a visit to Hitler's 'Wolf's Lair' headquarters and reported only good news, Goebbels remained uncharacteristically hesitant to embrace the mood. He first summarised Dietrich's glowing report in his diary. 'The Führer was in excellent form. The offensive operations were progressing forward as hoped and the opinion was expressed that at least military action in the Soviet Union could be concluded in the course of November.' Yet Goebbels then conceded: 'I am in this regard still somewhat sceptical. The eastern campaign has presented us with so many puzzles and surprises that it is good to arm oneself with doubt.'[52]

If Hitler and his generals at the OKW were inclined towards optimism, they were by no means the only ones. At the OKH Halder was conceiving of operations well beyond simply the investment of Moscow, and on 19 October he expressed his thoughts to Greiffenberg, Army Group Centre's chief of staff. Halder's newest suggestion reflected once again his disturbing predilection for wildly ambitious operations, recalling the many overestimations and dangerous misconceptions which underscored the whole planning process for Operation Barbarossa. Halder proposed 'before the end of the autumn period' to conduct a new operation for an 'enormous encirclement' (*Riesenkessel*) to the north and north-east of Army Group Centre. Launching from Kalinin, Halder wanted first to destroy the enemy in front of Army Group North and then gain a new line centred on Vologda – no less than 350 kilometres (linear distance) north-east of Kalinin. Not only did Halder appear to believe that such an operation was possible before the onset of winter, but he also assured Greiffenberg that once established in this new position 'harassment by the enemy from the deep Russian hinterlands would be as much as possible prevented and tie down the smallest possible number of our own forces'.[53] While the German high command planned fanciful operations and Hitler looked forward to an end of hostilities in November, others were observing events with distinct trepidation. On the same day that Halder was setting out his plans for an 'enormous encirclement' (19 October) the Italian foreign minister wrote in his diary: 'The approach of winter is viewed with great concern by all. Too many illusions have been built up, purposely or involuntarily, on the shortness of the conflict and on a victory which was supposed to be easy.'[54] Ciano also appeared to be better informed as to Germany's military situation. The day before

(18 October) he had already observed: 'the Germans are starting to slow down before Moscow. Isn't this a case of their having sung their hymn of victory too soon?'[55]

As Hoepner was just beginning his attack towards Moscow after the conclusion of the fighting at Viaz'ma, a corps of Reinhardt's Panzer Group 3 had just seized Kalinin after a long march of more than 150 kilometres. Arriving unexpectedly in the city on the morning of 13 October, the forward elements of Kirchner's XXXXI Panzer Corps soon found themselves engaged in heavy street fighting with many local people taking up arms against the Germans.[56] After taking control of the city and being resupplied, Kirchner had orders to continue his advance towards Torzhok, another 60 kilometres to the north-west. The OKH was looking to roll up the right flank of the Soviet North-Western Front and, while Bock had supported Reinhardt's offensive as far as Kalinin, he had since had second thoughts and feared his strength was being dangerously dissipated. On 14 October a new directive arrived from the OKH ordering all of Strauss's Ninth Army to march north-east and assemble in the Kalinin–Staritsa–Torzhok area, while at the same time suggesting that Guderian's Second Panzer Army might have to extend its right wing down as far as Voronezh, more than 250 kilometres south-east of Orel. Bock's fears appeared to be confirmed and he fumed in his diary. 'Like after Smolensk, once again the army group is to be scattered to the four winds and thus seriously weakened in its main direction of advance.'[57] Yet precisely because of his experience at Smolensk, not to mention the high command's habitual tendency to overestimate the strength of the *Ostheer*, Bock should hardly have been surprised that his army group might obtain new objectives pushing it well beyond the limit of its endurance. Indeed, given the dire implications of what the OKH was ordering and the resultant loss of strength this would entail for Moscow – the single most important objective of Operation Typhoon – Bock's reluctant acceptance was a distinctly half-hearted response for the 'Holy Fire of Küstrin'.

Having broken into Kalinin, Krüger's 1st Panzer Division found itself involved in a major operation to clear the city. Even twenty-four hours after arriving in the city the division's war diary spoke of the 'toughest house fighting' against 'rapidly formed groups of enemies – even workers and women take part in the fighting'. As a result, the diary noted, ground could only be won slowly.[58] While Kirchner's XXXXI Panzer Corps consisted of Krüger's 1st Panzer Division,

Ottenbacher's 36th Motorised Infantry Division and Krause's motorised infantry regiment 'Lehrbrigade 900', none of these units arrived in Kalinin with their full complement of equipment and manpower as regiments had been 'lightened' in the rush to reach the city. Far from simply storming the undefended Soviet hinterland, Kirchner's men now found themselves in a resource-intensive city battle. Supplies and reinforcements were en route to Kalinin, especially since the end of the fighting at Viaz'ma freed Schaal's LVI Panzer Corps, but these suffered greatly over the long distances from the worsening weather and deteriorating road conditions.

Another problem which hounded German movement on the road to Kalinin was the resurgent strength of the Soviet air force. The planes of Kesselring's Air Fleet 2, covering Army Group Centre, operated from distant airfields, utilising earth runways with few hangars and only the most basic infrastructure. Not surprisingly the number of sorties flown was increasingly limited, which contrasted starkly with the Soviet air force, which benefited from the numerous modern airfields around Moscow with concrete runways and large aircraft hangars.[59] In early October Kesselring's Air Fleet 2 managed more than 1,000 sorties per day, but after the weather turned the figure dropped to 559 on 8 October and just 269 on 9 October.[60] The war diary for Kirchner's XXXXI Panzer Corps noted on 14 October that Soviet planes had air superiority 'for the majority of the day' leading to 'tangible losses'.[61] The problem became a common one for the Germans throughout the battle for Kalinin and dangerously impeded the amount of supplies reaching the city. Soviet bombers concentrated their efforts over the 70 kilometres of road between Staritsa and Kalinin where countless German vehicles presented slow or even immobile targets.[62] As Kesselring noted: 'Army units were constantly calling for protection against the very low-flying Russian ground-strafer attacks, and sorties had to be flown to keep them quiet, though with little effect.'[63]

As part of Zhukov's reorganisation of the defences in front of Moscow, he sent Konev, at that time his deputy at Western Front, to manage the defences around Kalinin. He also diverted substantial reinforcements (to include the newly allocated Twenty-Second, Twenty-Ninth and Thirtieth Armies) to ensure the line was held. On 17 October these forces were grouped into the new Kalinin Front with Konev in command.[64] At Army Group Centre, Bock noted the marshalling of new Soviet forces in the north with evident unease. Writing on

15 October Bock observed: 'Panzer Group 3 is fighting hard at Kalinin; the enemy is bringing in reinforcements from all sides, even from Moscow, in order to regain possession of this important point.'[65] With much of Strauss's Ninth Army heading north to reinforce Reinhardt, Kalinin was becoming less the springboard for a drive into the open flank of the Soviet North-Western Front and more a major battle in itself. Recognising the difficulties of this battle and the need to ensure a unified command as Reinhardt's and Strauss's divisions crossed with one another, Bock resubordinated Panzer Group 3 to the Ninth Army on 16 October.[66]

While enemy forces were closing in on Kalinin from the north, east and south-west, Reinhardt took his chance to regain the initiative on 16 October and ordered Krüger's 1st Panzer Division along with Krause's 'Lehrbrigade 900' to strike out for Torzhok.[67] It was the kind of bold decision that so often set the panzer troops apart, but on this occasion it also reflected their rash imprudence. Using almost every drop of fuel available to the panzer corps and ignoring the increasingly dire position within Kalinin itself, Reinhardt authorised the offensive. By the following day (17 October) the advance had reached the village of Mednoye, 30 kilometres north-west of Kalinin and halfway to Torzhok, but there it ceased. The offensive ran into stiff enemy resistance and lacked the ammunition to go on attacking.[68] More worryingly, Soviet forces had broken through behind the spearhead, cutting Krüger and Krause off from Kalinin, while Major-General Hans Gollnick's[69] 36th Motorised Infantry Division was under increasing pressure defending the city.[70] To make matters even worse, aerial intelligence indicated that a 'very strong' enemy column numbering around 1,000 trucks together with another 3,000 assorted vehicles was heading towards Torzhok.[71] With no credible alternative, 1st Panzer Division's war diary noted it was with a 'heavy heart' that the attack towards Torzhok would have to be abandoned.[72] Reinhardt told Strauss that owing to the shortage of fuel and ammunition a further attempt to advance on Torzhok would now be impossible.[73] The implications of this failure effectively ruined the German plan for rolling up the southern flank of the Soviet North-Western Front and rendered Kalinin an extraordinarily costly detour from Operation Typhoon's main objective – Moscow. Not only was the German plan for the north a non-starter but, just as Halder refused to withdraw from the costly yet obsolete bridgehead at Dnepropetrovsk during the battle of Kiev, so too did the Army High Command go on insisting Kalinin be held and even reinforced. Hitler also attached great importance to a thrust north of Kalinin and welcomed the OKH's plans.[74] Bock also obliged and, in spite of his earlier complaints about his army group being 'scattered to the four winds',[75] he nevertheless resolved to muster more strength for a renewed offensive in the north. On 19 October Bock told Strauss at Ninth Army 'that Kalinin would long remain "the bleeding wound" of his army if strong infantry forces were not sent there very soon'.[76]

Of course movement in Russia during the *rasputitsa* – to say nothing of rapid movement – was precisely the problem. Even getting men and materiel to Kalinin was enough of a challenge without then trying to launch an offensive through the muck against strengthening Soviet defences. Moreover, it did not seem to occur to anyone in Army Group Centre or the OKH that the element of surprise had passed and that the Soviet North-Western Front was no longer going to be taken off guard by an offensive which was still days away at best. The 4,000 vehicles heading for Torzhok seemed to suggest that the Soviet command was aware of the danger to their flank and were adopting countermeasures. Indeed the preoccupation with operations to the north appears to have eclipsed other options. Major Carl Wagener, the operations officer at Panzer Group 3, noted after the war: 'Kalinin remained a secondary objective; the centre [where Kluge and Hoepner were attacking] was all that could produce results: [therefore Panzer Group 3 should] defend the northern flank of the deciding offensive to Moscow.'[77] Hoepner shared this view of Panzer Group 3 and the Ninth Army's deployment, writing in a report: 'It again seems to me that one sets objectives which, in relation to our strength, are too distant; one seeks too many objectives at the same time.'[78]

One of the greatest challenges confronting Strauss was the issue of supply. Not only was Panzer Group 3 in desperate need of almost all essential items (fuel and munitions above all), but also, with three corps of infantry marching north, along with Schaal's LVI Panzer Corps, maintaining effective supply was destined to worsen. Strauss resolved to establish an airfield south of Kalinin to allow the Luftwaffe to fly in supplies almost directly to the front lines. Yet Konev was moving faster than Strauss and the ring around Kalinin was tightened so rapidly that by 20 October only a narrow corridor was being held open to the southwest (see Map 12). The German airfield was within this corridor and the planes were effectively on the front line. The desperation of the

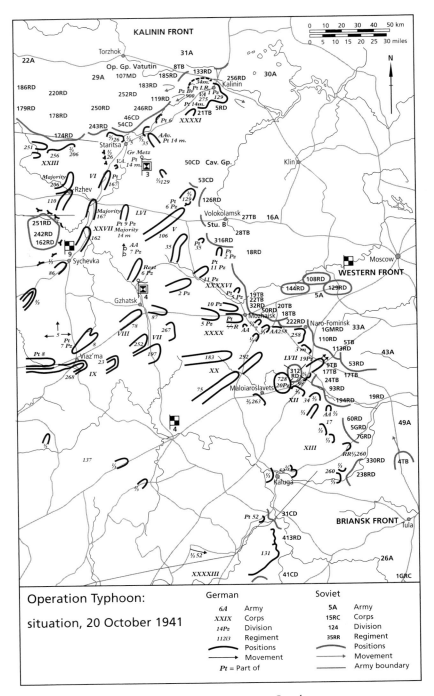

Map 12 Dispositions of Army Group Centre, 20 October 1941

fighting was described by Hans Rudel, one of the German pilots flying from the Kalinin airfield:

> The Soviets are attacking the airfield with tanks and infantry, and are less than a mile away. A thin screen of our own infantry protects our perimeter; the steel monsters may be upon us at any moment. We Stukas are a Godsend to the ground troops defending the position ... The ground personnel are able to follow every phase of the battle. We are well on the mark, for everybody realizes that unless the tanks are put out of action we have had it.[79]

Other German positions were not so lucky and on 18 October a single KV-1 tank broke through the German lines and drove into the streets of Kalinin, unable to be stopped. The tank subsequently destroyed countless vehicles and weapons including anti-tank guns and rocket launchers.[80] As Rudel observed when he heard about the rampaging tank in the city: 'Anything can happen here in Kalinin.'[81] With the battle for the city proving so costly, there was an urgent need for replacement equipment as well as supplies. In the fighting around the city and then the abortive drive to Torzhok, Krüger's 1st Panzer Division lost forty-five tanks in just five days, leaving the division with just thirty-four serviceable tanks (eight Mark IIs, twenty-two Mark IIIs and four Mark IVs) by 19 October.[82] At the same time the division reported having lost 548 men and 34 officers since it had arrived in Kalinin.[83] Indeed a number of combat battalions in Kirchner's XXXXI Panzer Corps, which normally fielded around 750 men, were down to 100 to 200 men.[84] Similarly, some companies with a pre-invasion strength of around 150 men now fielded just 25 to 30 men.[85] As Colonel Hans Röttiger, the chief of staff of the XXXXI Panzer Corps, noted: 'Our own losses increased seriously. The numerically low combat strength compelled certain units to merge their forces.'[86]

Of course any continuation of the attack north of Kalinin depended on the resupply of Kirchner's XXXXI Panzer Corps (Schaal's LVI Panzer Corps was still struggling north). Yet the average amount of fuel supplied daily by the Luftwaffe to the Kalinin airfield was 30 to 50 cubic metres, and the average 24-hour consumption of a panzer division was about 220 cubic metres.[87] The bulk of supplies were supposed to be brought up by the trucks of the *Grosstransportraum* from a newly established railhead (as of 18 October) at Sychevka. Yet Sychevka was still 150 kilometres south-west of Kalinin, and in the conditions it took many days for each individual load to arrive. To make matters worse, only 200 tons of supplies for Panzer Group 3 were arriving daily at the main exchange in Viaz'ma, and this was barely enough to meet day-to-day needs with nothing remaining to stockpile for a renewed offensive. Attempting to alleviate the problem, Reinhardt's *Grosstransportraum* was instructed to dispatch a portion of its strength all the way back to Smolensk in order to bring up more supplies to Viaz'ma.[88] This, however, took no account of the cost-to-gain ratio for each delivery and resulted in only a very small net return. In fact Panzer Group 3's *Grosstransportraum* was in a dreadful state. On 18 October Army Group Centre rebuked Strauss's Ninth Army for the 'terrible state of things' on the road leading to Kalinin where chaos in traffic control reigned. 'On this stretch the whole Ninth Army lives and dies!'[89] Yet the conditions were extraordinary and there was simply no precedent in the German army for what was being attempted. In one particularly bad area an estimated 1,000 trucks were bogged down.[90] As Bock observed on 19 October, 'the army group is stuck fast in muck and mire. No fuel is reaching Panzer Group 3.'[91] The situation was becoming so critical that Strauss queried whether fuel supplies destined for Panzer Groups 2 and 4 could be redirected to Panzer Group 3. Bock abruptly dismissed the request, but as a small consolation on the same day some 200 cubic metres of fuel were discovered in Rzhev (115 kilometres north of Viaz'ma).[92] Overall, Kirchner's XXXXI Panzer Corps viewed the situation as sufficiently dire to preclude any offensive 'for the time being'. The corps's war diary then illustrated the growing difficulties of the men by the appearance of signs which read, for example: 'Who will exchange 10 litres of petrol for one loaf of bread?'[93]

The process of moving supplies up to Kalinin suffered not only from the seasonal conditions, but also from enemy fire. The narrow corridor supplying the city was a gauntlet of Soviet artillery, mortar and aircraft fire, which inflicted heavy costs. Flying over the city, Hans Rudel noted, 'our supply lines are not functioning any too smoothly, because the main communications road from Staritsa to Kalinin runs right in front of the town in the hands of the enemy who exerts a continuous pressure from the east on our front line. I can soon see for myself how difficult and confused the situation is.'[94] As a result of enemy fire, Gollnick's 36th Motorised Infantry Division lost in just the first week in Kalinin eighty-four trucks, twenty-one cars, three tractors, fifteen motorcycles and five field kitchens.[95] The chief of staff of the XXXXI Panzer Corps noted that, once the Soviets had crossed the Volga River to the south-east and almost cut off the city, penetration into the vital German supply route 'could be sealed off only in an inadequate manner. As a result, the supply shipments to Kalinin continued to be at a standstill during this period, and could only be carried out under heavy convoy guard.'[96] Beyond the direct threat of interdiction by regular forces of the Red Army, individual vehicles and small convoys were also attacked by partisans or cut-off Soviet soldiers on the long road through the newly occupied area.[97] Even the Ninth Army's chief of staff, Colonel Kurt Weckmann, was attacked on the street in Sychevka while walking at night. He was hit over the head and stabbed a number of times (but survived the assault).[98]

Of course the dire state of Panzer Group 3's logistics reflected many of the wider problems within Army Group Centre and indeed the whole *Ostheer*. The hubris that reigned in the army's planning was nowhere better seen than in the private letters of the senior quartermaster-general, Major-General Eduard Wagner, who wrote on 12 October: 'The whole front is moving! Unbelievable this theatre of war. Every day I am asked: How far will you get? I always say: So far I have not left anyone in the lurch!'[99] By 20 October, however, Wagner's self-assured tone was changing as even the die-hard optimists within the German high command could not deny the effects of the *rasputitsa*. 'It can no longer be concealed', Wagner wrote; 'we are hung up in the muck, in the purest sense.'[100]

Bock's flagging offensive – pushing his army and his luck to Moscow

While the attack on Moscow by Hoepner's Panzer Group 4 was faltering and Reinhardt's Panzer Group 3[101] was halted at Kalinin, Guderian's Second Panzer Army, along with elements of Weichs's Second Army, were just concluding the fighting at the Briansk pocket. Lemelsen's XXXXVII Panzer Corps along with Model's 3rd Panzer Division (from Schweppenberg's XXIV Panzer Corps) were free to reinforce the stalled push on Tula. Yet it was not just the encirclement battle at Briansk that had delayed Guderian. Only half of his panzer army ever took part in the battle, while he attempted to press the attack in the east with the remainder of his forces. Langermann-Erlancamp's 4th Panzer Division (from Schweppenberg's XXIV Panzer Corps) was bottled up at Mtsensk and, far from advancing north-east towards Tula, was under intense pressure just retaining control of the town. As Hans Schäufler noted:

> We spent six days living like cave men in the wet and cold caves.[102] We barricaded the entrance to the courtyard, since the Russian heavy tanks continued to enter the city again and again. *Teller* mines[103] were placed at the entrance to the basement, armed and ready, since they were the only means with which we could combat those heavy monsters.[104]

In contrast to the ease of the 4th Panzer Division's earlier drive on Orel, the enemy was proving more than a match for the weakened forces of Langermann-Erlancamp's division. The divisional war diary noted that the enemy was a 'well-led, hard-fighting opponent who is determined to take back Mtsensk'.[105] In his memoir Guderian noted how in the fighting around Mtsensk some of his best officers at the 4th Panzer Division were starting to lose hope. They were continually being ordered to achieve new objectives with fewer and fewer resources, to which Guderian commented: 'What a contrast to the high spirits in evidence at the OKH and Army Group Centre!'[106] Yet it was Guderian issuing their orders, and his private correspondence from the time reveals that his own estimation of events was much more in line with the OKH than with his officers at the 4th Panzer Division. Writing to his wife on 11 October, Guderian claimed that recent German operations 'have now destroyed the great mass of the Russian army. There cannot be too many good [Soviet units] left.' Even after days of rain and snow Guderian then expressed the hope that the campaign could be won in as little as two weeks: 'Now we are hoping for good, dry weather at least for fourteen days; then is the main task probably achieved.'[107] The overriding question for the officers at the 4th Panzer Division was how this might be achieved. On 12 October Langermann-Erlancamp retained just forty serviceable tanks in his division, and stocks of munitions were noted to be 'very tight for all calibres'. Soviet aircraft were also very active around Mtsensk and, in spite of some Luftwaffe presence, 'the impression is of Russian air superiority'.[108] The state of the roads was a further major concern, which Army Group Centre's war diary noted would delay the transfer of reinforcements to Mtsensk after the conclusion of the fighting in the Briansk pocket.[109]

More importantly, the distance from Mtsensk to Tula was some 120 kilometres, and it is a further 170 kilometres from Tula to Moscow. Bock's orders as of 14 October stated that the Second Panzer Army was to 'encircle the city [of Moscow] in the south and east',[110] which, given the distances involved, the state of the roads, the strengthening of Soviet resistance and the fact that reinforcements for Guderian were still days away, rendered the whole undertaking remarkably naive.

By 20 October, despite a week with no forward movement, Langermann-Erlancamp had managed to return just 6 tanks to operational service, giving him a total of 46 tanks from an original strength of 170 plus a late September consignment of 35 replacements. His artillery listed forty-one guns from a starting strength of fifty-seven and his losses in personnel left 'only a few old officers and non-commissioned officers available'. The fighting units themselves contained 'a considerable percentage of replacements with correspondingly little training and combat experience'. Moreover, with no winter clothes, the troops were noted to be 'very stressed'. Ammunition supply trucks were down to just 18 per cent of normal establishment, while fuel trucks were at 40 per cent.[111] It was not a division that Langermann-Erlancamp now commanded, indeed in some respects it was barely a regiment, but this did not change his orders or the expectation that these should be carried out. The German offensive towards Tula was not subject to an investigation into Schweppenberg's strength in materiel or manpower; for Hitler and the OKH the triumph of the 'will' and the 'natural' superiority of the German soldier were enough.

While Schweppenberg's XXIV Panzer Corps was stalled at Mtsensk, it was not the only offensive the Second Panzer Army was attempting to manage. In the south, Kempf's XXXXVIII Panzer Corps was endeavouring to advance on Kursk from the town of Dmitriev-Lgovskiy 85 kilometres north-west of Kursk. Here again Army Group Centre was attempting an overblown objective, which considerably extended the length of its front. Kursk was no less than 460 kilometres south of Moscow (linear distance) and, if one then factors in the additional distances to Kalinin and then to Ostashkov (at the border to Army Group North), Army Group Centre was proposing to maintain a line nearly 800 kilometres (linear distance) in length. Meanwhile Kempf's panzer corps was still a long way from Kursk and suffering badly from the slogging fighting over a bridgehead that Hubicki's 9th Panzer Division was maintaining just east of Dmitriev-Lgovskiy.

Hubicki's panzer division had been in almost constant combat since it broke out of the Kremenchug bridgehead during the battle of Kiev a month earlier and its fitness for combat was exhausted. On 16 October the divisional war diary spoke of a 'general state of exhaustion' in which 'many examples of fatigue arise'. At the same time the strength of the forward units was noted to be 'sinking by the hour',[112] and the XXXXVIII Panzer Corps's war diary spoke of the 'critical' situation on Hubicki's front.[113] By 20 October Hubicki was protesting his orders to continue with the offensive and cited three key reasons: firstly, any further advance would only lengthen his flanks for which there were no additional forces; secondly, the appalling state of the roads did not permit an advance; and, thirdly, his regiments were militarily very weak. As an example of the last Hubicki reported that the division had a total of only seven serviceable tanks, while one of the motorised infantry regiments, which was supposed to operate with 287 trucks, was down to just 51.[114] Clearly Hubicki's 9th Panzer Division, with just seven tanks, was a panzer division only in name.

In addition to his three panzer corps Guderian's Second Panzer Army also commanded Waeger's XXXIV Army Corps and Kaempfe's XXXV Army Corps. Together these two corps included some six infantry divisions (45th, 95th, 134th, 262nd, 293rd and 296th) as well as the 1st Cavalry Division. As of 19 October Guderian's Second Panzer Army was reinforced by a further two corps, Weisenberger's LIII Army Corps (56th, 112th, 167th and one-third of the 52nd Infantry Division) and Heinrici's XXXXIII Army Corps (31st and 131st Infantry Divisions).[115] The infantry were in some respects more mobile than the motorised and panzer troops, given their principal form of movement was marching, yet the conditions still presented problems for the horses and heavy wagons, while also reducing marching speeds. Waeger's XXXIV Army Corps, for example, could move at an average of only 1 kilometre an hour.[116]

Even more seriously, because the infantry were exposed to a far greater extent to the frigid air and wet conditions, while wearing inadequate clothing and with their feet perpetually in cold mud and water, sickness soon took a crippling toll on the men. By 18 October Kaempfe's XXXV Army Corps had an average combat strength within its companies of just fifty men.[117] Yet in the *Ostheer* only the most serious illnesses could have a man excused from duty, and therefore many sick men remained at their posts despite suffering from flu or bronchitis.[118] In a study of 1.5 million German medical cases registered between 1 September 1941 and 31 August 1942 50 per cent of all reported illnesses were related to the cold weather.[119] The diary of Hans Efferbergen included an entry on 10 October in which he wrote: 'From time to time the Russian artillery would growl and rumble and we would throw ourselves into the indescribable mud ... Something ails every one of us now; the change in the weather has poisoned everybody's life.'[120] Similarly, Harald Henry wrote home in a letter on 18 October about the physical difficulties encountered on the march and the effects these were having:

> Our company ... went into the woods until we were over our knees in snow, which filled our boots. Across frozen marshes that broke open so that icy water ran into our boots. My gloves were so wet that I could not bear them any longer. I wound a towel around my ruined hands ... My face was contorted from tears, but I was already in a sort of trance. I stamped forward with closed eyes, mumbled senseless words and thought that I was experiencing everything only in a sleep as a dream. It was all like madness ... Agony without end ... We are all more or less sick.[121]

Heinrici, in command of the XXXXIII Army Corps, noted in a letter to his wife on 16 October how much the men under his command had suffered in the cold. 'No one has any idea what these men have to endure in this weather, this terrain, these conditions and these battle requirements.'[122] Ernst Guicking, a soldier serving in Weisenberger's LIII Army Corps, noted on 17 October that since the start of Operation Typhoon on 2 October he had not had a day without fighting.[123] Another soldier described the conditions in a letter home on 15 October: 'We have duty day and night, there is little sleep and warm food only on occasion.'[124] Given the harsh conditions as well as the punishing routine of duty it was small wonder that the men of Army Group Centre were falling sick in record numbers, yet this was still only the middle of October and the worst was yet to come.

While the men of the infantry suffered, they nevertheless fared better than the tens of thousands of horses pulling their guns, supplies and assorted equipment. At Panzer Group 3 Wagener stated that horses were dying at a rate of 1,000 a day.[125] A report from Weisenberger's LIII Army Corps in mid October noted that the horses pulling the artillery were 'very exhausted' and that half of them had to be left behind in Briansk.[126] As an alternative the army enlisted the locally raised panje horses, which were small but extremely hardy. Yet panje horses were much too weak to haul German artillery and could manage only small wooden carts. Transporting the standard German artillery piece, a 105mm gun, required no less than six healthy draft horses and the heavier 150mm gun required a team of eight horses. Nor could the panje horses draw the heavy steel wagons which the army needed to transport the infantry's munitions and equipment.[127] The smaller, lighter loads, which the panje horses could manage, fared much better during the period of the *rasputitsa*, making them an important aid to the army's transportation problem, but certainly no replacement for the loss of its heavier West European breeds.

Even before the drop in temperatures and the onset of the autumn rains, Lieutenant-General Karl von Oven's 56th Infantry Division (belonging to Weisenberger's LIII Army Corps) reported the 'heavy fallout of horses even on good roads'.[128] The months of campaigning and excessive demands made on the horses had weakened them to such an extent they were literally dying in the harness. As Horst Lange wrote in his diary on 22 October: 'The horses have to work an enormous amount. The bad drivers lash the teams of horses senselessly. The forest echoes with shouts.'[129] Helmut Pabst observed another problem afflicting the horses: 'Some of the horses still have summer-shoes and they keep slipping and falling.'[130] In a letter on 20 October Hans Meier-Welcker recorded the effect this was having on the horses of the Ninth Army: 'The roads quickly became icy and our route was lined by dead horses that had broken their legs or collapsed through sheer exhaustion.'[131] As the summer months passed and the pace of the advance slowed, fodder was increasingly difficult to come by and the horses were reduced to eating birch twigs, tree bark and the old straw roofs of peasant houses.[132] Yet as Max Kuhnert, who served in Major-General Kurt Feldt's 1st Cavalry Division, observed, the mud presented the greatest difficulty for the horses. As Kuhnert wrote: 'The mud was of course the largest obstacle for everyone, most of all for the horses. Not only had they to carry us, but they had no proper rest or food. Everything was sticky and wet, there was nowhere to shelter. The conditions were impossible for man and beast.'[133] Another account spoke of the horses on the road to Moscow being 'skeleton-thin, emaciated, lame and powerless'.[134] As a result of such poor treatment as well as the seasonal conditions, General of Infantry Hermann Geyer, commanding the IX Army Corps, noted that by late October: 'The losses in horses were frightening.'[135] The veterinary company of Lieutenant-General Kurt von Tippelskirch's 30th Infantry Division treated 1,072 horses between 16 September and 30 November 1941, but only 117 of these were for wounds sustained from enemy fire; the rest were suffering from exhaustion. Despite the addition of replacement horses sent east from Germany throughout the campaign by early November the infantry divisions of the *Ostheer* retained only an estimated 65 per cent of their horse-drawn transportation.[136]

As the infantry divisions of the Second Panzer Army grappled to maintain their mobility and strength, both Guderian's infantry and panzer corps shared one very profound problem, which, with the conclusion of the fighting at Briansk, threatened to derail any renewed offensive. On 19 October Army Group Centre determined that the state of the roads had deteriorated to such an extent as to constitute 'a severe crisis in the supply of the troops with provisions, munitions and above all with fuel'.[137] On the same day (19 October) the quartermaster-general at Second Panzer Army declared that the supply of fuel being brought forward was 'completely inadequate'[138] and Guderian informed Army Group Centre that '[w]ide ranging operations are currently not possible.'[139] Not surprisingly, Guderian's earlier expression of hope that the campaign might be completed in two weeks was now undergoing something of a reappraisal. Writing to his wife on 15 October the panzer commander suggested: 'The victory here will certainly not fall into our lap ... The war will be continually harder the longer it lasts.'[140] Experiencing the difficulties firsthand, the quartermaster-general at Model's 3rd Panzer Division noted that on the muddy roads 'a tragedy is taking place, nobody helps'.[141] On 19 October, Model determined that success could be achieved only by a prolonged period of frost to harden the ground,[142] a view which was shared at Schweppenberg's XXIV Panzer Corps.[143] Further south, Hubicki's 9th Panzer Division complained as early as 12 October that forward movement in the area of Kempf's XXXXVIII Panzer Corps was possible only with tracked vehicles and tractors.[144] For this purpose, the Luftwaffe had to drop bundles of rope to the stricken vehicles.[145] Lemelsen's XXXXVII Panzer Corps drew its supplies from a railhead at Roslavl some 170 kilometres away and everything flowed along one main road. A single journey Roslavl–Briansk–Karachev took three days.[146] Given the developing supply crisis across the length of Army

Group Centre's front and the fact that movement was so seriously constrained by the conditions, it is hardly surprisingly that the wisdom of continuing with the offensive was now being questioned at senior levels. Certainly many of the cold, wet and exhausted soldiers favoured a halt. One soldier wrote: 'We can't go on. There is no more petrol and nothing is coming up behind us. The route is long and the roads even worse over the last few days. The snow has melted and worsened the muck. Rations still do not arrive. And we sit in the filth the entire day.'[147] Another soldier perceptively suggested that the constant advance into the depths of the Soviet Union was less an example of conquest than a case of being 'drawn in' to the enemy's advantage. Addressing his letter to Russia itself the soldier wrote: 'Russia, you bearer of bad tidings, we still know nothing about you. We have started to slog and march in this mire and still have not fathomed you out. Meanwhile you are absorbing us into your tough and sticky interior' (see Illustration 14).[148]

Inevitably, after the war historians and former German officers debated Army Group Centre's strategic alternatives in the second half of October, and some concluded that Germany should have halted its offensive operations and begun preparing winter positions. While hindsight might suggest this to be the most prudent step the Germans could have taken, at the time it was simply unthinkable to the panzer generals, Bock, Halder and Hitler. Stalemate in the east and a winter campaign were to be avoided at all costs. Moreover, backing away from Moscow after seemingly eliminating the Soviet armies protecting the city was incomprehensible. Indeed, beyond continuing the offensive, there was no discussion of another strategic option within Army Group Centre or the German high command until the end of October.

While Guderian grappled with the almost insurmountable logistic challenges, throughout the Second Panzer Army these were exacerbated by the considerable strength of cut-off Soviet forces as well as the first fledgling partisan movements in the Briansk area. The war diary of Nehring's 18th Panzer Division noted on 16 October that in the rear areas a 'superior enemy strength' still predominated and that this presented a manifest problem to the division's isolated and immobile transport columns.[149] Aerial intelligence indicated that in one forested area of the highway an estimated 1,000 Soviet troops were plundering a column of German trucks. Nearby, five bypassed Soviet tanks had taken to the highway and were heading east along a road where countless

14 As the autumn *rasputitsa* took hold in the east, wheeled transport in many areas of Army Group Centre became impossible. Only with the help of tanks or tractors could individual vehicles be brought forward.

more German trucks were stuck fast in the mud. In another small town to the south, a column with forty to fifty German vehicles was surrounded and under attack by a superior enemy force.[150] The attacks continued, and on 20 October Lemelsen's XXXXVII Panzer Corps noted that Nehring's 18th Panzer Division had lost the greater part of three supply columns as well as a motor repair company.[151] On the same day (20 October) the war diary of Kempf's XXXXVIII Panzer Corps reported that the 'supply services of the [9th Panzer] division remain far behind in combat with partisans'.[152] At Army Group Centre, Bock observed the situation with growing alarm. Supply via Briansk, he noted, remained 'unbelievably difficult', while enemy activity had resulted in thirty-three demolitions, including eleven large bridges, which would have to be repaired or rebuilt.[153] Overall the situation remained extremely precarious and even the die-hard optimists at the OKH were at last beginning to comprehend the scale of the undertaking. Wagner, the army quartermaster-general, wrote in a letter on 17 October:

> In the highly tense situation … I am the most sought-after man and the commanding officer [Brauchitsch] wants to see me every day. Tremendous achievements are demanded [to continue the

advance], which go to the limit of human, materiel and horses; the theatre of war in the centre is at the moment a mixture of muck, snow, ice and cold. So pretty much everything a soldier does not need.[154]

Gaining a sense of the challenges afoot did not mean the OKH was any closer to finding solutions or even reducing their expectations on Bock's army group. Indeed, far from learning the lessons of the preceding months and guarding against the dangers of overextension, the OKH was just as complicit as Hitler in failing to understand Clausewitz's concept of 'the country'.

While the state of the Soviet roads, inclement weather and the rapidly declining strength of the German panzer groups posed serious complications to Operation Typhoon, such difficulties were not allowed to impede the enthusiasm of Nazi propaganda. The victories at Viaz'ma and Briansk were complemented by the fighting in the Nogai Steppe in which Rundstedt's Army Group South won a significant victory in the battle on the Sea of Azov. Here two more Soviet armies (the Ninth and Eighteenth) of Lieutenant-General D. I. Riabyshev's Southern Front (I. T. Cherevichenko replaced Riabyshev on 5 October) were encircled by the rapid southern swing of Kleist's First Panzer Army. On 11 October the Germans reported 106,332 Soviet POWs and 212 tanks and 672 guns destroyed or captured.[155] Following up this success was the final act in the long-drawn-out and remarkably costly Romanian siege of Odessa. Having sealed off all land routes to the city in early August, the Romanians conducted a number of major offensives against the city, which ground down Soviet defences, but did not succeed in taking control of the city. Finally, with troops urgently needed for the defence of Crimea, the Soviet Black Sea Fleet evacuated Lieutenant-General G. P. Sofronov's Coastal Army from Odessa between 2 and 16 October. On 17 October the Romanians entered Odessa.[156] Goebbels immediately issued another *Sondermeldung* proclaiming the success of their ally, while German radio played the Romanian national anthem.[157] Hitler's euphoria took no account of the fact that Antonescu's army had suffered a staggering 98,000 casualties in less than two months of fighting at Odessa and that there were some 80 per cent casualties in the twelve divisions which took part.[158] As Hitler himself observed back in September, 'Antonescu is using in front of Odessa the tactics of the First World War.'[159] For Antonescu's part, he too was heedless of the cost and organised a grand parade in Bucharest for 8 November attended by the chief of the German Wehrmacht, Field Marshal Keitel, and King Michael.[160]

While the Axis powers celebrated their victories in the east, not everyone was quite so convinced by the veneer of success. In Italy Ciano noted in his diary on 20 October:

> Alfieri reports a long conference with von Ribbentrop, who has sung his usual song: victory is achieved, the Russian army crushed, England has reached the end of her days. And yet Moscow puts up very strong resistance and the armoured divisions are at a standstill, many German soldiers are bound to die with their mother's name on their lips before the flag of the Reich flies over the Kremlin. Meanwhile, winter is drawing near, and military operations will soon become very limited.[161]

No such qualms, however, dampened the popular mood in Germany, where the secret SD reports told of widespread euphoria stemming from the recent flood of *Sondermeldungen*. The war had after all, according to Nazi newspapers, been 'decided'. The SD poll from 16 October claimed that people took great heart from reports that the battlefields at Viaz'ma and Briansk were already 'far behind the front', and many comparisons were now being made with the final phase of the war in France, which suggested that the capture of Moscow, like the capture of Paris, would soon be followed by an armistice.[162] Goebbels observed such exaggerated expectations with growing trepidation, knowing that unless Soviet resistance soon collapsed, the German leadership's soaring public approval would. The German propaganda minister lamented that the term 'decision of the war' was being confused with 'ending of the war' and declared that the most important thing now was that the eastern front come to a 'definitive' conclusion.[163] In this respect it was not just the Soviets that stood to lose something in the fighting before Moscow. Germany had overplayed its hand in its public declarations by such a terrific extent that the prestige of the whole Nazi state, including its much-vaunted Wehrmacht, was now exposed to a very public defeat. Seizing Moscow would only confirm Germany's claims of triumph, while failure raised the prospect of a seemingly stunning Soviet victory, snatched, as it were, from the very jaws of defeat.

In spite of the evident optimism in German public opinion and the expectation that the Soviet Union had in fact been brought to its knees, it was precisely the audacity of such a claim that convinced record numbers of Germans to tune into foreign radio broadcasts.[164] Exposing the credibility gap in Nazi reporting on the war was proceeding apace, and Goebbels noted with evident alarm on 22 October that the stalling of Bock's front constituted 'a gigantic propaganda service' to the Allies. For this Goebbels found it convenient to blame 'General Winter'; however, the real culprit was the unrestrained hubris of his own propaganda ministry aided to no small extent by the reckless plans and heedless direction of the war by the German high command. Foreign propaganda, Goebbels observed, was now infused with 'new hope',[165] while Germans everywhere were beginning to wonder what had happened to their much-promised victory. As Ingeborg Ochsenknecht recalled from October 1941: 'For the first time I asked myself whether this "Führer", whom we admired so much, really knew what he was doing.'[166] At the same time British radio fed the worst fears of the German population by playing on the enormity of the Wehrmacht's losses in the east. The BBC Foreign Service broadcast the sound of a ticking clock and after every seventh tick a German voice stated: 'Every seven seconds a German dies in Russia. Is it your husband? Is it your son? Is it your brother?'[167]

Nor was Allied propaganda only targeting the German home front. Soldiers on the eastern front were often fed exaggerated reports about the effectiveness of British bombing, which, given Bomber Command's limited success in 1941, may well have proved a more potent contribution than the relatively inconsequential physical destruction caused.[168] As one German soldier in the east noted:

> We heard very little news from home, only snatches now and then over the wireless. What we heard wasn't always good – the bombing of our towns and cities was well known to us, and many of our first-line soldiers were in despair, especially those who had had bad news of their families in the bombed areas. A soldier was supposed to fight on the front and defend his country, and such demoralising news made our fight here in Russia a mockery.[169]

Airdropped Soviet leaflets further contributed to the propaganda offensive and similarly emphasised a fictitious level of destruction carried out by British bombing. One leaflet claimed that the German newspapers were withholding the true scale of the British aerial offensive, which included 1,000 tons of bombs being dropped on Cologne over a six-day period in July 1941, 500 tons of bombs being dropped on Bremen and more than 2,000 tons on the industrial area of the Ruhr. 'The bombardment will kill your parents, your wives, your children. The human victims are countless.'[170] Another leaflet described abysmal working conditions for German women who were said to be working for just 40 per cent of a man's income, while putting in ten- to twelve-hour days. German children were reported to be going hungry, and therefore youth crime was rising rapidly along with instances of child sexual exploitation and child prostitution. 'What is happening with your family?', the leaflet asked.[171]

From 1 August 1941 the Soviets even attempted to maintain regular leaflet drops to German lines providing propaganda under the title *Auslands-Nachrichten (Foreign News)*. Each leaflet included a series of short articles such as 'America Helps the USSR', 'Uprising in Yugoslavia', 'Romanian Oilfields in Flames', 'Czechoslovakian and Romanian Hospitals Overflowing with German Wounded', 'Peru Cuts Ties to Germany' and 'Hopkins Is Impressed on His Trip to Moscow'.[172] Another recurring Soviet leaflet dropped on German lines was *Nachrichten von der Front (News from the Front)*, which also included a series of short articles detailing military news from the eastern front. Articles appeared with titles such as 'Smashing the 307 IR [Infantry Regiment] of the 163 Infantry Division', 'Losses of the 312 IR', 'Success of the Red Partisans' and 'German Soldiers on the Losses of the Eastern Front'.[173] Other Soviet leaflets were more straightforward with simple satirical images such as Hitler standing on a great mound of German bodies and broken equipment looking into the distance through a telescope; behind him Göring and Goebbels are asking: 'Do you see victory yet, Adolf?' (see Illustration 15).[174] More macabre was a picture of skeletons lying in a foxhole with German helmets and the caption 'View into the Future', followed by the warning: 'This also awaits you if you continue this senseless war against Soviet Russia.'[175] Complementing this depiction was another leaflet with smiling German soldiers who had surrendered; the caption read: 'They will not die. Follow their example.'[176]

Many of the Soviet forays into propaganda were dismissed by German soldiers as crude, and at times even humorous, attempts at deception. Hellmuth H. wrote in a letter home on 23 October about a 'brisk paper war' that was being waged in the east. The Soviets, he stated, offered: '"*News from the Homeland*", "*Foreign News*" and even

Siehst Du schon den Sieg, Adolf?

15 In the autumn of 1941 Soviet aircraft dropped propaganda leaflets to German soldiers, mocking Hitler's claims of a quick victory over the Soviet Union.

"*News from the Front*" ... All these with passes to the Reds; there is absolutely no hope that anyone falls for it; the Russian seems to have no idea of crowd psychology or rather psychology at all.'[177] Yet if there was one chink in the amour of German morale in 1941 it was their losses. It was a point that Soviet propaganda repeatedly emphasised and was the one claim that even the most ardent Nazi officers found difficult to refute. Paul Stresemann noted how in the autumn of 1941: 'I had become resigned to losing my life … The stupidity and enormity of that war [were] really coming home to me, but I could see no way out. I could not desert, so what hope was there? I felt trapped, as did millions of my comrades.'[178] It was this sense of being trapped and constantly threatened by mortal peril that led increasing numbers of men to undertake radical measures. Erich Hager, a tanker with Arnim's 17th Panzer Division, noted in his diary on 20 October: 'Thomas shot himself in the leg. The left leg, with a Russian rifle.'[179] On the same day (20 October) Wilhelm Prüller, serving in Clössner's 25th Motorised Infantry Division, noted in his diary that a lieutenant had lost his nerve during a Russian attack and fled with all his men. Furthermore, Prüller noted that two non-commissioned officers were discovered to have shot themselves in the hand. 'Out of fear for their personal safety and hoping in this way to be able to lead a quieter and less dangerous life … It's scandalous, not only for themselves, but for the companies.'[180] Such behaviour was perhaps scandalous for the German army's much hallowed sense of honour, but when increasing numbers of men were prepared to shoot themselves in the belief that they were more likely to survive the war, the perils of the eastern front were starkly underlined. As Henning Kardell recalled from his experiences in the east in 1941: 'You knew it would be your turn one day. You didn't reckon to get to the end of the war alive.'[181]

Even given the distorted beliefs of the Nazi elite, the losses on the eastern front could hardly be ignored. In late September, before Operation Typhoon had even begun, Hitler observed: 'We've forgotten the bitter tenacity with which the Russians fought us during the First World War. In the same way, coming generations will see in the campaigns now in progress only the magnificent operation that it will have been, without giving any more thought to the numerous crises that we had to overcome by reason of this tenacity.'[182] Indeed by the middle of October Kluge, whose Fourth Army was directing the main drive on Moscow, made reference to an emergent crisis of confidence in the whole German operation to seize Moscow. On 15 October Army Group Centre's war diary noted: 'In the opinion of Field Marshal von Kluge the "psychologically most critical moment of the eastern campaign" had begun.' Kluge referred to the absence of winter clothing and shelter for the men, the difficulties of movement and the tough enemy resistance, which 'greatly hindered the continued advance of the weak attack groups'.[183]

That Kluge was having serious reservations about the course of the war is made clear by his decision to dispatch his trusted aide, Lieutenant Fabian von Schlabrendorff, to make contact with opposition groups in Germany in order to find out whether opposition was crystallising and assure them that '"one" was ready to act'.[184] The former diplomat and prominent anti-Hitler conspirator Ulrich von Hassell welcomed Kluge's offer of support, but the field marshal's queries about whether there was any guarantee that Britain would make peace soon after a change of regime was effected reminded Hassell 'with what naiveté the generals approach this problem'. Writing in his diary, Hassell recorded his reply: 'I told him [Kluge] there were no such guarantees and that there could be none ... The whole incident is gratifying because, for the first time, some kind of initiative comes from that source ... If we wait until the impossibility of victory becomes clear to the whole world we shall have lost the chance for an acceptable peace.'[185] Clearly the war in the east was having a polarising effect within the German leadership, with a spectrum of opinion ranging from those willing to proclaim imminent victory to those foreseeing Germany's impending doom. In reality, however, there was little ambiguity about Germany's perilous strategic predicament and, with Army Group Centre's great offensive now faltering, this would only become increasingly more evident.

A study of German field post by Martin Humburg referred to an 'autumn crisis' in 1941, which asserted that the many trials of the German advance through the Soviet Union had resulted in two psychological episodes affecting the mood of German soldiers. The first was the disappointment of hopes for outright victory in 1941, and the second was the realisation that a winter campaign had become inevitable.[186] The physical strains of the German advance with constant combat and sacrifice were often sustained by the promise of an eventual victory and release from the torments of war. Already during the summer months the mental strains of the eastern campaign had been excessive, but now with conditions steadily worsening and the war promising to continue through the long months of a Russian winter German morale suffered a blow that even the recent victories at Viaz'ma, Briansk, the Sea of Azov and Odessa could not counteract. The problem was that the *Ostheer* appeared to be winning all the battles, but not the war itself. As Helmut

Pabst complained in a letter home: 'What a country, what a war, where there's no pleasure in success, no pride, no satisfaction; only a feeling of suppressed fury.'[187] Similarly Harald Henry complained that after all the battles he had taken part in there was still no discernible end in sight. In a letter home on 20 October Henry wrote: 'How much longer shall it take! It must finally come to an end or at least we should get some relief. At all the great encirclement battles of Army Group Centre, Belostok, Minsk, Mogilev, Roslavl, Desna, Viaz'ma and Briansk we were out-standing and took part with heavy losses. For once one must allow us to have a break. It is not bearable any longer.'[188]

For the German soldier enduring the awesome pressures of combat, climate and the unrelenting order to advance, warfare in the east entailed a daily routine of great physical strain and severe mental hardship. Ernst Guicking noted on 19 October 'Here one goes crazy. Here one needs damn good nerves.'[189] Helmut Günther reflected on how the strains of war changed the men and the brutalising effect this had had. 'We had long since ceased to be the fellows who crossed the Bug River on 26 June 1941 at Brest-Litovsk. The constant being on-the-go, and the inexorable battle with mud, rain, snow and cold had burnt us out. We had become hard, hard towards others and towards our-selves.'[190] Max Kuhnert also alluded to the dropping morale and how this was linked to the diminishing prospects of ending the war and escaping the torments of the eastern front. 'Tempers were high because everybody was starving and dead tired besides being soaked to the skin; and the Russian artillery kept pumping shells in our direction, which of course did not help our morale ... We not only lost men and materials, even things like trucks, but most of all we lost a great deal of hope of ever getting out of such a darned mess.'[191] Rumours of relief, being brought off the line and rested, or even being transferred out of the Soviet Union altogether and assigned occupation duty in France were a common occurrence on the eastern front and appear to have pervaded most of the divisions. By the autumn of 1941, however, such rumours had often circulated so often that many disregarded such ideas in order to save themselves the eventual disappointment. Helmut Günther noted: 'At first, we still had a few hopes. Rumours made the rounds about our relief to France. Now we ... only believed what was at hand. Faith was generally a thing of the past!'[192]

In fact, in the middle of October 1941 a number of major formations were ordered back to the west from Bock's army group.

It was another element of the OKH's overreaction to the successes at Viaz'ma and Briansk and another dramatic weakening of Army Group Centre. Four infantry divisions and Feldt's 1st Cavalry Division were supposed to be transferred to France,[193] but as difficulties mounted and Bock's advance stalled only Feldt's 1st Cavalry Division was withdrawn from the front on 25 October (to be reorganised as the new 24th Panzer Division). In November Lieutenant-General Johann Sinnhuber's badly depleted 28th Infantry Division and most of Major-General Gustav Höhne's 8th Infantry Division followed suit and were sent to France for rebuilding. More worryingly, in November Bock would also see Kesselring, the command staff of Air Fleet 2 and Loerzer's II Air Corps (with thirteen air groups) all transferred to the Mediterranean, leaving Army Group Centre only Richthofen's VIII Air Corps.[194] While the prospect of a transfer to a far quieter and warmer part of Europe fed hopes of salvation within Army Group Centre's rank and file, in fact the withdrawal of Feldt's and Sinnhuber's divisions only increased the burden on the men who remained.[195]

At the same time, the constant losses steadily worsened the conditions and workload of the men left behind. The same distance of front always had to be held, only by fewer troops. Rest periods became shorter as labour-intensive tasks, such as sentry duty, digging entrenchments, ammunition distribution, conducting patrols and gathering local intelligence, rotated much faster among the men of the understrength and overstretched companies. Horst Lange's diary described the mood of the men including one young lieutenant as 'alarming' and went on to state that they 'cannot be bothered anymore with the war. They speak openly about "running away" during the next attack. One can hold them together only with force and unwavering determination.'[196] Although such flagrant acts of insubordination remained the exception rather than the rule, it does however highlight the depths to which German morale was sinking by the fourth month of the war in the east. More commonly German soldiers simply suffered through their daily torments, some still hoping for an outright victory and others preferring not to think beyond their own personal circumstances. Helmut Pabst addressed the question directly in a letter home: 'Have I had enough? No. What has to be, must be. We have to push on with all our energy.' He then, however, ominously drew attention to his veiled sense of foreboding: 'But there's another part of us which wakes us up at night and makes us restless – all of us, not just me.'[197] Even Léon Degrelle, a prominent Belgian fascist leader fighting with the volunteer Waffen-SS and recently arrived on the eastern front, wrote: 'Optimism was still very great, but one noted that certain things were passed over in silence.'[198]

Even success on the battlefield proved a relative, and not always positive, experience for the soldiers who endured the brutality and terror of the fighting. After one night attack Gottlob Bidermann, a German infantryman, described dark forms littering the battlefield with wounded enemy soldiers 'thrashing in agony before our positions'. This, however, was only the prelude to repeated Soviet assaults, all of which ended in failure. Describing the gruesome scene of the next attack, Bidermann's account continued:

> Within minutes we again faced another onslaught, and the sun climbed above the horizon to reveal the full horror of the battlefield. Pushed to hatred … their loud screams of "Urrah!" again lost in the deafening roar of exploding weapons. Over the din I heard the machine gunner cry, "I can't just keep on killing!" as he squeezed the trigger and held it tightly, sending a stream of bullets from the smoking MG barrel into the masses of attackers. Our Pak[199] projectiles screamed and tore holes in the collapsing ranks. This attack ground to a halt hardly fifty paces from the muzzle of our gun.[200]

Fresh attacks soon followed, with innumerable numbers of men thrown against the German lines in massed waves. The assaults continued for many hours until, sometime in the afternoon, the attacks ceased and Bidermann took stock of the shattering toll. '[W]e hardly remained conscious as we staggered through air thick with cordite fumes, ears ringing, bodies overcome and exhausted by the exertion and terror of battle.' He then drew attention to the appalling sight of bodies stacked high before the German positions. 'I recalled a story of how some defenders of a fortress during the Middle Ages stacked the dead in rows to be used as emergency defences. Now a comparison came to mind.' The cost to Soviet forces had been appalling, but Bidermann noted that his battalion had also suffered numerous casualties with Soviet forces managing to penetrate a section of the German line and having to be repulsed in costly hand-to-hand fighting. However, what was to higher authorities another victorious defensive battle left its mark on the weary and shaken defenders. 'Our only thoughts were to flee this nightmare, to escape from this place of filth, misery, and death, far away where no shells would fall.' However, the horror of such battles did not end for many of the men who witnessed and survived them. As Bidermann concluded; 'Long afterwards I could still hear the words of the machine gunner in my sleep, "I just can't keep killing!"'[201]

Because Hitler's war in the east so drastically exceeded what his hard-pressed armies could ever hope to achieve, he taxed his soldiers to the very limits of their physical and psychological capacity. Already in the middle of August Halder warned that Army Group Centre could sustain one last major offensive, and after this was directed into Ukraine (for the battle of Kiev) yet another was formulated towards Moscow as Operation Typhoon. Now that Typhoon was approaching the limits of its advance, as a result of German fatigue, lack of supplies, bad weather, woeful German strategic direction and stout Soviet resistance, it was the exhausted German soldier who was once again expected to bear up and achieve ever more with increasingly less. A breaking point was inevitable and soon the German command would have to accept the verdict that its forces could no longer advance in spite of their orders. In the meantime the men of Army Group Centre trudged forward as best they could, wondering what their fate would be as the Russian winter drew closer and difficulties mounted. For one German soldier writing home on 18 October there was only one sure salvation, 'when we one day leave this baneful country'.[202]

7 WEATHERING THE STORM

'Wait, for I'll return, defying every death' (Konstantin Simonov)

For all the problems Army Group Centre was confronting on the road to Moscow, from the Soviet perspective it became evident by the second week of October that the Soviet capital would soon be on the front line. Stalin was so concerned at the inexorable advance of German forces that on 15 October he ordered the evacuation of the government to Kuibyshev some 2,500 kilometres east of Moscow.[1] There were also orders issued to begin dismantling and transporting major industrial enterprises to the east, while those that could not be saved, including some 1,119 educational, administrative and industrial institutions, were to be fitted with explosives and prepared for destruction.[2] Such measures, however, should not be understood as an abandonment of Moscow. There was certainly no intention of surrendering the city, only salvaging what could be saved and denying the rest to the Germans. There is no greater symbol of Stalin's determination to defend Moscow than his decision to remain in the Kremlin even after the evacuation orders had been issued. Many have claimed this decision galvanised resistance within the Red Army, inspiring hopes that the city could in fact be saved and elevating Stalin to the status of a front-line commander.[3] It was in the fighting before Moscow that the popular rallying cry 'Stalin is with us!' was born.[4]

Yet Stalin's refusal to leave the city did not avert the scenes of panic which erupted throughout the city on 16 October. Understanding the roots of the Moscow panic tells us much about the Soviet government's mismanagement of the crisis rather than, as some have suggested, a collapse of morale among the city's population. Indeed the very idea of a 'Moscow panic' suggests that the motive for the looting and lawlessness was fear and, while this was no doubt part of the equation, a good deal of the disorderly conduct could better be characterised as anger and frustration at being abandoned by party officialdom and factory managers. In this sense it was not, as the Germans believed, 'the appearance of an anti-Soviet mood in the population', rather the wholesale desertion of the city by the civil and political leadership, which sparked much of the 'panic'. As the Russian historian Mikhail Gorinov observed: 'the "hysteria" was passed to the masses "from above"; in this way the "flight from Moscow" was initiated by the leaders of the factories, having suggested by their own efforts that the workers evacuate to the east'.[5] After months of official declarations calling for the greatest sacrifices and insisting upon an iron resolve in the face of the enemy, the flight of the Soviet elite now smacked of an insufferable hypocrisy. On 17 October N. K. Verzhbitskii described the deeply resentful mood among the masses: 'They began to remember and count up all the insults, oppression, injustices, pressure, bureaucratic machinations of officialdom, contempt and self-puffery of party members, draconian orders, deprivations, systematic deception of the masses, the newspapers' braying self-congratulations ... Can a city really hold out when it's in such a mood?'[6]

In fact for a significant portion of the population it was precisely their determination to defend their homes that fuelled their anger. Hundreds of thousands had been working long days digging anti-tank defences on the immediate approaches to the city; prior to this many had been working themselves to exhaustion in the armament factories, while at night they endured the Luftwaffe's bombing. To these people it was simply inconceivable that Moscow could suddenly be abandoned, and even though this was not the Soviet leadership's intention, the perception was enough to spark revolt. Although the evacuation of the Soviet government, foreign missions and the city's major industrial enterprises constituted a prudent step in the face of the emergent threat to the city, it was neither explained to the people of Moscow nor managed in a manner befitting the sensitivities of its population. To the city's exasperated onlookers it was the Soviet elite who had asked so much and sacrificed so little and who, in the face of real danger, were now seen to be abandoning Muscovites to their fate by saving themselves first.

Beyond the perceived injustice of Moscow's evacuation, another important aspect in understanding the advent of the city's panic was the very real fear that people felt. This, however, was also greatly exacerbated by the gross incompetence and blatant mismanagement of the crisis by the Soviet government. Since the start of October Soviet authorities had been deliberately coy on the exact developments taking place on the central part of the front, reluctant to reveal the scope of yet another devastating defeat. The population was still absorbing the news of deep German advances in Ukraine as well as the recently undertaken siege of Leningrad in the north. Indeed it was only on 7 October that the first official Soviet reference was made to the new German offensive towards Moscow, which referred to 'heavy fighting in the direction of Viaz'ma'.[7] On the same day (7 October) Lozovsky, the Soviet deputy minister of foreign affairs, curiously announced that the capture of any one Soviet city would not determine the outcome of the war, which, as the BBC correspondent Alexander Werth noted, 'was as if he was already preparing the press for the possible loss of Moscow.'[8]

While the true depths of the calamity engulfing the Western, Reserve and Briansk Fronts went largely unreported in Moscow, the population was well informed by unofficial sources that the situation at the front was developing into another debacle. Peter Miller, a well-known historian living in Moscow, recorded on 7 October: 'The silence of the SovInformBuro [Soviet Information Bureau] is irritating, although people no longer read [its] communiqués ... There is a mood of catastrophe and fatalism. The shops are empty, even coffee has disappeared ... There is a feeling of approaching catastrophe in the air and endless rumours: Orel has been surrendered, Viaz'ma has been surrendered, the Germans have got to Maloiaroslavets ... The mood is particularly bad today.'[9] While wild rumours and unsubstantiated gossip fuelled a rising sense of panic, the absence of official statements to confirm or deny a true picture of events only contributed to people's worst fears. Such absurdities reached new heights when on 8 October the lead article in *Pravda*, the Soviet daily newspaper, concerned 'The Work of Women in War Time'.[10] To counter the spread of rumours about a crisis at the front Soviet officials began issuing warnings that enemy spies and agents were attempting 'to disorganise the rear and to create panic'. Even so by 12 October *Pravda* was itself making reference to the 'terrible danger' threatening the country.[11] Yet as far as most people knew the fighting was concentrated around Viaz'ma, and indeed this is where the Germans were tied up for some time eliminating the pocket they had created there. Yet when German forces suddenly appeared at Mozhaisk, only 100 kilometres from the Soviet capital, confirmation that another disaster had befallen the Red Army appeared irrefutable. This, coupled with the sudden rush to evacuate the government quarter and mine hundreds of prominent buildings, only acted to confirm the danger Moscow was in. It seemed to many that German tanks would reach the capital within a day or two and that the city itself might well fall to the Germans directly off the march just as Orel, Viaz'ma, Briansk and Kalinin all had. As Olga Sapozhnikova recalled, from 16 October: 'There was a feeling the Germans might appear in the street at any moment.'[12] Likewise, Stephan Mikoyan noted: 'Rumours of the proximity of the Germans spread like wildfire alongside the news that major industries had been evacuated and the city's most important buildings mined. This sparked a general panic.'[13]

Contributing to the spiralling sense of dread within the city was an alarming mix-up, never fully explained, at the SovInformBuro radio network. On 16 October, the opening day of the Moscow panic, the loudspeakers broadcasting the morning news suddenly broke off and a song began playing. Many at first assumed it to be the patriotic Soviet song, 'The March of the Airmen', but the melody was wrong and only some recognised it as the 'Horst Wessel Lied', the anthem of the Nazi party from 1930 to 1945. Had the Germans already begun to take over the city? Moments later the song cut out and the announcer returned to the morning news without any explanation.[14] Such events further intensified the already wildly extravagant rumours and led to suggestions that Stalin had been arrested in a coup d'état and that the Germans had reached Fili, where the Mozhaisk highway enters Moscow.[15] Others even suggested that German paratroops had landed in Red Square and that German troops wearing Red Army uniforms had already entered Moscow.[16] Overwrought nerves were stretched to breaking point and, when people began to vent their fears and frustrations in acts of public disobedience, mobs quickly fired the wave of discontent and the results were manifest in riots, looting and frantic attempts to flee the city. There were even public instances of people denouncing Soviet power, cries of support for Hitler and calls to 'Beat the Jews.'[17]

For all that the Moscow panic might suggest about the public mood, one should beware of paying too much attention to its more extreme elements.[18] Much of the disorder passed without violence, and many more people observed the unruly behaviour than took part in it.[19] Even more to the point, what took place could be characterised more by the fear that the capital was being surrendered to the Germans and by frustration at the departure of ruling elites.[20] There is far less evidence of a pervasive anti-Soviet sentiment within Moscow; in fact the young Russian urban working class constituted the most active supporters of the Soviet state in 1941.[21] There was also no collapse in the resolve of average Muscovites to pursue the war with Germany, only dismay at how that war was being managed.[22] When on 16 October there were no newspapers, no shops open, no metro and no money for wages, and workers turned up to factories that were either locked and abandoned or being fitted with explosives, it appeared to many that the city was being left to its doom. In this sense, the ensuing chaos was largely a response to the perceived neglect of the city's defence[23] and not, as some have claimed, a panic induced simply by the approach of German forces.[24]

As the city descended into turmoil, on 16 October Stalin hosted a meeting in which he ordered the immediate return of services to the city. The metro was to operate again, unpaid workers were to receive their money and shops were to reopen.[25] Moreover, A. I. Shakhurin, the commissar for the aviation industry, made a public address on 17 October appealing for calm and assuring the population that Moscow would be defended 'stubbornly, fiercely, to that last drop of our blood'.[26] These measures did not completely put an end to the unrest, but they did ensure that the disorder had peaked by 17 October.[27] Indeed when on 16 October Stalin was told of the disturbances and lawlessness, including suggestions of widespread looting, his reaction was, for a man so insistent on absolute obedience, remarkably sedate. The Soviet dictator told Shakhurin: 'Well, that's not so bad. I thought things would have been worse.'[28] Yet parallel to his more benevolent measures to appease the population of Moscow Stalin never lost faith in the more trusted methods of the NKVD, which were also working to restore order.[29] One such officer, Mikhail Ivanovich, recalled after the war: 'It was necessary, absolutely necessary, to establish order. And yes, we did shoot people who refused to leave the shops and offices where food and other goods were stored.'[30]

By 19 October the unrest in Moscow had ceased. In a 24-hour period from 19 to 20 October city authorities detained 1,530 people, of whom 1,442 were soldiers absent without leave from their units; the remainder, fewer than one hundred people, were arrested for vandalism and disturbing the peace – a remarkably low figure for a city of Moscow's size. Indeed the only conceivable threat stemmed from the fourteen people arrested for being '*agents provocateurs*' – enemy agents. Accordingly Stalin's decision on 20 October proclaiming Moscow to be in a 'state of siege' and authorising draconian measures, including summary executions, was more a response to the approaching German threat rather than a reaction to internal strife.[31] The so-called state of siege was a new emergency designation for strategically important areas, aimed to guarantee maximum mobilisation of resources, while also ensuring swift measures for provocateurs, spies and anyone propagating unrest.[32] Six days after Moscow's 'state of siege' was declared (on 26 October) Tula also received the designation and three days after that (on 29 October) the whole of Crimea was determined to be under siege.[33]

While the episode of the Moscow panic caused a serious disturbance to the operation of the Soviet capital for a period of two to three days it was little more than that and should not be construed as any kind of substantive challenge to Soviet power or cast doubt on the resolve of average Muscovites to go on prosecuting the war against Germany. The chaos which erupted on 16 October was built on a rising amount of discontent, which the Soviet authorities fed by their gross mismanagement of the crisis confronting the city and the rampant, if unfounded, fear that German forces were about to break into the city. In fact Stalin was preparing for two eventualities: first, providing everything possible for Moscow's defence and, secondly, being able to continue governing the Soviet Union in case of the loss of the city. Without knowing the true extent of the difficulties confronting Bock's army group, Stalin's decision to evacuate the Soviet government, essential industry and foreign missions to Kuibyshev was altogether prudent. At the same time the Soviet contingency to fall back towards the east demonstrates the folly of German hopes that the seizure of Moscow might somehow force an end to the war. That hope was in any case predicated on the idea that the battle for Moscow could be won by Germany and, given that Bock had almost exhausted his strength 100 kilometres from the city, Army Group Centre was going to have a hard time just reaching the city, to say nothing of conquering it. In the meantime Moscow was being transformed into a colossal battleground for urban warfare so that if, contrary to Hitler's current order, German forces did indeed attempt to take the city by storm they would be made to pay dearly for it.

The shoulders upon which the defence of Moscow most directly rested were those of the gifted, but utterly ruthless Marshal Zhukov. Born in 1896, Zhukov came from the town of Strelkovka, which derives its name from the Russian word *streltsy* (archers) because Ivan the Terrible established his archers' camp here to defend Moscow from invading Tatars.[34] Headstrong and uncompromising, Zhukov was at the best of times a demanding superior, but at the worst he could also be brutal and outright pitiless in the sacrifice of his men. Yet these were precisely the traits which endeared him to Stalin and caused him to entrust Zhukov with the most critical sectors of the Soviet front. Accordingly on 13 October Zhukov issued orders demanding the summary execution of 'cowards and panic-mongers that leave the battlefield and retreat from their positions without permission'. Nor was this an idle threat: a week later Zhukov had the commander of the 17th Rifle Division executed without trial for having allowed his forces to withdraw on a number of occasions without permission from above.[35] Yet, perhaps because of his ruthlessness, Zhukov projected a certain unflappable self-belief in his abilities, which in some instances in his career allowed for gross overconfidence, but in a crisis such as at Moscow in October 1941 meant there was no hint of defeatism at the top. In late October, with Soviet forces still doggedly on the defensive before Moscow, Zhukov was already thinking ahead to an offensive against Bock. Writing to A. A. Zhdanov at the Leningrad Front war council, Zhukov boldly asserted: 'I have cobbled together a reasonable organization and have virtually stopped the enemy advance, and you know how I propose to go on: I will wear him out and then beat him.'[36] Zhukov's resolve to beat the Germans, while they were still advancing on Moscow, probably contains more than a touch of bravado, but the idea that Zhukov could defend Moscow was hardly baseless.

By 20 October half a million Muscovites had been mobilised to dig a total of 8,000 kilometres of trenches and anti-tank ditches on the immediate approaches to the city. In addition some 300 kilometres of barbed wire were laid out.[37] As Zhukov himself recalled: 'In those days I saw thousands and thousands of Moscow women, who were unused to heavy labour and who had left their city apartments lightly clad, work on those impassable roads, in that mud, digging anti-tank ditches and trenches, setting up anti-tank obstacles and barricades, and hauling sandbags.'[38] Inside the city itself a myriad of roadblocks were set up, and countless strong points were built on top of buildings and inside people's apartments. Roads were mined and bridges fitted with explosives. The city was defended by an outer 'main' defensive line running in a semi-circle around Moscow for a radius of 16 kilometres. This was then augmented by three separate 'urban' lines inside the city itself, which were designated 'circular railway line', 'urban ring A' and 'urban ring B'.[39] The Moscow City Council directed construction and each district was issued detailed instructions on what to build and where.[40] Irina Bogolyubskaya recalled soldiers coming into her family's apartment and setting up a machine-gun emplacement at one of their windows overlooking the street. 'They were preparing for street fighting', she noted.[41] There was talk at the time of Moscow being transformed into a 'super Madrid', a reference to Madrid's role in the Spanish civil war, which held out under siege from November 1936 until its fall in March 1939.[42]

Emergency measures were taken to produce rudimentary weapons for the new volunteer units being raised around the city. I. E. Kozlov, the director of a popular soft-drink factory, began adapting his production lines to turn out half-litre 'Molotov cocktails'. Likewise, many of Moscow's concrete and metallurgical factories were instructed to start producing 'hedgehogs',[43] barbed-wire entanglements, reinforced-concrete pillboxes and fortified gun emplacements.[44] As one official Soviet account claimed: 'Muscovites made their city into an unassailable fortress … Every building became a bastion, every street a fortified area. Moscow bristled with barricades, metal tank traps and barbed wire.'[45] Even if Soviet-era claims are prone to a degree of embellishment, there can be no question that Moscow was preparing itself for a mighty struggle. Indeed, when one looks at the gruelling German experience of urban warfare in 1941 at the Brest fortress, Mogilev and Dnepropetrovsk, not to mention Romania's experience at Odessa, capturing a city of Moscow's size block by block would surely have proven prohibitively costly (see Illustration 16).[46]

Even assuming, however, that the Germans did manage to seize control of Moscow L. P. Beria, the head of the NKVD, was preparing to mimic the success at Kiev by mining dozens of prominent city buildings in anticipation of German occupancy. The Bolshoi Theatre, for example, was fitted with explosives in new specially developed anti-magnetic containers, which made the mines much more difficult to

16 As Army Group Centre approached Moscow, the Soviet capital became increasingly fortified with roadblocks, tank traps, mines and concealed firing positions.

detect.[47] Even before the German occupation the NKVD had planned for more than 1,000 of Moscow's prominent buildings and enterprises to be destroyed.[48] In addition, throughout the last two weeks of October some 200 trains and 80,000 trucks left Moscow for the Volga and the Urals transporting the essential equipment of nearly 500 factories.[49] As one historian concluded: 'Had the Germans actually taken Moscow, they would have found a desert.'[50] The Soviet security services also cultivated special 'stay-behind teams', which were to act in a range of roles including gathering intelligence, conducting sabotage and carrying out targeted assassinations. One troop of four performers was recruited by the NKVD to stage shows for the Germans hoping to be successful enough to gain an audience with high-level Nazi or Wehrmacht officials. In this case they were to conclude their show by hurling disguised grenades into the audience and killing as many Germans as possible.[51] However, the defence of the city depended far more on the Red Army than the NKVD.

At the start of 1941 Moscow had a population of 4.2 million people, but a combination of military service, industrial relocation and civilian evacuation[52] had reduced this to 3.1 million by October

1941.[53] To augment Zhukov's forces, each of Moscow's twenty-five districts was instructed to raise one battalion of so-called *opolchenie* – a form of people's militia that usually consisted of poorly equipped volunteers with little or no military training. There were some 7,963 volunteers in the first week of the appeal, which, given that those inclined to volunteer for military service had already had ample opportunity to do so, was not a bad result, but still well short of the desired total. The volunteers were assembled into the 3rd Communist Division and committed to the front at the end of the month.[54] Another five Moscow rifle divisions were created from volunteers, subunits of the regular army, new conscripts and so-called destruction battalions[55] established earlier in the war.[56] An additional 100,000 workers started military training in their free time, while some 17,000 women signed up to train as nurses and medical assistants.[57] As Zhukov observed, many of his new troops 'had a lot to learn', but, he added, 'all of them were distinguished by common traits – a high degree of patriotism, an unshakable determination and confidence in ultimate victory. It was no accident that these voluntary units became outstanding fighting forces after they had gained some military experience.'[58] Putting aside the Soviet-era bravado of Zhukov's claim, the fact was that he desperately needed all the reinforcements he could get and even the dubious *opolchenie* units were better than nothing.[59] In Zhukov's favour the fighting had transformed into a slogging series of German frontal attacks along the main roads leading to Moscow. With the German panzer forces deprived of their dangerous fast-moving envelopments, even *opolchenie* units could play a role, although a costly one, in Moscow's defence.

When Zhukov took over the Western Front defending the approaches to Moscow, he commanded just eleven rifle divisions, sixteen armoured brigades and more than forty artillery regiments, approximately 90,000 men in total. The Mozhaisk Defensive Line was the rallying point for all these forces, with Lieutenant-General K. K. Rokossovsky's Sixteenth Army defending Volokolamsk, Major-General D. D. Leliushenko's Fifth Army covering Mozhaisk, Major-General K. D. Golubev's Forty-Third Army manning positions at Maloiaroslavets and Lieutenant-General I. G. Zakharkin's Forty-Ninth Army defending Kaluga.[60] Yet from mid October these forces were augmented not only by newly raised forces from Moscow, but also by units rushed from the Soviet interior.[61] By the end of October some thirteen additional rifle divisions and five armoured brigades were delivered to Zhukov's front.[62] Moreover, Lieutenant-General M. G. Efremov's newly formed Thirty-Third Army was inserted into the line at Naro-Fominsk between Leliushenko's Fifth and Golubev's Forty-Third Armies.[63] By 20 October much of the Mozhaisk Defensive Line was in German hands, but Bock's army group had only pushed Zhukov's forces back and were still almost 100 kilometres from Moscow. The battle for the Soviet capital was still only just beginning, but a week after Nazi propaganda had proclaimed the eastern campaign to have been 'decided' Zhukov was effectively halting German progress. With their backs to Moscow the military council of the Western Front extolled its soldiers to maximum effort to halt the German advance once and for all. 'The homeland calls on us to stand like an indestructible wall and to bar the Fascist hordes from our beloved Moscow. What we require now, as never before, are vigilance, iron discipline, organization, determined action, unbending will for victory and a readiness for self-sacrifice.'[64]

Such stirring speeches, intended to inspire the men of the Red Army to glorious deeds on the battlefield, were a common theme of Soviet historiography, but a recent study by Roger Reese suggests new insights into the morale and motivation of the average Soviet soldier. Reese rejects both 'draconian punishment' and 'love of country' as the popular, but contrasting explanations for the Red Army's effectiveness in World War II. His study suggests that the Soviet soldier's performance depended far more upon extrinsic influences like good leadership, thorough training and support within both his primary group and the society at large, as well as intrinsic motivations such as patriotism, hatred of the enemy and the moral justification of a just war.[65] Such research takes us much closer to an explanation of the radically different responses within the Red Army to the German invasion in 1941 and suggests that painting a picture of the Red Army's motivations in broad brush strokes is inherently problematic. It also conclusively rejects the popular Nazi image of the Soviet soldier, which has found its way into numerous post-war German memoirs,[66] as an ostensibly mechanical being devoid of independent reason and even the primal instinct for self-preservation.

There can be no question that the Red Army suffered remarkable losses in 1941. In the first six months of the war the Soviet Western Front alone suffered 956,000 irrecoverable losses – almost double its initial starting number, meaning it was nearly completely wiped out twice in 1941 alone.[67] Yet in contrast to another Nazi-era myth the Soviet Union's survival was not just a matter of dragooning ever more masses of men into the ranks from an ostensibly endless manpower reserve; new recruits had to want to fight the German enemy.[68] Here in many respects was the real source of strength for the Soviet state. Not because the men of the Red Army wanted to fight for Stalin's regime – many of course had good cause to revile it[69] – but because the Soviet state benefited from a wider range of emotions, which transcended any singular national, ideological or political construction. In other words many people did fight for socialism, just not always Stalin's particular brand of it, while others fought, in spite of the socialist system, for their homeland and in the hope of increased political freedoms after the war.[70] As one Soviet citizen summed up his feelings:

> Even those of us who knew that our government was wicked, that there was little to choose between the SS and NKVD except their language, and who despised the hypocrisy of Communist politics – we felt that we had to fight. Because every Russian who had lived through the revolution and the thirties had felt a breeze of hope, for the first time in the history of our people. We were like the bud at the tip of a root which had wound its way for centuries under rocky soil. We felt ourselves to be within inches of the open sky.
>
> We knew that we would die, of course. But our children would inherit two things: A land free of the invader; and time, in which the progressive ideals of communism might emerge.[71]

Stalin shrewdly stimulated a degree of cultural liberalisation to exploit historical and religious sentiments which he correctly judged would add support to his war effort. There was also something of a cultural offensive launched in 1941 to garner support from every possible sector of the creative intelligentsia, whether it was fine arts or the humanities. Historians stressed patriotic themes and suggested a continuity between the previously taboo Russian imperial past and the Soviet present. Composers brought the suffering and heroism of the war to the stage with works such as Shostakovich's 'Leningrad' Symphony and Prokofiev's opera *War and Peace*. Film directors started work on new war epics such as Ilya Kopalin and Leonid Varlamov's 1942 masterpiece *Moscow Strikes Back*.[72] Perhaps most influential of all, however, were the Soviet writers, many of whom became popular war correspondents with huge followings. The best known were Ilya Ehrenburg, Vasily

Grossman and Konstantin Simonov. Their poems, newspaper articles, pamphlets and fictional pieces all dramatically depicted the wartime themes of loss, pain, patriotism, conviction, revenge and service to the state.[73] Aleksei Surkov's 1941 *A Soldier's Oath* also faithfully illustrates many of these themes and delivers them in the bombastic, but highly effective prose of the time:

> I am a Russian man, a soldier of the Red Army. My country has put a rifle in my hand, and has sent me to fight against the black hordes of Hitler that have broken into my country. Stalin has told me that the battle will be hard and bloody, but that victory will be mine.
>
> I heard Stalin, and know it will be so. I am the 193 million of free Soviet men, and to all of them Hitler's yoke is bitterer than death …
>
> Mine eyes have beheld thousands of dead bodies of women and children, lying along the railways and the highways. They were killed by the German vultures … The tears of women and children are boiling in my heart. Hitler the murderer and his hordes shall pay for these tears with their wolfish blood; for the avenger's hatred knows no mercy.[74]

Demonising the Germans and extolling the men of the Red Army to serve as avengers was one side of the Soviet cultural offensive, but providing support and buttressing the sorrow of its increasingly brutalised people was equally important. In the six months and nine days of the war in 1941 the Soviet Union suffered the staggering loss of 4,473,820 fighting men and women.[75] With losses on such an unprecedented scale, the need for public coping mechanisms, in place of officially prohibited religious and spiritual references, presented Soviet writers with a unique challenge. Yet Simonov's masterful poem 'Wait for Me', which first appeared in the autumn of 1941, was a form of secular prayer combining boundless faith with irrational conviction. The poem professed that a lost loved one would in fact return so long as hope was never abandoned.[76] The poem was an immediate success, and countless women waiting for news from lost loved ones recited it almost like a mantra throughout 1941 and 1942.

> Wait for me, and I'll return, only wait very hard.
> Wait, when you are filled with sorrow as you watch the yellow rain;
> Wait, when the wind sweeps the snowdrifts,
> Wait in the sweltering heat,
> Wait when others have stopped waiting, forgetting their yesterdays.

Wait even when from afar, no letters come to you,
Wait even when others are tired of waiting.
Wait even when my mother and son think I am no more,
And when friends sit around the fire, drinking to my memory.
Wait and do not hurry to drink to my memory too;
Wait, for I'll return, defying every death.
And let those who did not wait say that I was lucky;
They will never understand that in the midst of death,
You, with your waiting, saved me.
Only you and I will know how I survived:
It's because you waited as no one else did.[77]

'A combination of states has at last been formed against Hitlerism' (Viacheslav Molotov)

While Bock's armies desperately fought their way to Moscow, a more immediate threat to the people of the city was posed by Kesselring's bombers. Since July when Air Fleet 2 acquired air bases within range of the Soviet capital, Moscow had come under sporadic attack with seventy-six night raids and eleven day missions between 21 July 1941 and 5 April 1942.[78] Although it was extraneous to the Luftwaffe's dual tasks of suppressing Soviet air activity and providing tactical support to the army, Hitler insisted upon a strategic bombing campaign as a reprisal for Soviet attacks on Bucharest and Helsinki.[79] The first German air raid against Moscow on the night of 21–22 July was also the largest the *Ostheer* ever undertook, involving 195 bombers and dropping 104 tons of high explosives along with 46,000 incendiary bombs. By 25 October bombers had conducted fifty-nine air raids and dropped a total of 1,000 tons of high explosives, which amounted to only half of what the Royal Air Force would drop in a single night during their strategic bombing campaign over Germany in 1944. Indeed many of Kesselring's air raids were decidedly weak numerically. Of the seventy-five raids conducted up to 6 December 1941, just three involved more than one hundred aircraft, six involved more than fifty bombers, nineteen between fifteen and forty planes, and fifty-nine German air raids contained between three and ten aircraft.[80] It was nowhere near enough to devastate Moscow. Even the first large raid on 21–22 July resulted in only 130 people killed and 241 wounded and 37 buildings destroyed.[81] One figure put the total damage to the city as a result of

German bombing at just 3 per cent.[82] Yet the resources the bombing campaign demanded constrained Kesselring's other operations and led to what he referred to as a 'harmful dissipation'.[83] Another problem was that the Luftwaffe's air bases were still a long way from Moscow, meaning that bombs had to be substituted for extra fuel, with the result that the tonnage dropped on the Soviet capital could not always justify the heavy losses in aircraft. By the autumn the aircraft sometimes had to be dug out of overnight snow, and the cold made it difficult to get the engines started.[84] As Hans Rudel noted of the autumn conditions: 'Gradually the cold weather sets in and we get a foretaste of approaching winter. The fall in the temperature gives me, as engineer officer of the squadron, all kinds of technical problems, for suddenly we begin to have trouble with our aircraft which is only caused by the cold.'[85] By the beginning of October the serviceability rate throughout the Luftwaffe's bomber force had sunk to just 40 per cent and was continuing to decline, reaching 32 per cent by December 1941. Indeed the Luftwaffe was losing an average of 268 bombers, either as total losses or from damage, every month between June and November 1941.[86]

Soviet countermeasures ensured that the approaches to Moscow were defended by almost 800 medium anti-aircraft guns, more than 600 large searchlights and nearly 600 fighter planes. Inside the city itself more anti-aircraft guns were positioned on the top of buildings, along with smaller searchlights and more than 100 barrage balloons intended to make the Germans fly high and to confuse their aim.[87] As squadron commander Hans-Georg Bätcher stated: 'The night raids against Moscow were the most difficult missions that I ever flew on the Eastern Front ... The anti-aircraft fire was extremely intense and the gunners fired with frightening accuracy.'[88] Likewise, Richard Wernicke described the fear he experienced while flying over Moscow. 'It was terrible: the air was full of lead, and they were firing very accurately. We hadn't seen anything like this before.'[89] In fact Moscow's air defences far exceeded even those of London during the Blitz. The American war correspondent Henry Cassidy was surprised after the first German air raid on Moscow by how little damage there had been. 'What had seemed to be a withering raid turned out to be a light one. Most of the impression of intensity ... came from the violence not of the bombing, but of the anti-aircraft defences.'[90] The strength of Moscow's aerial defence shocked even the German air crews who had flown over London. 'The raids on Moscow caused me great anxiety. Crews shot down had to be written off, the effectiveness of the Russian anti-aircraft guns and searchlights impressing even our airmen who had flown over England. Also as time went on Russian defence fighters appeared in increasing numbers.'[91] Indeed some of those fighters towards the end of 1941 were British Hurricanes and American Tomahawks shipped to the Soviet Union as part of the Lend-Lease deal.[92] Another feature of the first German raid over Moscow was that it included one of the first recorded instances of a Soviet pilot ramming a German aircraft, which Soviet sources claim occurred some 300 times during the course of the war. On this occasion Boris Vasiliev flying a Yak-1 fighter used his propeller to saw off the tail of a German bomber.[93]

While the strategic bombing campaign was much weaker than the London Blitz, and Moscow was far better defended, it was still a harrowing experience for the city's population.[94] Incendiary bombs caused hundreds of fires which sometimes suffocated people hiding in their air-raid shelters, while others were buried alive when high explosive bombs demolished whole apartment buildings. The Kremlin itself suffered some damage, as did the Bolshoi Theatre,[95] but, as in London, life in the air-raid shelters soon took on a routine of its own. Indeed, after a time the risk was judged sufficiently low that there were those who simply refused to seek the safety of the underground bunkers. One engineer at a tank factory observed the development: 'They bombed the city, but the designers and the copyists did not leave work.'[96] Stalin himself took refuge in the Kirovskaia metro station where he was provided with a specially prepared compartment of a train hidden from view by plywood panelling. On another occasion Stalin felt sufficiently safe to observe an air raid while returning to his dacha outside the city in the early hours of the morning.[97] Of course German propaganda told a very different story, insisting that their air raids were highly effective. On 5 August German radio announced: 'Strong units of German aviation are each night subjecting this major industrial centre of the country to devastating bombardment. Factories and plants on the outskirts of Moscow are destroyed, the Kremlin is destroyed, Red Square is destroyed ... Moscow has entered into a final phase of ruination.'[98] Contrastingly the news of German raids on Moscow had a distinctly humbling effect on the British public, as one banner hanging in a London street read: 'Quiet nights, thanks to Russia.'[99]

By October 1941 Kesselring's aerial campaign mimicked the exhaustion and overextension of Bock's armies. Already in the summer

Field Marshal Erhard Milch, the inspector-general of the Luftwaffe, had reported on the scores, even hundreds, of damaged and inoperable aircraft littering the eastern air fields.[100] By November 1941 continued heavy losses depleted aircraft strengths to the point where reserve stocks were exhausted and production could not keep pace with losses.[101] The advent of bad weather further compromised serviceability rates and slowed the pace of operations, prompting Major-General Hoffman von Waldau, the chief of the operations department of the Luftwaffe, to comment in his diary on 16 October: 'Our wildest dreams have been washed out by rain and snow.'[102] Between 22 and 25 October, Kesselring's Air Fleet 2 was able to conduct only between 614 and 662 sorties a day, which was a small fraction of what it had achieved at the start of the eastern campaign.[103] Moreover, with winter looming, worse was to come, and when the recently appointed inspector-general of fighters, Colonel Werner Mölders (who was the Luftwaffe's top-ranking fighter ace with 101 accredited 'kills'), commissioned a study on the likely effects of winter on the Luftwaffe's eastern operations and sent the damning results to Hitler, Göring, Keitel, Brauchitsch and the chief of staff of the Luftwaffe, General of Aviation Hans Jeschonnek, there was upheaval. Göring, as head of the Luftwaffe, was incensed at Mölders's actions and strongly chided him for causing such alarm.[104] Clearly, even the high standing and remarkable influence of a man like Mölders was welcome only so long as his news supported what the high command wanted to hear. Dire predictions were analogous to defeatist thinking, and there was no room for that in the Third Reich's celebrated triumph of the will. As Mölders told his wife: 'The *Reichsmarschall* [Göring] always says: My Führer, we can do this, we can do that. But, Ponny – we cannot do more.'[105]

When German bombers attacked the Soviet capital for the first time in July Lieutenant-General Semyon Zhavaronokov, the commander of the Soviet Naval Air Force, decided to organise reprisal attacks on Berlin. Although he knew the physical damage from such attacks would be minimal, he was motivated by the potential blow to German prestige as well as the corresponding boost to Soviet morale by taking the war to Germany. With the Wehrmacht already deep inside Soviet borders, the only access point to Berlin was from an airfield on the Estonian island of Saaremaa, and Zhavaronokov dispatched his first raid of fifteen DB-3T bombers on 7 August 1941. As expected, the damage was largely insignificant, but all the planes hit their target area and returned home safely. Berlin's air defences, on the other hand, were taken completely by surprise, with their early warning systems directed overwhelmingly towards the west. On the following night (8–9 August) Zhavaronokov repeated the raid, dropping 72 bombs and 2,500 propaganda leaflets, but this time lost 1 aircraft. Just seven more raids would follow before the Germans invaded Saaremaa. In total the Soviets flew fifty-four sorties against Berlin and lost twenty aircraft, yet Zhavaronokov had made his point and, if nothing else, achieved a much-needed propaganda coup.[106]

Another audacious act of Soviet aviation in 1941 was the formation of three all-women bomber regiments on 8 October. The most famous of these was the 588th Night Bomber Regiment, later known as the 46th Guards Night Bomber Aviation Regiment, which flew in old PO-2s, two-seater biplanes made of plywood and canvas. The regiment flew some 24,000 sorties during the war and mainly concentrated on bombing German forward positions with ordnance payloads of up to 400 kilograms. As Nadezhda Popova noted: 'The Germans knew all about us. They called us "night witches".' All the women were volunteers and the regiment, right down to the aircraft mechanics, had no males. The planes flew at night so as not to present easy targets for the much faster German fighters, yet the open cockpits of the biplanes made flying conditions for the women extremely uncomfortable, especially in the freezing winter months. There was also the danger of getting lost or not finding the airfield after a mission as the aircraft had no special equipment for night flying. 'It was not an easy job', Popova recalled; 'almost every time we had to sail through a wall of enemy fire.' Yet in spite of the regiment's at times heavy losses, Popova concluded: 'we practised our "witchcraft" almost from the first to the last days of the war'.[107]

While Soviet bombers did their best to retaliate for the German air offensive against Moscow, there were other aspects of the Soviet war machine that caused more serious problems for the *Ostheer*. Foremost among these were the increasing numbers of Soviet T-34 tanks, against which the Germans had few adequate defences. As the months went by, the older and much less effective Soviet tanks (T-26s and BT series) were less and less a feature of the Soviet tank arsenal as Soviet factories steadily replaced production with T-34s, KV-1s and the light T-60 tank. Some 500 new tanks were produced in October alone[108] and, despite the turmoil of industrial evacuation, during the final quarter of 1941 some 441 KV-1s, 765 T-34s[109] and 1,388 T-60s were produced.[110]

Hitler was sufficiently aware of the problem to insist that units on the eastern front be uniformly equipped with 88mm Flak guns to deal with the 'remarkable number of heavy tanks appearing over those previously'.[111] While 88mm Flak guns were highly effective in a defensive posture, the attacking German panzer divisions often had few alternatives in direct confrontations with T-34s.[112] Tank for tank the Germans were simply outclassed, as one report from Langermann-Erlancamp's 4th Panzer Division on 22 October makes clear: 'Time and again our tanks have been split right open by hits from the front and the commander's cupolas on the Mark III and IV tanks have been completely blown off, proof that the armour plating is inadequate and that the fastening on the cupolas is faulty, and also proof of the great accuracy and penetration of the Russian (T-34) 7.62 cm tank cannon.'[113] In one soldier's words the 'T-34 knocked off our tanks like rabbits.'[114] Kesselring described how difficult it proved for ground-strafes to engage T-34s from the air. In the first instance he stated that pilots had to fly 'recklessly' to hit them, but even then the effect was minimal. According to Kesselring: 'we continued to attack the tanks from the air, but we could not, and did not, do them any serious damage'.[115] The result was an instrument of war which German tankers genuinely feared. As one tanker from the 4th Panzer Division stated:

> There is nothing more frightening than a tank battle against superior force. Numbers – they do not mean so much, we were used to it. But better machines, that's terrible ... The Russian tanks are so agile, at close ranges they will climb a slope or cross a piece of swamp faster than you can traverse the turret. And through the noise and the vibration you keep hearing the clangour of shot against armour. When they hit one of our panzers there is often a deep long explosion, a roar as the fuel burns, a roar too loud, thank God, to let us hear the cries of the crew.[116]

Soviet artillery was another bane of the *Ostheer*. Unlike the newer Soviet tanks, it was not so much that the Red Army's artillery was better, but their vast reserves of guns and shells often ensured a preponderant advantage in firepower.[117] In June 1941 the Red Army possessed a staggering total of 112,800 guns and mortars and, even though losses over the next five months eliminated most of these, frantic production ensured that by December 1941 the Red Army still dominated with some 70,100 guns and mortars at its disposal.[118] The German infantry was often, therefore, outgunned, but this mattered less in the early stages of the war when the front was still fluid and the Soviet ability to range and co-ordinate their guns proved frequently very poor. As the front settled down, however, and Soviet commanders grew in experience the consequence for the *Landser* was harrowing bombardments. As Hans Roth wrote in his diary: 'Let's not forget to mention the artillery, those God damned Bolshevik batteries which are considerably greater in strength than we ever imagined. Their weapons of all calibres seem infinite; we encounter them even on the smallest stages ... Single batteries with missiles are occasionally encountered. Ammunition is available in good quantity and quality.'[119] Henning Kardell noted after the war: 'That was something we'd learned from the Russians: the deeper you were dug in, the greater the chance of survival.'[120]

New Soviet infantry weapons were also appearing in 1941, such as the PPSh-41, which was to become the Red Army's iconic submachine gun for the rest of the war. Production of the PPSh-41, which was durable in combat and simple to make, began towards the end of 1941 and by spring of 1942 was running at three thousand a day.[121] Like many other successful Soviet weapons, it was not uncommon for German infantrymen to seek to replace their own weapons with captured Soviet models. As Gottlob Bidermann wrote: 'I took one of the submachine guns and several drum magazines from one of the prisoners for my own use, as I no longer placed much faith in the slow-firing 98k carbine for close combat. I felt more confident equipped with the high-capacity automatic weapon, and it was to remain with me for many months.'[122]

Yet successful combat was about more than just weaponry and, while the Wehrmacht deservingly retains the mystique of being the best-trained and most professional army in 1941[123] (at least in the mid to lower ranks), this did not mean, however, there was nothing to learn from the Red Army. In many respects it was precisely the numerous deprivations of the Red Army that forced the Soviet soldier to become an expert at improvisation and, as the *Ostheer* experienced its own rapid demodernisation over the course of 1941, adapting the art of self-sufficiency became a priority for the Wehrmacht. One example of Soviet improvisation was a special construction of landmines in which the casings and parts were fashioned completely out of wood so that they were almost undetectable.[124] The same soldier's letter which reported encountering the wooden mines also expressed wonderment at other Soviet constructions: 'The irreproachable work of the Russians again excited astonishment and admiration. The Russian is a master in the construction of field positions and camouflage.'[125] Another German soldier noted: 'We learned the art of improvisation and self-sufficiency from the enemy.'[126] Indeed as the winter took hold an increasing number of the *Ostheer*'s survival skills would be learned from the Red Army. Yet the Red Army improvised to kill as well as to survive. At dawn on 14 October a group of Soviet soldiers disguised with German uniforms approached a forward posting of *Brigadeführer*[127] Walter Krüger's 4th SS 'Polizei' Division and killed all the unsuspecting soldiers.[128] In other instances Soviet soldiers pretended to surrender only to attack their would-be captors at close range.[129] As one German soldier concluded: 'I have never seen such tough dogs as the Russians, and it is impossible to tell their tactics in advance.'[130] Another feature commonly highlighted was the fearlessness and audacity of the Soviet enemy. 'The Russians are not the cowards they are represented to be', concluded another German soldier in a letter home.[131]

While in the earliest stages of the war the Red Army seemed capable of a wide range of responses when engaged by German forces – from passive surrender to bitter resistance – by the autumn there was much greater consistency among Soviet units in adopting the latter course of action. While the determination and toughness of the Soviet infantryman inspired grudging respect from some within the *Ostheer*, many German soldiers instead adopted popular Nazi conceptions which sought to explain Soviet 'toughness' as a primitive predilection typical of a supposed lower racial ordering or the effects of Bolshevism.[132] Hans Roth wrote in his diary on 29 September:

> Bolshevism has consciously destroyed everything soulful,
> everything individual and private that also makes up the character
> and the value of a human being. What is left is the animal in the
> Bolshevik, who, however, does not have its finer instincts. Humans
> in the state of animals are much lower than the actual animal. That
> is why the animal Bolshevik is so hard and bloodthirsty, cruel and
> stubborn against the enemy and against himself. This is how to
> understand the demeanor of the Soviet in this war. What looks like
> braveness is brutality![133]

Nor were such viewpoints simply the preserve of the rank and file. Nazi ideals were not imposed upon the *Ostheer*; they were organic to it, and the dissemination of such propaganda was actively initiated by many of the generals.[134] Even after the war Kleist, the commander of the First Panzer Army in October 1941, told an interviewer: 'The Russians are so primitive that they won't give up even when they are surrounded by a dozen machine guns. I would say it is a difference between German and Russian bravery in the sense that the former is logical and the latter is brutal.'[135] German soldiers also expressed astonishment that the men of the Red Amy fought so hard to defend such a poverty-stricken country, which Albert Neuhaus concluded could result only from 'stupidity or organised hate'.[136] The idea of Bolshevism as the ruin of civilisation was the view that Hitler expounded on the night of 17–18 October when told his inner circle: 'Everything that resembles civilisation, the Bolsheviks have suppressed it, and I have no feelings about the idea of wiping out Kiev, Moscow or St Petersburg.'[137] Indeed in his new eastern empire Hitler foresaw only the most base and subservient role for the enslaved Slavic peoples:

> We shan't settle in the Russian towns, and we'll let them fall to pieces without intervening. And, above all, no remorse on this subject! We're not going to play at children's nurses; we're absolutely without obligations as far as these people are concerned. To struggle against the hovels, chase away the fleas, provide German teachers, bring out newspapers – very little of that for us! We'll confine ourselves, perhaps, to setting up a radio transmitter, under our control. For the rest, let them know just enough to understand our highway signs, so that they won't get themselves run over by our vehicles!
>
> For them the word 'liberty' means the right to wash on feast days … There's only one duty: to germanise this country by the immigration of Germans, and to look upon the natives as Redskins.[138]

Hitler's views of *Lebensraum* in the east, backed by the army's criminal orders and the inherent brutalising effect of war, informed the thinking of German soldiers in the east and radicalised their behaviour towards the Soviet people.[139] The groundwork had been laid by Brauchitsch who told senior commanders of the *Ostheer* on 27 March 1941: 'The troops have to realise that this struggle is being waged by one race against the other, and proceed with the necessary harshness.'[140] From the first days of the war, Rudolf Lange's diary revealed a great compulsion to kill and destroy. Writing on 27 June he stated: 'We felt no compassion but only a great urge to destroy. My fingers itched to shoot off my pistol into the crowd. Soon the SS will come along and smoke out all of them. We are fighting for the greatness of Germany. The Germans cannot have communion with these Asiatics, Russians, Caucasians and Mongols.'[141] While many perceptions of the Soviet Union and its peoples were heavily coloured by Nazi ideology, not all Germans expressed such disdain for the Soviet people, and a few even appreciated the many differences.[142] Johannes Huebner wrote home on 18 October: 'It has now been almost four months and the "holiday trip" in the Soviet paradise has surely meant a lot to everyone. For me personally I feel quite well among the Russian people. Their simple lifestyle is attractive and admirable.'[143] Another soldier referred to the friendly attitude of the local population, but was forced to wonder how genuine it was and whether it was sometimes just inspired by fear.[144]

Clearly the German image of the enemy (*Feindbild*) in the east was influenced by many factors, and not all of them were necessarily negative, but the overriding depiction was extremely hostile.[145] This is not surprising based on both the content of Nazi propaganda and its proliferation within the Wehrmacht.[146] Accounting for the widespread adoption of Nazi precepts pertaining to the Soviet enemy need not mean that the great majority of German soldiers were at the same time avid Nazi party supporters. The eastern front provided even experienced German soldiers with a new set of very disturbing challenges, and the Nazis' *Feindbild* simply provided much-needed coping strategies, which allowed German soldiers to make sense of the war, while also rationalising their own role in it. Dehumanising the Soviet enemy legitimated the killing process and allowed it to proceed without remorse. It also avoided, or at least ameliorated, feelings of guilt for the frequent cruelties the German soldiers observed and at times took part in. Another powerful motive in the *Ostheer*'s *Feindbild* was the Red Army's willingness to perpetuate brutish crimes against captured German soldiers, for which there was also frequent evidence. This rapidly dispelled feelings of sympathy for the enemy and encouraged hateful acts of vengeance even by those who had not personally witnessed Soviet atrocities. Ernst Guicking observed a group of Soviet soldiers who appeared 'happy to have come over to us', and may have just defected; nevertheless he concluded in favour of their guilt: 'These bandits, it is always the same. The horrors they did to our comrades, we do not forget so soon.'[147] The Nazi *Feindbild* received widespread acceptance on the eastern front because it made the tasks of the German soldier easier to perform, while, at the same time, presenting the average *Land-ser* as a victim of the enemy's barbarous injustice. In this way the *Ostheer* was psychologically strengthened against 'weakness' and encouraged to perform as an aggressive and unremitting destructive force (see Illustration 17).

While the *Ostheer* was indeed a formidable fighting force, it was precisely the perceived threat to the Soviet Union that reconciled former rivals in east and west and allowed the forging of a powerful new alliance against Hitler's Germany. From June 1941 Churchill, Roosevelt and Stalin shared the defeat of Nazism as their one overriding

17 Germany's war of annihilation against the Soviet Union ran parallel to its military campaign. Here suspected partisans are publicly hanged. The sign reads: 'Such is the end for partisans.'

goal, eclipsing their previous differences and allowing an unprecedented spirit of co-operation. Nothing symbolised the new determination to work together more than the outcome of the Three-Power Conference, which agreed on vast sums of Allied aid to the Soviet Union under the terms of an extended Lend-Lease agreement. Known as the First Protocol and signed on 1 October 1941, the agreement stated that Britain and the United States undertook to provide the Soviet Union with 400 aircraft and 500 tanks a month in addition to vast stocks of other weapons, raw materials, foodstuffs, medical supplies and military equipment.[148] Upon concluding the agreement the Soviet foreign minister, V. M. Molotov, declared: 'A combination of states has at last been formed against Hitlerism.'[149] It was not always a happy alliance, but it endured for the rest of the war and, through Lend-Lease supplies, gave the west an indirect, but nonetheless important role in the fighting on the eastern front.

Stalin himself wrote to Churchill on 3 October to express his gratitude, but also to ask that 'the British and American governments will do all they can to increase the monthly quotas and also to seize the slightest opportunity to accelerate the planned deliveries right now, because the Hitlerites will use the pre-winter months to exert the utmost pressure on the USSR'.[150] Churchill's reply three days later (6 October) emphasised his willingness to comply by outlining ambitious plans to run a continuous cycle of convoys leaving every ten days.[151] This placed the British Admiralty under enormous pressure, given that they had anticipated convoys leaving every forty days.[152] Yet Churchill, recognising the dire importance of events in the Soviet Union, insisted his timetable be met. The second convoy to the Soviet Union (the first, codenamed 'Dervish', having left on 21 August) departed at the end of September, transporting 193 fighter planes and 20 tanks. Starting with this second convoy, the Admiralty instituted a new lettered system for each convoy: 'PQ' followed by a numbering sequence for convoys running to the Soviet Union and 'QP' for those returning to the UK.[153] PQ.1 sailed from Hvalfjord in Iceland with eleven merchantmen plus escorts and successfully made the passage to Archangel unmolested by German ships or aircraft. PQ.2 left Scapa Flow on 17 October with six ships plus escorts and arrived equally unscathed.[154] According to Churchill's telegram to Stalin, PQ.2 transported 140 heavy tanks, 200 Universal Carriers[155] and 100 Hurricane fighters.[156] The Arctic convoys were off to a good start, but from the beginning Stafford

Cripps, the British ambassador in Moscow, warned that 'after the spectacular success of the [Three-Power] conference, the time of disappointment will come when things do not arrive'.[157] Indeed, despite the Admiralty's best efforts it was simply not possible to meet Churchill's demand for a convoy to depart every ten days, and PQ.3 did not get underway until 9 November, twenty-three days after PQ.2. In total seven convoys with a total of fifty-three merchantmen departed for the Soviet Union in 1941 and four convoys with thirty-four merchantmen sailed in the reverse journey. Remarkably, none of the ships were lost and the greatest difficulty in getting the cargo into Soviet hands came at the end of the year when pack ice closed Archangel's port; the ships were directed to Murmansk which had extremely poor port facilities.[158]

British tanks supplied to the Soviet Union consisted of the medium Valentine and heavy Matilda models, which did not compare favourably to the T-34 and KV-1, but generally outperformed the older Soviet model tanks as well as the light T-60. Before British tanks could take their place at the front, a crash-course training programme was instituted at the Kazan training centre with the first twenty Lend-Lease tanks. Some 1,600 Soviet personnel were trained in the operation of British tanks in courses lasting just fifteen days. The Soviets complained about the small size of the 40mm (2-pounder) gun and there were even proposals to upgrade the Valentine to a 45mm and the Matilda to a 75mm main armament. Yet, probably due to the urgent need for armoured support at Moscow, these ideas came to nothing. The Soviets were also disappointed by the slow cross-country performance of the British tanks, which averaged only 24 kilometres per hour. This was less than half of what the T-34 could manage (51 kilometres per hour) and also inferior to the far heavier KV-1, which managed 35 kilometres per hour. Overall, British tanks were clearly not equal to the best Soviet models, but then the British did not have to engage these on the battlefield, and against the German Mark III and Mark IV panzers the Valentines and Matildas compared more favourably. On another level, the battlefield success of British tanks on the eastern front in 1941 was probably less important than the boost they offered to Soviet morale as well as the tangible commitment they represented to the newly forged alliance.[159] While some 466 British tanks arrived in the Soviet Union during the course of 1941, only 27 American M3 light tanks reached Soviet shores in the same period, leaving Soviet officials to conclude: 'Overall US deliveries are being conducted most unsatisfactorily.'[160]

The Allied aircraft shipped to the Soviet Union in 1941 started arriving in September and were initially concentrated at the Vianga airfield (27 kilometres north-east of Murmansk on the Barents Sea) where Soviet pilots were trained by elements of the accompanying British 151st Fighter Wing.[161] The initial Dervish convoy carried Hawker Hurricanes and Curtiss Tomahawks, meaning both British and American fighters would be active on the eastern front in the autumn of 1941. For all that the Royal Air Force's Hurricane had achieved in the Battle of Britain, the fact remained that by the autumn of 1941 the aircraft was fast approaching obsolescence. The Hurricane was significantly slower than the better German fighters (Bf 109E/Fs) and its machine guns fired small 7.7mm rounds that Soviet pilots joked were good only for spoiling the Germans' paint. Yet it was not all bad news for the Soviet pilots. Every Hurricane was equipped with a two-way radio, whereas only one in every three Soviet aircraft at the start of the war had a radio and even then many only had receivers, not transmitters. Soviet planes were also plagued by poor-quality canopy transparencies, which meant Hurricanes, with their superior armoured glass, offered pilots much greater visibility and protection. Overall, however, the Hurricane was unpopular with Soviet pilots. It was marginally superior to the LaGG-3, but outclassed by the Yak-1 and MiG-3. Nevertheless, the deficiencies of the aircraft did not stop a number of Soviet pilots from reaching the status of 'ace'. Captain Sergei Kurzenkov completed 225 missions in his Hurricane, downing twelve German aircraft and destroying another five on the ground. He was awarded the title 'Hero of the Soviet Union' on 24 July 1943.[162]

The American Tomahawk was considered a solid and capable fighter by Soviet pilots. It was not quite the equal of the Yak-1 and MiG-3 or even the German Bf 109E/Fs, but better than the Hurricane. It was extremely robust, capable of sustaining remarkable battle damage, and powerfully armed with six high-calibre machine guns. Drawbacks included a slower speed than the Bf 109s and sluggish performance at altitudes above 15,000 feet (although most aerial combat on the eastern front took place at low altitude). Lend-Lease planners also failed to provide sufficient spare parts for the Tomahawks, rendering many planes inoperable because rudimentary replacement parts were not available. While the first Soviet pilots began training in Tomahawks on 15 September, they were soon switched to the Moscow Air Defence Zone and saw their first action on 12 October. Owing to its solid combat performance, the Tomahawk produced a higher share of fighter 'aces' than the Hurricane. Petr Belyasnik claimed seven 'kills' in the battle of Moscow and another four at Stalingrad, becoming a 'Hero of the Soviet Union' on 28 April 1943 and ending the war with twenty-six individual or shared 'kills'. Another Soviet pilot, Stepan Ridnyi, shot down six German planes in the battle of Moscow and already had twenty-one individual or shared 'kills' before his conversion to the Tomahawk. Ridnyi, however, was killed on 17 February 1942, when his Tomahawk suffered engine failure on take-off and crashed.[163]

While the initial strength of the Grand Alliance was to no small extent forged on the back of Lend-Lease agreements, the Soviet Union was still shouldering the overwhelming weight of the war against Nazi Germany, and this quickly led to undercurrents of tension between London and Moscow. To Churchill's mind, he was already pushing the limits of what the Royal Navy could muster, while at the same time denying his air force and army hundreds of replacement aircraft and tanks. Additionally, in the wake of the Anglo-Soviet occupation of Iran, on 12 October Churchill, hoping to free up more units for the hard-pressed Red Army, offered to replace the five Soviet divisions on garrisoning duties with additional British troops.[164] From the Soviet point of view, however, this indicated that there were clearly still limits on the British commitment to the war in the east, which tended to reinforce the idea, held by some in the Soviet government, that Britain was prepared to fight to the last Red Army soldier. Suspicions surrounded Churchill's offer in Iran and the question was asked why, if the British were so eager to aid their ally, did they not send their additional forces directly to the Soviet southern front?[165] Stalin also noted British reluctance to declare war on Finland, Romania and Hungary, which had all been fighting against the Soviet Union since the launch of Operation Barbarossa.[166] Churchill was reluctant in the case of Finland and Romania since both, initially at least, were waging wars of liberation to take back territory aggressively seized by the Soviets only the year before.[167] There was also the consideration that once war was declared these countries would be bound to Hitler and the possibility of influencing them back towards the Allied camp would be forever lost. Yet Stalin interpreted British hesitancy as a lack of commitment to the alliance, which undermined his confidence, especially when the month before Churchill had utterly dismissed the prospect of launching a second front in Europe in 1941 and the North African front had been largely quiet since the failure of

Britain's Battleaxe offensive in June. Accordingly, when Churchill concluded his 12 October telegram to Stalin with the insistence, 'Words are useless to express what we feel about your vast heroic struggle. We hope presently to testify by action',[168] Stalin may well have felt a sense of bitter irony.

Stafford Cripps, the British ambassador now working from the reserve Soviet capital at Kuibyshev, was at pains to point out to Churchill how damaging the perception of British inaction was to Anglo-Soviet relations. Writing to the prime minister on 26 October, Cripps declared: 'They [the Soviets] are now obsessed with the idea that we are prepared to fight to the last drop of Russian blood ... and they interpret every action either from this point of view or else from the point of view that we are sitting back and resting while they are doing the fighting.'[169] Churchill justifiably took exception at being called out for inaction by the Soviets when they themselves had been, only five months before, Hitler's economic and political ally against an isolated Britain.[170] Still, beyond the already vast commitments of the First Protocol, Churchill was not prepared to do more. Only in response to the rising clamour for British troops to be deployed to the Soviet Union, not just from the Soviet government, but supported by Cripps, Secretary of State for Foreign Affairs Anthony Eden and large sections of the British public, did Churchill concede to Oliver Lyttelton, minister of state in the Middle East, that British troops might indeed have to be moved from the Mediterranean to the eastern front. As Churchill wrote Lyttelton: 'I am confronted with Russian demands for a British force to take its place in the line on the Russian left flank at the earliest moment. It will not be possible in the rising temper of the British people against what they consider our inactivity to resist such a demand indefinitely.'[171]

By late October it was already clear that the Grand Alliance, in spite of agreement on the First Protocol at the start of the month, was going to have to overcome a number of new challenges, which would be complicated by old suspicions. Yet October 1941 was also an especially difficult time for the alliance. Stalin was worried he was about to lose Moscow, and the dire news from eastern Ukraine and Crimea only heightened his sense of urgency and frustration. At the same time Churchill was irritated by the constant delays to the upcoming Crusader offensive in North Africa[172] and, having already given up so much to support the Red Army, he now feared Britain's own war effort might be compromised for the Soviet cause. In other words, the sudden tension in Anglo-Soviet relations was as much a result of the divisive issues themselves as the external circumstances in which the disputes were taking place. Neither nation, however, ever questioned the value of their alliance nor did the discussions become acrimonious or hostile. Indeed, if the clouds hanging over the alliance in October had a silver lining, it was the closely guarded secret revealed by the Enigma decrypts, which indicated that Germany's Typhoon offensive was running out of steam.[173] Even more encouraging were the buoyed hopes of US belligerency after news on 17 October that the USS *Kearney* had been torpedoed with the death of eleven American sailors. This was followed on 31 October by the sinking of the USS *Reuben James* by another German torpedo, resulting in the loss of 115 sailors.[174] Such incidents suggested the United States' entry into the war was only a matter of time and, with Allied aid now flowing to the east, the mutual interdependency of the Grand Alliance proved superior to its difficulties. On 10 October a BBC radio broadcast picked up and recorded in Army Group Centre's war diary reported on the Soviet defence of Moscow and concluded: 'They are standing with their backs to the wall and are defending themselves as best they can, but behind this wall stands Great Britain with the United States of America.'[175]

8 RUNNING ON EMPTY

Flogging the dead horse – Army Group Centre's stalled advance

On 19 October 1812, after having occupied Moscow for thirty-four days (beginning on 15 September), Napoleon began his long retreat from Russia. By this point the French emperor was already counting his losses while seeking to escape the dreaded effects of a Russian winter. On 19 October 1941 Hitler's armies were struggling east to reach Moscow and they were still a long way from capturing it. Indeed on 20 October Schroeck's 98th Infantry Division, one of the easternmost divisions in Bock's Army Group Centre, found a sign indicating it was still 69 kilometres short of its goal.[1] At the same time on a hill near Tarutino the Germans passed a victory column commemorating Tsar Alexander I's 1812 triumph over the French.[2] For Bock's armies, opposed by stiffening resistance and viscous mud, the omens of a defeat on the road to Moscow were very much apparent.

From his headquarters at Smolensk Bock surveyed the deteriorating strength of his army group with increasing desperation. Only ten days before, he had looked like the irresistible conqueror of Moscow, but the pendulum had swung, the army group was bogging down and Bock was looking for any expedient to maintain his advance. He prepared an order instructing motorised units, 'which are paralyzed because of the road conditions', to give up their vehicles 'and be put together as infantry with limited artillery'. Yet, when Bock approached Brauchitsch for his consent, the commander-in-chief of the army wholly refused.[3] In a telephone conversation on the following day (22 October)

Brauchitsch, like so many in the German high command, simply could not believe that things had reached such a low point that the very instruments of modern mobile warfare should simply be abandoned. Indeed, it appears Brauchitsch still held out hope for an improvement in the weather.[4] The fact was that the German high command had completely underestimated, and was continuing to do so, the all-pervasive nature of the Russian *rasputitsa*. As the chief of staff of the Fourth Army, Blumentritt, observed, the reality of the *rasputitsa* really had to be experienced to be truly understood. Writing of the October conditions after the war, Blumentritt explained:

> We had anticipated this [the *rasputitsa*] of course, for we had read about it in our studies of Russian conditions. But the reality far exceeded our worst expectations … It is hard to convey a picture of what it was like to anybody who had not actually experienced it … The infantryman slithers in the mud, while many teams of horses are needed to drag each gun forward. All wheeled vehicles sink up to their axles in the slime. Even tractors can only move with great difficulty. A large proportion of our heavy artillery was soon stuck fast and was therefore unavailable for the Moscow battle. The quality of the mud may be understood when it is realised that even tanks and other tracked vehicles could only just get along and were frequently and repeatedly mired. The strain that all this caused our already exhausted troops can perhaps be imagined.[5]

Certainly Bock, like many of the commanders at the front, had had a much sharper learning curve than the men of the OKH and OKW. Even Goebbels, who had previously expressed serious concerns about the seasonal conditions in the east and received daily military briefings detailing the problems, still refused to accept that weather could prevent a German victory. Writing on 21 October, Goebbels noted: 'We have to try to obtain victory even against the weather. That is indeed more difficult than we originally thought, but ultimately the war cannot be allowed to fail on account of weather.'[6] Indeed weather was not the only factor impeding Bock's progress, and for this reason the post-war assertion that the bad October weather was Operation Typhoon's solitary Achilles heel simply does not withstand examination. Zhukov was opposing Bock with everything at his disposal and bringing up his reserves in identical conditions. Indeed Army Group Centre's 'overall conclusion' on 21 October was that the Soviets were deploying every available unit to the front and especially their artillery was again proving strong. There was also a constant appearance of mechanised units, and hastily dug fieldworks were being encountered everywhere.[7] Not surprisingly, Army Group Centre's offensive was floundering. As Bock noted on 21 October, Guderian's Second Panzer Army and Reinhardt's Panzer Group 3 'are essentially at a standstill'. Indeed Guderian had ceased his attacks towards Tula and was gathering strength for a new effort due to be launched on 23 October. Reinhardt's forces in and around Kalinin, on the other hand, were under immense pressure just holding their positions against a vigorous Soviet counter-offensive launched by Konev's new Kalinin Front. At the centre of Bock's front Kluge's Fourth Army, with Hoepner's Panzer Group 4, was still managing 'limited progress', but that evening Kluge emphasised to Bock 'the tremendous difficulty of any movement'.[8] Indeed on the following day (22 October) Bock opened his diary entry with the blunt observation: 'No significant progress anywhere.'[9]

At Panzer Group 4 Hoepner described, in a letter on 19 October, the joint problem of dreadful roads and stiffening enemy resistance:

> Since 13.10 I am still in the same place. As a result of the abysmal roads we go forward slowly. In addition the resistance of the Moscow defensive zone is very strong. The Russians have been able to deploy a division from the Far East in time … Then they have brought up ten completely new tank brigades = 1,000 tanks. It is astonishing. I have the toughest battles at Mozhaisk because the strongest constructions and bravest defence are on the roads. Because of the roads, bypassing these causes progress to be slow.[10]

At Vietinghoff's XXXXVI Panzer Corps, on Hoepner's northern flank, forward movement was constrained not only by bad roads and Soviet resistance, but also by lack of fuel, which, even before Bock's rebuff by the OKH, had resulted in orders for the forward battle groups to abandon their vehicles and proceed on foot.[11] The only method of bringing up supplies was towing trucks with tractors; even teamsters could hardly get their wagons through because the hooves of the horses sank so deeply into the mire.[12] On one occasion Bock observed for himself that a single gun was being hauled forward by a team of twenty-four horses.[13] Across the front of the XXXXVI Panzer Corps there were profound problems (see Map 13). By 22 October Vietinghoff had hoped

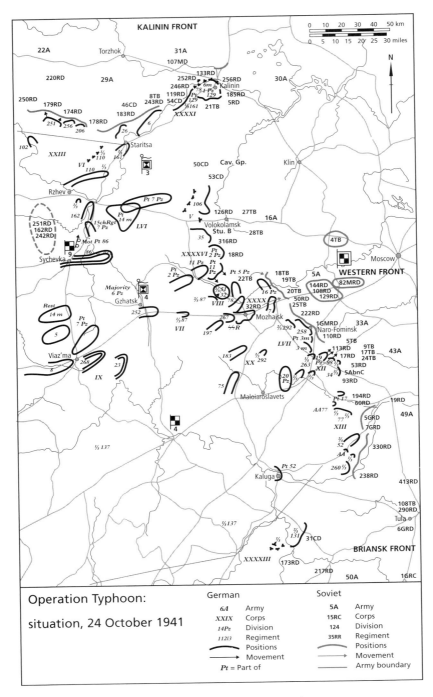

Map 13 Dispositions of Army Group Centre, 24 October 1941

he could at least use the tanks of Fehn's 5th Panzer Division in the attack, but with only a quarter-consignment of fuel (good for a 25-kilometre advance in good conditions) this was deemed 'impossible'. On the same day (22 October) in the area of Major-General Walter Scheller's 11th Panzer Division[14] a new concentration of some 100 Soviet tanks was reported.[15] Additionally Veiel's 2nd Panzer Division reported constant attacks by Soviet planes and noted: 'Fighters urgently necessary.'[16] The ground at nearby German airfields, however, had suffered from days of rain and had reached a point where the planes could no longer gather enough speed to take off. By 26 October the war diary of Vietinghoff's panzer corps recounted a depressing picture of extraordinary hardship:

> As a result of the renewed rains the roads have reached a point of marshiness that is unknown in Central Europe. Even panje wagons, which are widely used, are getting stuck on the most travelled roads. It sometimes happens that a horse sinks up to its neck in the mud and must be shot. On the advance route stand numerous trucks, some of which sit up to the body in the swamp so that they can no longer be pulled out by tractors/tanks. On the roads only heavy tractors get through; the feared result for the overburdened supply traffic will be heavy fallouts. The corduroy roads, which are built over long distances, are after a short time already covered with 30–40 cm of watery mud that squeezes through the gaps between the logs.[17]

In many ways Vietinghoff's corps, like all of Kluge's Fourth Army, was essentially pulling itself apart. The enormous strain of pushing the front forward only contributed to the distance which supplies and reinforcements had to travel.[18] In the appalling conditions motors failed, horses died of exhaustion and men suffered untold hardships marching in the mud, freezing in the cold, attacking Soviet positions and, if wounded, waiting for many hours, or even days, to reach aid stations.[19] Even food was now becoming a scarce commodity, as the advance was too slow to continue the earlier practice of living off the land, and supply from the rear had all but ceased to function.[20]

To the south of Vietinghoff's XXXXVI Panzer Corps was Stumme's XXXX Panzer Corps which had recently battled its way through the heavily fortified Soviet line at Mozhaisk, sustaining heavy losses in the process. In a week of fighting Bittrich's 'Das Reich' suffered

1,242 casualties (including 270 killed), while Fischer's 10th Panzer Division took another 776 casualties (including 167 killed).[21] Even after such gruelling combat, there could be no let-up in pursuing the enemy and Stumme pushed his men forward in spite of the fact that on 19 October the war diary of the XXXX Panzer Corps noted that 'the mass of the vehicles of the two motorised divisions are stuck'.[22] For most of the men, therefore, the advance continued on foot as *Obersturmführer* Günther Heysing wrote:

> These infantrymen, all with the same facial expression under their faded field caps, stamp silently through the mud, step by step to the east. The loamy liquid runs into the top of their boots. What does it matter! Their feet have been sopping wet for days anyway. Wet too are the trousers which lie round their knees like cold compresses each night. The coats are also wet, smeared with clay. The only things dry and warm are the glimmering cigarette butts hanging from the corner of their mouths and their hearts pounding in their breasts.[23]

Not only had the advance slowed in tempo, but in contrast to the rapid strategic envelopments of early October, Stumme's panzer corps was largely bound to the Smolensk–Moscow highway, which meant the direction of his attacks was entirely predictable. Frontal assaults still favoured the better-trained and more experienced German forces, but the cost of battling through constantly recurring Soviet defensive lines for another 80 kilometres to Moscow was prohibitively high. On 23 October the XXXX Panzer Corps's war diary listed the many difficulties of the attack. Bridges and roads were blown up to hinder movement, while the area was filled with 'very numerous' numbers of mines, some even set with time-delayed fuses. The Soviets also began deploying multiple heavy tanks, Katyusha rocket launchers and launching 'squadron-strength' attacks by enemy fighters and bombers.[24] Boris Baromykin, who fought the XXXX Panzer Corps on the retreat from Borodino and the Mozhaisk Defensive Line, remembered after the war: 'The Germans kept trying to finish us off ... As we moved down the Smolensk–Moscow highway their tanks were hard on our heels. But we resisted doggedly. We frequently turned our guns and fired point blank to beat off their pursuit. We counter-attacked against their infantry ... To slow the German advance, we set light to everything, so that the enemy would not have it. We were determined not to let them through.'[25]

As Fischer's 10th Panzer Division and Bittrich's 'Das Reich' repeatedly attempted to breach Soviet lines, the toll on their already depleted combat units was excessive. Towards the end of October when Fischer reported his effective strength to Stumme, the corps commander is said to have exclaimed: 'Good God, this is no more than a reinforced reconnaissance patrol.'[26]

Hoepner's third panzer corps operating on the southern flank of Panzer Group 4 was Kuntzen's LVII Panzer Corps, with two panzer and one motorised infantry division.[27] Having seized Maloiaroslavets on 18 October, Kuntzen's spearhead (Knobelsdorff's 19th Panzer Division) managed to advance another 30 kilometres to just outside the town of Kamenskoye, some 70 kilometres to Moscow. Here, however, the advance stopped and would not move again in October. Knobelsdorff's 19th Panzer Division was acting alone, as Thoma's 20th Panzer Division, which was down to thirty-four tanks on 16 October, had been left in the rear to rest and refit.[28] As Thoma's war diary summed up the problem: 'The spirit is willing, but the truck is weak.'[29] At Kamenskoye Knobelsdorff's division again encountered stiff Soviet resistance as well as some of the most sunken roads in Army Group Centre. The war diary of Kuntzen's LVII Panzer Corps noted that even tractors and tanks could not get through in some areas.[30]

By 25 October the advance on Kuntzen's front had been stalled for almost a week, but the panzer corps was at least now gaining support on the flanks from the continued arrival of infantry divisions from Kluge's Fourth Army. Any hope, however, for a renewal of the offensive was shattered, along with any lingering illusions about a defeated Soviet enemy, when the Western Front launched an offensive against Kluge's southern front. As Bock noted at Army Group Centre: 'The enemy has moved in new forces from Siberia and from the Caucasus and has launched counterattacks on either side of the roads leading southwest from Moscow. The southern half of the Fourth Army, with a major element of its artillery delayed by the muddy roads, has been forced onto the defensive.'[31] The offensive was launched on both sides of Naro-Fominsk, with Schroth's XII Army Corps taking the heaviest losses on 25 October while being pushed back between 2 and 3 kilometres. By the end of the day one company in the corps was reported to have only twelve men left.[32] On the following day (26 October) the offensive expanded, requiring Kluge to order Schroth's XII Army Corps, Felber's XIII Army Corps and General of Infantry

Friedrich Materna's XX Army Corps all over to the defensive. Kluge also committed his two reserve divisions (Lieutenant-General Ernst-Eberhard Hell's 15th Infantry Division and Major-General Richard Stempel's 183rd Infantry Division)[33] to the fighting and even asked Bock for the additional release of the army group reserve.[34] Hardest hit on 26 October was Schroeck's 98th Infantry Division, which was attacked by T-34 and KV-1 tanks, overrunning the front lines so quickly that a blockhouse housing a battalion staff was crushed with the occupants inside.[35] Only the commitment of the panzer regiment from Knobelsdorff's nearby 19th Panzer Division restored the situation.[36] Yet the cost was dire: in the 290th Infantry Regiment companies ended the day with strengths of just twenty men. Colonel Martin Gareis, commander of the 282nd Infantry Regiment on 26 October, recalled it as 'a black day'. Moreover, he determined 'That this day will bring a decision, that the advance on Moscow will find its final end and that the division's offensive momentum will be broken for long weeks to come.'[37]

While the shattered remains of an infantry division certainly drove home the challenges of continuing the drive on Moscow, the fact remains that one did not need to await such disasters to determine that Bock's army group, far from seizing the Soviet capital, was crossing a dangerous Rubicon into being overextended, immobilised and increasingly exposed to Soviet countermeasures. Moreover, only a trickle of supplies was now reaching the front, causing munitions stocks to become dangerously low and forcing many soldiers to go hungry. As a sign of the extraordinary disconnect between the events at the front and the understanding of the high command, Wagner, the army quartermaster-general, noted in a letter on 24 October: 'At the front it is going very well before Moscow. If the weather was better even faster. We can be satisfied and one hardly thinks that since 2 October we have another 300 kilometres behind us.'[38] In fact as early as 4 October, Panzer Group 4 had complained that only 50 per cent of its motorised transport was still serviceable and four days later Kluge's Fourth Army had complained about the small number of fuel trains arriving in the rear area.[39] Indeed while the overall number of trains reaching the eastern front in September had proved inadequate (2,093) there were even fewer in October (1,860).

Poor planning, operating difficulties and low transport capacity meant that the October supply crisis was a preordained fact, exacerbated by the bad weather, but not caused by it. The extension of the front to the east strained resources even further so that by the beginning of November Army Group Centre required at least thirty-two trains a day just to meet its operating costs, but only sixteen were arriving.[40] With grossly insufficient supplies reaching the forward railheads, the army group then faced the secondary problem of moving the provisions they did get to the front. Part of the problem was the distance which supplies were being transported because the railheads could not keep pace with the advance. Hell's 15th Infantry Division, for example, was receiving part of its supplies from as far back as Smolensk, some 350 kilometres from its current position.[41] At the same time Schroeck's 98th Infantry Division was transporting its munitions from between 300 and 400 kilometres in the rear.[42] Even with the completion of the planned railhead to Viaz'ma (as of 23 October) the front was still another 115 kilometres eastwards at its nearest point and 200 kilometres to Kalinin in the north. Even under normal circumstances these were protracted distances, but in the prevailing conditions there could be no question of a workable supply system. Accordingly, although the German command refused to accept it, Operation Typhoon's drive on Moscow was largely doomed.

Already at the front there were signs of real desperation. One soldier recalled: 'There were many times in that first autumn when we had no bread for a few days at a time and there was little that could be requisitioned or even bought from the civil population.'[43] Even the typically well-resourced Waffen-SS were suffering serious shortages. Günther Heysing from 'Das Reich' noted: 'Ammunition, fuel for our vehicles, and bread soon became as rare as gold. We could not even transport our wounded to safety.'[44] It even proved impossible to bring up a specially ordered field cot for Field Marshal Kluge.[45] Many thousands of Army Group Centre's trucks, necessary to provide the bridge between Bock's railheads and the front, began Operation Typhoon with extremely limited life spans. Many functioned only because of highly provisional repairs or were 'hybrid trucks' rebuilt and maintained from whatever parts could be improvised or fitted from other vehicles or machinery. The reliability of such trucks, heavily weighed down with supplies and travelling long distances over bad roads, was exceptionally poor. Indeed many of the vehicles that were having to be pulled along on the sunken roads would not have moved much faster on dry roads. An assessment of the vehicles belonging to one unit in Vietinghoff's

XXXXVI Panzer Corps showed that some models in service were 'completely unsuited' for the east with more than 50 per cent at any one time in the repair station. More worryingly, with movement now dependent on tractors for pulling the trucks through the marshiest areas, the results showed a very heavy fallout rate in the tractor fleet. Of the forty vehicles used for this purpose, by 20 October only four or five were still operational.[46] The inability of the army to provide replacement parts was one of the biggest problems for the repair crews, which, given the culture of self-sufficiency practised on the eastern front since the summer months, saw, in extreme instances, trucks being dispatched all the way back to Germany to procure necessary parts.[47]

The real secret to the continued mobility of many units on the eastern front was their relentless seizure of captured Soviet equipment, especially in the aftermath of major battles such as Viaz'ma and Briansk. As Georg Lehrmann recalled, his unit quickly learned new lessons to help retain their mobility:

> We were told by another division, if your vehicles won't work, try
> to find Russian tanks; and so we went off to find some, there were
> enough of them lying around. When we found tanks that were
> not burned out, we stacked up sticks of dynamite to blow out
> the drive shaft where the gun was mounted and used these to tow
> the other vehicles. We had 10-ton tractors to tow the artillery guns
> and we used these as recovery vehicles. There were so many
> abandoned Russian tanks that other divisions were able to fetch
> their own. We knew exactly where they were and in this way
> we managed to drag ourselves out of the mud. But it was a
> tremendous effort.[48]

Another German soldier reported on 17 October that his unit came across 300 abandoned Soviet trucks and took a few with them; however, he also added, 'in this weather they too do not get any further'.[49] Gottlob Bidermann noted the unofficial lines of supply that sustained many units, 'as the troops learned to live from the land and from captured enemy resources'.[50] Captured Soviet trucks may have helped slow the rate of demotorisation within the *Ostheer*, but neither these seizures nor the limited deliveries of new trucks from Germany could arrest the absolute decline in vehicle numbers on the eastern front (see Illustration 18). From a starting total of 600,000 vehicles[51] at the

18 Two captured Soviet T-26 tanks, each painted with a swastika and pressed back into service on the Finnish front in Karelia.

beginning of Operation Barbarossa the *Ostheer* was down to just 75,000 serviceable vehicles by mid November 1941.[52]

Even as Hoepner's Panzer Group 4 became stuck in the autumn mire, it was still the most formidable panzer formation on the eastern front. Losses at the battle of Viaz'ma had been minimal. Fehn's 5th Panzer Division, for example, had lost just two Mark II and six Mark III tanks by 14 October.[53] Yet with a combined total of some 780 tanks at the opening of Operation Typhoon[54] Hoepner's subsequent drive east was especially demanding in fuel consumption. There were also the inevitable fallout rates resulting from the 100-kilometre advance from Viaz'ma as well as the heavy losses sustained during the frontal attacks against the Mozhaisk Defensive Line. By 24 October Fischer's 10th Panzer Division had a strength of ninety-two tanks (forty-four of which were Mark I or Mark IIs) and had lost forty tanks in the fighting. At the same time Veiel's 2nd Panzer Division had total losses of 13 tanks and 40 were out of service, leaving 149 operational panzers. Scheller's 11th Panzer Division had total losses of sixty-four tanks, forty-five were out of service and another ninety were operational.[55] Thoma's 20th Panzer Division, which by 25 October had been resting and refitting for a week, was up to sixty-five operational tanks.[56]

Thus it was not for want of raw firepower that Hoepner's panzer group could not drive forward and, given that tracked vehicles were still largely mobile on the main roads leading to Moscow, it was not the *rasputitsa* preventing their use; rather it was the inability of the army to supply them with fuel and munitions. There were too few trains arriving at the railheads and even the inadequate quantities that were being delivered could not be transported to the front by the army group's immobilised *Grosstransportraum*. The heavy rains and thick mud were therefore preventing movement in both a direct and an indirect manner. Even the arduous process of towing the fuel and supply trucks to the front was a self-defeating process, as one soldier explained: 'Engineers, flak and tank regiments send their heavy tracked vehicles to the rear in order to put them in front of supply vehicles and tow them forward. But it is all to no avail. The fuel brought forward in this manner is just enough to supply the towing detachments.'[57] In many ways maintaining the advance to Moscow was a vicious circle of cause and effect that undercut many of Hoepner's best efforts. Moving supplies required trucks, the trucks needed roads, the roads required tracked vehicles and the tracked vehicles needed fuel. Yet none of these problems were able to be solved any time soon. As Wilhelm Prüller observed: 'Everything is grey, dark and impenetrable. The whole of Russia is sunk in mud.'[58] Likewise, Albert Neuhaus noted in a letter on 27 October: 'You cannot imagine what kind of difficulties we have to overcome. We have to wade through muck almost to the knee and then you have to imagine the vehicles and especially the heavy vehicles.'[59]

While Hoepner's panzer group was stalled well short of Moscow, in the north Reinhardt's Panzer Group 3 was fighting desperately at Kalinin. Kirchner's XXXXI Panzer Corps was almost completely encircled as attacks by Konev's Kalinin Front pressed in from all sides. Reinhardt's other corps, Schaal's LVI Panzer Corps, had been delayed much longer at the battle of Viaz'ma and was now struggling north on the bad roads to assist Kirchner with a battle group formed from Landgraf's 6th Panzer Division. An even smaller advanced detachment had left for Kalinin on about 13 October and arrived in the city on 16 October. Yet the battle group's progress was hardly much faster than that of the marching infantry.[60] Gerhard vom Bruch, who took part in the march, wrote on 20 October: 'More and more time is being lost – and we are suffering endless halts. During the day the snow thaws somewhat; in the night it freezes again, and fresh snow sweeps over the flat countryside.' He then concluded: 'Was it merely an illusion that we would be able to defeat this Russian colossus in just a few months?'[61] Major-General Erhard Raus, a brigade commander in the 6th Panzer Division, wrote of the autumn conditions: 'Motor vehicles broke down with clutch or motor trouble. Horses became exhausted and collapsed. Roads were littered with dead draft animals. Few tanks were serviceable. Trucks and horse drawn wagons bogged down.'[62] Schaal's LVI Panzer Corps also commanded Funck's 7th Panzer Division, which sent at least one of its grenadier regiments north to Kalinin, but the bulk of the division, including the panzer regiment, remained resting and refitting at Viaz'ma until 25 October. When at last the division did depart for the north it found the roads extremely hard going,[63] and a letter from Karl Fuchs, a tanker in the division's panzer regiment, indicates just how hard movement was. Writing on 26 October Fuchs explained: 'Rain, rain, nothing but rain! The countryside looks like an endless grey swamp. The roads, at least what's left of them, have become totally impassable. Even walking has become a feat. It is very difficult to stay on your feet – that's how slippery it is.'[64] By the following day (27 October) an entry in the war diary of Panzer Group 3 stated that no less than 50 per cent of the 25th Panzer Regiment (belonging to the 7th Panzer Division) had already fallen out as a result of the roads and conditions.[65]

While Schaal's panzer corps played almost no role in the fighting at Kalinin until the very end of the month, by 20 October Kirchner's XXXXI Panzer Corps had been in uninterrupted battle for seventeen days, and with Soviet pressure increasing there was no sign of relief.[66] On 21 October Krüger's 1st Panzer Division was still on the northern bank of the Volga some 10 kilometres from Kalinin and was fighting its way back to the city after being cut off during its abortive advance on Torzhok. The divisional war diary noted that the condition of the men gave cause for 'serious worries' and that the division was attempting to get back over the Volga 'without too many material losses'.[67] Yet Krüger's division had been devastated in the fighting. On 14 October the 1st Panzer Division had seventy-nine serviceable tanks,[68] but by 21 October that figure had shrunk to just twenty-four.[69] Two days (23 October) later it was reported that a further eight tanks had been lost, four to enemy action and four blown up to avoid capture after breaking down.[70] At the same time the division reported having lost 765 men and 45 officers between 13 and 20 October.[71] Losing more than 800 men in just one week was serious enough, but since 22 June 1941 the division had lost 265 officers (from a starting complement of 387) and 4,935 non-commissioned officers and men.[72] As Hans Röttiger, the chief of staff of the XXXXI Panzer Corps, noted: 'Due to the heavy Russian pressure against the road Mednoye–Kalinin (Mednoye is a village half way to Torzhok), the [1st Panzer] Division had to confine its withdrawal to a very narrow strip along the northern bank of the Volga. As a result, a great number of men and particularly materiel was lost.'[73]

The defensive perimeter around Kalinin was held by Gollnick's 36th Motorised Infantry Division, the withdrawn remnants of Krüger's 1st Panzer Division and Krause's 'Lehrbrigade 900' (which had also taken part in the drive to Torzhok), an advanced detachment from the 6th Panzer Division and a newly arrived advanced detachment from Major-General Stephan Rittau's 129th Infantry Division. Helmut Pabst, whose unit reached Kalinin on 23 October, wrote in a letter the following day: 'Since last night we have been in Kalinin. It was a tough march, but we made it. We're the first infantry division here … We marched up the road which stretches into this bridgehead like a long arm, without much covering on either flank. The bridgehead must be held for strategic and propaganda purposes. The road bears the stamp of war: destroyed and abandoned equipment, tattered and burnt-out houses, enormous bomb craters, the pitiful remains of men and animals.'[74] The situation was frequently desperate, as Konev's Kalinin Front launched relentless assaults and carried them out, according to Hans Röttiger, 'without regard to casualties'.[75] One captured Soviet officer claimed Stalin had demanded the retaking of Kalinin by 27 October or else the commanding officer, presumably Konev, would be shot.[76] Earlier in the month Stalin had considered having Konev shot for the debacle at Viaz'ma, making such a threat not beyond the realm of possibility, but Kalinin was not retaken by the stated date and Konev was not shot. However, if true, it says much about Stalin's method of 'motivation'.

By 22 October Ninth Army reported to Army Group Centre that, unless Soviet forces to the south and south-east of the city could be pushed back, Kalinin could not be held indefinitely, and certainly no further offensives could be undertaken.[77] This, however, conflicted with Hitler's latest thinking, which Kesselring had expressed to Bock the day before (21 October). Not only was Hitler still envisaging an offensive from Kalinin, but rather than the 60-kilometre advance to Torzhok, which had in any case proved beyond Kirchner's corps, the dictator was now proposing an advance to the north-eastern town of Bezhetsk some 110 kilometres away. Bock was flabbergasted. 'We are pushed back to Kalinin; first we must hold Kalinin! I have always remarked that this will be the bloody wound of the Ninth Army.'[78] On 23 October Bock discussed his orders for the Ninth Army with Halder at the OKH. The army group headquarters had not yet received instructions from Hitler demanding an advance towards Bezhetsk, so Bock insisted his first priority was to eliminate Soviet forces striking across the Volga and secure Kalinin from the south. Bock, however, then reiterated his desire for another offensive towards Torzhok.[79] By 25 October Soviet attacks south of Kalinin, far from abating, were striking with renewed vigour across the Volga from the west. Bock, on the other hand, took some heart from the fact that two corps from Ninth Army (General of Engineers Otto-Wilhelm Förster's VI Army Corps and General of Infantry Albrecht Schubert's XXIII Army Corps) were making some progress towards Torzhok from the south.[80] Yet these were still some 40 kilometres from the town, and Schubert's corps reported on the following day (26 October) that even its horse-drawn vehicles were now stuck in mud up to 1 metre deep.[81]

On 26 October Hitler met with Brauchitsch to discuss plans for renewed offensives on Bock's flanks. Hitler appeared to think Kluge's Fourth Army could operate without Hoepner's Panzer Group 4 before Moscow, in spite of the fact that their combined attack had been stopped in the south and slowed to a crawl in the north. However, Hitler wanted action on the wings, and in the north his thoughts turned again to Bezhetsk. This time he determined that the primitive roads would not support motorised units so that the advance would have to be undertaken by the infantry of Strauss's Ninth Army. At the same time Strauss would also have to ensure that Kalinin was defended from the west. Meanwhile, Reinhardt's Panzer Group 3 and Hoepner's Panzer Group 4 would be combined for a new operation towards Yaroslavl–Rybinsk some 250 kilometres north-east of Kalinin.[82] Army Group Centre was requested to provide information on the logistical feasibility of the proposed operations, to which Bock added the precautionary note in his diary: 'I promised to examine the situation on the northern wing, but pointed out that at the moment an advance by motorized forces in the strategic sense was out of the question as they were all buried up to their axles in the mud.'[83] Yet in contrast to Bock's previous protests about Kalinin being the Ninth Army's bleeding wound, not to mention the state of the roads and the great distances, Bock suddenly evinced a degree of support for Hitler's ideas. Continuing in his diary entry for 26 October, Bock wrote:

> If I am to advance on Bezhetsk, whether with infantry or with tanks, I first have to have Torzhok and have to screen my left flank … I will examine whether it is possible to force two armoured groups northeast between Moscow and the Volga and supply them. Halder replied that he didn't think it would work. But we have to reach the area of Rybinsk and Yaroslavl' somehow, in order to eliminate the enemy northeast of this line for the continuation of the war in the coming year.[84]

If the hubris inherent in German strategic planning allowed many of the ultimate flaws in Operation Barbarossa to pass unnoticed and unattended, Operation Typhoon confirmed that the same men had learned little from the previous four months of campaigning in the east. The day-to-day situation reports at Kalinin – the Soviet attacks, the shortage of German supplies, the difficulty of movement – simply cannot be reconciled with the strategic discussions taking place within the German high command. Even if one contends that Hitler and the generals of the OKW and the OKH remained somewhat insulated from the daunting reality of the autumn conditions in the east, it was Bock who insisted upon seizing Torzhok and then 'somehow' reaching the area of Rybinsk and Yaroslavl. Even Halder, who harboured his own wildly optimistic illusions about what Army Group Centre could achieve, considered the new plans doubtful, and all this was taking place independently of the faltering drive on Moscow as well as the other far-fetched offensive in the army group's south. If the battles of Viaz'ma and Briansk provided the mainstays of Operation Typhoon's success, they may paradoxically have also fed the hubris which provided for its ultimate failure.

When Reinhardt's Panzer Group 3 caught wind of the plans under discussion within the high command, there was thinly disguised exasperation. The supply of Kirchner's XXXXI Panzer Corps at Kalinin was proving demanding enough without the prospect of extending operations, especially given the current state of the roads. To make the point absolutely clear, the panzer group reported the fuel reserves of each division and how far these could reach in the current road conditions. The 1st Panzer Division could only travel a maximum of 20 kilometres, while the 36th Motorised Infantry Division and the 129th Infantry Division could travel at best 30 kilometres. The mass of Landgraf's 6th Panzer Division was still well south of Kalinin and had enough fuel to travel only 60 kilometres, which would not even take it all the way to the city. Funck's 7th Panzer Division was the closest to the rear area supply dumps and therefore had fuel for up to 180 kilometres, but this would only take it as far as Kalinin.[85] Even independent of practical considerations such as the strength of Konev's Kalinin Front, which did not feature in the discussions of the high command, there was simply no fuel for deep operational thrusts. Supplies of munitions were similarly affected: stockpiles were very low and limiting German defensive fire in and around Kalinin. Food supplies had been exhausted for some days and by 25 October the Luftwaffe took to throwing bread from low-flying aircraft.[86] As Reinhardt wrote of his panzer group's supply status in the second half of October:

> As a result of the weather it was almost impossible to supply the troops in and around Kalinin even with the most basic battle and food requirements. He who has not undergone it cannot imagine what kind of experience every movement by roads demands from mid October to the beginning of November, even on the so-called good roads. What was achieved in this time, especially by the drivers, to bring up supplies for hundreds of kilometres through the mud and snow sludge was astonishing. In the end only the panje columns, and sometimes boats on the Volga, remained to bring up the most important goods.[87]

While the panje columns constituted the most effective form of transportation the panzer group's war diary also made clear that for an advance to Bezhetsk there was 'no satisfactory possibility for the use of panje vehicles'.[88] Clearly the disconnect between the German high command and the conditions on the ground considerably undermined the chances of Typhoon's continuing success. In the aftermath of the battles at Viaz'ma and Briansk, the scope of operations needed to be reduced and given a clear central focus. Even so, with ground conditions proving so problematic the effort invested had to be balanced with the projected gains, which could by no means be guaranteed, especially with stiffening Soviet resistance. The fighting at Kalinin was a good example; the city had been seized by a bold advance exploiting the breach in the Soviet lines north of Viaz'ma, but retaining control of the city was bleeding Kirchner's XXXXI Panzer Corps white and requiring more and more strength from Strauss's Ninth Army to hold. The bloody urban fighting on the banks of the Volga, which famously destroyed the German Sixth Army in 1942–1943, was actually prefaced in 1941 by another urban battle on the banks of the same river. While the battle of Stalingrad doomed Army Group South's Operation Blue in 1942, in 1941 Kalinin was doing much the same for Army Group Centre's Operation Typhoon.

The last charge – Guderian's drive on Tula

The difficulties of Army Group Centre may have unconsciously bypassed the German high command, but Goebbels's propaganda ministry had a purposeful role in overstating the case for Moscow's fall as well as touting the impending victory of the *Ostheer*. Indeed since Hitler was a keen follower of Goebbels's weekly newsreels, it is not too much to suggest that the dictator was quite literally influenced by his own propaganda. Certainly the SD reports showed that much of the German population was still expecting decisive results in the very near future. The penetration of the Mozhaisk Defensive Line, together with the news that the Soviet government and foreign diplomatic missions had fled the capital, inspired even more confidence. On 23 October the latest SD reports read: 'The battle in the middle section [of the eastern front] is followed with eagerness. The declaration of Moscow being in a "state of siege", the departure of the diplomatic corps and the flight of the Soviet government to Samara have reinforced the opinion of the population that Moscow is already strongly threatened and the conquest of the Russian capital lies in the not too distant future.'[89] This of course was hardly in keeping with events at the front, and the radio fanfare trumpeting the victorious march to Moscow was received by many of the troops with mockery and disgust. One lieutenant taking part in the drive on Tula wrote home on 25 October about the 'Hurrah patriotism' on the home front, which he said sounded like the work of a radio play or a propaganda company and to which 'one can only shake the head'.[90]

Guderian had postponed Second Panzer Army's drive on Tula until 23 October in order to bring up supplies, which were moving no better in his area. Heinrici, the commander of the XXXXIII Army Corps which was pushing towards Tula from the west, wrote to his family on 23 October that trucks required 36 hours to travel 35 kilometres. He also noted that the roads were strewn with dead horses and broken-down trucks, which resulted not only from the strain brought on by the conditions, but also by half-metre deep craters in the road which were filled with water, disguising their depth. Heinrici also confirmed that the panje columns formed the basis of all movement, but added that running supplies for distances of 100 to 120 kilometres each way was hardly feasible.[91] Given such difficulties it is not surprising that on 23 October Guderian's spearhead 3rd Panzer Division was complaining that the attack could not go ahead on account of a shortage of fuel.[92] Yet Guderian was adamant and Schweppenberg's XXIV Panzer Corps was ordered onto the offensive. The first obstacle was crossing the Zusha River north-west of Mtsensk, which commenced in preliminary operations on the night of 22–23 October. The attack was driven forward, meeting costly resistance from Soviet infantry and T-34 tanks. Minefields were another problem, so German tanks followed as closely as possible to the tracks of the sacrificial lead vehicle. This thankless task was assigned to the small Mark I tanks, which soon suffered losses.[93] It took until 25 October to capture the town of Chern, just 28 kilometres north-east of Mtsensk and another 95 kilometres to Tula.[94]

Nevertheless Guderian was at last moving forward after being halted for almost two weeks at Mtsensk. He had also broken the main Soviet defensive line south of Tula and was now battling bad roads, blown bridges, minefields and fuel shortages as much as the sporadic appearance of the Red Army. Corduroy roads had to be built for long distances to maintain movement, and the spearhead was now reordered into a battle group led by Colonel Heinrich Eberbach. As Guderian recalled: 'The strength of the advancing units was less dependent on the number of men than on the amount of petrol on hand to keep them going.'[95] Yet Eberbach also adopted Soviet tactics and had a battalion of Hörnlein's Infantry Regiment 'Grossdeutschland' ride on the tanks, while the Luftwaffe prioritised the battle group with close air support.[96] Transport planes were also able to fly enough fuel to Chern to refill the equivalent of two panzer regiments.[97] By 27 October Eberbach's battle group had taken Plavsk, some 36 kilometres north-east of Chern, and was still pushing forward faster than Soviet defences could be organised to stop it. It was a remarkable achievement given the seasonal conditions, but made possible by advancing almost entirely on the main Orel–Tula–Moscow road, which allowed enough movement to maintain momentum. The late October weather also included some light frosts and a brief reprieve from the continual rain soaking the ground.[98] By 29 October Eberbach's lead tanks had driven to within 5 kilometres of Tula and attempted to seize the city directly off the march, as Orel had been taken at the start of the month. Yet at Tula Soviet defences had been prepared, and the German advance was stopped by strong anti-tank and anti-aircraft fire, which inflicted heavy losses on Eberbach's advanced detachment.[99]

The results of Eberbach's advance had no doubt been impressive, but Tula was to prove the high-water mark of Guderian's autumn advance.[100] Model's 3rd Panzer Division was at the end of its fuel supplies and, given the additional distance to the railhead, there could be no question of a speedy replenishment.[101] Moreover, the division's 6th Panzer Regiment retained just forty serviceable tanks.[102] At the same time Soviet resistance at Tula benefited from being much closer to its sources of supply. Tula was also a major population centre with more than a quarter of a million inhabitants and was supported by a heavy armaments industry that was able to service and supply the defending Soviet Fiftieth Army directly from its factories.[103] Beyond the immediate situation on the ground, the strategic implications of Guderian's drive to Tula increased the pressure on Moscow, but not greatly. Tula was still 175 kilometres south of Moscow, and Soviet opposition, organised by the Briansk Front, had been weakened by losses sustained in the encirclements around Briansk, but not destroyed. There was little that could be expected from the battered and badly depleted divisions, many with as few as 3,000 men,[104] but Eberbach's battle group was itself barely of regimental strength. Additionally, just as Eberbach finally reached Tula, the defending Soviet Fiftieth Army began to receive sizeable reinforcements from Soviet reserves.[105] Guderian's offensive had reached its culminating point, which, as Clausewitz determined it, was the point at which the strength of the attack was superseded by the power of the defence. Indeed the drive to Tula was in many ways the last whirlwind of Army Group Centre's Typhoon. Yet this was not the conclusion drawn by the German high command, which only saw evidence that attacks could indeed be pushed long distances even in the appalling conditions.

Even before Guderian launched his drive on Tula, the Army High Command was pushing Bock for offensives towards Kursk in the south, Moscow in the centre and, most recently, Bezhetsk in the north. Bock was extremely sceptical and told Halder on 23 October that given the circumstances he could not sustain three separate offensives in three different directions. As Bock concluded: 'If I extend myself in all three directions the attack on Moscow will have to suffer.'[106] Yet only the day before (22 October) Brauchitsch had enquired as to Bock's opinion on a new operation in the south towards the city of Voronezh with Kempf's XXXXVIII Panzer Corps. At this time Kempf's only panzer division (Hubicki's 9th) was stalled about 85 kilometres northwest of its current objective at Kursk, and by 24 October its 33rd Panzer Regiment was down to just eleven serviceable tanks.[107] Brauchitsch's proposed offensive to Voronezh, an idea which originated with Hitler, would entail an advance of 285 kilometres (linear distance) to the southeast. Not surprisingly Bock rejected the idea, 'since the fighting strengths of the armoured and motorized divisions were only those of regiments, and finally that the corps would become stuck in the mud east of Kursk just as it presently was west of the town'.[108] Yet Bock's advice was disregarded, and two days later on 24 October Army Group Centre received orders to restructure its southern forces and drive on Voronezh 'as soon as possible'.[109] Hitler was hardly opposed to overruling his field commanders and remained utterly convinced of his own infallibility. On the night of 21–22 October he told his inner circle: 'A war-leader is what I am against my own will. If I apply my mind to military problems, that's because for the moment I know that nobody would succeed better at this than I can.'[110] With such conceited bravado, and not a word of dissent from the submissive generals of the OKW, Hitler's self-deception went unchallenged. Moreover, since the August showdown with the generals of the OKH Hitler had completely cowed Brauchitsch, who had lost any stomach for further conflict and preferred to ferry messages and pass on any objections rather than make them himself. Halder, on the other hand, was a stronger character, but was also infected by the allure of sweeping victories built on the back of successes at Viaz'ma and Briansk. Thus it came down to Bock, whose rejections and excuses suggested only a lack of the necessary fortitude to overcome the difficulties and force the operations through with resourcefulness and ardent determination. Indeed, having seen his well-founded objections to the Voronezh operation overruled may well have influenced Bock's later decision not to oppose the outlandish proposal to drive Reinhardt's Panzer Group 3 all the way north to Yaroslavl. On this occasion the field marshal argued that the first objective should be the much closer town of Torzhok, which he may well have calculated would present enough of a challenge.

With the authorisation of the Voronezh operation, Army Group Centre's southern wing was reorganised to provide forces for two simultaneous offensives at Tula and Voronezh. Guderian's Second Panzer Army was stripped of Kempf's XXXXVIII Panzer Corps, Waeger's XXXIV Army Corps and Kaempfe's XXXV Army Corps and handed to Weichs's Second Army to direct operations in the south.[111] Uncharacteristically, Guderian appears to have accepted the loss of these forces from his panzer army, which may suggest he had his own doubts about the wisdom of the operation or simply that he had his hands full with the battle to reach Tula. In any case Weichs's Second Army was now tasked with reaching the general line Kursk–Maloarchangelsk (some 90 kilometres away) and then pushing on to Voronezh. Bock accepted the decision with bitter resignation and commented in his diary on 25 October: 'The splitting apart of the army group together with the frightful weather has caused us to be bogged down. As a result the Russians are gaining time to bring their shattered divisions back up to strength and bolster their defence, especially since they have most of the rail lines and roads around Moscow. That is very bad!'[112] Yet as bad as things were, the self-inflicted wound of the German high command's strategic mismanagement was by no means over.

On 26 October while Guderian's panzer army was still straining every effort to reach Tula, new information reached Bock's headquarters from Heusinger at the OKH that new discussions had taken place between Hitler and Brauchitsch in which the dictator expressed the opinion that Tula should no longer be Guderian's objective. After three days on the offensive Hitler thought it best that Guderian be halted, turned around and directed back to the south to assist Weichs in capturing Voronezh. Hitler's reasoning, according to Heusinger, was twofold; on the one hand, the panzer army's lack of bridging equipment prevented it from crossing the many streams and rivers on Guderian's northern course. On the other hand, Hitler apparently believed that the right wing of Kluge's Fourth Army, which was now on the defensive and committing all its reserves just to hold its positions, still possessed the strength to take over Guderian's task of enveloping Moscow from the south.[113] Bock was aghast, and even though no formal order had arrived instructing Bock to halt Guderian's attack the commander of Army Group Centre immediately called Halder and told him:

> I have no idea what the objective of the Second Panzer Army's departure for Voronezh is. It is essential at Tula and farther north-east. The situation is such that the southern half of Fourth Army between the Oka [River] and the highway has been forced onto the defensive by the increasingly strong enemy ... Relief for the Fourth Army and a possible resumption of the attack can only come through a continuation of the panzer army's advance through Tula to the north-east. Turning this army is unjustifiable.[114]

Halder claimed to agree with Bock; however, late on the following day (27 October) an order arrived from the OKH instructing Army Group Centre to halt Guderian's advance. Bock at once tried to contact Halder, but could only reach Heusinger. The commander of Army Group Centre was in utter disbelief and protested the order to the point of insubordination. As Bock regarded the decision, 'halting the panzer army means ceasing the attack on the entire army group front'.[115] Bock again restated all the reasons against such a move and then, in an extraordinary act of defiance for the field marshal, he refused point-blank to pass on the order. Writing in his diary, Bock declared: 'If the army command wants to do it, it will have to tell the [panzer] army itself. The advance by the panzer army, including its infantry corps, has been started through unspeakable effort and after overcoming great difficulties. If I now order it to halt, they will think me mad.'[116] Certainly there was a degree of madness in the dithering German strategy and the almost daily improvisation of new plans, none of which reflected an understanding of the conditions confronting Army Group Centre. The emotional strain this placed on Bock, in addition to the already enormous demands of the campaign, only added to his burden. During the course of the night of 27–28 October, two more telegrams arrived at Army Group Centre, both insisting that Guderian's Second Panzer Army be halted, but Bock stubbornly refused to pass them on.[117] Finally, on the afternoon of 28 October, the OKH sent an order consenting to Second Panzer Army's continued drive on Tula 'so as not to lose time'.[118] Although Bock did not record a response to this new development, what the field marshal must have made of yet another about-face in the orders of his superiors one can only imagine. Bock did, however, allude to difficulties over the question of Voronezh between Hitler and the OKH. Yet there seems little chance that Hitler would allow himself to be prevented from turning Guderian around by the opposition of Halder or Brauchitsch at the OKH. It is therefore much more likely that Hitler was simply won over by Guderian's surprisingly good progress towards Tula. Whatever the case, it stands as a telling indictment of the conduct of the German high command that the only offensive on Bock's front to make good progress against both the resurgent Red Army and the awful conditions was almost halted by internal wrangling and strategic indecision.

While the meddling of the high command and their insistence on operations on the flanks acted as an extrinsic brake on Bock's operations, combat losses proved an intrinsic restraint. In the month of October the *Ostheer* lost another 41,099 men killed,[119] while total losses for the period up to 6 November came to a staggering 686,108 casualties. In straightforward terms one in every five men who entered the Soviet Union on 22 June 1941 was now a casualty, and the dangerous winter period was yet to begin.[120] Indeed in the fourth quarter of 1941 the *Ostheer*'s daily rate of loss would equal 1,300 men killed every day.[121] A letter from Lieutenant-General Kurt Himer, commanding the 46th Infantry Division, noted that stiff Soviet resistance had resulted in his combat battalions being reduced to between 180 and 200 men. Himer then explained the difficult nature of the fighting: 'The Russians are resisting with unparalleled tenacity. Strong point after strong point has to be captured individually. As often as not, we can't get them out even with flame-throwers, and we have to blow the whole thing to bits.'[122] Similarly, Ernst Kern noted that on 15 October: 'Our recently reinforced company had shrunken to a miserable small group. The battle for this village had cost us forty lives.'[123] Helmut Günther, who served in 'Das Reich', recalled both the high losses and the absence of reinforcements. 'We drew ever closer to the Russian capital. The recent fighting had again demanded its tribute: Our outfit was noticeably smaller. There was no thought of replacements.'[124] What became clear in the second half of October was that even after the heavy fighting at such major battles as Viaz'ma and Briansk, Army Group Centre was continuing to shed large numbers of men in countless smaller encounters on the Mozhaisk line, around Kalinin and on the approaches to Kursk and Tula.

Moreover, Operation Typhoon's victorious battles and advancing armies came at a cost that was seldom appreciated in the plans and objectives of the German command. As one regimental commander from the hard-pressed 98th Infantry Division questioned: 'Does one "above" know the magnitude of the infantry's steady loss of strength from July to October?'[125] Certainly the Soviets had a sense of what was happening and did their best to exploit it with their propaganda. One airdropped Soviet leaflet depicted the eastern front as a giant skull surrounded by fire into which a column of German troops marched.[126] Nor was such a dramatisation a long way from the truth. Bock noted in his diary on 30 October that throughout the army group there were more than twenty battalions under the command of lieutenants.[127] Even veteran soldiers were expressing shock at the number of dead. Horst Lange wrote in his diary on 7 October: 'My tentmate came back yesterday from a car ride to the front (25 kilometres away) and told me full of shock (as far as that is still possible) how our dead are lying there.'[128] Two weeks later a letter from Kurt Miethke to his wife stated that he had to stand guard at a post where 2,000 men were buried. 'But that cannot shock us any more; one gets used to it.'[129] Another German soldier simply stated: 'Russia, the grave of our youth.'[130]

Part of the reason for the high October death toll was the fact that many of the wounded could not be transported quickly back to aid stations and then on to field hospitals. Ingeborg Ochsenknecht, a German nurse serving in a field hospital behind Army Group Centre in October 1941, noted: 'The dressings were full of dirt that stuck to the wounds, the stench of rotting flesh, the maggots which had spread around under a plaster cast, the cries of pain from the soldiers – that was hell.'[131] Not only did it take an inordinate amount of time to get the wounded back to the hospitals, but German medical services behind the eastern front were uniformly underequipped and poorly resourced. Each division had just two medical companies and one field hospital, which often could not cope with the deluge of wounded in periods of heavy fighting.[132] Max Kuhnert recalled:

> The worst was always the pitiful sight of the wounded; there was very little comfort – medicaments and bandages were getting short in supply ... It was simply indescribable, not only to see, but to hear their groans and even worse. Transportation was just too difficult, and carrying the wounded sometimes did more harm than good,

especially when they had internal injuries. We tried very hard to get straw or anything to bed them down on, to protect them from the sleet and snow. Several tarpaulins were erected to make a first aid tent, but I am afraid that it was in no way sufficient ... I could not but admire the field doctors; they worked inexhaustibly in atrocious conditions and seemingly without sleep or even rest.[133]

The wounded were tagged according to three categories relating to their transportation: two red stripes on the tag meant not transportable, one red stripe meant transportable and no red stripes placed the man among the walking wounded.[134] In the October conditions many German soldiers regarded it as a death sentence when a comrade was wounded at the front and immediately issued a tag with two red stripes. Severe wounds could only be treated with first aid, and with no possibility of transporting the man to the rear he usually died of his injuries. Aid stations were extremely rudimentary; there were no sterilised instruments and no gloves, so hands were washed in alcohol. The emphasis was on speed, patching up the wounds as quickly as possible and getting the men back to hospitals for their operations. Stomach wounds were often the most serious cases, requiring immediate surgery.[135] At the field hospitals the backlog of urgent cases meant that doctors often amputated limbs which under normal circumstances could have been saved. The strain on the medical staff often extended to the point of absolute exhaustion. Ingeborg Ochsenknecht recalled a surgeon who repeated after each operation, 'I cannot stand this much longer. This is hell.'[136]

As countless thousands of wounded inundated field hospitals in the east, packed hospital trains ferried the wounded back to Germany, which soon too found its hospitals unable to cope. Rudolf Stützel, who arrived in Germany to recover from his wounds, found himself in a converted field hospital at Bad Lausick near Leipzig. 'The whole complex was clearly recently converted into a field hospital, just like many health centres, schools and other facilities. A necessity resulting from the many wounded that are rolling out of Russia and arriving in Germany.'[137] Indeed some of the new hospitals had been made available by the Nazi Aktion T4 programme, which organised the murder of incurably sick and mentally handicapped patients.[138] In 1941 Anna Wendling was working as a nurse in Germany and recalled the changes that Operation Barbarossa brought. 'The routine did not vary very much until the summer of 1941 when there was a great influx of military wounded who had overflowed from hospitals in the east. There were some very awful sights to see and I had to steel myself, as despite my experiences, these things were worse.' As the year continued Wendling noted that new measures were adopted to try and provide an improvised form of mobile surgical hospitals operating further east. 'When contrary to expectations the war in Russia did not end, we were told that special teams would be formed to deal with the wounded on a mobile basis ... We packed into a car or van with all our equipment and rushed off somewhere, to various districts but always outside the city and usually miles to the east, where we would set up shop in all kinds of temporary quarters to carry out operations.' Yet Wendling concluded that, even with these expedients, 'The organisation broke down and was insufficient to take such large numbers of casualties.' Moreover, Wendling noted that the workload was increased by the addition of wounded Soviet soldiers, although she believed that most of these were never brought to the hospitals and rather 'left to die in the field' (see Illustration 19).[139]

Beyond the wounds that had to be treated by the medical services on the eastern front, there were also a variety of illnesses not typically found in Central Europe. Typhus was the most dangerous and,

19 A sports hall used as an improvised German field hospital in the rear of Army Group Centre.

Table 4 *German losses on the eastern front, June 1941 to June 1942*

	Losses[a] due to:	
	Sickness/frostbite	Weapons
Killed in action	–	23%
Died of sickness/wounds	1%	9%
Unfit for military service	1%	2%
Fit for labour and garrison service	5%	10%
Restored to active service	93%	56%
Average time in case of sick and wounded men restored for active service	27 days	98 days

Source: Adapted from Bernhard R. Kroener, 'The Winter Crisis of 1941–1942: The Distribution of Scarcity or Steps Towards a More Rational Management of Personnel' in Militärgeschichtliches Forschungsamt (ed.), *Germany and the Second World War. Volume V/I. Organization and Mobilization of the German Sphere of Power* (Oxford, 2000) p. 1012.
[a] For every 1 loss due to weapons, 1.9 losses occurred due to sickness and frostbite.

although less of a problem in 1941, it would develop into a full-scale epidemic with tens of thousands of cases in 1942.[140] In fact the *Ostheer* would suffer some 10,000 fatalities as a result of typhus in 1941 and 1942.[141] Also prevalent in the Soviet Union were many of the diseases commonly associated with camp life and low hygiene levels such as typhoid, paratyphoid and dysentery. By the late nineteenth century cholera was much less a feature of European warfare,[142] but there were still cases reported within the German army in 1941.[143] A small number of 'trench foot' cases developed in October once the autumn rains started and soldiers could not dry their feet for days on end.[144] Malaria had been a problem in the dense swamplands of the Soviet Union, but the colder weather eliminated this problem. Venereal diseases were also reported in the east, but with much lower frequency than among the occupying troops in the west.[145] Overall, during the first year of the war in the east less than 1 per cent of all reported cases of serious illness resulted in death, although another 6 per cent were deemed permanently unfit for active service. Most importantly for the *Ostheer*, men reported as sick were on average able to be returned to duty twenty-seven days after receiving treatment (see Table 4).[146]

While the overwhelming bulk of sick soldiers would eventually return to duty, their increasing number placed a further strain on the *Ostheer*'s manpower resources, especially as the winter took hold. Lieutenant-General Walter Graf von Brockdorff-Ahlefeldt, commanding the II Army Corps, wrote on 28 October: 'The health of the men and horses is deteriorating due to the wretched housing facilities ... The men have been lying for weeks in the rain and stand in knee-deep mud. It is impossible to change wet clothing. I have seen the soldiers and spoken with them. They are hollow-eyed, pale, many of them are ill. Frostbite incidence is high.'[147] Much of the field post in October speaks of the increasing difficulty of finding quarters now that it was too cold and wet to sleep outside. Harald Henry wrote on 20 October that his unit's quarters 'were almost getting worse by the day, usually thirty men lying on the floor in a farmhouse room. The air is terrible.' To make matters worse Henry noted that all the men, including himself, had diarrhoea and stomach pains.[148] In another instance on the night of 16–17 October a battalion commander in Kluge's Fourth Army radioed his superior at regimental headquarters with the request: 'We're freezing, want to attack!' Then came the somewhat baffled reply: 'Attack where to?' The battalion commander answered: 'Doesn't matter, need quarters!' The regiment therefore authorised an attack on the village of Avdotnya, which the battalion promptly seized.[149] Part of the problem was that the Red Army was implementing a ruthless scorched-earth policy as they withdrew leaving little shelter for the advancing Germans. Max Kuhnert recalled the difficulty of finding refuge on the road to Moscow. 'It wouldn't have been so bad if, after a long period of marching, a dry shelter awaited us, but no such luck ... All the barns we came upon had long been destroyed and although we were now allowed in the houses, they were not adequate to accommodate everyone.'[150]

While the homes of Russian peasants offered German soldiers a welcome shelter, they also introduced new problems for the men, which is why some commanders had previously forbidden their men to sleep in them. To begin with, peasant houses in much of the Soviet Union were primitive, but highly effective constructions, especially for the long winter months. Peasant homes seldom consisted of more than a single large room in which all activity was centred. The thick walls were made of either mud bricks or field stones cemented together with mud. The roof was thatched and on the inside there was no ceiling. Most houses had only one or two small windows, so as not to lose too much heat in winter. The glass was fixed directly into the walls so that windows could never be opened. At the centre of the room was a large clay stove which took up about one-third of the room and contained many niches for storage and valuables. The stove was used for warmth and cooking, but at night it was covered with animal skins and blankets to become the heated base of the family bed. Light was provided by means of candles, lamps or a simple contraption dubbed a 'smoking candle', which consisted of a vodka bottle filled with oil and fitted with a wick of twine, rag or felt that protruded out of the bottle. The toilet was outside and in most cases consisted only of a hole with two boards.[151] Many homes dated back a century or two, reflecting the few changes that had affected peasant lives in the modern era. Indeed for the poorest peasants who had no barn to keep their animals, the chickens, geese, pigs and even on occasion cows would share the family home in winter.

The reaction this provoked from the German soldiers, especially as they took over or shared family homes, was often indignant. Karl Fuchs noted in a letter to his wife: 'Hygiene is something totally foreign to these people … These people here live together with the animals, indeed they live like animals.'[152] Staying a single night in a peasant home, Wilhelm Prüller and his comrades could not stand the foul smell and, frustrated that they could not open a window, simply smashed the glass.[153] Of course, not all Russian peasants lived in such primitive circumstances. On his march to Kalinin, Helmut Pabst noted passing through villages with two-storeyd brick homes and noted: 'I've seen houses furnished with excellent taste, shining with cleanliness, with floors scrubbed white, hand-woven rugs, white Dutch stoves with brass fittings, clean beds, and people dressed plainly but well. Not every house is like this, but many are. The people are generally helpful and friendly.'[154] While not entirely devoid of some fear or suspicion, Russian peasants tended to be much more receptive to the arriving Germans than their urban countrymen. This was largely due to the dual Soviet policies of collectivising the land and suppressing the Orthodox Church, of which many Russian peasants had been devout members. In fact it was suggested that many peasants mistook the black cross of the Wehrmacht (the *Balkenkreuz*) for a sign of Christian liberation.[155]

With German soldiers routinely inhabiting peasant homes, a new and potentially deadly pest was introduced into the German army. As Helmut Günther observed: '[I]t was no secret that we were infested with lice ever since the time the cold drove us into the buildings and it was no longer possible to sleep under the open sky.'[156] Wagener, the operations officer at Panzer Group 3, noted that from the middle of October about 80 per cent of the infantry had lice.[157] Nor was it hard to see why, since accounts from German soldiers speak of rampant infestations within some peasant homes. Helmut Pabst wrote of hanging a pair of socks out to dry and the next morning finding that they were white with lice eggs.[158] Erich Hager wrote in his diary on 15 October after a night in a peasant house: 'Lice, bugs, fleas. Armies of them!'[159] Indeed it was not the lice that the soldiers encountered first upon entering some of the houses. There were all sorts of insects and rodents occupying them. Helmut Pabst noted: 'I stood alone in a house and lit a match, and the bugs fell from the ceiling. On the walls and floor regiments of vermin were crawling. By the fireplace it was quite black: a horrible, living carpet. When I stood still, I could hear it rustle and grate unceasingly.' Yet Pabst then added his quiet resignation and acceptance. 'Nitchevo [Nothing] – it doesn't upset me anymore. I just wonder and shake my head.'[160] Not surprisingly, many German soldiers soon contracted lice, which, without proper treatment, proved almost impossible to expel and were potentially life-threatening. The human body louse is the only vector of *Rickettsia prowazekii*, a bacterium that causes epidemic typhus.

While epidemic typhus was the most common of louse-borne diseases on the eastern front, it was not the only disease transmitted by the lice. *Rickettsia quintana* caused trench fever and *Borrelia recurrentis* relapsing fever. There was also spotted fever, but this was spread by mites, ticks and fleas, not lice.[161] Heinrich Haape, a doctor in Auleb's 6th Infantry Division, worried about the possible health implication of such diseases and berated his orderlies for the poor state of the men, especially the increasing prevalence of lice. 'Whole armies have been wiped out in no time at all with spotted fever. You may think the Russians defeated Napoleon, well I'm telling you now that spotted fever, more than the Russians, drove Napoleon back from Moscow. The same thing could happen to our army.'[162] The men were therefore instructed to keep themselves free of lice, but this proved almost impossible without mobile delousing stations, which did not appear on the eastern front until the end of 1942.[163] One of the main problems was that in the colder weather the men bathed much less frequently and were less inclined to strip down and pick out the lice from their armpits and groin where they multiplied and spread. There was also much less washing of clothes, especially as the men were continuously cold and often forced to wear everything that they possessed. Ernst Kern noted that the lice were relatively unobtrusive outside in the cold, 'but as soon as we came into a warm room and were longing for rest or sleep, their crawling and the itching drove us to despair'.[164] When the opportunity presented itself, the men often competed with each other to find and remove the highest number of lice. In one such competition Ferdinand Melzner noted finding twenty-six lice in his shirt and pullover, but noted that was nothing compared with some who removed them in 'company strength' (150).[165]

While German troops improvised makeshift, and largely inadequate, solutions for ridding themselves of lice, in many ways it was only a small example of a much wider problem that saw the *Ostheer* adapting to unforeseen circumstances with seemingly no concept of what they were to encounter. There were seldom contingency plans because many of the problems were unanticipated in the first place or it was simply believed that the war would be won before serious complications arose. At its root, the German invasion of the Soviet Union was plagued by manifest and systematic failures in intelligence, which pervaded almost every aspect of planning and operations in the east. The central military intelligence-gathering and -assessment body within the OKW was Admiral Wilhelm Canaris's Office of Foreign and Counterintelligence. Yet Canaris was considered a poor organiser who made bad appointments to senior postings and favoured so many personal friends for the roles that general-staff officers referred to his department as 'Canaris and Son, Inc.'.[166] In fairness to Canaris, German intelligence on the Soviet Union had been extremely poor even before his appointment in 1935 and, as was subsequently discovered, the Polish and French intelligence services had had little more luck penetrating Soviet security. Indeed Lieutenant-General Ernst Köstring, who was born in Russia and had been the German military attaché in Moscow from 1931 to 1933 and again from 1935 to 1941, told Canaris that 'it would be easier for an Arab in flowing burnous to walk unnoticed through Berlin, than for a foreign agent to pass through Russia!'[167] Even so, such was the confidence of the German high command in the prelude to Operation Barbarossa that the head of the Wehrmacht's Operations Department, Colonel-General Jodl, informed Canaris in January 1941 that information was not required on the Red Army and that he should limit agent activities to the border regions.[168] This task was facilitated by a small number of agents that Germany operated in the Baltic states and what had formerly been eastern Poland,[169] yet once these areas were overrun Germany found it extremely difficult to operate new agents in the Soviet Union. The training programme for agents had in fact been rapidly expanded in 1941, and attempts were made to use agents from Romania, China and Japan. Soviet counterintelligence, however, proved extremely effective in eliminating such men. This was due in part to the NKVD's rigorous security procedures, but was also the result of faulty German documentation, which often contained minor errors on identification papers, party cards, travel passes and military orders. Another factor was the paranoid overreaction of the Soviet state to the scale of the problem, leading to tens of thousands of its own citizens and soldiers being wrongly denounced and shot as spies. In response, German intelligence switched to recruiting Soviet POWs. This posed the problem of securing the candidate's loyalty, which was solved, according to one method, by having him shoot a fellow POW while the act was photographed. Thousands of Soviet POWs agreed to work for the Germans, many simply to escape their harsh life of captivity, yet upon reaching Soviet territory large numbers turned themselves in to Soviet counterintelligence.[170]

In addition to the OKW's Office of Foreign and Counterintelligence, the OKH operated its own intelligence apparatus, broken down into two main branches: 'Foreign Armies West', covering the British Empire and the United States, and 'Foreign Armies East', focused on Eastern Europe, Scandinavia, Japan, China and, most importantly, the Soviet Union. Colonel Eberhard Kinzel headed Foreign Armies East from November 1938 to March 1942, yet he had no specialist intelligence training, did not speak Russian and had no previous familiarity with the country.[171] Prior to 22 June 1941, Foreign Armies East pieced together a basic picture of the Red Army's order of battle in the western districts from radio interceptions and radio direction finders. This method, however, was limited in range and hampered by the fact that the Red Army was still deficient in radio technology and reliant on the telegraph and telephone. There were also a few Soviet defectors who aided the Germans as well as the co-operation of the intelligence services from Finland, Hungary, Romania and Japan. Overall, Foreign Armies East formed a reasonably accurate picture of the Soviet dispositions in the border areas, but had little idea of what was to be encountered in the Soviet interior.[172] Indeed the Soviet reserves allowed for an unprecedented rate of force generation, which German intelligence utterly failed to foresee. In July 1941 no fewer than thirteen new field armies appeared, and in August another fourteen came into service. This continued throughout 1941 and early 1942, allowing the Red Army to grow in size in spite of its tremendous losses. In October the Soviets added another four armies to their order of battle and eight more in November and December (mostly deployed to the Moscow region).[173]

Foreign Armies East also failed to accurately assess how the climate and topography of the Soviet Union would affect the operation of aircraft, motor vehicles and tanks. Moreover, there was a glaring deficiency in cartographic intelligence, which aerial photographic intelligence could hardly remedy given the size of the country. As Peter von der Osten-Sacken noted: 'The available maps were very outdated and inaccurate. A number of small villages were not even shown.'[174] In spite of the large gaps in German intelligence, the army's confidence in the success of Operation Barbarossa remained unshaken because all that was not known about the Soviet Union was offset by Nazi precepts about Slavs and the general staff's traditional, and largely disparaging, view of Russia.[175] Such unfavourable views were used to gloss over more positive and even worrying depictions of the Red Army, which were by no means absent from the planning process. The Walther memorandum from the German embassy in Moscow (October 1940) foresaw no chance of an internal Soviet collapse and argued that Ukraine, Belarus and the Baltic states would probably be more of a burden than a benefit to Germany's economic situation.[176] Moreover, Köstring, the German military attaché in Moscow, warned Halder in September 1940 of the demands that the Soviet Union's terrain and climate would make on the *Ostheer*.[177] The following month Köstring stressed the defensive qualities of the Red Army, while again emphasising the absence of roads and the extremes in weather, which he concluded were the Soviet Union's greatest allies, along with time and space.[178] In spite of such well-reasoned objections the German general staff operated in reverse order, planning its operations first and then using intelligence to assess the enemy's most damaging reaction instead of having intelligence shape the operational concept from the beginning.[179]

Certainly many of Köstring's fears were confirmed during the course of Operation Barbarossa and, in terms of climate and the absence of roads, doubly so in Operation Typhoon. Yet Army Group Centre was facing a new problem by the end of October. The deficiency of German intelligence had been somewhat offset in the early months of the campaign by the *Ostheer*'s rapid movement, which provided a stream of captured Red Army documents as well as high-ranking captives.

With the stalling of the campaign, the best source of operational intelligence for the forward elements of Canaris's agency (the *Frontaufklärungskommandos* and *Frontaufklärungstrupps*) dried up. Shortly thereafter the Soviets launched a sweeping intelligence offensive deploying large numbers of agents behind German lines and ordering a major expansion in sabotage and diversionary operations by the fledgling partisan movement. This was particularly damaging since the Germans did not possess any mobile military counterintelligence units to help resist such attacks, leaving the field units, once again, to improvise solutions.[180] This was often undertaken with the well-known ruthlessness and brutality of the Wehrmacht. One report from Funck's 7th Panzer Division during the battle of Viaz'ma noted: '[W]e picked up a boy aged between 13 and 15, carrying on him low level codes, instructions on the use of radio sets and on signalling with lamps. He was trying to get into the encircled areas. Having been proved guilty beyond doubt, he was shot.'[181]

While the Germans struggled to conduct and repel intelligence operations into and out of the Soviet Union, their failings extended well beyond the eastern front because British cryptologists working on the Ultra project at Bletchley Park had decrypted the German Enigma codes. Acting on such intelligence without betraying their knowledge of it was a dilemma that would occupy the British for the rest of the war, yet this did not stop them from passing highly sensitive information to the Soviets. On 24, 25 and 27 September, the British relayed information warning of the German build-up in Bock's army group. The Soviets recognised the value of such intelligence and requested from the British more information on German casualties, the order of battle of German formations and the organisation of Romanian and Italian forces fighting on the eastern front. As Operation Typhoon progressed in the first half of October, the War Office in London authorised more information for the Soviet command, which, British records indicate, 'gave the outline German plan and grouping of their armoured divisions for their attack on Moscow'. The Soviet high command was noted to be 'very pleased' with this information.[182]

Of course the Soviets had their own sources of information and, while there was nothing to rival the success of the Ultra project, their network of spies was second to none. The most successful, and important, for the battle of Moscow was undoubtedly the spy ring led by Richard Sorge from the German embassy in Tokyo.[183] He had already gained a high measure of credibility from his repeated warnings in June that the Germans were about to attack the Soviet Union (which at the time Stalin angrily rejected).[184] Many histories credit Sorge with providing the vital intelligence in September and October 1941 that convinced Stalin that the Japanese would not attack in the Far East, thereby freeing him to authorise the transfer of Siberian divisions to the Moscow front. Such an interpretation, however, tends to overstate the impact of Sorge's role, as there were a number of influencing factors.[185] To begin with, there were a number of other indications that the Japanese were preparing for a strike into south-east Asia and not against the Soviet Union. Moreover, the idea of Japan launching an invasion of eastern Russia as late as October was considered increasingly unlikely and, in any case, there could be no question that the defence of Moscow was more important to the Soviet Union than that of Vladivostok.[186] Thus, while Sorge provided the Soviet command with much vital intelligence on German and Japanese intentions, his arrest on 18 October was hardly the end of Soviet espionage. In Germany Soviet intelligence gained information from what the Gestapo called the *Rote Kapelle* (Red Orchestra) spy ring[187] and in Switzerland the much more effective Lucy spy ring.[188] Given the gulf in the effectiveness of intelligence gathering between the Allied powers and Nazi Germany it is small wonder that in October 1941 Hitler and his high command did not appear to know just how imperilled their war effort really was.

9 THE EYE OF THE STORM

The culminating point of the attack – Army Group Centre halts

With Army Group Centre's three panzer groups stalled on all fronts and the Soviet Western, Kalinin and Briansk Fronts receiving reinforcements at a much faster rate, Operation Typhoon was becoming an offensive only in name. By the last week of October, Bock's dispositions on the map remained virtually unchanged from one day to the next and his overall strength was in a slow but steady state of decline. Not only was Feldt's 1st Cavalry Division being transferred out of Army Group Centre, but the newly arrived Spanish Blue Division, redesignated the 250th Infantry Division, which had originally been assigned to Bock, was at the last minute redirected to Leeb's Army Group North. The Blue Division, commanded by General Muñoz Grandes, was a volunteer division made up largely of veterans from Spain's recent civil war and was at full strength with over 18,000 men (641 officers, 2,272 NCOs and 15,780 other ranks).[1] Yet during their month-long march to the front the division's wily and seemingly ill-disciplined behaviour led to many disparaging reports from the German liaison officers, one of which from early September Bock recorded in his diary:

> The Spanish view grooming the horses as a bother, feeding them unnecessary. Belts and suspenders are cut from new harnesses. Gas mask containers are often used as coffee pots. Dust and driving glasses are cut from the gas masks themselves. If a Spaniard has corns, he cuts appropriate holes in his shoes and boots to keep them

from chafing. Rifles are often sold. New bicycles are thrown away as they find tire repair too boring. The MG 34 [a machine gun] is often assembled with the help of a hammer. Parts left over during assembly are buried. They consider all women fair game. In Grodno there were orgies with Jewesses, who were also taken along in their vehicles.[2]

The Spanish were supposed to be assigned to Kluge's Fourth Army; however, once Kluge heard of the Spaniards' unruly behaviour he took the extraordinary step of rejecting their inclusion in his own army, rhetorically asking: 'Are these soldiers or gypsies?'[3] The Spaniards were therefore assigned to Strauss's Ninth Army, but even here the army's war diary made it clear that almost nothing was expected in terms of fighting qualities. 'The deployment of the division from Spain is less a military advantage than a political and propaganda effect. Therefore, despite any lack of ability, they should be welcomed as comrades in arms.'[4] At the last minute, however, Hitler decided to bolster Leeb's long right wing with Muñoz's Blue Division,[5] denying Bock another division, which in combat would prove itself of far more worth than many of the early German reports had suggested. One German officer recalled from October 1941: 'The Spaniards performed well in front of the enemy; they held on to their defensive area in spite of heavy losses.'[6] Even Goebbels, who earlier in the month had fumed at Franco's intransigent attitude towards the Axis war effort[7] and referred to the Spanish Blue Division as a mixture of soldiers and 'unbelievable criminal types',[8] noted its 'contrasting' successes in the heavy October fighting.[9]

While Bock missed out on receiving help from the Spaniards, on 22 October he was informed by the OKH that he would receive the newly formed Légion des Volontaires Français contre le Bolchevisme (Legion of French Volunteers Against Bolshevism, or LVF). Yet while the Spanish deployed a whole division to the eastern front, the French, under much tighter constraints imposed by the German occupation authorities, were able to raise only some 3,000 men. The result was barely a regimental-sized force (with only two infantry battalions) under the command of Colonel Roger Henri Labonne. The LVF, soon redesignated the 638th Infantry Regiment, was assigned to Lieutenant-General Eccard Freiherr von Gablenz's 7th Infantry Division. Yet difficulties in transportation meant that the regiment was broken up on the march to

20 Members of the Légion des Volontaires Français contre le Bolchevisme (Legion of French Volunteers Against Bolshevism) who in October 1941 were assigned to Bock's front for the battle of Moscow.

the front, and I Battalion did not manage to reach the eastern front until 24 November, while II Battalion took until 3 December. Even then, some 605 men were still somewhere in the rear.[10] If Bock had had to wait a long time for what was in any case one of the smallest foreign formations sent to the eastern front, he was to be even more disappointed by its performance. Labonne's regiment performed so poorly in its early battles and suffered so many casualties (some 450 men in two weeks) that it was soon withdrawn from the eastern front and never again employed against the Red Army (see Illustration 20).[11]

The LVF was not the only contingent of foreign volunteers to reach the eastern front in the autumn. The Belgian Légion Wallonie, which consisted of a single battalion, reached the eastern front in late October and over the next six months performed reasonably well as part of both Kleist's First Panzer Army and Hoth's Seventeenth Army.[12] The 369th Reinforced Croatian Infantry Regiment reached the front at the start of October after a 750-kilometre march from Bessarabia and also served in Hoth's Seventeenth Army.[13] *Brigadeführer* Felix Steiner's 5th SS Division 'Wiking' was conceived of as the first truly international division of the Waffen-SS and, while propaganda made much of its international make-up with recruits from the Netherlands, Norway, Denmark, Belgium and Finland plus a few *Volksdeutsche* from the Balkans, in 1941 the division remained overwhelmingly staffed with Germans (some 90 per cent).[14] While the various volunteer units added a guise of credibility to Hitler's 'European crusade against Bolshevism', their performance varied greatly. The LVF, for example, performed poorly as did the Croatians at first, but with time as foreign volunteer forces gained in experience and expanded in number (more formations appeared in 1942 and 1943) they made an increasingly significant contribution to the *Ostheer*.

Beyond the small volunteer units, by far the most important foreign contributions came from the Axis armies serving within Rundstedt's Army Group South as well as on the Finnish front in the distant north. The highest casualties were borne by Romania because of the staggeringly costly siege at Odessa, which claimed almost 100,000 men between August and October. After Romania's short campaign to free the annexed Soviet territories of Bessarabia and Northern Bukovina, Hitler had been keen to retain the aid of Antonescu's armies both to ease the strain on the *Ostheer* and to ensure no armed hostilities developed between Romania and Hungary. In 1940 Romania had been forced to cede Northern Transylvania to Hungary in the Second Vienna Award; however, far from resolving tension between the two countries, the threat of confrontation had increased. Once Operation Barbarossa began, Hitler sought to compensate Romania by granting it the whole of the Black Sea coast up to the Dnepr River,[15] which Antonescu accepted without relinquishing his rejection of the Second Vienna Award. The capture of Odessa in mid October therefore completed the conquest of Romania's new territory and contributed to the victory euphoria in the east. Hitler declared on 17 October that, 'With the fall of Odessa, the war will be practically over for Romania. All that's left for the Romanians to do is to consolidate their position.'[16] In Bucharest Mihail Sebastian noted on 14 October: 'News placards in the street: "The Decisive Hour Is Approaching." "Peace is Approaching."' Three days later (17 October) he continued: 'Odessa has fallen. The streets are decked with flags.'[17] A German report from 25 October on the state of the Romanian Fourth Army at Odessa told of just how exacting the battle had been. The army's sole panzer division, which in any case started the war with just seventy tanks, was down to ten by the middle of September. Some of the infantry were said to be marching barefoot, while others were armed only with bayonets.[18] Yet Romania's war in the east was far from over, with the Romanian Third Army fighting in the Crimean campaign and losing a further 10,000 men by the beginning of November.[19] Nor did Antonescu shy away from fighting his own parallel war against Soviet Jews. In the aftermath of Odessa's conquest Romanian forces shot 19,000 of the city's Jews,[20] and in the course of World War II a total some 300,000 Jews died under Romanian occupation.[21]

While the Romanians celebrated the fall of Odessa, Mussolini lamented the news, seeing himself as taking second place to Antonescu and venting his frustration upon the Italian generals.[22] In fact the three divisions of Messe's CSIR had performed rather well given their small size (in comparison to the Romanians) and adverse circumstances.[23] By the time Odessa fell, the CSIR had travelled 1,400 kilometres across Eastern Europe, fought a number of successful actions, captured 12,000 Soviet POWs and shot down 33 enemy aircraft.[24] By the end of October the CSIR had also played an important role in the capture of Stalino.[25] Yet Mussolini insisted upon a dramatic upscaling of Italian forces on the eastern front and on 22 October rashly instructed Ciano to inform Hitler that a further fifteen Italian divisions would be made ready for the eastern front. Indeed the Italian high command exhibited even more delusional tendencies with the chief of the Italian Supreme Command, General Ugo Cavallero, absurdly claiming that he would have ninety-two new divisions ready for use by the spring of 1942. At the same time Cavallero proclaimed that the solution to Italy's dire lack of motorisation would be to increase the daily marching distance of the troops from 18 kilometres to 40. In his diary Ciano denounced such 'artificial, hypocritical and servile optimism' as 'unbearable'.[26]

While Antonescu and Mussolini pressed ahead with their commitment to Hitler's war in the east, the Hungarian leader, Admiral Miklós Horthy, had already unsuccessfully attempted to extract his elite Mobile Corps during discussions with Hitler in early September. Hitler attempted to placate the Hungarians with promises of new war materiel and equipment for the establishment of an armoured division, but Horthy, like many in his high command, feared the damaging consequences of a long war in the east, which the Romanian example already appeared to confirm. A new Hungarian proposal was therefore sent to the German high command, which proposed the withdrawal of the Mobile Corps and two brigades of the 'Carpathian Group' in exchange for four new brigades committed to occupation purposes. The Hungarian intent was clear: to maintain their numerical commitment in the east, while exchanging the high-intensity war against the Red Army for a far less costly role in the rear areas. The German response reflected the growing manpower crisis in the east by again rejecting any withdrawals, but willingly accepting the deployment of four new brigades.[27] Part of the problem was that the Mobile Corps of General Béla Miklós was well regarded by both Kleist's First Panzer Army and Hoth's Seventeenth Army.[28] Yet Miklós himself had no illusions as to the nature of the German–Soviet war and made his opinion known to Horthy during a return visit on 30 October: 'A long and bloody war, the outcome of which is questionable, awaits Germany. Hungary should have nothing to do with this war; we can only lose!'[29] A week earlier the chief of the Hungarian general staff, Lieutenant-General Ferenc Szombathelyi, had expressed the view 'that Hungary would gradually have to fight the war with all its forces at the side of Germany'.[30] With such dire warnings the Hungarian government pushed relentlessly for withdrawal, and in early November the OKW finally approved the withdrawal of Miklós's Mobile Corps in exchange for two new brigades destined for security duties in the rear area. By the time of its withdrawal the Mobile Corps had suffered 4,500 casualties (from 26,000 men), and lost 90 per cent of its tanks and 30 per cent of its aircraft, yet the Hungarians had escaped the fighting on the eastern front for the time being, leaving the *Ostheer* to cover yet another gap in the line.[31]

Slovakia's commitment to Germany's war in the east echoed that of Hungary in that the initial enthusiasm to commit a large force to the war was soon overtaken by practical realities. In Slovakia's case this stemmed first from domestic economic pressures (there were not enough men left to bring in the harvest) and, secondly, from fears that the high number of reservists in the army (66 per cent) meant that it was ill disposed to cope with a costly war which few supported. Indeed the poor performance of the Rapid Brigade's first major encounter with the Red Army at the battle of Lipovec on 22 July, in which almost 250 men were killed or wounded, underscored the danger.[32] The Slovaks had initially deployed some 41,000 men to the eastern front, but in August the majority of the reserves were sent home, leaving the new Mobile Division (with only 8,500 men), built around the former Rapid Brigade, and a security division for use in the rear area (with 8,000 men). By October the Slovak contribution to the eastern front had been cut by almost two-thirds, and the only combat formation, the Mobile Division, was judged by the German Army Mission in Slovakia as unequal to a German division and suitable only 'for military objectives of a not too difficult character'.[33]

On the far north of the eastern front, Finland was fighting for the territory it had lost during the Winter War with the Soviet Union in 1939–1940. For this reason the Finnish liked to refer to their war as 'the Continuation War' and viewed their participation as something separate from Germany's wider European war aims. To the Finns it was therefore a joint war against a common enemy. Accordingly, Finland declined to be seen as a German ally, and never joined the Axis, but styled its relationship as that of a 'co-belligerent'.[34] With a country of only 3.9 million people the Finns fielded an army of 476,000 men, and by late summer there were some 650,000 people working directly for the armed forces constructing fortifications, roads and bridges or working as nurses or air-raid wardens and in supply services. The manpower drain placed a massive burden on the Finnish economy, with industry having lost 50 per cent of its workers and agriculture about 70 per cent.[35] The result was that by October Finland was forced to appeal to Germany for 175,000 tons of grain in order to survive until the 1942 harvest. Meanwhile, the threat of a declaration of war from Britain and the United States was growing, as Finland refused to halt its advance even after it had reoccupied its 1939 frontier established by the Peace of Tartu in 1920. Up until this point the western powers had tolerated Finland's co-belligerency despite strenuous Soviet objections, but were not prepared to endanger relations further for a 'Greater Finland'.[36] Militarily the war was also proving extremely costly for the Finns (some 75,000 casualties were experienced in 1941 alone) and, coupled with the worsening economic crisis, was hardly sustainable beyond 1941. The much-anticipated quick victory over the Soviet Union had failed to materialise, and the result demanded major structural changes as well as a comprehensive demobilisation of the army. Between the end of 1941 and the spring of 1942, the Finnish army shrank to just 150,000 men occupying defensive positions on what was to become a relatively quiet and inactive front.[37] This permitted Allied Lend-Lease supplies to flow unhindered from the northern ports, eased the pressure on Leningrad and freed Soviet troops for deployment on other, more critical fronts. Thus, in the course of 1941 Germany's single biggest contributor of foreign troops to the war against the Soviet Union had transformed itself from an aggressive co-belligerent to a passive advocate.

Clearly Nazi Germany's war against the Soviet Union had rapidly proven an unpopular one among many of Hitler's supporters and allies. By the end of the autumn only Romania and Italy remained firmly committed to the war in spite of its heavy cost and uncertain course. It was Operation Typhoon that was supposed to provide closure and stamp the summer battles of 1941 with a resounding mark of victory. Yet by the final week of October Army Group Centre's drive on Moscow was only slowly plodding forward on Kluge's northern wing. His southern wing was defending desperately against heavy Soviet counterattacks. Indeed for all the power of Hoepner's panzer group – the strongest on the eastern front at that time – Kluge's Fourth Army was making slower progress heading east than Napoleon's marching infantry had retreating west 129 years before. Clearly Zhukov's Western Front was again proving its resilience after being almost annihilated for the second time in four months (the first time was in the battle of Minsk). Even more remarkably, Zhukov was already returning to the offensive and placing Kluge under tremendous pressure. The war diary of Thoma's 20th Panzer Division recorded radio reports from its forward regiment defending a bridgehead over the Nava River on 26 October: 'Very heavy losses. Units mixed. Bridgehead can hardly be held.'[38] Kluge had already committed all his reserves, and on 27 October Bock was considering, 'in view of the anticipated attrition' and the absence of support from Guderian's distant panzer army, committing Army Group Centre's last remaining reserve divisions (Hellmich's 23rd Infantry Division and Lieutenant-General Erich Straube's 268th Infantry Division).[39]

Characteristic of the German high command, however, the emphasis was on the attack rather than defence. On 27 October Ruoff's V Army Corps took Volokolamsk in the north (see Map 14), the last remaining defensive region on the Mozhaisk Defensive Line (after Mozhaisk, Maloiaroslavets and Kaluga).[40] The next day (28 October) orders were issued to the Fourth Army for the capture of Klin, another 60 kilometres to the north-east. Yet there was now an important difference, which for the first time offered some measure of recognition of the incredibly arduous conditions. The Fourth Army's orders for the next stage of the offensive were only to 'make preparations so that in the event of a freeze it can resume the attack at clear points of main effort north and south of the [Moscow] highway with no loss of time'. This in effect suspended Kluge's advance until the ground had sufficiently hardened. It was precisely what many panzer commanders had been insisting upon as the only option for restoring the vital speed and 'shock' to their attacks. Yet as the war diary for Vietinghoff's XXXXVI Panzer Corps pointed out: 'The hope for a quick continuation of the corps after an intensification of the frosts can, however, not be realised because the fuel situation is continually worsening.' The diary also mentioned shortages in the supply of food and munitions, which would first have to be brought up to sustain the advance.[41] On 30 October the war diary of Panzer Group 4 was even more specific, stating that a continuation of the attack was dependent upon supplies because 'at the moment the troops have none'. Furthermore the panzer group estimated that once a permanent frost took hold it would require about six days for the necessary minimum of supplies to be brought up for a new attack. Of course there was no guarantee as to when the frosts would become permanent and, in the meantime, the war diary noted that the enemy 'directs all attainable strength here'.[42]

At the same time that Operation Typhoon was being put on hold Hitler was becoming increasingly frustrated at the slow pace of the attack and may have even suspected that the generals of the OKH were again trying to manipulate him, as they had attempted to do in July and August, to gain favour for their strategic preferences. Hitler had been seeking the redirection of Guderian's Second Panzer Army from Tula to Voronezh, but the OKH, backed by Bock's outright refusal to implement the order, had argued that Tula was the more important objective and that Kluge's drive on Moscow now required the support of Guderian's army. In spite of Hitler's order, the Second Panzer Army never turned south and simply drove until Guderian closed in on Tula, and Hitler, presented with a *fait accompli*, saw little choice but to acquiesce. With the OKH still pressing for Guderian's advance towards Moscow, Hitler wanted to know the real condition of Kluge's army, but no longer trusted the reports of the army command. Bock was told that in order for the Führer to find out, Kluge was to fly immediately to Hitler's headquarters, but that the OKH was not to be informed of this action.[43] There is no record of Kluge's discussion with Hitler, but the Fourth Army commander told Bock upon his return that Hitler had asked for a detailed account of the battle conditions, especially the state of the roads and the impact of the weather. As Bock wryly commented in his diary: 'He [Hitler] probably refused to believe the written reports, which is not surprising, for anyone who has not seen this filth doesn't think it possible.'[44]

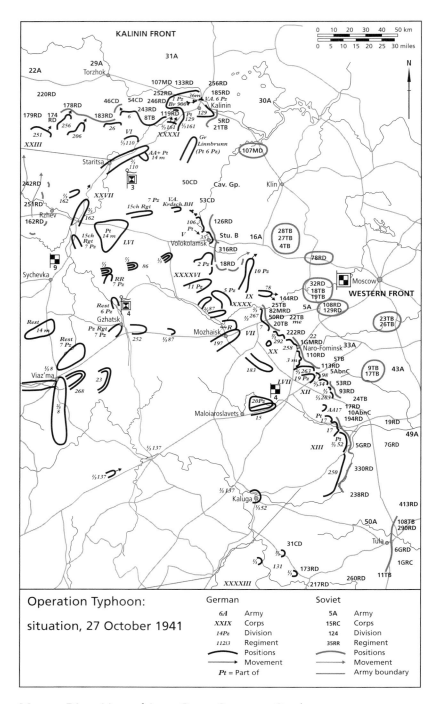

Map 14 Dispositions of Army Group Centre, 27 October 1941

In any case Kluge's report seems to have confirmed the problems raised by the OKH and thereby averted a widening rift in the German high command. Yet Kluge was also in a unique position to influence German strategy. The field marshal was a much more cautious attacker than many of the other senior commanders in Army Group Centre, and his army was suffering from a myriad of problems. It is therefore highly likely that he lobbied for a pause in operations until the ground hardened and also pressed for Guderian's continued drive north-east to assist the Fourth Army at Moscow. That Hitler was amenable to what Kluge had to say is suggested by both the length of the field marshal's stay (three nights and two days) as well as the subject of one of his nightly monologues in the presence of the Fourth Army commander. On the evening of 29 October Hitler suddenly appeared to reject the very notion of mobile warfare, which may well have stemmed from Kluge's reports on the battlefield conditions. Hitler stated:

> In a campaign, it's the infantryman who, when all's said, sets the tempo of the operations with his legs. That consideration should bid us [to] keep motorisation within reasonable limits. Instead of the six horses that used to pull an instrument of war, they've taken to using an infinitely more powerful motor-engine, [with] the sole objective of making possible a speed which is, in practice, unusable – that's been proved. In the choice between mobility and power, the decision in peace-time is given too easily in favour of mobility.[45]

Certainly Kluge was at times extremely critical of the aggressive mobile warfare practised by the panzer troops, and he had already butted heads with Guderian, Hoth and Hoepner during the eastern campaign. Kluge also displayed a distinctly servile acquiescence around Hitler in spite of the fact that Kluge already had dealings with the resistance movement and claimed to despise Hitler's regime. Yet Kluge could never quite bring himself to act against Hitler and soon became known in resistance circles as the *der Kluge Hans* (Clever Hans), an unflattering reference to his fence-sitting indecision. Despite his private views, Kluge's duplicity in Hitler's company and his highly regarded performance in the Polish and French campaigns endeared him to the German dictator.[46] Kluge was also one of the few generals to have supported Hitler's decision to redirect Guderian into Ukraine in August, which resulted in the victory at Kiev.[47] Now, with Operation Typhoon stalled, Hitler trusted Kluge's advice above that of many of the other generals.

In a telephone conversation with Goebbels towards the end of October, Hitler judged the military situation as 'extremely positive'. Goebbels then drew attention to Hitler's willingness to accept a pause in operations. 'We are waiting for dry [conditions] or even frost. When the panzers can use their engines again and the roads are free of mud and muck, then Soviet resistance will be broken in a relatively short time.'[48] Yet while Goebbels faithfully reproduced Hitler's opinion and tried to sustain himself with his master's emphatic confidence, in truth Goebbels saw the eastern front in a much darker – albeit realistic – light. On 31 October the propaganda minister noted in his diary: 'At the moment the general situation offers little joy. Even though considerable progress is made here and there the planned grand offensive, which was supposed to lead to a complete annihilation of the last battle-worthy Bolshevik divisions, is currently stuck in the mud ... Gradually it seems necessary to me that we and also our people need to abandon the idea that in this winter the ambitious objectives will be obtained and start anew in the coming spring.'[49] Of course the implications of having to retract statements about impending conquests, not to mention the fact that the whole campaign had already been pronounced 'decided', which most people understood as 'finished', caused Goebbels unending anxiety. On 30 October he noted in his diary: 'The damage caused from a somewhat too optimistic assessment of the situation has to be corrected as soon as possible.'[50] Yet, short of the Red Army's collapse or the conquest of Moscow, there was no word-twisting antidote to the fever-pitch expectations of the German people, and the SD report of 30 October detected for the first time since early September a 'certain disappointment' (gewisse Enttäuschung) and a 'somewhat reduced mood' within the population.[51] It was the beginning of a long fall from grace for the Nazi leadership in the opinion of the victory-minded German public.

At the front, the harsh conditions had long since affected the mood of the men, but opinions ranged widely from optimism to despair largely because the men lacked an overview of the army group's situation. One lieutenant wrote at the end of October: 'Who is left? We are all in God's hands, surrounded by a thousand dangers ... One hangs onto life. Still 70 kilometres to Moscow. When will the advance continue? What is happening in the big picture? Is everyone so miserably battered as us?'[52] Another soldier, Gerhard vom Bruch, noted on 26 October: 'We hear the wildest rumours, that Stalin has already fled the city and that within a few weeks the Soviet state will be brought to its knees. But in reality, things seem rather less rosy.'[53] Lieutenant Walther Schaefer-Kehnert of the 11th Panzer Division recalled the increasingly bitter reaction of the men to the German propaganda: 'For weeks they had been trumpeting in Germany that we had already won the war. That's what the *Völkischer Beobachter* actually announced. Our troops were furious. They said: "They should come and take a look for themselves!"'[54] As the advance ground to a halt, Blumentritt at Fourth Army made a similar claim in his post-war writings, which also alluded to the miscalculations and oversights of the army's command:

> We discovered to our surprise and dismay that the defeated Russians had not ceased to exist as a military force, and the intensity of the battles increased every day … All this came as a complete surprise to us. We could not believe that the situation had changed so radically after our decisive victories when, it seemed, the capital was almost in our hands. The troops recalled with indignation the bombastic announcement made in October by our Propaganda Ministry.[55]

Even at this point, however, many lessons remained unlearned and there was still a sense that the next offensive would achieve a decisive result. Writing a letter on 30 October, Hoepner noted that after the victory at Viaz'ma everything had got bogged down in the impenetrable mud. He then concluded: 'Dear God give us fourteen days of frost! Then we will surround Moscow.'[56]

 While Hoepner still foresaw an offensive solution to the army group's problems and seemed to believe that all his difficulties could be solved if only the roads would harden, he was soon to be granted his wish for an offensive, but not towards Moscow. The fighting around Kalinin had already drawn in Kirchner's XXXXI Panzer Corps and the whole of Strauss's Ninth Army, yet the situation had not improved, and in fact by 27 October Konev's Kalinin Front was in danger of cutting off the city completely. As Bock noted in his diary, 'Things don't look good at Kalinin. To the west the enemy has driven across the Volga and is trying to seal off the city from the south.'[57] Indeed the fighting south of Kalinin was desperate and extremely bloody. In only four days between 25 and 28 October Recke's 161st Infantry Division lost some 1,450 men bringing the division's total casualties at Kalinin to some 2,000 troops.

At the same time the total losses for Gollnick's 36th Motorised Infantry Division at Kalinin stood at 960 men, while Rittau's 129th Infantry Division had lost a further 550 men.[58] Reports in the war diary of Kirchner's XXXXI Panzer Corps speak of extreme shortages in munitions at the height of the defensive fighting, leading to increased casualties and local breakthroughs. On 29 October the diary noted: 'The defence of Kalinin is exclusively a question of munitions supply, which at the moment is not nearly sufficient.' The diary went on to cite instances of gun batteries with just forty shells at the height of the Soviet attacks.[59] It was desperate fighting and everywhere units had to be amalgamated to make them operational again, but the net loss of strength proved crippling. Krüger's 1st Panzer Division reported that its losses had been so severe that it was in need of a complete organisational overhaul, requiring five days out of the line to conduct.[60] At the same time an advanced battle group of Landgraf's 6th Panzer Division (from Schaal's LVI Panzer Corps) was driving north to Kalinin but, as Major-General Raus reported, its tanks were in a sorry state. By the end of October the division's surviving tanks had averaged a distance of 11,500 kilometres for the Mark IIs, 12,500 kilometres for the Czech 35(t)s and 11,000 kilometres for the Mark IVs. There were so few spare parts remaining that in the case of the Czech 35(t) Raus reported that from forty-one broken-down tanks only ten could be repaired by cannibalising the others. As Raus concluded, 'perhaps the armoured hulls are still salvageable'.[61]

On 28 October, as Strauss's Ninth Army and Kirchner's XXXXI Panzer Corps fought desperately at Kalinin, the OKH sent orders to Army Group Centre confirming the new operation of Panzer Group 3, together with Panzer Group 4, for an advance towards Yaroslavl–Rybinsk (250 kilometres north-east of Kalinin) and later on to Vologda (350 kilometres north-east of Kalinin).[62] With Kalinin far from secure, the Ninth Army expressed a degree of consternation at the thought of such a distant offensive. 'The [Ninth] army confirmed that all other thoughts concerning a wide-ranging advance now must be subordinated to the main task at hand: defence of Kalinin.'[63] Reinhardt in command of Panzer Group 3 did not agree. He judged the enemy forces attacking south of Kalinin as 'fragmented parts of units' and insisted to Bock: 'There is no difficulty with the enemy!'[64] He set the date for the new offensive on 4 November even though that was too soon to allow Schaal's LVI Panzer Corps to reach the staging areas for the attack and

Kirchner's battered XXXXI Panzer Corps would have to proceed alone, supported only by forward elements of the 6th Panzer Division and three infantry divisions (86th, 129th and 162nd).[65] On the following day (30 October), however, Strauss overruled Reinhardt and forbade the use of his infantry divisions for the attack. Strauss viewed the whole offensive as foolhardy, especially when Panzer Group 3's own war diary acknowledged that the desperate situation around Kalinin remained 'unchanged'. Strong Soviet attacks had been held to the north of the city, but south of Kalinin the enemy was now making progress driving to the west and south-west.[66] Bock was also worried and spoke of a 70-kilometre gap between Volokolamsk and Kalinin, which neither Kluge nor Strauss had extended themselves to cover and was now attracting the enemy's attention.[67] This now constituted Bock's greatest worry, but his field commanders were reluctant to deal with the problem as their forces were stretched enough as it was. Strauss was struggling to hold the army group's northern flank and now had orders for a wildly ambitious offensive. Yet on 31 October Bock determined that the Ninth Army now treat the northern flank as a secondary front and deploy everything Strauss could spare to close the gap between Kalinin and Yaropolets (a small village 15 kilometres north-west of Volokolamsk). Reinhardt, for his part, was still focused on launching his offensive to Yaroslavl–Rybinsk and showed little interest in closing the gap to the east unless it were 'linked with his attack to the northeast'. Bock, however, was tiring of the panzer commander's blind ambivalence to the army group's problems. 'I had stated and restated to him that we must lose no time in clearing the eastern flank, while Reinhardt's attack was out of the question until lasting cold arrived. Strauss agreed.'[68] Indeed, beyond the sheer weakness of Reinhardt's forces at Kalinin as well as the strategic sense of preventing the developing Soviet bulge in the army group's front, Panzer Group 3's war diary makes clear that there was neither the fuel nor the munitions to support Reinhardt's reckless bid for a further offensive. Even the German airfield at Kalinin, which had been receiving direct deliveries from Ju-52 aircraft, was now closed as a forward supply base on account of heavy aircraft losses.[69]

While much of the history of the German panzer troops in the early years of World War II highlights their daring boldness in achieving success against the odds, the eastern front in 1941 also provides many examples where boldness crossed the fine line into recklessness. Hoepner

claiming he could seize Moscow if only he had been granted two weeks
of frost and Reinhardt seeking to drive 250 kilometres to Yaroslavl–
Rybinsk with one understrength panzer corps are cases in point. Here
the caution and attention to more immediate dangers, as advocated
by the much-maligned infantry generals, were surely appropriate
and acted, at least in some instances, as an essential brake on overly
ambitious motorised operations. Yet far greater constraints on the
panzer groups in October 1941 were the combined effects of Russia's
rasputitsa and the often-undervalued role of the Red Army in the early
weeks of the battle for Moscow. The Western, Briansk and Kalinin
Fronts doggedly held the line on the approaches to Moscow and could
not simply have been supplanted by mud and cold weather alone.
Indeed already at the end of October Kluge and Strauss were busy
repelling heavy Soviet counterattacks from both Zhukov's and
Konev's respective fronts.

Army Group Centre's October offensive had promised so much
and the scale of the victories in the first half of the month had seemingly
provided the essential precondition for wide-ranging advances and
major conquests. By the end of the month, however, many of the old
problems from Operation Barbarossa – logistical weakness, inadequate
transportation, poor roads, weakened combat units and stiff Soviet
resistance – were compounded by the sodden ground, endless mud
and freezing temperatures. It was enough to halt the almost two million
men of Bock's army group and stop Operation Typhoon. The operation
was not formally called off – local attacks and opportunities for
advance were still to be exploited – but major operations were no longer
expected until the ground hardened. With profound regret, Bock wrote
on the first day of November:

> Kluge spoke once again about the possibilities of attacking. He said
> that if he drove his forces forward now there might be a gain of a
> few kilometres then that would be it again because artillery and
> motorized weapons became stuck. I told him that we would gain
> nothing by that. Naturally we must stay alert to any weakening of
> the enemy and strike there immediately. But in general the army
> had to, as per orders, make thorough preparations for an attack
> as soon as the cold sets in. This time benefits the enemy but
> unfortunately there is no other solution.
>
> The situation is enough to drive one to despair and filled with
> envy I look to the Crimea, where we are advancing vigorously in

the sunshine over the dry ground of the steppe and the Russians are scattering to the four winds. It could be the same here if we weren't stuck up to our knees in the mud.[70]

That Bock felt somewhat hard done by only reflects the misplaced expectations of the single most important German commander in the east. Bock, like so many in the high command, seemingly had little real understanding of what a motorised campaign through central Russia might encounter in the autumn period, and his envy, borne of his own ignorance, for the 'sunshine' and 'dry ground' of battlefields more than 1,000 kilometres to the south only indicates the misconceptions upon which operations proceeded. Indeed Bock's observation that scattering Russians to the four winds 'could be the same here', if not for the mud, seems an entirely moot point, perhaps analogous to hoping that the Russian winter would not be cold. Yet Bock at least recognised the uselessness of struggling against both the intractable conditions and the Red Army, but there was no thought yet of adopting winter quarters. The end of October halt was only a pause in operations, not a cessation of the offensive. November would present new challenges and demand new sacrifices, especially once the offensive resumed and Bock discovered how correct he had been in stating that the pause would also benefit the enemy. In the final days of October, however, the men of Army Group Centre welcomed a much-needed rest, which for many was their first chance to wash, rest and keep warm since Typhoon began.

With the widespread pause of Army Group Centre, many of the men took the opportunity to write letters home, putting their thoughts about their present circumstances and hopes for the future into words. Adolf B. happily reported that he and his comrades now spent their time reading and playing chess: 'militarily the war is already decided and whether we are employed again is still a question'.[71] Perhaps some of the men wanted to spare their loved ones unnecessary worry, but for many men within Army Group Centre there was still an enduring belief that victory was to be obtained at Moscow and that this goal was seemingly now very close at hand. Karl Fuchs wrote his father about the successful battle he had taken part in at Viaz'ma and then continued: 'We have never before struck the enemy with such crushing defeats. I guess the Russians never dreamed that we would engage in this kind of offensive prior to winter. I'm convinced that the last cohesive forces of the enemy have been decimated and once again our Führer has proven to the world that the German soldier can do incredible tasks.'[72] Another solder wrote on 29 October that he was taking part 'in the last great battle for Moscow', which he hoped would be over 'before the onset of winter'.[73] Yet, while optimism was sustained by the hope of impending victory, those who could not see an end in sight were more typically beset by depression and even despair. Martin Gareis wrote that the unceasing torments of the war were an unbearable strain: 'Who can hold out for weeks without becoming weak in rain, cold, hunger and thirst, in battle and under threat of death, in dirt and filth, with fleas, lice, bugs and without any cleanliness, with hours spent daily standing or crouching in water?'[74] Even beyond the personal torments of the men, the vastness of the Russian landscape mired in miles of mud and bleak interminable sameness gave an impression of the unending, the unreachable horizon, where the war could not be escaped. Hans Roth noted in his diary on 27 October: 'It is always the same: a dreary leaden sky driven by strong winds and alternating snow and rain showers. The roads and fields are the same: far and wide nothing but mud and muck, sometimes up to a meter in depth' (see Illustration 21).[75]

21 German soldiers dressed in some of the few winter uniforms to reach Bock's front in October 1941. Yet even for the best-equipped German troops, the camouflaging white sheets draped over the half-track suggest improvisation was always a necessary skill in the *Ostheer*.

The war was also taking place in increasing darkness as the days shortened and night fell by five o'clock in the afternoon.[76] Since the first days of Operation Barbarossa two and half hours of daylight had been lost in the morning and darkness fell three and a half hours earlier.[77] Already by the middle of October there were only ten hours of daylight a day, hampering offensive operations and aiding the clandestine work of partisan groups who were becoming increasingly bold in Army Group Centre's rear.[78] In one attack on 31 October twenty-one German soldiers were killed 15 kilometres north of Briansk, while countless ambushes dogged the supply columns upon which so much depended.[79] Not surprisingly, German countermeasures were both swift and violent, often resulting in the complete destruction of nearby settlements.[80] Yet closer to the front new orders were being issued in the area of Stumme's XXXX Panzer Corps forbidding the 'senseless destruction of villages through shooting or burning because the troops urgently need quarters'.[81] Indeed in many areas local fighting increasingly centred on the possession of villages for the warmth they offered. One German doctor noted that, whenever a German attack sought to force the Red Army out of a village, 'they would fight like tigers for the comfort of a night spent round a peasant's huge stove'.[82] Yet for all the murderous savagery with which the Nazi–Soviet war was being fought, by the autumn of 1941 a new phenomenon was beginning to take place both within Army Group Centre and in places all along the inactive parts of the eastern front.[83] Small unofficial ceasefires were cautiously being agreed, often with an unspoken accord, by German and Soviet soldiers. Human exhaustion, an inability to break the stalemate of positional warfare and the mutual acceptance of a common gain produced the circumstances which enabled varying periods of harmony for each side. At the Malakova ravine, Wolfgang Reinhardt recalled:

> We were stationed there from the autumn of 1941 … The position was fairly quiet; we'd built it up with bunkers. The Russians were 200 metres away across the ravine and they had done the same. So we were positioned very close, close enough to hear the balalaika music they played for us in the evening. There was a sawmill below and it produced wooden posts. We had an unwritten law that in the mornings we would go down and fetch posts to build our bunkers with, and in the afternoon the Russians would fetch posts in their turn. Nothing bad happened, we were in total agreement with one another.[84]

Robert R. noted that he forbade his machine-gunners to shoot Soviet soldiers who sought only to sit on warm house ovens exposed to German fire in no man's land. 'A small ceasefire', he noted in a letter home.[85] Yet as the front settled down across large stretches of Army Group Centre, in late October 1941 local ceasefires were very much the exception rather than the rule, and the fighting continued from fixed positions in local probing actions, night-time raids and sporadic shelling and gunfire.

Another reminder of the war for the German troops was the increasingly one-sided activity of the Soviet air force operating from Moscow's many well-resourced airfields. The forward German positions typically did not have enough Flak or fighter protection to shield them from what Vietinghoff's XXXXVI Panzer Corps described as the 'lively enemy activity of fighters and bombers'.[86] In fact in only a few days at the end of October Veiel's 2nd Panzer Division suffered more than 100 casualties from aerial attacks alone,[87] which the Fourth Army reported were the highest losses of this kind since the start of the war.[88]

Just as Operation Barbarossa had withered and died short of its objective, so too was Operation Typhoon now drawing to a halt and in danger of becoming an offensive only in name. By the end of October the constant flow of orders from Army Group Centre pressing the attack forward ceased, and static positions were quickly adopted almost everywhere along the vast front. Officially this was only a 'pause' in operations, but getting the front moving again would prove harder and take longer than Bock anticipated. Moreover, the strength that Bock so desperately hoped to gain by halting Typhoon was taking him dangerously close to the ravages of a Russian winter, while his army group still had no prepared positions or winter equipment. At the same time Zhukov benefited from Moscow's expansive logistic infrastructure to prepare for the November offensive he knew to expect. The 1941 German offensive in the east was not yet over, but October was the last month of the great victories and deep advances (for the German–Soviet front at the start of November, see Map 15).

Operation Typhoon was conceived by the German high command to be an all-out final attempt to end the war against the Soviet Union in 1941. A winter campaign had never been anticipated and even the preparations underway by the end of October were still hopelessly inadequate to sustain the three million men of the *Ostheer* in the field. Yet far from restraining German ambitions, adversity tended only to

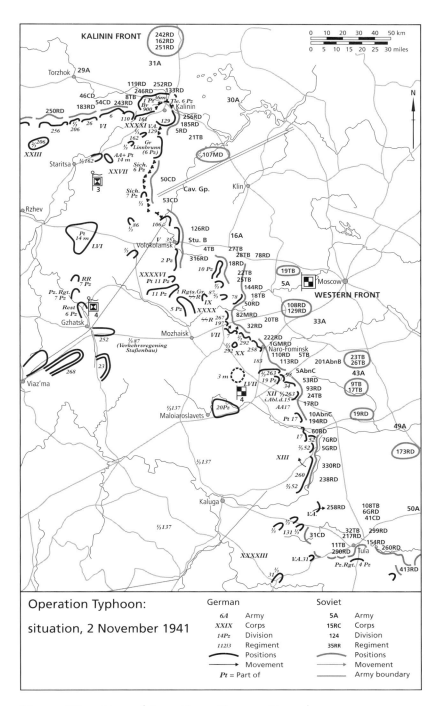

Map 15 Dispositions of Army Group Centre, 2 November 1941

radicalise the army's plans and reinforce the resolution to press once again for another decisive 'final' blow against the Soviet Union. This was the consistent pattern of response seen again and again throughout the eastern campaign as each new operation – at Minsk, Smolensk and Kiev, and now the drive on Moscow – was followed by a pause in which the failure to break Soviet resistance was ignored and a new offensive was simply concocted. Of course on the surface each operation, just as at Viaz'ma and Briansk, netted remarkable totals of Soviet prisoners of war and destroyed vast sums of Soviet equipment. One can, however, win battles and lose a war, which is perhaps nowhere better illustrated than on the eastern front in 1941. By the end of October the German high command found itself, once again, at the end of another operational success, albeit one which was still very far from the stated goal of ending Soviet resistance.

Indeed in spite of the offensives launched by the Western and Kalinin Fronts in the second half of October there was still no serious thought given to the Red Army's capacity for seizing back the initiative or launching any kind of winter offensive. The only questions the German command was asking itself were how far a renewed German offensive could penetrate and along which axis of advance such an attempt should be directed. At the end of October it was already strikingly apparent that any new operation would enjoy an even more perilous margin for success than the already overly ambitious hopes invested in Operation Typhoon. It was now a race to build up for the battle of Moscow, and in that regard Zhukov enjoyed many advantages over Bock. Army Group Centre was overstretched, underresourced and at the end of long and tenuous supply lines. A visit to Army Group Centre by Lieutenant-Colonel Bernhard von Lossberg, who worked for Jodl at the OKW, led to discussions with Lieutenant-Colonel Henning von Tresckow, the first general-staff officer at Army Group Centre. According to Lossberg, Tresckow stated that in his opinion the troops were in a worse state than the German western army in September 1918. 'It was therefore high time to end the mobile operations in the east for this year and commit the troops to building winter positions.'[89] Yet most of the men in the German high command did not think in such terms. If Germany held the initiative, the army would attack, and even if the odds were stacked against them the German military culture or 'way of war' still tended to overwhelmingly favour an offensive solution.[90]

The experience of a winter campaign had proved devastating to Charles XII and Napoleon I, heralding the demise of their respective empires. Yet in the minds of the German generals it was the fate of the Soviet empire that was now being decided. Some, however, were perceptive enough to foresee another reality and, like Tresckow, question whose fate was actually being decided. Lieutenant-Colonel Oskar Munzel, the commander of the 6th Panzer Regiment in Model's 3rd Panzer Division, concluded at the end of October that Operation Typhoon had run its course. 'The great attack towards Moscow failed on the overestimation of our strength and, above all, on account of the yearly climate and terrain difficulties. The culminating point of the campaign in the east had already been surpassed.'[91]

CONCLUSION

The opening phase of Operation Typhoon confirmed Germany's enduring operational superiority in the east. Bock's new offensive soon overwhelmed the defending Soviet fronts and created two large pockets filled with anywhere between 750,000 and 1,000,000 Soviet troops. Few in the German high command doubted that another immense hole in the Soviet front – coming so soon after the great encirclement at Kiev – would permit both Bock's rapid advance to Moscow as well as threaten the flanks of the remaining Soviet fronts to the north and south. Throughout the OKH and OKW there was an overriding feeling of excitement and expectation. It appeared as though the back of the Red Army's resistance had at last been broken, and Hitler felt sufficiently confident to authorise a statement claiming that the war in the east had been 'decided'. It appeared Moscow would fall within the coming week or two and that the war in the east would start to wind down. Yet, as we have seen, none of this happened. The campaign was far from decided, Moscow was not about to fall and, far from winding down, Germany's war in the east was only in its opening phase.

According to many of the German generals, the answer to what went wrong was simple. They were thwarted by the arrival of the autumn rains, which paralysed all movement both at the front and in the forward movement of supplies. Thus at the Red Army's nadir 'General Mud', aided later by 'General Winter', acted to save Moscow and the Soviet cause. Any accusation that the generals had left their drive on the Soviet capital too late in the year again elicited a simple explanation for their failure. In July and August the OKH as well as many of the commanders within Army Group Centre engaged in a bitter, and ultimately unsuccessful, dispute with Hitler for a continuation of the advance towards Moscow in the late summer months. This time the army's plans were thwarted by Hitler, who insisted upon the diversion of Bock's panzer divisions into Ukraine for the battle of Kiev, causing the delay that ultimately led to Operation Typhoon getting caught in the autumn rainy season. Thus, according to the popular post-war view espoused by the generals, the German army's victory in the 1941 campaign was prevented by circumstances entirely beyond their control and better judgement. Hitler's baneful interference followed by the harsh Russian weather had combined to snatch a victory for the Soviet Union from the very jaws of their defeat.

For many years after the war, this version of events was accepted in western historiography and formed a cornerstone of our understanding for Operation Barbarossa's failure. It was certainly not uncommon for historians to assert that if only Hitler had listened to his generals the war may well have ended in victory in 1941.[1] Until 1991 the dismissal of this view by eastern bloc historians centred on the role of the Red Army in frustrating the German plan for a blitzkrieg victory in the east. The official view was that Soviet countermeasures as well as the dogged resistance of the Red Army foiled German plans. There was also a fervent rejection of the notion that the outcome of the war could ever have been determined by German strategic choices.

In the post-Cold War era scholars have tempered the extremes of each position, yet the discussion today has tended more towards highlighting the role of Soviet resistance and the *Ostheer*'s operational problems over a reconsideration of German strategic options and subsequent decisions. This is not to suggest any kind of revival in the Marxist-Leninist historical worldview, but rather recognition of the fact that events on the ground were impacting upon the strategic circumstances of the war to a much greater extent than the decisions of the German high command. In other words, the German generals did not control the course of the war to anywhere near the extent that they believed they did, either at the time or in their subsequent post-war analysis.

Yet east/west historiography still produces widely divergent views. Official Soviet, and later Russian, histories contend that the Germans won the crushing victories at Viaz'ma and Briansk largely as a result of superior numbers. While Bock's reinforced army group certainly did outnumber his rivals in the opposing Western, Reserve and Briansk Fronts, official Russian sources nevertheless include exaggerated figures of German strengths. Thus, instead of 1,500 German tanks Russian sources report 1,700 and in place of 1,000 German aircraft Russian historians mention 1,390. The most inaccurate figure is for German artillery, which Russian sources suggest amounted to some 14,000 guns, but in reality numbered no more than 3,000. Only in raw manpower do Russian sources actually underestimate the size of Bock's army group, suggesting a force of 1.8 million troops (100,000 men fewer than German files indicate).[2] While Bock's numerical superiority certainly played a role in the victories at Viaz'ma and Briansk, it alone did not account for Germany's initial success. Bock's superiority in central Russia amounted to about 500 more tanks, some 350 more aircraft and roughly 650,000 more men. Yet the German–Soviet front before Moscow had remained largely unchanged since late July, which should have allowed for better defensive works as well as a better awareness of German concentrations and strategic intentions. Stalin simply did not expect the Germans to launch an operation of this scale so late in the year. In late August and early September he anticipated that Guderian's drive into Ukraine was only a ruse to draw off Soviet forces and conceal a renewed offensive towards Moscow. In the meantime Stalin ordered the Dukhovshchina and Yel'nya offensives (28 August to 10 September) in order to disrupt and even push back Bock's army group. These offensives certainly cost the German Ninth and Fourth Armies dearly, but they did not win much ground and were even more costly to the already depleted Soviet armies that would soon be defending Moscow. Thus by October the great majority of the Soviet divisions in central Russia were dangerously under strength or filled with poorly trained reserves and recently recruited militia units.

While Stalin had incorrectly judged the direction of Guderian's operations in August and September, he then compounded this decision by refusing to allow the withdrawal of the Soviet South-Western Front from its deep salient defending Kiev. The rapid destruction of this force with the loss of four Soviet armies again deceived Stalin, as well as the Stavka, as to where to expect the next German offensive. With eastern Ukraine and southern Russia now largely exposed, not to mention the seemingly imminent fall of Leningrad in the north, there seemed little doubt that German offensives could continue on either end of the eastern front, but not in the middle. Indeed Army Group South did press its advantage, with Kleist's panzer group and Field Marshal Erich von Manstein's Eleventh Army combining in early October to destroy the Soviet Ninth and Eighteenth Armies in the battle on the Sea of Azov. Yet an offensive on the scale of Typhoon in the centre of the German front was completely unexpected by the Soviet command.[3] Poor Soviet intelligence no doubt played a role in this catastrophic oversight and one cannot expect the Soviet command to have anticipated the bitter German strategic disputes, which led to a confused and changing set of directives for the *Ostheer*, but nevertheless Stalin and the Stavka bear considerable responsibility for the disasters at Viaz'ma and Briansk. Soviet strategic deployments repeated many of the mistakes from June 1941, with Soviet armies committed in bulk across the breadth of the German front. This facilitated German encirclements especially when the Stavka stubbornly insisted upon holding the line even after multiple breakthroughs by panzer forces had been achieved. Screening the front with lighter forces while holding back larger reserves to identify and counterattack German penetrations would have proved far more effective and should have been part of the Soviet learning curve after more than three months of repeated German offensives. Instead, Stalin followed the same road that had led to encirclement and disaster at Kiev. In the critical period before the German panzer groups linked up behind the Soviet front, desperate requests for withdrawals were refused in spite of the fact that no reserves were available to block or counterattack German breakthroughs. It was a catastrophic series of errors made worse by the fact that they had all been made before.

While official Russian histories have tended to blame German numerical superiority for the creation of encirclements on the road to Moscow, the fighting to eliminate those pockets has resulted in further divergent east/west views. Western historians have typically adopted the view, first expounded by the German generals, that the battles at Viaz'ma and Briansk represented overwhelming battlefield triumphs with few parallels in history. Russian historians, on the other hand, tend to follow the view advanced by some of the leading Soviet generals, including Zhukov, that the extended fighting at Viaz'ma and Briansk delayed German forces long enough to allow reserves to arrive and halt the German attack on Moscow. Placed in the wider context of the battle for Moscow, this allows the battles at Viaz'ma and Briansk to be seen as an expensive, but ultimately essential price to pay for the defence of the Soviet capital.

In many respects both perspectives have their merits depending on whether one takes a shorter (operational) or longer (strategic) view of the events. Indeed it may well be argued that the October fighting was on many levels a reflection of Germany's 1941 campaign, in which the Soviets suffered grossly disproportionate losses, but the ultimate cost to the *Ostheer* denied it victory. Perhaps the most balanced appraisal of the October fighting comes from the deputy chief of the Soviet general staff and head of the Operations Staff, Lieutenant-General A. M. Vasilevsky, who summed up the momentous implications of Operation Typhoon for both sides:

> In appraising the outcome of the events in October it should be said that it was very unfavourable to us. The Soviet army had suffered severe losses. The enemy had advanced nearly 100 miles. But the aims of Operation Typhoon had not been achieved. One of Bock's groupings had become hopelessly bogged down near Tula, another beyond Mozhaisk, and yet another in the upper reaches of the Volga [at Kalinin]. The staunchness and courage of the defenders of the Soviet capital stopped the Nazi hordes.[4]

Nor do such depictions belong exclusively to Soviet accounts. Lieutenant-General Kurt von Tippelskirch, who was a divisional commander in October 1941 and rose to become an army and even army group commander by the end of the war,[5] wrote of Germany's position in the autumn of 1941. 'The magnitude of the local successes spoke for Hitler, but only the outcome of the war could prove whether the extent of the tactical victories on the battlefields was in proportion to the resultant time lost for the continuation of the operation. Should the goal of the campaign not be attained then the Russians had lost a battle, but won the war.'[6] In a similar vein, Kesselring's account of Operation Typhoon dismisses any notion of the Soviets snatching a victory from the jaws of defeat. In his account the outcome of the October fighting was less a matter of the *rasputitsa*'s arrival and much more a matter of strategic factors. According to Kesselring:

> For this task [deep panzer thrusts in October] the panzer groups were too weak. Our strategic mechanised forces had to be proportionate to the depth and breadth of the area to be conquered and to the strength of the enemy, and we had not anywhere near this strength. Our fully tracked vehicles, including tanks, were not

adequately serviceable. There were technical limitations to constant movement. A mobile operation in 1,000 kilometres depth through strongly occupied enemy territory requires vast supplies, especially if there is no chance of falling back on large and useful enemy stores. Our lines of communication and our airfields lay mostly in enemy threatened country, and were insufficiently protected.[7]

Highlighting such strategic factors goes a long way to a fuller understanding of Operation Typhoon's failure and suggests that the operational perspective, so prevalent within the Wehrmacht, came at the expense of a more lucid assessment of the war's possibilities. Indeed Operation Typhoon, for all its success at Viaz'ma and Briansk, further exemplified the German command's inability to grasp warfare beyond the operational level, leading to a repetition of mistakes seen throughout Operation Barbarossa. In the aftermath of Viaz'ma and Briansk, for example, Hitler and the OKH were not merely concerned with Moscow; they also wanted Bock to launch simultaneous offensives in the north as well as the south to capitalise on the breach his army group had created and roll up more of the Soviet front. This forestalled a concentrated push on Moscow and overextended Bock's increasingly limited strength.

In drawing any definitive conclusions about the October fighting, it becomes clear, given the lofty aims of the Typhoon offensive and its subsequent additions, that much of the German command was deceived by the guise of success and poorly informed as to their real options and circumstances in the war. After three months of battlefield victories, Operation Typhoon needed to achieve something much more wide-ranging than just another battlefield success without decisive military or political implications for the outcome of the war. A major winter campaign was to be avoided at all costs, Moscow was to be surrounded and cut off, if not captured, and the Soviet front needed to be splintered beyond repair. None of these resulted from the October fighting and the costs to Army Group Centre suggested that a renewed offensive in November was even less likely to be successful. No one can deny the imposing scale of Bock's early successes in Operation Typhoon, but crushing the Soviet front attains less significance when that front was rebuilt again by the end of the month and when Army Group Centre's offensive had ground to a halt far short of its stated objectives. It is important to remember that battles are not ends in themselves and should not be viewed as such. A comprehensive victory over the Soviet Union was the overriding measure of success for the *Ostheer* in 1941 and, in spite of what some early histories concluded was an unbroken string of successes for the Wehrmacht, by the end of October the preconditions of a decisive victory were in fact far from being met. Even if Bock had reached Moscow in October the outcome would hardly have been more favourable. As Sir Ian Kershaw correctly concluded: 'Had the Wehrmacht reached the city, in the absence of a Luftwaffe capable of razing Moscow to the ground (as Hitler wanted), the result would probably have been a preview of what was to eventually happen at Stalingrad. And even had the city been captured, the war would not have been won.'[8]

Bock's October offensive was a failure at two important levels. Militarily Army Group Centre was fought to a standstill in front of Moscow. As Zhukov concluded: 'Petering out day by day, the German offensive finally stopped by the end of October at a front line running through Turginovo, Volokolamsk, Dorokhovo, Naro-Fominsk, a point west of Serpukhov and Aleksin. The Kalinin Front's defensive area near Kalinin had been stabilized as well.'[9] Given the seasonal difficulties, the tenacious resistance of the Red Army and the ability of the Soviet state to muster reserves, this is hardly a surprising outcome. Bock was always going to encounter problems on the road to Moscow, especially once opposed by a commander of Zhukov's expertise and unscrupulousness, but Bock's advance was further complicated by the inability of his army group to maintain a functioning logistics network as well as the erratic and overzealous demands of Hitler and the OKH. Thus militarily Army Group Centre was opposed by formidable forces, but further hindered by self-inflicted constraints.

The second German failure of October 1941 was no less decisive, but entirely self-inflicted. After the war Blumentritt complained about the German propaganda ministry trumpeting the successes of the *Ostheer* with 'a bombastic statement' declaring the Red Army to be 'practically annihilated'.[10] The fallout from Dietrich's bombshell was a frenzy of grandiloquent headlines claiming the war in the east to have been decided and declaring the brilliance of Adolf Hitler. The self-congratulatory tone of the pronouncements reflects both the extent of the high command's departure from reality and the heights from which German public opinion would soon sink. The short-term boon to German morale would soon transform into an albatross for exploitation by enemy propaganda, which dashed the hopes of the population but, more importantly, decisively contributed to the realisation, within both Germany and occupied Europe, that the Nazi state had fundamentally underestimated its enemy in the east. Paul Schmidt, the chief foreign ministry interpreter, observed the radical transformation in the messages being broadcast by Nazi propaganda during the final months of 1941. As Schmidt recalled: 'Instead of "We have won the war", foreigners now heard "We shall win the war", and finally "We cannot lose the war."' In Schmidt's words: 'The gramophone records were being changed.'[11]

While I have argued in my previous books that the turning point in Germany's war occurred as early as August 1941,[12] this by no means renders the later battles and campaigns of the *Ostheer* irrelevant or extraneous. Despite the fact that Operation Typhoon did not alter the course of the war in Germany's favour, as Evan Mawdsley correctly noted the battles of Viaz'ma and Briansk together stand as 'one of the greatest successes of German arms in the entire Second World War'.[13] Yet these battles, much like the battle of Kiev, have often been subsumed into the wider German offensive of 1941 and have seldom been the subject of specific attention. One of the German army's more remarkable features in this period is its seemingly irrational devotion to the offensive. In the midst of the Russian *rasputitsa* with knee-deep mud and only the most meagre supplies, whole panzer divisions were pressed into the attack with only small groups of marching infantry, very little heavy weaponry and whatever tanks still had fuel. Even at the end of October, when the offensive had finally been halted, there was no discussion of adopting winter positions but only of planning for the next offensive. As Robert Citino explained, 'the notion of calling a halt ran contrary to everything this officer corps believed: the importance of will and aggression, and especially the importance of finishing the war in a single campaign'.[14] Not only was there a refusal to give up the offensive in 1941, but at no point in the year was there any serious acknowledgement that Germany's war effort was in serious trouble.

While some may claim that such a recognition comes only with the benefit of hindsight, the fact remains that even as late as 1944 comparatively few of the German generals gave voice to such 'defeatist talk' and even fewer contemplated independently surrendering their commands until after Hitler was dead. It has sometimes been maintained that the German generals of this later era were more 'Nazi' than those in 1941, but the notion that there was ever a non-Nazi German officer corps within the Wehrmacht during World War II is something of a post-war myth. Halder himself, whose active service ended in September 1942, argued after the war in a private letter to Blumentritt that there was no cause for surrender at any point in the war regardless of the military situation. 'The question of when the last war had to be seen as lost makes no sense. A war is a political act and can be militarily hopeless for the longest time while it still offers political chances. Such chances can even come up unexpectedly, as the Seven Years War [1756–1763] proved. So the correct answer remains: a war is only lost when one gives up.'[15] Yet the unpopular nature of such a viewpoint was not lost on Halder and he felt it necessary to add: 'Naturally a German soldier cannot give such an answer to a foreigner, however, without putting that man-eating German militarism on trial again.'[16] Indeed there were many aspects of their leadership during the war that the German generals sought to remain discreetly tight-lipped about after 1945. The life-and-death struggle against Bolshevism and the active support of the generals for Hitler's war of annihilation meant that surrender was simply not one of the political options available to the high command. Indeed, the unwillingness even to consider surrender, unlike in the militarily hopeless situations of 1806 and 1918, only further highlights the high command's ties to Hitler.

While this study has been an operational and strategic analysis of Operation Typhoon, there has also been an attempt to include a perspective on the fighting from the everyday *Landser*'s point of view. Illustrating the broader narrative of events in Hitler's war in the east is no less important than telling the human story of that conflict, replete with all its suffering and torment. At the conclusion to his landmark study of the so-called *Bloodlands* in the east, Timothy Snyder observed: 'The Nazi and Soviet regimes turned people into numbers ... It is for us as scholars to seek these numbers and to put them into perspective. It is for us as humanists to turn the number back into people.'[17] For those researching Hitler's war against the Soviet Union, the single most striking feature is the sheer scale of its violence. No other war in history produced so much hardship, destruction and death. Soviet losses alone have been estimated at some twenty-seven million people.[18] Turning numbers of this size back into people will require more than the scope of any single book, but Snyder's point is well taken – numbers do matter. In assessing the military history of the Nazi–Soviet war one must be careful to point out that, unlike the rather clear distinctions in *Bloodlands*, soldiers in the east often served as both victims and perpetrators. Illegal killings were frighteningly commonplace and, with both sides distributing hate propaganda, brutality and violence were often viewed as 'necessary' and even 'acceptable'. Violence was seen as a means of survival, and without question the soldiers of the Red Army and the Wehrmacht, to varying degrees and in different circumstances, contributed to each regime's destructive capabilities. Charting the human tragedy of the Nazi–Soviet war is therefore more complex because its perpetrators often became its victims and vice versa. The cycle of violence left few innocent or guiltless and fed a culture of criminal behaviour that perverted otherwise reasonable men and led them to perform acts of untold cruelty.

Warfare is a brutalising process stripping the soldier and his opponent of their shared humanity, while eroding reason and compassion. Hitler's war in the east was the epitome of this process and for that reason alone deserves intensive study. As Willy Peter Reese reflected during a pause in the fighting:

> The armour of apathy with which I had covered myself against terror, horror, fear, and madness, which saved me from suffering and screaming, crushed any tender stirring within me, snapped off the green shoots of hope, faith, and love of my fellow men, and turned my heart to stone ... At the same time, I bore in mind that I was fighting men I didn't hate, who were never enemies to me, who in their destiny were more like brothers; and that I was only trying to perform an imposed duty.[19]

Yet Reese was resigned to his fate as a soldier, all the while aware of its destructive implications. Before his death at the age of just twenty-three, Reese wrote in his journal: 'We served the imperative of history as specks of dust in the whirlwind and were privileged to participate in the end of our world.'[20]

NOTES

Introduction

1 Rüdiger Overmans, *Deutsche militärische Verluste im Zweiten Weltkrieg* (Munich, 2000) p. 279.
2 I use 'Soviet' as the generic adjective unless the people or place in question is Russian, Ukrainian etc. Germans of the era typically referred simply to 'Russians' instead of 'Soviets' and that is maintained in all my translations.
3 Panzer Group 2 commenced its part of the offensive two days earlier on 30 September.
4 See David Stahel, *Operation Barbarossa and Germany's Defeat in the East* (Cambridge, 2009); David Stahel, *Kiev 1941. Hitler's Battle for Supremacy in the East* (Cambridge, 2012). For a summary of the events encapsulated in these two books, see David Stahel, 'Radicalizing Warfare: The German Command and the Failure of Operation Barbarossa' in Alex J. Kay, Jeff Rutherford and David Stahel (eds.), *Nazi Policy on the Eastern Front, 1941. Total War, Genocide and Radicalization* (Rochester, 2012) pp. 19–44.
5 Elke Fröhlich (ed.), *Die Tagebücher von Joseph Goebbels Teil II Diktate 1941–1945 Band 2 Oktober–Dezember 1941* (Munich, 1996) p. 40 (3 October 1941).
6 Albert Axell, *Stalin's War. Through the Eyes of His Commanders* (London, 1997) p. 13. Unfortunately, it is unclear when this statement was made.
7 Thanks to Yan Mann for helping with this translation. See also Evan Mawdsley, *Thunder in the East. The Nazi–Soviet War 1941–1945* (London, 2005) p. 115. It should be noted that Russian textbooks sometimes have the unfortunate tendency to record a paraphrased statement as direct speech. Zhukov's quotation may therefore be only an approximation of what was said.
8 In North Africa the British Eighth Army was preparing for a major new offensive with the aim of destroying Rommel's *Afrikakorps*. However, while Churchill was impatient for action, General Claude Auchinleck resisted any premature action

which might upset his careful planning, and Operation Crusader was not launched until 18 November 1941.

9 This is a Russian word, which refers to the biannual difficulties caused by heavy rains or melting snow in Russia, Belarus and Ukraine. The *rasputitsa* may be directly translated as 'quagmire season'.

10 In fact the Soviet–Japanese Neutrality Pact was signed on 13 April 1941.

11 Alexander Werth, *Russia at War 1941–1945* (New York, 1964) p. 228.

12 Henry Cassidy, *Moscow Dateline, 1941–1943* (London, 1943) p. 108.

13 Mawdsley, *Thunder in the East*, p. 112.

14 Cassidy, *Moscow Dateline, 1941–1943*, p. 108.

15 Gabriel Gorodetsky (ed.), *Stafford Cripps in Moscow 1940–1942. Diaries and Papers* (London, 2007) p. 171 (30 September–2 October 1941).

16 As James Lucas has argued: 'Assessing the situation at the end of the first phases of "Operation Barbarossa" [the] OKH, commanding the ground forces on the eastern front, could be pleased with the results gained and confident that these would be maintained for the next stage of operations ... Reflecting upon the losses which the Red Army had suffered, the planners at [the] OKH could believe that they were well on the road to victory.' See James Lucas, *War of the Eastern Front 1941–1945. The German Soldier in Russia* (London, 1980) p. 183. At around the same time Harrison E. Salisbury, who authored the landmark study of the siege of Leningrad, *The 900 Days*, as well as a more concise account of the fighting in the east in *The Unknown War*, concluded that the German plan for the investment of Moscow was based on a 'simple plan and the Germans had every reason to believe that it would succeed' (Harrison E. Salisbury, *The Unknown War* (London, 1978) p. 71). Finally, the once-prominent military historian David Irving suggested that, with the forces assembled for the start of Operation Typhoon, Hitler could be sure: 'Only the weather could now thwart him' (David Irving, *Hitler's War. Volume I* (New York, 1977) p. 347).

17 Elisabeth Wagner (ed.), *Der Generalquartiermeister. Briefe und Tagebuchaufzeichnungen des Generalquartiermeisters des Heeres General der Artillerie Eduard Wagner* (Munich, 1963) pp. 202–203 (29 September 1941).

18 Walter Görlitz, *Paulus and Stalingrad* (London, 1963) pp. 132–133.

19 David M. Glantz and Jonathan House, *When Titans Clashed. How the Red Army Stopped Hitler* (Lawrence, 1995) pp. 81–82.

20 For many of the command appointments used in this study, see Andris J. Kursietis, *The Wehrmacht at War 1939–1945. The Units and Commanders of the German Ground Forces During World War II* (Soesterberg, 1999) p. 167.

21 Stahel, *Kiev 1941*, pp. 338–339.

22 Helmut Pabst, *The Outermost Frontier. A German Soldier in the Russian Campaign* (London, 1957) p. 29.

1 Contextualising Barbarossa

1 Carl von Clausewitz, *On War*, Michael Howard and Peter Paret (eds.) (New York, 1993) pp. 88–89.

2 Filaret's 17-year-old son Michael I had been crowned tsar in July 1613, but upon Filaret's return from Polish imprisonment in 1618 he assumed primary control until his death in 1633.

3 'Muscovy' is the name most commonly used to refer to the early modern empire centred on Moscow. 'Russia' or the 'Russian empire' emerged with the reforms and expansion of Peter the Great's rule.

4 William C. Fuller Jr, *Strategy and Power in Russia 1600–1914* (New York, 1992) pp. 1–14 and 21–34.

5 See the discussion of the Thirteen Years' War and Muscovy's war against the Crimean Tatars in David R. Stone, *A Military History of Russia. From Ivan the Terrible to the War in Chechnya* (Westport, 2006) pp. 34–43.

6 Commonly known as Peter the Great.

7 Paul Bushkovitch, 'The Romanov Transformation 1613–1725' in Frederick W. Kagan and Robin Higham (eds.), *The Military History of Tsarist Russia* (New York, 2002) pp. 31–45.

8 Fuller, *Strategy and Power in Russia 1600–1914*, p. 80.

9 For more on this battle, see Peter Englund, *The Battle that Shook Europe. Poltava and the Birth of the Russian Empire* (New York, 2003). Alternatively, see http://www.battle.poltava.ua/english/history.htm.

10 Stone, *A Military History of Russia*, pp. 56–57.

11 John P. LeDonne, *The Grand Strategy of the Russian Empire, 1650–1831* (Oxford, 2004) p. 40.

12 See the discussion on instructional and institutional reforms within the Russian army in Bruce W. Menning, 'The Imperial Russian Army 1725–1796' in Kagan and Higham (eds.), *The Military History of Tsarist Russia*, pp. 48–75.

13 Commonly known as Frederick the Great.

14 See Dennis Showalter, *The Wars of Frederick the Great* (London, 1996).

15 Commonly known as Catherine the Great.

16 Stone, *A Military History of Russia*, pp. 84–89.

17 Frederick W. Kagan, 'Russia's Wars with Napoleon, 1805–1815' in Kagan and Higham (eds.), *The Military History of Tsarist Russia*, pp. 117–118.

18 Dominic Lieven, *Russia Against Napoleon. The Battle for Europe, 1807 to 1814* (London, 2010) p. 151.

19 For an excellent account of the campaign, see Adam Zamoyski, *1812. Napoleon's Fatal March on Moscow* (London, 2004).

20 Lieven, *Russia Against Napoleon*, p. 353.

21 See Fuller, *Strategy and Power in Russia 1600–1914*, pp. 14–23.

22 See Stahel, *Kiev 1941*.

23 Between 1935 and 1990 the Russian city of Samara was named Kuibyshev in honour of the Bolshevik leader Valerian Kuibyshev.

24 Chris Bellamy, *Absolute War. Soviet Russia in the Second World War* (New York, 2007) pp. 283–284.

25 Both divisions had taken part in the Balkan campaign in April 1941 and had to be refitted back in Germany. The 5th Panzer Division had originally been earmarked for deployment to North Africa, and its tanks were sent to the eastern front still bearing their desert paint scheme. See Robert Kirchubel, *Operation Barbarossa 1941 (3). Army Group Centre* (Oxford, 2007) p. 73.

26 Rolf-Dieter Müller, 'The Failure of the Economic "Blitzkrieg Strategy"' in Militärgeschichtliches Forschungsamt (ed.), *Germany and the Second World War. Volume IV. The Attack on the Soviet Union* (Oxford, 1998) p. 1129.

27 See my discussion in Stahel, *Kiev 1941*, p. 339.

28 Ernst Kern, *War Diary 1941–1945. A Report* (New York, 1993) p. 11.

29 Ty Bomba, 'Proud Monster: The Barbarossa Campaign Considered' in Command Magazine (ed.), *Hitler's Army. The Evolution and Structure of the German Forces, 1933–1945* (Cambridge, MA, 2003) pp. 133–134.

30 See also my discussion in Stahel, *Operation Barbarossa and Germany's Defeat in the East*, pp. 135–136.

31 '3rd Pz. Gr. KTB Nr.2 1.9.41–31.10.41' BA-MA Microfilm 59060 (13 and 29 September 1941). This diary is recorded in the reference books of the BA-MA as missing. It did in fact survive the war and exists on microfilm. The microfilm can be misleading as it consists of many handwritten notes and combat reports from units in Panzer Group 3. Only towards the end of the microfilm does the 'Ia' war diary for Panzer Group 3 begin. The diary has no folio stamped page numbers so references must be located using the date.

32 J. P. Stern, *Hitler. The Führer and the People* (Berkeley, 1992) ch. 7, 'Hitler's Ideology of the Will'. Even after the war Halder wrote in the preface to a study by Colonel-General Erhard Raus: 'It becomes very clear that a strong military leader with great powers of motivation is the most important factor for success' (Peter Tsouras (ed.), *Panzers on the Eastern Front. General Erhard Raus and His Panzer Divisions in Russia 1941–1945* (London, 2002) p. 9).

33 Franz Halder, *Kriegstagebuch. Tägliche Aufzeichnungen des Chefs des Generalstabes des Heeres 1939–1942. Band III Der Russlandfeldzug bis zum Marsch auf Stalingrad (22.6.1941–24.9.1942)*, Hans-Adolf Jacobsen and Alfred Philippi (eds.) (Stuttgart, 1964) p. 53 (8 July 1941) (hereafter cited as Halder, *KTB III*). Hitler did, however, make an exception to his rule in July, releasing a total of eighty-five tanks after Halder pleaded 'the urgent needs of the front'. See Halder, *KTB III*, p. 54 (8 July 1941).

34 *Ibid.*, p. 233 (15 September 1941).

35 Müller, 'The Failure of the Economic "Blitzkrieg Strategy"', p. 1127.

36 Ernst Klink, 'The Military Concept of the War Against the Soviet Union' in Militärgeschichtliches Forschungsamt (ed.), *Germany and the Second World War. Volume IV*, p. 318.

37 Halder, *KTB III*, p. 242 (20 September 1941).

38 *Ibid.*, p. 233 (15 September 1941).

39 Horst Boog, 'The Luftwaffe' in Militärgeschichtliches Forschungsamt (ed.), *Germany and the Second World War. Volume IV*, p. 764.

40 David Irving, *The Rise and Fall of the Luftwaffe. The Life of Erhard Milch* (London, 1973) p. 131.

41 Adam Tooze, *The Wages of Destruction. The Making and Breaking of the Nazi Economy* (London, 2006) p. 432.

42 See Richard Overy, 'Statistics' in I. C. B. Dear and M. R. D. Foot (eds.), *The Oxford Companion to the Second World War* (Oxford, 1995) Table 2, 'Military production' p. 1060 (reproduced here as Table 1).

43 Michael Burleigh, *The Third Reich. A New History* (London, 2001) pp. 491–492.

44 Georg Thomas, *Geschichte der deutsch Wehr- und Rüstungswirtschaft (1918–1943/45)*, Wolfgang Birkenfeld (ed.) (Boppard am Rhein, 1966) p. 467.

45 Halder, *KTB III*, p. 260 (30 September 1941). This does not include men listed as 'ill' or casualties from Germany's Axis allies.

46 Franz Halder, *Kriegstagebuch. Tägliche Aufzeichnungen des Chefs des Generalstabes des Heeres 1939–1942. Band II Von der geplanten Landung in England bis zum Beginn des Ostfeldzuges (1.7.1940–21.6.1941)*, Hans-Adolf Jacobsen (ed.) (Stuttgart, 1963) p. 422 (20 May 1941).

47 Halder, *KTB III*, p. 170 (11 August 1941).

48 Günther Blumentritt, 'Moscow' in William Richardson and Seymour Freidin (eds.), *The Fatal Decisions* (London, 1956) pp. 51–52.

49 'Kriegstagebuch Nr.1 Panzergruppe 2 Band II vom 21.8.1941 bis 31.10.41' BA-MA RH 21–2/931, fol. 220 (15 September 1941).

50 Elke Fröhlich (ed.), *Die Tagebücher von Joseph Goebbels Teil II Diktate 1941–1945 Band 1 Juli–September 1941* (Munich, 1996) p. 419 (15 September 1941).

51 Hans Pichler, *Truppenarzt und Zeitzeuge. Mit der 4. SS-Polizei-Division an vorderster Front* (Dresden, 2006) p. 94 (22 August 1941).

52 Hermann Geyer, *Das IX. Armeekorps im Ostfeldzug 1941* (Neckargemünd, 1969) pp. 122–125.

53 *True to Type. A Selection from Letters and Diaries of German Soldiers and Civilians Collected on the Soviet–German Front* (London, undated) p. 107 (8 September 1941). This book makes no reference to its editor or date of publication.

54 Peter G. Tsouras, 'Introduction' in Peter G. Tsouras (ed.) *Fighting in Hell. The German Ordeal on the Eastern Front* (New York, 1998) p. 6.

55 Heinz Guderian, *Panzer Leader* (New York, 1996) p. 142.

56 Blumentritt, 'Moscow', pp. 34–35. See also Blumentritt's comments in Basil Liddell Hart, *The Other Side of the Hill* (London, 1999) p. 284.

57 In 1812 Clausewitz left Prussia for service in Alexander's army.

58 Armand de Caulaincourt, *At Napoleon's Side in Russia* (New York, 2008) pp. 53–55 and 58–59.

59 Alexander Stahlberg, *Bounden Duty. The Memoirs of a German Officer 1932–1945* (London, 1990) p. 161.

60 Field Marshal Ewald von Kleist commented after the war: '[The Soviet] equipment was very good even in 1941, especially the tanks. Their artillery was excellent, and also most of the infantry weapons – their rifles were more modern than ours, and had a more rapid rate of fire' (as cited in Liddell Hart, *The Other Side of the Hill*, p. 330). See also R. Koch-Erpach, '4th Panzer Division's Crossing of the Dnepr River and the Advance to Roslavl' in David M. Glantz (ed.), *The Initial Period of War on the Eastern Front 22 June–August 1941* (London, 1997) p. 404; Erhard Rauss [Raus], 'Russian Combat Methods in World War II' in Tsouras (ed.), *Fighting in Hell*, pp. 35–36. Note that Raus's name is spelled incorrectly in the aforementioned title.

61 Tsouras, 'Introduction', p. 5.

62 See my discussion in Part I of Stahel, *Operation Barbarossa and Germany's Defeat in the East*.

63 In Operation Barbarossa Kleist, at that point a colonel-general, was the commander of Panzer Group 1 operating in Ukraine as part of Army Group South.

64 As cited in Leon Goldensohn, *Nuremberg Interviews. An American Psychiatrist's Conversations with the Defendants and Witnesses* (New York, Robert Gellately (ed.) 2004) p. 341 (25 June 1946).

65 Harrison E. Salisbury (ed.), *Marshal Zhukov's Greatest Battles* (London, 1971) p. 14. If indeed Zhukov did know Clausewitz as well as Salisbury claimed it probably counted less in the battle for Moscow in 1941 than in the Red Army's subsequent advance across Eastern Europe from 1943 to 1945.

66 For a full listing of the *Ostheer*'s order of battle see Klink, 'The Military Concept of the War Against the Soviet Union', pp. 222–223.

67 Mark Axworthy, Cornel Scafes and Cristian Craciunoiu, *Third Axis Fourth Ally. Romanian Armed Forces in the European War, 1941–1945* (London, 1995) p. 45.

68 Jürgen Förster, 'The Decisions of the Tripartite Pact States' in Militärgeschichtliches Forschungsamt (ed.), *Germany and the Second World War. Volume IV*, pp. 1028–1029.

69 Ciro Paoletti, *A Military History of Italy* (Westport, 2008) p. 176.

70 Mark Axworthy, *Axis Slovakia. Hitler's Slavic Wedge 1938–1945* (New York, 2002) p. 95; Förster, 'The Decisions of the Tripartite Pact States', p. 1034.

71 George H. Stein, *The Waffen SS. Hitler's Elite Guard at War 1939–1945* (New York, 1984) chs. 6 and 7.

72 For the Spanish 'Blue' Division (soon designated the 250th Infantry Division), see Gerald R. Kleinfeld and Lewis A. Tambs, *Hitler's Spanish Legion. The Blue Division in Russia* (St Petersburg, FL, 2005); Xavier Moreno Juliá, *La División Azul. Sangre española en Rusia, 1941–1945* (Barcelona, 2005).

73 On the Finnish front the Germans deployed four divisions and the Finns fifteen: Olli Vehviläinen, *Finland in the Second World War. Between Germany and Russia* (New York, 2002) pp. 90–91; Manfred Menger, 'Germany and the Finnish "Separate War" Against the Soviet Union' in Bernd Wegner (ed.), *From Peace to War. Germany, Soviet Russia and the World, 1939–1941* (Oxford, 1997) pp. 525–539. For German operations, see Earl F. Ziemke, *The German Northern Theater of Operations 1940–1945* (Washington, DC, 1959) ch. 8.

74 For the most useful studies on the role of non-German forces on the eastern front, see Jürgen Förster, 'Volunteers for the European Crusade Against Bolshevism' in Militärgeschichtliches Forschungsamt (ed.), *Germany and the Second World War. Volume IV*, pp. 1049–1080; Rolf-Dieter Müller, *An der Seite der Wehrmacht. Hitlers ausländische Helfer beim 'Kreuzzug gegen den Bolschewismus' 1941–1945* (Berlin, 2007); Richard L. DiNardo, *Germany and the Axis Powers. From Coalition to Collapse* (Lawrence, 2005).

75 Burkhart Müller-Hillebrand, *Das Heer 1933–1945. Band III. Der Zweifrontenkrieg. Das Heer vom Beginn des Feldzuges gegen die Sowjetunion bis zum Kriegsende* (Frankfurt am Main, 1969) p. 205; reproduced in Bryan I. Fugate, *Operation Barbarossa. Strategy and Tactics on the Eastern Front, 1941* (Novato, 1984) p. 349.

76 David M. Glantz, 'The Border Battles on the Bialystok–Minsk Axis: 22–28 June 1941' in Glantz (ed.), *The Initial Period of War on the Eastern Front 22 June–August 1941*, p. 187.

77 For maps, see David M. Glantz, *Atlas and Operational Summary of the Border Battles 22 June–1 July 1941* (privately published by David M. Glantz, 2003).

78 Christian Hartmann, *Wehrmacht im Ostkrieg. Front und militärisches Hinterland 1941/42* (Munich, 2010) pp. 259–267; Albert Axell, *Russia's Heroes 1941–1945* (New York, 2001) ch. 2, 'The Hero Fortress'; Salisbury, *The Unknown War*, ch. 3, 'Bravery at Brest'. See also the first-hand accounts provided in Robert Kershaw, *War Without Garlands. Operation Barbarossa 1941/42* (New York, 2000) pp. 47–51, 59–60, 65–67, 78–79; Constantine Pleshakov, *Stalin's Folly. The Tragic First Ten Days of World War II on the Eastern Front* (New York, 2005) pp. 238–245.

79 '3rd Pz. Gr. KTB 25.5.41–31.8.41' BA-MA Microfilm 59054, fol. 36 (22 June 1941).

80 The German tanks of the *Ostheer* can be divided into seven main models: Marks I, II, III, IV, 35(t), 38(t) and the StuG III. No fewer than half of these were light

and relatively obsolete models, drafted into service to make up the numbers for Operation Barbarossa. This left Germany with only 1,673 modern tanks, especially the Mark III, IV and StuG IIIs. See my discussion of German tank models in Stahel, *Operation Barbarossa and Germany's Defeat in the East*, pp. 107–112.

81 'Kriegstagebuch Nr.3 der 7.Panzer-Division Führungsabteilung 1.6.1941– 9.5.1942' BA-MA RH 27–7/46, fol. 21 (28 June 1941).

82 Department of the US Army (ed.), *Small Unit Actions During the German Campaign in Russia* (Washington, DC, 1953) pp. 91–92. See also Horst Zobel, '3rd Panzer Division's Advance to Mogilev' in Glantz (ed.), *The Initial Period of War on the Eastern Front 22 June–August 1941*, pp. 393–394.

83 Horst Zobel, '3rd Panzer Division Operations' in Glantz (ed.), *The Initial Period of War on the Eastern Front 22 June–August 1941*, p. 242.

84 Johannes Hürter (ed.), *Ein deutscher General an der Ostfront. Die Briefe und Tagebücher des Gotthard Heinrici 1941/42* (Erfurt, 2001) p. 62 (23 June 1941).

85 Underlining in the original; 'Tagesmeldungen der Heeresgruppe Mitte vom 22.6.41 bis 15.7.41' BA-MA RH 19 II/128, fol. 138 (3 July 1941).

86 'KTB 3rd Pz. Div. I.b 19.5.41–6.2.42' BA-MA RH 27–3/218 (17 July 1941). This war diary has no folio stamped page numbers so references must be located using the date.

87 As cited in James Lucas, *Das Reich. The Military Role of the 2nd SS Division* (London, 1991) pp. 61 and 63.

88 'KTB Nr.1 Panzergruppe 2 Bd.II vom 22.7.1941 bis 20.8.41' BA-MA RH 21–2/ 928, fols. 49–50 (26 July 1941).

89 Fedor von Bock, *Generalfeldmarschall Fedor von Bock. The War Diary 1939– 1945*, Klaus Gerbet (ed.) (Munich, 1996) pp. 273–274 (5 August 1941) (hereafter references for Bock's diary will be cited as Bock, *War Diary*); 'Tagesmeldungen der Heeresgruppe Mitte vom 16.7.41 bis 5.8.41' BA-MA RH 19 II/129, fol. 223 (5 August 1941).

90 While no exact figures are available, Kesselring estimated that 'over 100,000' fled the pocket: Albrecht Kesselring, *The Memoirs of Field-Marshal Kesselring* (London, 1988) p. 93.

91 Glantz and House, *When Titans Clashed*, pp. 67–68.

92 Michael Geyer, 'German Strategy in the Age of Machine Warfare, 1914–1945' in Peter Paret (ed.), *Makers of Modern Strategy. From Machiavelli to the Nuclear Age* (Oxford, 1999) p. 591.

93 David M. Glantz, *Barbarossa. Hitler's Invasion of Russia 1941* (Stroud, 2001) p. 68. See also Mawdsley, *Thunder in the East*, pp. 112–113.

94 Halder, *KTB III*, p. 145 (2 August 1941).

95 Tooze, *The Wages of Destruction*, p. 437.

96 Halder, *Kriegstagebuch: Tägliche Aufzeichnungen des Chefs des Generalstabes des Heeres 1939–1942. Band II*, p. 422 (20 May 1941).

97 Halder, *KTB III*, p. 266 (4 October 1941).

98 A recently published study by David Glantz concludes: 'the Wehrmacht and Red Army would fight a complex series of battles across a front of roughly 645 kilometres known collectively as the battle of Smolensk. As they did, they knew full well they were engaging in a struggle that could determine the ultimate outcome of the war.' David M. Glantz, *Barbarossa Derailed. The Battle for Smolensk 10 July–10 September 1941. Volume 1. The German Advance, the Encirclement Battle, and the First and Second Soviet Counteroffensives, 10 July–24 August 1941* (Solihull, 2010) p. 135. See also David M. Glantz, *Barbarossa Derailed. The Battle for Smolensk 10 July–10 September 1941. Volume 2. The German Offensives on the Flanks and the Third Soviet Counteroffensive, 25 August–10 September 1941* (Solihull, 2012).

99 'Kriegstagebuch Nr.1 (Band August 1941) des Oberkommandos der Heeresgruppe Mitte' BA-MA RH 19II/386, p. 364 (22 August 1941).

100 'The Germans in Russia' LH 15/4/40. See the file entitled 'von Rundstedt writes home' p. 2 (12 August 1941).

101 Müller, 'The Failure of the Economic "Blitzkrieg Strategy"', p. 1128.

102 Hans-Adolf Jacobsen (ed.), *Kriegstagebuch des Oberkommandos der Wehrmacht (Wehrmachtführungsstab), Band I/2: 1. August 1940–31. Dezember 1941* (Munich, 1982) p. 661 (26 September 1941) (hereafter cited as *KTB OKW*, vol. II); 'Heeresgruppe Süd Kriegstagebuch II.Teil Band 4, 16 Sept.–5 Okt. 1941' BA-MA RH 19-I/73, fol. 132 (26 September 1941).

103 See my previous volume, Stahel, *Kiev 1941*. For the most complete collections of maps of the battle, see David M. Glantz, *Atlas of the Battle for Kiev Part I. Penetrating the Stalin Line and the Uman' Encirclement 2 July – 9 August 1941* (privately published by David M. Glantz, 2005) p. 8 (7–14 July 1941); David M. Glantz, *Atlas of the Battle for Kiev Part II. The German Advance to the Dnepr River, 9–26 August 1941* (privately published by David M. Glantz, 2005); David M. Glantz, *Atlas of the Battle for Kiev Part III. The Encirclement and Destruction of the Southwestern Front, 25 August–26 September 1941* (privately published by David M. Glantz, 2005).

104 'Kriegstagebuch Nr.1 Panzergruppe 2 Band II vom 21.8.1941 bis 31.10.41' BA-MA RH 21-2/931, fols. 322–323 (27 September 1941). The totals reported in this file are slightly different, but the addition of the figures is sometimes in error.

105 Müller-Hillebrand, *Das Heer 1933–1945. Band III*, p. 205.

106 Because the order of battle changed for each of the three panzer groups between 22 June and 2 October, it should be understood that my starting totals here are calculated for each panzer group's order of battle as it existed for Operation Typhoon. For the estimated strengths of the panzer divisions, see my discussion in Stahel, *Kiev 1941*, pp. 323–325.

107 Franz Halder, *Hitler als Feldherr* (Munich, 1949) p. 43.

108 Halder, *KTB III*, p. 233 (15 September 1941).

109 On 22 June 1941 the panzer divisions subsequently assigned to Bock for Operation Typhoon had the following panzer strengths: 1st Panzer Division, 154; 3rd Panzer Division, 198; 4th Panzer Division, 169; 6th Panzer Division, 254; 7th Panzer Division, 299; 9th Panzer Division, 157; 10th Panzer Division, 206; 11th Panzer Division, 175; 17th Panzer Division, 180; 18th Panzer Division, 200; 19th Panzer Division, 239; 20th Panzer Division, 245. See Müller-Hillebrand, *Das Heer 1933–1945. Band III*, p. 205.

110 Walter Chales de Beaulieu, *Generaloberst Erich Hoepner. Militärisches Porträt eines Panzer-Führers* (Neckargemünd, 1969) pp. 191–192.

111 'Kriegstagebuch Nr.1 (Band Oktober 1941) des Oberkommandos der Heeresgruppe Mitte' BA-MA RH 19-II/411, fols. 525–526 (2 October 1941). One source claims that Army Group Centre in fact possessed only 549 serviceable aircraft (including 158 bombers and 172 fighters) for Operation Typhoon. See Christer Bergström, *Barbarossa: The Air Battle. July–December 1941* (Hersham, 2007) p. 90.

112 Glantz, *Barbarossa*, pp. 141–143.

113 Walter S. Dunn Jr., *Hitler's Nemesis. The Red Army, 1930–1945* (Mechanicsburg, 2009) p. 29.

114 Klaus Reinhardt, *Moscow. The Turning Point. The Failure of Hitler's Strategy in the Winter of 1941–1942* (Oxford, 1992) p. 59.

115 Bock, *War Diary*, p. 317 (24 September 1941).

116 Guderian, *Panzer Leader*, pp. 224–225.

117 Bock, *War Diary*, p. 317 (24 September 1941).

118 Heinz Rahe, Museumsstiftung Post und Telekommunikation, Berlin, 3.2002.0985 (26 September 1941) (hereafter cited as MPT).

119 Ortwin Buchbender and Reinhold Sterz (eds.), *Das andere Gesicht des Krieges. Deutsche Feldpostbriefe 1939–1945* (Munich, 1982) p. 82 (24 September 1941).

120 *Ibid.* (24 September 1941).

121 Alois Scheuer, *Briefe aus Russland. Feldpostbriefe des Gefreiten Alois Scheuer 1941–1942* (St Ingbert, 2000) pp. 41–42 (28 September 1941).

122 Heinz Boberach (ed.), *Meldungen aus dem Reich. Die geheimen Lageberichte des Sicherheitsdienstes der SS 1938–1945. Band 8* (Berlin, 1984) p. 2795, Document 223 (25 September 1941).

123 *Ibid.*, p. 2809, Document 224 (29 September 1941).

124 Fröhlich (ed.), *Die Tagebücher von Joseph Goebbels Teil II Band 1*, p. 505 (27 September 1941).

125 Konrad Elmshäuser and Jan Lokers (eds.), *'Man muß hier nur hart sein'. Kriegsbriefe und Bilder einer Familie (1934–1945)* (Bremen, 1999) p. 141 (28 September 1941).

126 Jürgen Kleindienst (ed.), *Sei tausendmal gegrüßt. Briefwechsel Irene und Ernst Guicking 1937–1945* (Berlin, 2001). Accompanying this book is a CD-ROM with some 1,600 letters mostly unpublished in the book. The quoted letter appears only on the CD-ROM and can be located by its date (29 September 1941).

127 Hellmuth H., MPT, 3.2002.7139 (30 September 1941).

128 Graham A. Loud, *The Crusade of Frederick Barbarossa: The History of the Expedition of the Emperor Frederick and Related Texts* (Farnham, 2010).

129 Förster, 'Volunteers for the European Crusade Against Bolshevism', pp. 1050–1051.

2 Operation Typhoon

1 Max Domarus, *Hitler. Speeches and Proclamations 1932–1945. The Chronicle of a Dictatorship. Volume IV. The Years 1941 to 1945* (Wauconda, 2004) pp. 2484–2485 (2 October 1941).

2 *Ibid.*, p. 2486 (2 October 1941). Reprints of Hitler's proclamation were posted on noticeboards along the eastern front, but after a few weeks the mistaken prophecies had become an embarrassment and special orders were issued for the proclamation to be removed.

3 As cited in Michael Jones, *The Retreat. Hitler's First Defeat* (London, 2009) p. 32.

4 *Ibid.*

5 Heinrich Haape with Dennis Henshaw, *Moscow Tram Stop. A Doctor's Experiences with the German Spearhead in Russia* (London, 1957) p. 109.

6 Ernst Kern, *War Diary 1941–1945*, p. 12.

7 Halder, *KTB III*, p. 263 (2 October 1941).

8 As cited in Michael Jones, *The Retreat*, p. 35.

9 Pabst, *The Outermost Frontier*, p. 30.

10 Bismarck was only a temporary divisional commander taking over from Lieutenant-General Horst Stumpff on 10 September and handing command of the division over to Major-General Wilhelm Ritter von Thoma on 14 October 1941.

11 '20.Pz.Div. KTB vom 15.8.41 bis 20.10.41 Band Ia.' BA-MA RH 27–20/25, fol. 108 (2 October 1941).

12 Halder, *KTB III*, p. 264 (2 October 1941).

13 'Kriegstagebuch Nr.2 XXXXVII.Pz.Korps. Ia 23.9.1941–31.12.1941' BA-MA RH 24–47/258, fol. 19 (2 October 1941).

14 Halder, *KTB III*, p. 264 (2 October 1941).

15 'Anlage zum KTB Pz.Gruppe 4 Meldungen von unten 20.9.41–14.10.41' BA-MA RH 21–4/37, fol. 82 (2 October 1941).

16 Halder, *KTB III*, p. 265 (2 October 1941).

17 '3rd Pz. Gr. KTB Nr.2 1.9.41–31.10.41' BA-MA Microfilm 59060 (2 October 1941).

18 'Anlagen zum Kriegstagebuch Tagesmeldungen Bd.I 1.9–31.10.41' BA-MA RH 21-3/70, fol. 48 (2 October 1941).

19 'Kriegstagebuch Nr.3. des XXXXVI.Pz.Korps vom 24.08.41–31.12.41' BA-MA RH 24–46/21, fol. 61 (2 October 1941).

20 '5. Panzer Division KTB Nur.8 vom 11.9.41–11.12.41' BA-MA RH 27–5/29, fol. 16 (2 October 1941).

21 Bock, *War Diary*, p. 320 (2 October 1941).

22 'Anlage zum KTB Pz.Gruppe 4 Meldungen von unten 20.9.41–14.10.41' BA-MA RH 21–4/37, fol. 82 (2 October 1941).

23 '3rd Pz. Gr. KTB Nr.2 1.9.41–31.10.41' BA-MA Microfilm 59060 (2 October 1941).

24 Pabst, *The Outermost Frontier*, p. 31.

25 *Ibid.*

26 'Armeeoberkommando 2. I.a KTB Teil.2 19.9.41–16.12.41' BA-MA RH 20–2/207, p. 26 (2 October 1941).

27 '18.Panzer Division, Abt.Ia KTB Teil III vom 30.9.–19.10.41' BA-MA RH 27–18/22, p. 14 (2 October 1941).

28 '9.Pz.Div. KTB Ia vom 19.5.1941 bis 22.1.1942' BA-MA RH 27–9/4, p. 125 (2 October 1941).

29 'Kriegstagebuch Nr.1 (Band Oktober 1941) des Oberkommandos der Heeresgruppe Mitte' BA-MA RH 19-II/411, fol. 530 (2 October 1941).

30 Domarus, *Hitler*, p. 2491 (3 October 1941).

31 *Ibid.* (3 October 1941).

32 *Ibid.* (3 October 1941).

33 *Ibid*, p. 2494 (3 October 1941).

34 H. C. Robbins Landon and Sebastian Leitner (eds.), *Diary of a German Soldier* (London, 1963) p. 110 (3 October 1941).

35 David Garden and Kenneth Andrew (eds.), *The War Diaries of a Panzer Soldier. Erich Hager with the 17th Panzer Division on the Russian Front 1941–1945* (Atglen, 2010) p. 53 (3 October 1941).

36 As cited in Michael Jones, *The Retreat*, p. 33.

37 Malcolm Muggeridge (ed.), *Ciano's Diary 1939–1943* (Kingswood, 1947) p. 379 (2 October 1941).

38 'Kriegstagebuch Nr.1 (Band Oktober 1941) des Oberkommandos der Heeresgruppe Mitte' BA-MA RH 19-II/411, fols. 537–538 (3 October 1941); Halder, *KTB III*, p. 266 (3 October 1941).

39 Hermann Geyer, *Das IX. Armeekorps im Ostfeldzug 1941*, p. 137.

40 A. Eremenko, *The Arduous Beginning* (Honolulu, 2004) p. 240; Glantz, *Barbarossa*, pp. 147–148.

41 Halder, *KTB III*, p. 266 (3 October 1941).

42 Antony Beevor and Luba Vinogradova (eds.), *A Writer at War. Vasily Grossman with the Red Army 1941–1945* (New York, 2005) p. 45.

43 Hans Schäufler (ed.), *Knight's Cross Panzers. The German 35th Panzer Regiment in WWII* (Mechanicsburg, 2010) p. 127.

44 Distances are worked out along straight lines or 'as the crow flies', thus real distances were somewhat longer in practice.

45 As cited in Janusz Piekalkiewicz, *Moscow 1941. The Frozen Offensive* (London, 1981) p. 109.

46 Wagner (ed.), *Der Generalquartiermeister*, p. 203 (3 October 1941).

47 Robert Cecil, *Hitler's Decision to Invade Russia 1941* (London, 1975) p. 134.

48 Halder, *KTB III*, p. 265 (3 October 1941).

49 'Kriegstagebuch 4.Panzer-Division Führungsabtl. 26.5.41–31.3.42' BA-MA RH 27–4/10, p. 189 (3 October 1941); *KTB OKW*, vol. II, p. 675 (3 October 1941).

50 'Anlagen zum Kriegstagebuch Tagesmeldungen Bd.I 1.9–31.10.41' BA-MA RH 21–3/70, fol. 53 (3 October 1941).

51 Karl Reddemann (ed.), *Zwischen Front und Heimat. Der Briefwechsel des münsterischen Ehepaares Agnes und Albert Neuhaus 1940–1944* (Münster, 1996) pp. 324–325 (3 October 1941).

52 Formed on 14 July 1941 in Madrid and commanded by Major Angel Salas Larrazábal, the Escuadrilla Azul consisted of seventeen pilots, all of whom were veterans of the Spanish Civil War. After some additional training, they departed for the eastern front on 26 September and, from their new base north-east of Smolensk, took part in the first day of fighting for Operation Typhoon. Overall, the Escuadrilla Azul was to have a poor operational record. In their first encounter on 2 October nine of their planes were surprised by Soviet fighters with one being shot down and their mission cancelled. By mid December 1941 only two planes remained and the unit was soon repatriated to Spain. See Bergström, *Barbarossa*, p. 90. See also Hans Werner Neulen, *In the Skies of Europe. Air Forces Allied to the Luftwaffe 1939–1945* (Ramsbury, 2000) pp. 277–279; Frank Joseph, *The Axis Air Forces. Flying in Support of the German Luftwaffe* (Santa Barbara, 2011), ch. 2, 'The Spanish Blue Squadron'.

53 Neulen, *In the Skies of Europe*, pp. 172–173.

54 Hermann Plocher, *The German Air Force Versus Russia, 1941* (New York, 1965) p. 230.

55 Richard Muller, *The German Air War in Russia* (Baltimore, 1992) p. 58.

56 Bergström, *Barbarossa*, p. 91.

57 Guderian, *Panzer Leader*, pp. 232–233.

58 John Weal, *More Bf 109 Aces of the Russian Front* (Oxford, 2007) p. 22. Mölders did, however, take part in numerous unofficial combat flights after his withdrawal and shot down an even higher number of enemy aircraft.

59 Halder, *KTB III*, p. 266 (3 October 1941).

60 Glantz, *Barbarossa*, pp. 147–148.

61 'Kriegstagebuch Nr.1 (Band Oktober 1941) des Oberkommandos der Heeresgruppe Mitte' BA-MA RH 19-II/411, fol. 545 (4 October 1941).

62 '3rd Pz. Gr. KTB Nr.2 1.9.41–31.10.41' BA-MA Microfilm 59060 (4 and 5 October 1941).

63 Beevor and Vinogradova (eds.), *A Writer at War*, p. 48.

64 A German weather report from central Russia on 4 October 1941 stated: 'Sunny day, almost summer warmth' ('Kriegstagebuch Nr.3. des XXXXVI.Pz.Korps vom 24.08.41–31.12.41' BA-MA RH 24–46/21, fol. 65 (4 October 1941)).

65 Halder, *KTB III*, p. 267 (4 October 1941).

66 Rudolf Steiger, *Armour Tactics in the Second World War. Panzer Army Campaigns of 1939–1941 in German War Diaries* (Oxford, 1991) p. 123.

67 'Kriegstagebuch Nr.1 (Band Oktober 1941) des Oberkommandos der Heeresgruppe Mitte' BA-MA RH 19-II/411, fol. 552 (5 October 1941).

68 Guderian, *Panzer Leader*, p. 232.

69 'Anlage zum KTB Panzer Gruppe 4: 20.9.41–14.10.41' BA-MA RH 21-4/34, fol. 52 (5 October 1941).

70 'Kriegstagebuch Nr.1 (Band Oktober 1941) des Oberkommandos der Heeresgruppe Mitte' BA-MA RH 19-II/411, fol. 552 (5 October 1941).

71 Wagner (ed.), *Der Generalquartiermeister*, p. 204 (5 October 1941).

72 Christine Alexander and Mark Kunze (eds.), *Eastern Inferno. The Journals of a German Panzerjäger on the Eastern Front, 1941–1943* (Philadelphia and Newbury, 2010) p. 117 (6 October 1941).

73 Guderian, *Panzer Leader*, p. 233.

74 'Kriegstagebuch 4.Panzer-Division Führungsabtl. 26.5.41–31.3.42' BA-MA RH 27–4/10, p. 196 (6 October 1941).

75 *Ibid.*, pp. 192 and 196 (4 and 6 October 1941).

76 The *Nebelwerfer* (literally 'fog-thrower') was a German weapon adapted to fire mortar shells or rockets.

77 See the tactical account given in Schäufler (ed.), *Knight's Cross Panzers*, pp. 131–133.

78 'Kriegstagebuch 4.Panzer-Division Führungsabtl. 26.5.41–31.3.42' BA-MA RH 27–4/10, p. 198 (6 October 1941).

79 Schäufler (ed.), *Knight's Cross Panzers*, pp. 135 and 138.

80 The war diary only states 'M.T.W.', which is an abbreviation for *Mannschaftstransportwagen*. Thanks to Dr Adrian Wettstein for his assistance here.

81 'Kriegstagebuch 4.Panzer-Division Führungsabtl. 26.5.41–31.3.42' BA-MA RH 27–4/10, p. 203 (9 October 1941).

82 Guderian, *Panzer Leader*, p. 235.

83 Department of the US Army (ed.), *Small Unit Actions During the German Campaign in Russia*, pp. 1–2. One former German soldier of the eastern front wrote of November 1941: 'Missions were carried out with a few men that would have seemed nearly incredible in earlier months and that would have occasioned an unbelieving smile from every teacher of tactics at the war college' (Helmut Günther, *Hot Motors, Cold Feet. A Memoir of Service with the Motorcycle Battalion of SS-Division 'Reich' 1940–1941* (Winnipeg, 2004) p. 207).

84 *Landser* is a colloquial German term for a soldier, particularly one who fought in World War II.

85 Robert Kershaw, *War Without Garlands*, p. 181.

86 '18.Panzer Division, Abt.Ia KTB Teil III vom 30.9.–19.10.41' BA-MA RH 27–18/22, p. 3 (5 October 1941).

87 For a diagram, see C. G. Sweeting, *Blood and Iron. The German Conquest of Sevastopol* (Washington, DC, 2004) p. 143. For individual encounters, see Hans von Luck, *Panzer Commander. The Memoirs of Colonel Hans von Luck* (New York, 1989) pp. 57–58; Paul Carell [Paul Karl Schmidt], *Hitler's War on Russia. The Story of the German Defeat in the East* (London, 1964) pp. 133–134; William Lubbeck with David B. Hurt, *At Leningrad's Gates. The Story of a Soldier with Army Group North* (Philadelphia, 2006) p. 112. Another source claimed that the dogs sometimes destroyed vehicles belonging to the Red Army. See Erhard Raus, *Panzer Operations. The Eastern Front Memoir of General Raus, 1941–1945*, Steven H. Newton (ed.) (Cambridge, MA, 2005) p. 87.

88 The famous Russian general Mikhail Kutuzov wrote some general rules for jaeger regiments in a 1789 handbook. He stressed craftiness, which included tricking the enemy by pretending to be dead. See Lieven, *Russia Against Napoleon*, p. 115.

89 Erich Kern, *Dance of Death* (New York, 1951) p. 50. For more such accounts, see Rauss, 'Russian Combat Methods in World War II', pp. 21–22; Günter K. Koschorrek, *Blood Red Snow. The Memoirs of a German Soldier on the Eastern Front* (London, 2002) pp. 69 and 152; Hürter, *Ein deutscher General an der Ostfront*, p. 70 (22 July 1941); Erich von Manstein, *Lost Victories* (Novato, 1994) pp. 180–181; Erich von Manstein, *Verlorene Siege. Erinnerungen 1939–1944* (Bonn, 1991) pp. 178–179.

90 Alexander and Kunze (eds.), *Eastern Inferno*, p. 104 (23 September 1941).

91 *Ibid.*, pp. 104–105 (23 September 1941).

92 '5. Panzer Division KTB Nur.8 vom 11.9.41–11.12.41' BA-MA RH 27–5/29, fol. 26 (6 October 1941).

93 John Erickson, *The Road to Stalingrad. Stalin's War with Germany. Volume One* (London, 1975) pp. 216–217.

94 Mawdsley, *Thunder in the East*, p. 95.

95 Glantz, *Barbarossa*, p. 148.

96 G. K. Zhukov, *The Memoirs of Marshal Zhukov* (London, 1971) pp. 320–321.

97 Viktor Anfilov, 'Zhukov' in Harold Shukman (ed.), *Stalin's Generals* (London, 1993) pp. 350–351.

98 Laurence Rees, *War of the Century. When Hitler Fought Stalin* (London, 1999) pp. 52–53.

99 Bellamy, *Absolute War*, p. 222.

100 As two leading experts have also noted: 'at the very least, this episode indicates that behind Stalin's image of implacable hostility to the invaders and iron determination to defend the Soviet motherland lay more complicated motives and intentions' (John Barber and Mark Harrison, *The Soviet Home Front 1941–1945. A Social and Economic History of the USSR in World War II* (London, 1991) pp. 54–55). For a more critical perspective, see Richard Overy, *Russia's War* (London, 1997) p. 96.

101 Anfilov, 'Zhukov', p. 351.

102 For a detailed account, see Zhukov, *The Memoirs of Marshal Zhukov*, pp. 321–327.

103 Mawdsley, *Thunder in the East*, p. 95.

104 Burleigh, *The Third Reich*, p. 502.

105 Erickson, *The Road to Stalingrad*, p. 217.

106 Andrew Nagorski, *The Greatest Battle. Stalin, Hitler, and the Desperate Struggle for Moscow that Changed the Course of World War II* (New York, 2007) pp. 216–218.

107 Thanks to Yan Mann for this information. According to Richard Evans, in the course of the battle for Moscow a total of some 400,000 soldiers, along with 1,000 tanks and 1,000 planes, would be transported across Siberia to take up positions around Moscow. See Richard J. Evans, *The Third Reich at War. How the Nazis Led Germany from Conquest to Disaster* (London, 2009) p. 205.

108 Erickson, *The Road to Stalingrad*, p. 218.

109 Bock, *War Diary*, p. 323 (5 October 1941).

110 *Ibid.*, pp. 322–323 (5 October 1941).

111 'Kriegstagebuch Nr.1 (Band Oktober 1941) des Oberkommandos der Heeresgruppe Mitte' BA-MA RH 19-II/411, fol. 565 (6 October 1941).

112 This was a special formation created from the infantry training school at Döberitz.

113 Bock, *War Diary*, p. 323 (5 October 1941).

114 *Ibid.*, p. 325 (6 October 1941).

115 Italics in the original. Telegram as cited in Alfred W. Turney, *Disaster at Moscow. Von Bock's Campaigns 1941–1942* (Albuquerque, 1970) p. 107.

116 Bock, *War Diary*, pp. 325–226 (7 October 1941).
117 Samuel W. Mitcham Jr, *The Men of Barbarossa. Commanders of the German Invasion of Russia, 1941* (Newbury, 2009) p. 38; Turney, *Disaster at Moscow*, p. 6.
118 Bock, *War Diary*, p. 226 (8 October 1941).
119 *Ibid.*, p. 324 (6 October 1941).
120 As cited in Heinrich Bücheler, *Hoepner. Ein deutsches Soldatenschicksal des 20. Jahrhunderts* (Herford, 1980) p. 149.
121 *Ibid.*
122 Guderian, *Panzer Leader*, p. 162.
123 Bock, *War Diary*, p. 304 (4 September 1941).
124 Guderian's memoir claims that in late July Panzer Group 2 was officially renamed 'Army Group Guderian', although the term is not used in Bock or Halder's diary or even subsequently in Guderian's memoir (Guderian, *Panzer Leader*, p. 184).
125 Halder, *KTB III*, p. 271, n. 1 (6 October 1941); Guderian, *Panzer Leader*, p. 233.
126 Guderian, *Panzer Leader*, pp. 235–236.
127 'Kriegstagebuch Nr.2 XXXXVII.Pz.Korps. Ia 23.9.1941–31.12.1941' BA-MA RH 24–47/258, fol. 24 (5 October 1941).
128 'Kriegstagebuch Nr.1 (Band Oktober 1941) des Oberkommandos der Heeresgruppe Mitte' BA-MA RH 19-II/411, fol. 564 (6 October 1941).
129 Beevor and Vinogradova (eds.), *A Writer at War*, p. 47.
130 Eremenko, *The Arduous Beginning*, p. 242.
131 Guderian, *Panzer Leader*, p. 233.
132 Robert Forczyk, *Moscow 1941. Hitler's First Defeat* (Oxford, 2006) p. 43.
133 Max Kuhnert, *Will We See Tomorrow? A German Cavalryman at War, 1939–1942* (London, 1993) p. 112.
134 See David M. Glantz, *Atlas of the Battle of Moscow. The Defensive Phase. 1 October–5 December 1941* (privately published by David M. Glantz, 1997) p. 19 (8 October 1941).
135 As cited in Robert Kershaw, *War Without Garlands*, p. 181.
136 Bellamy, *Absolute War*, p. 273.
137 Bock, *War Diary*, p. 324 (6 October 1941).
138 Chales de Beaulieu, *Generaloberst Erich Hoepner*, p. 197.
139 Luck, *Panzer Commander*, p. 61.
140 Glantz, *Barbarossa*, p. 149.
141 Mawdsley, *Thunder in the East*, p. 95.
142 See the daily weather reports provided in 'Kriegstagebuch Nr.3. des XXXXVI. Pz.Korps vom 24.08.41–31.12.41' BA-MA RH 24–46/21.
143 Fröhlich (ed.), *Die Tagebücher von Joseph Goebbels Teil II Band 2*, p. 44 (3 October 1941).

144 *Ibid.*, p. 50 (4 October 1941).

145 Bock, *War Diary*, p. 326 (7 October 1941).

146 'Kriegstagebuch Nr.3. des XXXXVI.Pz.Korps vom 24.08.41–31.12.41' BA-MA RH 24–46/21, fol. 69 (6 October 1941).

147 Haape with Henshaw, *Moscow Tram Stop*, p. 143.

148 Guderian, *Panzer Leader*, p. 234.

149 Landon and Leitner (eds.), *Diary of a German Soldier*, p. 111 (6 October 1941).

150 Kuhnert, *Will We See Tomorrow?*, p. 106.

151 Haape with Henshaw, *Moscow Tram Stop*, p. 141.

152 Bock, *War Diary*, p. 333 (15 October 1941).

153 Beevor and Vinogradova (eds.), *A Writer at War*, p. 52.

154 Halder, *KTB III*, p. 271 (6 October 1941).

155 '3rd Pz. Gr. KTB Nr.2 1.9.41–31.10.41' BA-MA Microfilm 59060 (7 October 1941).

156 Bock, *War Diary*, p. 325 (7 October 1941).

157 *Ibid.*, p. 326 (7 October 1941).

158 Michael Jones, *The Retreat*, p. 49.

159 Landon and Leitner (eds.), *Diary of a German Soldier*, p. 121 (2 November 1941).

160 'Kriegstagebuch Nr.1 (Band Oktober 1941) des Oberkommandos der Heeresgruppe Mitte' BA-MA RH 19-II/411, fol. 564 (6 October 1941).

161 Landon and Leitner (eds.), *Diary of a German Soldier*, pp. 111–112 (7 October 1941).

162 Empress Elizabeth was the wife of the Russian tsar Alexander I.

163 As cited in Lieven, *Russia Against Napoleon*, p. 240.

3 Viaz'ma and Briansk

1 Halder, *KTB III*, p. 267 (5 October 1941).

2 *Ibid.* (5 October 1941). See also Heinrich Bücheler, *Carl-Heinrich von Stülpnagel. Soldat – Philosoph – Verschwörer* (Berlin, 1989) pp. 225–228; Ernst Klink, 'The Conduct of Operations' in Militärgeschichtliches Forschungsamt (ed.), *Germany and the Second World War. Volume IV*, p. 608, n. 267.

3 'Personalakten für Hoth, Hermann' BA-MA PERS/6/38, fol. 21 (20 February 1941).

4 He also spoke French and some English.

5 Strauss had taken ill between 20 August and 5 September 1941. In January 1942 he again had to request a leave of absence on the basis of poor health, but this time his condition was much more serious. A doctor's report in April 1942 made

it clear that Strauss had suffered severe heart problems and that over the past four years he had been addicted to sleeping pills: 'Personalakten für Strauss, Adolf' BA-MA Pers 6/56, fol. 34 (14 April 1942).

6 'Personalakten für Hoth, Hermann' BA-MA PERS/6/38, fol. 21 (20 February 1941).

7 Bock, *War Diary*, p. 323 (5 October 1941).

8 '3rd Pz. Gr. KTB Nr.2 1.9.41–31.10.41' BA-MA Microfilm 59060 (9 October 1941).

9 'Personalakten für Reinhardt, Hans' BA-MA PERS/6/50, fol. 15 (no date provided).

10 'Kriegstagebuch Nr.1 (Band Oktober 1941) des Oberkommandos der Heeresgruppe Mitte' BA-MA RH 19-II/411, fol. 570 (7 October 1941).

11 Klaus Reinhardt, *Moscow*, p. 110, n. 43.

12 *Ibid.*, p. 86.

13 Hürter, *Ein deutscher General an der Ostfront*, p. 93 (8 October 1941).

14 *Ibid.*, p. 92 (8 October 1941).

15 Halder, *KTB III*, p. 274 (8 October 1941).

16 Guderian, *Panzer Leader*, p. 235.

17 Garden and Andrew (eds.), *The War Diaries of a Panzer Soldier*, p. 54 (9 October 1941).

18 Guderian, *Panzer Leader*, p. 236.

19 Eremenko, *The Arduous Beginning*, pp. 245–246.

20 'Kriegstagebuch Nr.1 (Band Oktober 1941) des Oberkommandos der Heeresgruppe Mitte' BA-MA RH 19-II/411, fol. 576 (9 October 1941).

21 Bock, *War Diary*, p. 327 (8 October 1941).

22 *Ibid.* (9 October 1941).

23 Forczyk, *Moscow 1941*, p. 48.

24 '3rd Pz. Gr. KTB Nr.2 1.9.41–31.10.41' BA-MA Microfilm 59060 (8 October 1941).

25 'Kriegstagebuch Nr.1 (Band Oktober 1941) des Oberkommandos der Heeresgruppe Mitte' BA-MA RH 19-II/411, fol. 576 (9 October 1941).

26 '5. Panzer Division KTB Nur.8 vom 11.9.41–11.12.41' BA-MA RH 27-5/29, fol. 35 (9 October 1941).

27 Bock, *War Diary*, p. 327 (9 October 1941).

28 Halder, *KTB III*, p. 275 (9 October 1941).

29 Rees, *War of the Century*, p. 65.

30 '3rd Pz. Gr. KTB Nr.2 1.9.41–31.10.41' BA-MA Microfilm 59060 (9 October 1941).

31 Underlining in the original; 'Kriegstagebuch Nr.1 (Band Oktober 1941) des Oberkommandos der Heeresgruppe Mitte' BA-MA RH 19-II/411, fol. 570 (7 October 1941).

32 Halder, *KTB III*, p. 271 (7 October 1941).

33 Bock, *War Diary*, p. 326 (8 October 1941).

34 *Ibid.* (8 October 1941).

35 Blumentritt, 'Moscow', p. 53.

36 'Kriegstagebuch Nr.1 (Band Oktober 1941) des Oberkommandos der Heeresgruppe Mitte' BA-MA RH 19-II/411, fol. 578 (9 October 1941).

37 Bock, *War Diary*, p. 327 (9 October 1941).

38 'Kriegstagebuch Nr.1 (Band Oktober 1941) des Oberkommandos der Heeresgruppe Mitte' BA-MA RH 19-II/411, fol. 579 (9 October 1941).

39 Müller, 'The Failure of the Economic "Blitzkrieg Strategy"', p. 1131.

40 Forczyk, *Moscow 1941*, pp. 23–24.

41 Alexander and Kunze (eds.), *Eastern Inferno*, p. 118 (8 October 1941).

42 Franz A. P. Frisch in association with Wilbur D. Jones Jr, *Condemned to Live. A Panzer Artilleryman's Five-Front War* (Shippensburg, 2000) p. 78.

43 Raus, *Panzer Operations*, p. 87.

44 Steiger, *Armour Tactics in the Second World War*, p. 97.

45 In the wake of Reinhardt's promotion to command Panzer Group 3 the XXXXI Panzer Corps was eventually handed to General of Panzer Troops Walter Model on 26 October 1941. Model, however, would not be able to leave his command of the 3rd Panzer Division and take up his new appointment until 15 November, and in the interim the panzer corps was commanded by Lieutenant-General Friedrich Kirchner. See Marcel Stein, *A Flawed Genius. Field Marshal Walter Model. A Critical Biography* (Solihull, 2010) p. 73. For the suggestion that Model's appointment to XXXXI Panzer Corps may have been an act of favouritism by Brauchitsch, see Steven H. Newton, *Hitler's Commander. Field Marshal Walter Model – Hitler's Favorite General* (Cambridge, MA, 2006) pp. 149–150.

46 'Anlagenband zum KTB XXXXI A.K. Ia 1. Durchbruch durch die Wop-Kokosch Dnjepr Stellung 2.10.41 bis 9.10.41. 2. Vorstoss auf Kalinin 15.10.41–20.10.41' BA-MA RH 24–41/14 (9 October 1941). This diary has no folio stamped page numbers so references must be located using the date.

47 '3rd Pz. Gr. KTB Nr.2 1.9.41–31.10.41' BA-MA Microfilm 59060 (9 October 1941).

48 *Ibid.* (8 October 1941).

49 'Anlagenband zum KTB XXXXI A.K. Ia 1. Durchbruch durch die Wop-Kokosch Dnjepr Stellung 2.10.41 bis 9.10.41. 2. Vorstoss auf Kalinin 15.10.41–20.10.41' BA-MA RH 24–41/14 (6 October 1941).

50 'Anlagen zum Kriegstagebuch Tagesmeldungen Bd.I 1.9–31.10.41' BA-MA RH 21–3/70, fol. 102 (8 October 1941).

51 As cited in Bücheler, *Hoepner*, pp. 150–151.

52 '11.Pz.Div. KTB Abt. Ia vom 1.5.41–21.10.41' BA-MA RH 27–11/16, fol. 148 (7 October 1941).

53 Backed by the 2nd SS Division 'Das Reich' and the 3rd Motorised Infantry Division.

54 'Gen.Kdo.LVII.Pz.Korps KTB Nr.1 vom 15.2.41–31.10.41' BA-MA RH 24–57–2, fol. 255 (8 October 1941).

55 '20.Pz.Div. KTB vom 15.8.41 bis 20.10.41 Band Ia.' BA-MA RH 27–20/25, fols. 119 and 123 (9 and 11 October 1941).

56 'Kriegstagebuch der O.Qu.-Abt. Pz. A.O.K.2 von 21.6.41 bis 31.3.42' BA-MA RH 21–2/819, fol. 177 (8 October 1941).

57 'KTB 3rd Pz. Div. I.b 19.5.41–6.2.42' BA-MA RH 27–3/218 (7 and 8 October 1941).

58 Forczyk, *Moscow 1941*, p. 23.

59 'Kriegstagebuch XXXXVIII.Pz.Kps. Abt.Ia Oktober 1941' BA-MA RH 24–48/30, fol. 5 (9 October 1941).

60 '9.Pz.Div. KTB Ia vom 19.5.1941 bis 22.1.1942' BA-MA RH 27–9/4, fols. 133 and 135 (7 and 10 October 1941).

61 '18.Panzer Division, Abt.Ia KTB Teil III vom 30.9.–19.10.41' BA-MA RH 27–18/22, p. 34 (8 October 1941).

62 As cited in Piekalkiewicz, *Moscow 1941*, p. 112.

63 Frisch in association with Jones, *Condemned to Live*, p. 78.

64 Edmund Blandford (ed.), *Under Hitler's Banner. Serving the Third Reich* (Edison, 2001) p. 127.

65 Léon Degrelle, *Campaign in Russia. The Waffen SS on the Eastern Front* (Torrance, 1985) p. 14.

66 Blumentritt, 'Moscow', p. 55.

67 When the British military historian Liddell Hart asked Kleist why the German invasion of the Soviet Union had failed in 1941 he was told: 'The main cause of our failure was that the winter came early that year' (Liddell Hart, *The Other Side of the Hill*, p. 265). Similarly, Hoepner wrote that the apparently unexpected rain 'snatched from German hands the victory that we had almost already won' (as cited in Catherine Merridale, *Ivan's War. Life and Death in the Red Army, 1939–1945* (New York, 2006) p. 117.

68 By the same token, subsequent claims by Hitler and many German officers that the Russian winter of 1941/1942 was unusually cold are fallacious. See Klaus Reinhardt, *Moscow*, pp. 170 and 255; Rolf-Dieter Müller and Gerd R. Ueberschär, *Hitler's War in the East 1941–1945. A Critical Assessment* (Oxford, 2009) p. 99.

69 Domarus, *Hitler*, p. 2491 (3 October 1941).

70 Fröhlich (ed.), *Die Tagebücher von Joseph Goebbels Teil II Band 2*, p. 61 (5 October 1941).

71 *Ibid.*, p. 73 (7 October 1941).

72 *Ibid.*, pp. 79–80 (9 October 1941).

73 Muggeridge (ed.), *Ciano's Diary 1939–1943*, p. 381 (9 October 1941).

74 Werth, *Russia at War 1941–1945*, p. 233.

75 Fröhlich (ed.), *Die Tagebücher von Joseph Goebbels Teil II Band 2*, p. 80 (9 October 1941).

76 Winston S. Churchill, *The Second World War. Abridged Edition* (London, 1959) p. 462.

77 Boberach (ed.), *Meldungen aus dem Reich*, Band 8, p. 2848, Document 227 (9 October 1941).

78 Ian Kershaw, *Hitler 1936–1945. Nemesis* (London, 2001) p. 951, n. 228. The battle of Königgrätz was the decisive battle of the Austro-Prussian War in 1866.

79 Walter Gorlitz [Görlitz] (ed.), *The Memoirs of Field-Marshal Keitel. Chief of the German High Command, 1938–1945* (New York, 1966) p. 160.

80 Nicolaus von Below, *Als Hitlers Adjutant 1937–1945* (Mainz, 1999) p. 292.

81 An SS-*Obergruppenführer* had a rank equivalent to an army lieutenant-general.

82 Otto Dietrich, *The Hitler I Knew. Memoirs of the Third Reich's Press Chief* (New York, 2010) p. 70.

83 Howard K. Smith, *Last Train from Berlin* (New York, 1943) p. 106.

84 Overy, *Russia's War*, p. 95.

85 Domarus, *Hitler*, p. 2497 (9 October 1941). Marshal S. K. Timoshenko had in fact been transferred to the command of the Soviet South-Western Front in mid September.

86 Overy, *Russia's War*, p. 95.

87 Piekalkiewicz, *Moscow 1941*, p. 113.

88 Mihail Sebastian, *Journal, 1935–1944* (London, 2003) p. 425 (10 October 1941).

89 Muggeridge (ed.), *Ciano's Diary 1939–1943*, pp. 381–382 (10 October 1941).

90 Piekalkiewicz, *Moscow 1941*, p. 85.

91 Cathy Porter and Mark Jones, *Moscow in World War II* (London, 1987) p. 103.

92 Overy, *Russia's War*, p. 95.

93 Nagorski, *The Greatest Battle*, p. 225.

94 Blumentritt, 'Moscow', p. 53.

95 Domarus, *Hitler*, p. 2497 (9 October 1941).

96 Fröhlich (ed.), *Die Tagebücher von Joseph Goebbels Teil II Band 2*, pp. 87–88 (10 October 1941).

97 In addition to Timoshenko no longer being in command of the Western Front, elements of five Soviet armies were encircled at Viaz'ma, not three.

98 Buchbender and Sterz (eds.), *Das andere Gesicht des Krieges*, p. 82 (9 October 1941).

99 Alexander and Kunze (eds.), *Eastern Inferno*, pp. 118–119 (10 October 1941).

100 Ingo Stader (ed.), *Ihr daheim und wir hier draußen. Ein Briefwechsel zwischen Ostfront und Heimat Juni 1941–März 1943* (Cologne, 2006) p. 41 (10 October 1941).

101 Fröhlich (ed.), *Die Tagebücher von Joseph Goebbels Teil II Band 2*, p. 91 (11 October 1941).

102 *Ibid.* (11 October 1941).

103 Howard K. Smith, *Last Train from Berlin*, p. 105; Oliver Lubrich (ed.), *Travels in the Reich. Foreign Authors Report from Germany* (Chicago, 2010) pp. 255–264.

104 Sebastian, *Journal, 1935–1944*, p. 425 (11 October 1941).

105 Alexander and Kunze (eds.), *Eastern Inferno*, p. 119 (11 October 1941).

106 Blumentritt, 'Moscow', p. 55.

107 Walter Bähr and Hans Bähr (eds.), *Kriegsbriefe Gefallener Studenten, 1939–1945* (Tübingen and Stuttgart, 1952) p. 77 (6 October 1941).

108 Martin Humburg, *Das Gesicht des Krieges. Feldpostbriefe von Wehrmachtssoldaten aus der Sowjetunion 1941–1944* (Wiesbaden, 1998) p. 219 (2 October 1941).

109 Howard K. Smith, *Last Train from Berlin*, pp. 109–110.

110 Boberach (ed.), *Meldungen aus dem Reich*, Band 8, p. 2865, Document 228 (13 October 1941).

111 Howard K. Smith, *Last Train from Berlin*, p. 108.

112 Fröhlich (ed.), *Die Tagebücher von Joseph Goebbels Teil II Band 2*, pp. 100–101 (12 October 1941).

113 Hugh Trevor-Roper (ed.), *Hitler's Table Talk, 1941–1944. His Private Conversations* (London, 2000) p. 57 (13–14 October 1941).

114 As cited in Marlis Steinert, *Hitlers Krieg und die Deutschen. Stimmung und Haltung der deutschen Bevölkerung im Zweiten Weltkrieg* (Düsseldorf and Vienna, 1970) pp. 232–233.

115 Trevor-Roper (ed.), *Hitler's Table Talk, 1941–1944*, p. 92 (26–27 October 1941).

116 Hugh R. Trevor-Roper (ed.), *Hitler's War Directives 1939–1945* (London, 1964) p. 137 (14 July 1941).

117 Tooze, *The Wages of Destruction*, p. 439.

118 Rolf-Dieter Müller, 'The Victor's Hubris: Germany Loses Its Lead in Armaments After the French Campaign' in Militärgeschichtliches Forschungsamt (ed.), *Germany and the Second World War. Volume V/I. Organization and Mobilization of the German Sphere of Power* (Oxford, 2000) p. 690.

119 As cited in Klaus Reinhardt, *Moscow*, pp. 130–131.

120 *Ibid.*

121 Tooze, *The Wages of Destruction*, p. 494.

122 Paolo Fonzi, 'The Exploitation of Foreign Territories and the Discussion of *Ostland*'s Currency in 1941' in Kay, Rutherford and Stahel (eds.), *Nazi Policy on the Eastern Front, 1941*, pp. 170–171.

123 Evans, *The Third Reich at War*, pp. 349 and 354–355.

124 Tooze, *The Wages of Destruction*, pp. 413–414.

125 Klaus Reinhardt, *Moscow*, p. 159, n. 85.

126 As cited in Joel Hayward, *Stopped at Stalingrad. The Luftwaffe and Hitler's Defeat in the East, 1942–1943* (Lawrence, 1998) p. 19.

127 Howard K. Smith, *Last Train from Berlin*, p. 141.

4 Carnage on the road to Moscow

1 As cited in Georg Meyer, *Adolf Heusinger. Dienst eines deutschen Soldaten 1915 bis 1964* (Berlin, 2001) p. 160 (8 October 1941).

2 Bock, *War Diary*, p. 326 (7 October 1941).

3 Blumentritt, 'Moscow', p. 53.

4 Heusinger's letter as cited in Meyer, *Adolf Heusinger*, p. 161 (14 October 1941).

5 *Ibid.* (no date provided).

6 'Anlage zum KTB Panzer Gruppe 4: 20.9.41–14.10.41' BA-MA RH 21–4/34, fol. 27 (10 October 1941).

7 '2. Panzer Division KTB Nr.6 Teil I. Vom 15.6.41–3.4.42' BA-MA RH 27–2/21 (10 October 1941). The diary has no folio stamped page numbers so references must be located using the date.

8 As cited in Rees, *War of the Century*, pp. 66–67.

9 Glantz, *Atlas of the Battle of Moscow*, p. 23 (10 October 1941).

10 'Kriegstagebuch Nr.1 (Band Oktober 1941) des Oberkommandos der Heeresgruppe Mitte' BA-MA RH 19-II/411, fol. 589 (10 October 1941).

11 Reddemann (ed.), *Zwischen Front und Heimat*, p. 327 (11 October 1941).

12 As cited in Robert Kershaw, *War Without Garlands*, pp. 182–183.

13 'Kriegstagebuch Nr.3 der 7.Panzer-Division Führungsabteilung 1.6.1941–9.5.1942' BA-MA RH 27–7/46, fol. 140 (10 October 1941).

14 The fighting at Yartseno was part of the battle of Smolensk. Here the 7th Panzer Division was attempting to close the northern arch of the encirclement while being attacked from the west by Soviet troops attempting to flee the pocket and, at the same time, resisting attacks from the east by Soviet units attempting to break into the pocket.

15 As cited in Robert Kershaw, *War Without Garlands*, p. 184.

16 As cited in Glantz, *Barbarossa*, p. 151.

17 As cited in Michael Jones, *The Retreat*, pp. 47–48.

18 Forczyk, *Moscow 1941*, p. 48.

19 Bock, *War Diary*, p. 329 (10 October 1941).

20 Horst Lange, *Tagebücher aus dem Zweiten Weltkrieg* (Mainz, 1979) p. 68 (11 October 1941).

21 Humburg, *Das Gesicht des Krieges*, p. 124 (11 October 1941).

22 '11.Pz.Div. KTB Abt. Ia vom 1.5.41–21.10.41' BA-MA RH 27–11/16, fol. 156 (11 October 1941).

23 As cited in Rees, *War of the Century*, p. 65.

24 '11.Pz.Div. KTB Abt. Ia vom 1.5.41–21.10.41' BA-MA RH 27–11/16, fol. 156 (11 October 1941).

25 '2. Panzer Division KTB Nr.6 Teil I. Vom 15.6.41–3.4.42' BA-MA RH 27–2/21 (11 October 1941).

26 'Anlage zum KTB Panzer Gruppe 4: 20.9.41–14.10.41' BA-MA RH 21–4/34, fol. 22 (11 October 1941).

27 Hans Reinhardt, 'Panzer-Gruppe 3 in der Schlacht von Moskau und ihre Erfahrungen im Rückzug', *Wehrkunde* Heft 9, September 1953, p. 1.

28 As cited in Robert Kershaw, *War Without Garlands*, p. 183.

29 'Kriegstagebuch Nr.3 der 7.Panzer-Division Führungsabteilung 1.6.1941– 9.5.1942' BA-MA RH 27–7/46, fol. 147 (12 October 1941).

30 Bock, *War Diary*, p. 330 (11 October 1941).

31 'Kriegstagebuch Nr.1 (Band Oktober 1941) des Oberkommandos der Heeresgruppe Mitte' BA-MA RH 19-II/411, fols. 583–584 (10 October 1941).

32 '18.Panzer Division, Abt.Ia KTB Teil III vom 30.9.–19.10.41' BA-MA RH 27– 18/22, p. 40 (10 October 1941).

33 *Ibid.*, p. 4 (11 October 1941).

34 Bock, *War Diary*, p. 329 (10 October 1941).

35 Glantz, *Atlas of the Battle of Moscow*, p. 22 (10 October 1941).

36 Kleindienst (ed.), *Sei tausendmal gegrüßt*, CD-ROM (10 October 1941).

37 'Kriegstagebuch Nr.1 (Band Oktober 1941) des Oberkommandos der Heeresgruppe Mitte' BA-MA RH 19-II/411, fols. 585–586 and 590 (10 October 1941).

38 Guderian, *Panzer Leader*, p. 236.

39 'Kriegstagebuch Nr.1 (Band Oktober 1941) des Oberkommandos der Heeresgruppe Mitte' BA-MA RH 19-II/411, fol. 593 (10 October 1941).

40 *Ibid.*, fol. 594 (11 October 1941).

41 Walther Lammers (ed.), '*Fahrtberichte*' *aus der Zeit des deutsch-sowjetischen Krieges 1941. Protokolle des Begleitoffiziers des Kommandierenden Generals LIII. Armeekorps* (Boppard am Rhein, 1988) p. 122.

42 Eremenko, *The Arduous Beginning*, pp. 247–248.

43 Guderian, *Panzer Leader*, p. 237.

44 Bock, *War Diary*, p. 330 (12 October 1941).

45 'Kriegstagebuch Nr.1 (Band Oktober 1941) des Oberkommandos der Heeresgruppe Mitte' BA-MA RH 19-II/411, fol. 576 (9 October 1941).

46 Edgar M. Howell, *The Soviet Partisan Movement 1941–1944* (Washington, DC, 1956) pp. 57–60.

47 'Gen.Kdo.LVII.Pz.Korps KTB Nr.1 vom 15.2.41–31.10.41' BA-MA RH 24-57-2, fols. 259 and 265 (10 and 12 October 1941).

48 As cited in Ben Shepherd, *War in the Wild East. The German Army and Soviet Partisans* (Cambridge, 2004) p. 89.

49 Italics in the original; Gerd R. Ueberschär (ed.), 'Armeebefehl des Oberbefehlshabers der 6. Armee, Generalfeldmarschall von Reichenau, vom 10.10.1941' in Gerd R. Ueberschär and Wolfram Wette (eds.), *'Unternehmen Barbarossa'. Der deutsche Überfall auf die Sowjetunion 1941* (Paderborn, 1984) pp. 339–340 (Document collection 20). See also the first-rate discussion in Geoffrey P. Megargee, 'Vernichtungskrieg: Strategy, Operations, and Genocide in the German Invasion of the Soviet Union, 1941' in *Acta of the International Commission on Military History's XXXIV Annual Congress* (Commissione Italiana di Storia Militare, 2009) pp. 459–464. Thanks to Geoffrey Megargee for providing me with a copy of this article.

50 For more on Reichenau, see Brendan Simms, 'Walther von Reichenau: der politische General' in Ronald Smelser and Enrico Syring (eds.), *Die Militärelite des Dritten Reiches. 27 biographische Skizzen* (Berlin, 1995) pp. 423–445; Walter Görlitz, 'Reichenau' in Correlli Barnett (ed.), *Hitler's Generals* (London, 1989) pp. 209–219.

51 Gerd R. Ueberschär (ed.), 'Befehl des Oberbefehlshabers der Heeresgruppe Süd, Generalfeldmarschall von Rundstedt, vom 12.10.1941' in Ueberschär and Wette (eds.), *'Unternehmen Barbarossa'*, p. 340 (Document collection 20).

52 As cited in Jürgen Förster, 'Securing "Living-space"' in Militärgeschichtliches Forschungsamt (ed.), *Germany and the Second World War. Volume IV*, pp. 1212–1213.

53 For key works in this area, see Gerhard L. Weinberg, 'The Yelnya-Dorogobuzh Area of Smolensk Oblast' in John A. Armstrong (ed.), *Soviet Partisans in World War II* (Madison, 1964) pp. 389–457; Kurt DeWitt and Wilhelm Koll, 'The Bryansk Area' in Armstrong (ed.), *Soviet Partisans in World War II*, pp. 458–516. For a useful map depicting Soviet partisan regions throughout the German occupied east in the winter of 1941–1942, see Kenneth Slepyan, *Stalin's Guerrillas. Soviet Partisans in World War II* (Lawrence, 2006) p. 29.

54 'Kriegstagebuch Nr.3. des XXXXVI.Pz.Korps vom 24.08.41–31.12.41' BA-MA RH 24-46/21, fol. 73 (9 October 1941).

55 '5. Panzer Division KTB Nur.8 vom 11.9.41–11.12.41' BA-MA RH 27-5/29, fol. 24 (5 October 1941).

56 '2. Panzer Division KTB Nr.6 Teil I. Vom 15.6.41–3.4.42' BA-MA RH 27-2/21 (13 October 1941).

57 'Anlagenband zum KTB XXXXI A.K. Ia 1. Durchbruch durch die Wop-Kokosch Dnjepr Stellung 2.10.41 bis 9.10.41. 2. Vorstoss auf Kalinin 15.10.41–20.10.41' BA-MA RH 24–41/14 (7 October 1941).

58 'Kriegstagebuch der O.Qu.-Abt. Pz. A.O.K.2 von 21.6.41 bis 31.3.42' BA-MA RH 21–2/819, fols. 174–175 (10 and 11 October 1941).

59 Lange, *Tagebücher aus dem Zweiten Weltkrieg*, p. 71 (12 October 1941).

60 Alexander Hill, *The Great Patriotic War of the Soviet Union, 1941–1945. A Documentary Reader* (Abingdon and New York, 2010) p. 55, Document 33.

61 Peter von der Osten-Sacken, *Vier Jahre Barbarossa. Authentische Berichte aus dem Russlandfeldzug 1941 bis 1945* (Frankfurt am Main, 2005) pp. 37–38.

62 Slepyan, *Stalin's Guerrillas*, p. 27.

63 Theo J. Schulte, 'Die Wehrmacht und die nationalsozialistische Besatzungspolitik in der Sowjetunion' in Roland G. Foerster (ed.), *'Unternehmen Barbarossa'. Zum historischen Ort der deutsch-sowjetischen Beziehungen von 1933 bis Herbst 1941* (Munich, 1993) p. 172.

64 Christian Gerlach, *Kalkulierte Morde. Die deutsche Wirtschafts- und Vernichtungspolitik in Weißrussland 1941 bis 1944* (Hamburg, 2000) pp. 618–619; Stephan Lehnstaedt, 'The Minsk Experience: German Occupiers and Everyday Life in the Capital of Belarus' in Kay, Rutherford and Stahel (eds.), *Nazi Policy on the Eastern Front, 1941*, p. 245.

65 Osten-Sacken, *Vier Jahre Barbarossa*, p. 38.

66 Kenneth Slepyan, 'The People's Avengers: The Partisan Movement' in David R. Stone (ed.) *The Soviet Union at War 1941–1945* (Barnsley, 2010) pp. 159–161. See also Alexander Hill, *The War Behind the Eastern Front. The Soviet Partisan Movement in North-West Russia 1941–1944* (Abingdon and New York, 2006); Howell, *The Soviet Partisan Movement 1941–1944*.

67 'Kriegstagebuch Nr.1 (Band Oktober 1941) des Oberkommandos der Heeresgruppe Mitte' BA-MA RH 19-II/411, fols. 575 and 584 (8 and 10 October 1941).

68 Erickson, *The Road to Stalingrad*, p. 218.

69 'Gen.Kdo.LVII.Pz.Korps KTB Nr.1 vom 15.2.41–31.10.41' BA-MA RH 24–57–2, fol. 257 (9 October 1941).

70 *Ibid.*, fol. 259 (10 October 1941).

71 *Ibid.*, fol. 260 (10 October 1941).

72 Willi Kubik, *Erinnerungen eines Panzerschützen 1941–1945. Tagebuchaufzeichnung eines Panzerschützen der Pz.Aufkl.Abt. 13 im Russlandfeldzug* (Würzburg, 2004) pp. 94–95 (2 October 1941). This diary also includes a few pictures of the tank.

73 'Gen.Kdo.LVII.Pz.Korps KTB Nr.1 vom 15.2.41–31.10.41' BA-MA RH 24–57–2, fol. 269 (13 October 1941).

74 '20.Pz.Div. KTB vom 15.8.41 bis 20.10.41 Band Ia.' BA-MA RH 27–20/25, fol. 129 (14 October 1941).

75 Guderian, *Panzer Leader*, p. 234.

76 Schäufler (ed.), *Knight's Cross Panzers*, p. 138.

77 Guderian, *Panzer Leader*, p. 235.

78 Schäufler (ed.), *Knight's Cross Panzers*, pp. 138–140.

79 'Kriegstagebuch 4.Panzer-Division Führungsabtl. 26.5.41–31.3.42' BA-MA RH 27–4/10, p. 206 (12 October 1941).

80 'Kriegstagebuch der O.Qu.-Abt. Pz. A.O.K.2 von 21.6.41 bis 31.3.42' BA-MA RH 21–2/819, fol. 174 (11 October 1941).

81 Guderian, *Panzer Leader*, p. 235. See also Kenneth Macksey, *Guderian. Panzer General* (London, 1975) pp. 155–156.

82 'Kriegstagebuch Nr.1 (Band Oktober 1941) des Oberkommandos der Heeresgruppe Mitte' BA-MA RH 19-II/411, fol. 594 (11 October 1941).

83 *Ibid.*, fol. 601 (11 October 1941).

84 'Kriegstagebuch XXXXVIII.Pz.Kps. Abt.Ia October 1941' BA-MA RH 24–48/30, fol. 7 (12 October 1941).

85 '9.Pz.Div. KTB Ia vom 19.5.1941 bis 22.1.1942' BA-MA RH 27–9/4, fol. 135 (11 October 1941).

86 Degrelle, *Campaign in Russia*, p. 17.

87 '9.Pz.Div. KTB Ia vom 19.5.1941 bis 22.1.1942' BA-MA RH 27–9/4, fol. 137 (12 and 13 October 1941).

88 'Kriegstagebuch Nr.7 des Kdos. Der 1.Panzer-Div. 20.9.41–12.4.42' BA-MA 27–1/58, fols. 11 and 14 (3 and 4 October 1941).

89 *Ibid.*, fol. 16 (6 October 1941).

90 'Anlagen zum Kriegstagebuch Tagesmeldungen Bd.I 1.9–31.10.41' BA-MA RH 21–3/70, fol. 65 (4 October 1941).

91 *Ibid.*, fol. 103 (8 October 1941).

92 Hans Röttiger, 'XXXXI Panzer Corps During the Battle of Moscow in 1941 as a Component of Panzer Group 3' in Steven H. Newton (ed.), *German Battle Tactics in the Russian Front 1941–1945* (Atglen, 1994) p. 23.

93 Siegfried Knappe with Ted Brusaw, *Soldat. Reflections of a German Soldier, 1936–1949* (New York, 1992) p. 229.

94 '3rd Pz. Gr. KTB Nr.2 1.9.41–31.10.41' BA-MA Microfilm 59060 (10 October 1941); Bock, *War Diary*, p. 329 (10 October 1941); Carl Wagener, *Moskau 1941. Der Angriff auf die russische Hauptstadt* (Dorheim, 1985) p. 72.

95 Röttiger, 'XXXXI Panzer Corps During the Battle of Moscow', p. 23.

96 Underlining in the original; 'Anlagen zum Kriegstagebuch Tagesmeldungen Bd.I 1.9–31.10.41' BA-MA RH 21–3/70, fol. 219 (11 October 1941).

97 Haape with Henshaw, *Moscow Tram Stop*, p. 141.

98 Röttiger, 'XXXXI Panzer Corps During the Battle of Moscow', p. 27.

99 Bock, *War Diary*, p. 330 (11 October 1941).

100 Röttiger, 'XXXXI Panzer Corps During the Battle of Moscow', p. 28.

101 Bock, *War Diary*, p. 330 (12 October 1941); '3rd Pz. Gr. KTB Nr.2 1.9.41–31.10.41' BA-MA Microfilm 59060 (12 October 1941).

102 'Kriegstagebuch Nr.7 des Kdos. Der 1.Panzer-Div. 20.9.41–12.4.42' BA-MA 27–1/58, fol. 26 (12 October 1941).

103 Gottlob Herbert Bidermann, *In Deadly Combat. A German Soldier's Memoir of the Eastern Front* (Lawrence, 2000) p. 46.

104 Wagener, *Moskau 1941*, p. 73.

105 As cited in Michael Jones, *The Retreat*, p. 51.

106 Röttiger, 'XXXXI Panzer Corps During the Battle of Moscow', p. 27 and n. 11.

107 'Ivan' was the nickname used by German troops to refer to the Soviet enemy. The Soviets adopted the name 'Fritz' for the Germans: Wagener, *Moskau 1941*, pp. 73–74.

108 Pabst, *The Outermost Frontier*, p. 34.

109 '3rd Pz. Gr. KTB Nr.2 1.9.41–31.10.41' BA-MA Microfilm 59060 (10 October 1941).

110 Röttiger, 'XXXXI Panzer Corps During the Battle of Moscow', pp. 27–28.

111 'Kriegstagebuch Nr.7 des Kdos. Der 1.Panzer-Div. 20.9.41–12.4.42' BA-MA 27–1/58, fol. 27 (13 October 1941).

112 Bock, *War Diary*, pp. 330–331 (12 October 1941).

113 Walter S. Dunn Jr, *Stalin's Keys to Victory. The Rebirth of the Red Army in WWII* (Mechanicsburg, 2006) p. 39.

114 Rolf-Dieter Müller, 'Beginnings of a Reorganization of the War Economy at the Turn of 1941/1942' in Militärgeschichtliches Forschungsamt (ed.), *Germany and the Second World War. Volume V/I*, p. 728.

115 Dunn, *Stalin's Keys to Victory*, p. 39.

116 Overy, 'Statistics', table 2, 'Military Production', p. 1060.

117 Porter and Jones, *Moscow in World War II*, pp. 68–71.

118 Glantz, *Barbarossa*, p. 166.

119 Fröhlich (ed.), *Die Tagebücher von Joseph Goebbels Teil II Band 2*, p. 70 (7 October 1941).

120 Werth, *Russia at War 1941–1945*, pp. 232–233.

121 Glantz, *Barbarossa*, p. 154.

122 Seweryn Bialer (ed.), *Stalin and His Generals. Soviet Military Memoirs of World War II* (New York, 1969) p. 285.

123 Glantz, *Barbarossa*, p. 148.

124 General N. F. Vatutin, the chief of staff of the North-Western Front, headed a separate group to defend Torzhok and later advance on Kalinin. See Keith

Cumins, *Cataclysm. The War on the Eastern Front 1941–1945* (Solihull, 2011) p. 55; David M. Glantz, 'Vatutin' in Shukman (ed.), *Stalin's Generals*, p. 292.

125 Erickson, *The Road to Stalingrad*, p. 219; Otto Preston Chaney, *Zhukov* (Norman, 1996) p. 167.

126 Bellamy, *Absolute War*, pp. 186–187; Rodric Braithwaite, *Moscow 1941. A City and Its People at War* (New York, 2006) pp. 204–205.

127 Porter and Jones, *Moscow in World War II*, p. 116.

128 Braithwaite, *Moscow 1941*, ch. 13, 'Evacuation'; Bellamy, *Absolute War*, p. 188.

129 Gorodetsky (ed.), *Stafford Cripps in Moscow 1940–1942*, p. 180 (11 October 1941).

130 Earl F. Ziemke and Magna E. Bauer, *Moscow to Stalingrad. Decision in the East* (New York, 1988) p. 39.

5 Bock's final triumph

1 Lieven, *Russia Against Napoleon*, pp. 264–265; Zamoyski, *1812*, p. 387.

2 Zhukov, *The Memoirs of Marshal Zhukov*, p. 331; Salisbury (ed.), *Marshal Zhukov's Greatest Battles*, pp. 51–52.

3 Ingeborg Ochsenknecht, *'Als ob der Schnee alles zudeckte'. Eine Krankenschwester erinnert sich an ihren Kriegseinsatz an der Ostfront* (Berlin, 2005) pp. 86–87.

4 Bock, *War Diary*, p. 330 (12 October 1941).

5 'Kriegstagebuch Nr.3. des XXXXVI.Pz.Korps vom 24.08.41–31.12.41' BA-MA RH 24-46/21, fol. 79 (12 October 1941).

6 Ernst Tewes, *Seelsorger bei den Soldaten. Erinnerungen an die Zeit von 1940 bis 1945* (Munich, 1995) p. 31.

7 '11.Pz.Div. KTB Abt. Ia vom 1.5.41–21.10.41' BA-MA RH 27–11/16, fols. 156–157 (12 October 1941).

8 'Anlage zum KTB Pz.Gruppe 4 Meldungen von unten 20.9.41–14.10.41' BA-MA RH 21-4/37, fol. 14 (12 October 1941).

9 *Ibid.*, fol. 10 (13 October 1941).

10 David M. Glantz, *Colossus Reborn. The Red Army at War, 1941–1943* (Lawrence, 2005) p. 123.

11 'Anlage zum KTB Pz.Gruppe 4 Meldungen von unten 20.9.41–14.10.41' BA-MA RH 21-4/37, fol. 10 (13 October 1941).

12 'Kriegstagebuch Nr.3. des XXXXVI.Pz.Korps vom 24.08.41–31.12.41' BA-MA RH 24-46/21, fol. 80 (12 October 1941).

13 As cited in Robert Kershaw, *War Without Garlands*, pp. 183–184. For the original German-language account, see Franz Josef Strauss, *Friedens- und*

Kriegserlebnisse einer Generation. Ein Kapitel Weltgeschichte aus der Sicht der Panzerjäger-Abteilung 38 (SF) in der ehemaligen 2. (Wiener) Panzerdivision (Neckergemünd, 1977) pp. 90–93.

14 As cited in Robert Kershaw, *War Without Garlands*, p. 184.

15 The available section of the diary does not specifically state that Krause belonged to the 35th Infantry Division, but he does give their distance from Viaz'ma, which could only be consistent with Weikersthal's division.

16 *True to Type*, p. 29 (12 and 13 October 1941).

17 It is also significant that Funck's panzer regiment was one of the most powerful on the eastern front, fielding 120 tanks on 14 October: '3rd Pz. Gr. KTB Nr.2 1.9.41–31.10.41' BA-MA Microfilm 59060 (14 October 1941).

18 Horst Fuchs Richardson (ed.), *Sieg Heil! War Letters of Tank Gunner Karl Fuchs 1937–1941* (Hamden, 1987) p. 142 (12 October 1941).

19 Steiger, *Armour Tactics in the Second World War*, p. 80.

20 '3rd Pz. Gr. KTB Nr.2 1.9.41–31.10.41' BA-MA Microfilm 59060 (16 October 1941).

21 Fuchs Richardson (ed.), *Sieg Heil!*, p. 143 (15 October 1941).

22 Fröhlich (ed.), *Die Tagebücher von Joseph Goebbels Teil II Band 2*, p. 109 (14 October 1941).

23 'Kriegstagebuch Nr.1 (Band Oktober 1941) des Oberkommandos der Heeresgruppe Mitte' BA-MA RH 19-II/411, fol. 601 (11 October 1941).

24 Nagorski, *The Greatest Battle*, pp. 116–117.

25 'Kriegstagebuch Nr.3. des XXXXVI.Pz.Korps vom 24.08.41–31.12.41' BA-MA RH 24–46/21, fol. 87 (13 October 1941).

26 Walter Neuser, MPT, 3.2002.0947 (15 October 1941).

27 As cited in Rees, *War of the Century*, pp. 65–66.

28 Reddemann (ed.), *Zwischen Front und Heimat*, p. 328 (14 October 1941).

29 As cited in Nagorski, *The Greatest Battle*, p. 118.

30 Lange, *Tagebücher aus dem Zweiten Weltkrieg*, p. 71 (12 October 1941).

31 Fuchs Richardson (ed.), *Sieg Heil!*, p. 143 (15 October 1941).

32 As cited in Michael Jones, *The Retreat*, p. 57.

33 Fuchs Richardson (ed.), *Sieg Heil!*, p. 143 (15 October 1941).

34 As cited in Rees, *War of the Century*, p. 67.

35 Bock, *War Diary*, p. 333 (14 October 1941).

36 Blumentritt, 'Moscow', p. 54.

37 Robert M. Citino, *Death of the Wehrmacht. The German Campaigns of 1942* (Lawrence, 2007) p. 44.

38 'Kriegstagebuch Nr.1 (Band Oktober 1941) des Oberkommandos der Heeresgruppe Mitte' BA-MA RH 19-II/411, fol. 611 (14 October 1941).

39 *Ibid.*, fol. 614 (15 October 1941).

40 Luck, *Panzer Commander*, p. 61.

41 As cited in Rees, *War of the Century*, p. 67.

42 As cited in Braithwaite, *Moscow 1941*, p. 195.

43 *Ibid.*, pp. 195–196.

44 As cited in Marius Broekmeyer, *Stalin, the Russians, and Their War 1941–1945* (London, 2004) p. 168.

45 As cited in Nagorski, *The Greatest Battle*, p. 118.

46 Slepyan, *Stalin's Guerrillas*, p. 34.

47 Glantz, *Barbarossa*, p. 153.

48 Braithwaite, *Moscow 1941*, p. 196.

49 Mawdsley, *Thunder in the East*, p. 95.

50 *KTB OKW*, Volume II, p. 693 (11 October 1941).

51 Klink, 'The Conduct of Operations', p. 685.

52 Geyer, *Das IX. Armeekorps im Ostfeldzug 1941*, p. 141.

53 Alexander and Kunze (eds.), *Eastern Inferno*, p. 93 (11 September 1941).

54 As cited in Lucas, *War of the Eastern Front 1941–1945*, p. 207.

55 Knappe with Brusaw, *Soldat*, p. 228.

56 Bidermann, *In Deadly Combat*, p. 52.

57 *True to Type*, p. 25 (there is no date listed, only 'Autumn 1941').

58 Fröhlich (ed.), *Die Tagebücher von Joseph Goebbels Teil II Band* 2, p. 124 (16 October 1941).

59 *True to Type*, pp. 146–147 (no date).

60 *Ibid.*, p. 147 (no date).

61 Ochsenknecht, '*Als ob der Schnee alles zudeckte*', pp. 92–93.

62 Luck, *Panzer Commander*, p. 61.

63 Henry Metelmann, *Through Hell for Hitler* (Havertown, 2005) p. 30.

64 As cited in Martin Gilbert, *The Second World War. A Complete History* (London, 2009) pp. 243–244.

65 As cited in Piekalkiewicz, *Moscow 1941*, p. 134.

66 'Kriegstagebuch Nr.1 (Band Oktober 1941) des Oberkommandos der Heeresgruppe Mitte' BA-MA RH 19-II/411, fol. 598 (11 October 1941).

67 '18.Panzer Division, Abt.Ia KTB Teil III vom 30.9.–19.10.41' BA-MA RH 27–18/22, pp. 48–49 (13 October 1941).

68 'Kriegstagebuch Nr.2 XXXXVII.Pz.Korps. Ia 23.9.1941–31.12.1941' BA-MA RH 24–47/258, fol. 45 (13 October 1941).

69 Bock, *War Diary*, p. 331 (13 October 1941).

70 'Kriegstagebuch Nr.1 (Band Oktober 1941) des Oberkommandos der Heeresgruppe Mitte' BA-MA RH 19-II/411, fol. 611 (14 October 1941).

71 Eremenko, *The Arduous Beginning*, p. 253.

72 'Kriegstagebuch Nr.2 XXXXVII.Pz.Korps. Ia 23.9.1941–31.12.1941' BA-MA RH 24–47/258, fol. 45 (13 October 1941).

73 'KTB 3rd Pz. Div. vom 19.9.41 bis 6.2.42' BA-MA RH 27–3/15, pp. 283–284 (13 October 1941). Guderian's memoir spoke of some 5,000 Soviet men: Guderian, *Panzer Leader*, p. 239.

74 Guderian, *Panzer Leader*, p. 237.

75 'Kriegstagebuch Nr.2 XXXXVII.Pz.Korps. Ia 23.9.1941–31.12.1941' BA-MA RH 24–47/258, fols. 46–47 (14 October 1941).

76 '18.Panzer Division, Abt.Ia KTB Teil III vom 30.9.–19.10.41' BA-MA RH 27–18/22, p. 6 (15 October 1941).

77 'Kriegstagebuch Nr.2 XXXXVII.Pz.Korps. Ia 23.9.1941–31.12.1941' BA-MA RH 24–47/258, fol. 48 (14 October 1941).

78 *Ibid.*, fol. 60 (19 October 1941).

79 Bock, *War Diary*, p. 333 (15 October 1941).

80 Kleindienst (ed.), *Sei tausendmal gegrüßt*, CD-ROM (16 October 1941).

81 Bähr and Bähr (eds.), *Kriegsbriefe Gefallener Studenten, 1939–1945*, p. 97 (16 October 1941).

82 Hans Bähr and Walter Bähr (eds.), *Die Stimme des Menschen. Briefe und Aufzeichnungen aus der ganzen Welt. 1939–1945* (Munich, 1961) pp. 113–114 (17 October 1941).

83 Kleindienst (ed.), *Sei tausendmal gegrüßt*, CD-ROM (15 October 1941).

84 As cited in Michael Jones, *The Retreat*, p. 60.

85 Roger R. Reese, *Why Stalin's Soldiers Fought. The Red Army's Military Effectiveness in World War II* (Lawrence, 2011) p. 85.

86 Bock, *War Diary*, p. 334 (17 October 1941).

87 Kleindienst (ed.), *Sei tausendmal gegrüßt*, CD-ROM (17 October 1941).

88 'Verlustmeldungen 5.7.1941–25.3.1942' BA-MA RH 21–2/757, fols. 15 and 17 (15 and 25 October 1941).

89 Guderian, *Panzer Leader*, p. 230.

90 '18.Panzer Division, Abt.Ia KTB Teil III vom 30.9.–19.10.41' BA-MA RH 27–18/22, p. 50 (14 October 1941).

91 'Kriegstagebuch Nr.1 (Band Oktober 1941) des Oberkommandos der Heeresgruppe Mitte' BA-MA RH 19-II/411, fols. 611–612 (14 October 1941).

92 Bock, *War Diary*, p. 335 (18 October 1941).

93 As outlined in Sergei M. Shtemenko, *The Soviet General Staff at War 1941–1945* (Moscow, 1975) pp. 45–46.

94 Glantz, *Barbarossa*, p. 153; Bellamy, *Absolute War*, p. 277.

95 '3rd Pz. Gr. KTB Nr.2 1.9.41–31.10.41' BA-MA Microfilm 59060 (19 October 1941); Bock, *War Diary*, p. 336 (19 October 1941).

96 Fröhlich (ed.), *Die Tagebücher von Joseph Goebbels Teil II Band 2*, p. 144 (20 October 1941). The announcement stated that 657,948 Soviet POWs had been captured, while 1,241 Soviet tanks and 5,396 guns were captured or destroyed.

97 'Kriegstagebuch Nr.1 (Band Oktober 1941) des Oberkommandos der Heeresgruppe Mitte' BA-MA RH 19-II/411, fol. 644 (19 October 1941). In addition the war diary noted 1,277 tanks, 4,378 guns, 1,009 anti-tank and anti-aircraft guns and 87 planes destroyed or captured. See also Bock, *War Diary*, p. 336 (19 October 1941).

98 For the best works on the treatment of Soviet POWs, see Christian Streit, *Keine Kameraden. Die Wehrmacht und die sowjetischen Kriegsgefangenen 1941–1945* (Bonn, 1997); Christian Streit, 'Soviet Prisoners of War in the Hands of the Wehrmacht' in Hannes Heer and Klaus Naumann (eds.), *War of Extermination. The German Military in World War II 1941–1944* (Oxford, 2006) pp. 80–91; Christian Streit, 'Die sowjetischen Kriegsgefangenen in der Hand der Wehrmacht' in Walter Manoschek (ed.), *Die Wehrmacht im Rassenkrieg. Der Vernichtungskrieg hinter der Front* (Vienna, 1996) pp. 74–89.

99 Sönke Neitzel, *Tapping Hitler's Generals. Transcripts of Secret Conversations, 1942–1945* (St Paul, 2007) p. 186, Document 100 (2–4 August 1944).

100 As cited in Michael Jones, *The Retreat*, p. 68.

101 Bock, *War Diary*, p. 337 (20 October 1941).

102 Roy Mark-Alan, *White Coats Under Fire. With the Italian Expedition Corps in Russia – 1941* (New York, 1972) pp. 37–38.

103 Nikolai I. Obryn'ba, *Red Partisan. The Memoir of a Soviet Resistance Fighter on the Eastern Front* (Washington, DC, 2007) p. 30.

104 Mark-Alan, *White Coats Under Fire*, pp. 37–38.

105 Streit, 'Soviet Prisoners of War in the Hands of the Wehrmacht', p. 81.

106 Konrad H. Jarausch (eds.), *Reluctant Accomplice. A Wehrmacht Soldier's Letters from the Eastern Front* (Princeton, 2011) pp. 306–307 (15 October 1941).

107 *Ibid.*, pp. 307 and 310 (23 and 25 October 1941).

108 Degrelle, *Campaign in Russia*, pp. 12–13.

109 For this reason there are no entries in Halder's war diary between 10 October and 3 November 1941. See Halder, *KTB III*, p. 277 (10 October 1941).

110 Bock, *War Diary*, p. 331 (13 October 1941).

111 Blumentritt, 'Moscow', p. 54.

112 As cited in Boog, 'The Luftwaffe', p. 794.

113 Piekalkiewicz, *Moscow 1941*, p. 117.

114 Fröhlich (ed.), *Die Tagebücher von Joseph Goebbels Teil II Band 2*, p. 105 (13 October 1941).

115 Bähr and Bähr (eds.), *Kriegsbriefe Gefallener Studenten, 1939–1945*, p. 63 (14 October 1941).

116 Humburg, *Das Gesicht des Krieges*, p. 126 (15 October 1941).

117 Bumke incorrectly recorded the date of the speech as 4 October.

118 *Ibid.*, p. 122 (18 October 1941).

119 Stader (ed.), *Ihr daheim und wir hier draußen*, p. 42 (17 October 1941).

120 For an excellent discussion of German myths surrounding their defeat in 1941 see Gerd R. Ueberschär, 'Das Scheitern des Unternehmens "Barbarossa": Der deutsch-sowjetische Krieg vom Überfall bis zur Wende vor Moskau im Winter 1941/42' in Ueberschär and Wette (eds.), '*Unternehmen Barbarossa*', p. 165. Following Napoleon's 1812 campaign a similar rationale for defeat was adopted. As Dominic Lieven observed: 'Subsequently Napoleon himself and some of his admirers were much inclined to blame the unusually cold winter for the destruction of his army. This is mostly nonsense' (Lieven, *Russia Against Napoleon*, p. 265).

121 Ferdinand Prinz von der Leyen, *Rückblick zum Mauerwald. Vier Kriegsjahre im OKH* (Munich, 1965) p. 37.

122 Alexander and Kunze (eds.), *Eastern Inferno*, p. 118 (7 October 1941).

123 Landon and Leitner (eds.), *Diary of a German Soldier*, p. 111 (7 October 1941).

124 *True to Type*, p. 13 (7 October 1941).

125 '3rd Pz. Gr. KTB Nr.2 1.9.41–31.10.41' BA-MA Microfilm 59060 (7 October 1941). Interestingly the same problem resulted in the deaths of numerous Frenchmen during Napoleon's retreat from Russia in the winter of 1812.

126 Bidermann, *In Deadly Combat*, p. 62.

127 DiNardo, *Germany and the Axis Powers*, p. 108.

128 These deaths were only the beginning of the German 'Hunger Plan' for the east; see Alex J. Kay, '"The Purpose of the Russian Campaign Is the Decimation of the Slavic Population by Thirty Million": The Radicalization of German Food Policy in Early 1941' in Kay, Rutherford and Stahel (eds.), *Nazi Policy on the Eastern Front, 1941*, pp. 101–129; Wigbert Benz, *Der Hungerplan im 'Unternehmen Barbarossa' 1941* (Berlin, 2011). For first-rate case studies reflecting the impact of these policies in 1941, see Jeff Rutherford, 'The Radicalization of German Occupation Policies: *Wirtschaftsstab Ost* and the 121st Infantry Division in Pavlovsk, 1941' in Kay, Rutherford and Stahel (eds.), *Nazi Policy on the Eastern Front, 1941*, pp. 130–154; Norbert Kunz, 'Das Beispiel Charkow: Eine Stadtbevölkerung als Opfer der deutschen Hungerstrategie 1941/42' in Christian Hartmann, Johannes Hürter and Ulrike Jureit (eds.), *Verbrechen der Wehrmacht. Bilanz einer Debatte* (Munich, 2005) pp. 136–144. The dimensions of the Hunger Plan and the 2 May 1941 meeting have recently come under attack from revisionist historians seeking to expunge the Wehrmacht's deep-seated involvement. The controversy can be followed in the *Journal of Contemporary History*; see Alex J. Kay, 'Germany's Staatssekretäre, Mass Starvation and the Meeting of 2 May 1941', *Journal of Contemporary History*, 41, 4 (October 2006) pp. 685–700; Klaus Jochen

Arnold and Gerd C. Lübbers, 'The Meeting of the Staatssekretäre on 2 May 1941 and the Wehrmacht: A Document up for Discussion', *Journal of Contemporary History*, 42, 4 (October 2007) pp. 613–626; Alex J. Kay, 'Revisiting the Meeting of the Staatssekretäre on 2 May 1941: A Response to Klaus Jochen Arnold and Gert C. Lübbers', *Journal of Contemporary History*, 43, 1 (January 2008) pp. 93–104.

129 Luck, *Panzer Commander*, p. 56. The fact that Luck choose to place the word 'requisition' in quotation marks implies the process may better be described as looting or plundering.

130 *Ibid.*, p. 63.

131 Mark-Alan, *White Coats Under Fire*, p. 37.

132 Hans Joachim Schröder, 'German Soldiers' Experiences During the Initial Phase of the Russian Campaign' in Wegner (ed.), *From Peace to War*, p. 320.

133 Bidermann, *In Deadly Combat*, p. 62.

134 Kuhnert, *Will We See Tomorrow?*, p. 113.

135 Erhard Rauss, 'Effects of Climate on Combat in European Russia' in Tsouras (ed.) *Fighting in Hell*, p. 18. Note that Raus's name is spelled incorrectly in the aforementioned title. See also Department of the US Army (ed.), *Effects of Climate on Combat in European Russia* (Washington, DC, 1952) p. 18.

136 Guderian, *Panzer Leader*, p. 234.

137 *Ibid.*, p. 237.

138 Neitzel, *Tapping Hitler's Generals*, pp. 226–227, Document 135 (25 April 1945).

139 Metelmann, *Through Hell for Hitler*, p. 35.

140 Landon and Leitner (eds.), *Diary of a German Soldier*, p. 108 (26 September 1941).

141 For evidence in support of this conclusion, see Jean Lévesque, 'A Peasant Ordeal: The Soviet Countryside' in Stone (ed.) *The Soviet Union at War 1941–1945*, pp. 192–193.

142 Hans Becker, *Devil on My Shoulder* (London, 1957) p. 30.

143 Thoma replaced the aforementioned Colonel Georg von Bismarck in command of the division on 14 October 1941.

144 Neitzel, *Tapping Hitler's Generals*, pp. 192–193, Document 107 (16–17 September 1944).

145 Kuhnert, *Will We See Tomorrow?*, p. 114.

146 While there can be no doubt about the criminal nature of German rule in the east, the question has recently been asked whether this resulted from radicalising external factors encountered by the Germans in the east (as argued by Jörg Baberowski and Klaus J. Arnold) or whether the radicalising factors were something imbued in Nazi ideology and German plans for the east (as far more convincingly argued by Alex J. Kay). See Jörg Baberowski, 'Kriege in

staatsfernen Räumen: Rußland und die Sowjetunion 1905–1950' in Dietrich Beyrau, Michael Hochgeschwender and Dieter Langewiesche (eds.), *Formen des Krieges. Von der Antike bis zur Gegenwart* (Paderborn, 2007), pp. 291–309; Klaus J. Arnold, *Die Wehrmacht und die Besatzungspolitik in den besetzten Gebieten der Sowjetunion. Kriegführung und Radikalisierung im 'Unternehmen Barbarossa'* (Berlin, 2005); Alex J. Kay, 'A "War in a Region Beyond State Control"? The German–Soviet War, 1941–1944', *War in History*, 18, 1 (January 2011) pp. 109–122.

6 Exploiting the breach

1 Bücheler, *Hoepner*, pp. 151–153.

2 As cited in Johannes Hürter, *Hitlers Heerführer. Die deutschen Oberbefehlshaber im Krieg gegen die Sowjetunion 1941/42* (Munich, 2006) p. 298.

3 Kuntzen was soon given command of the 19th Panzer Division, which had been held in Army Group Centre's reserve.

4 '20.Pz.Div. KTB vom 15.8.41 bis 20.10.41 Band Ia.' BA-MA RH 27–20/25, fols. 119 and 123 (9 and 11 October 1941).

5 'Kriegstagebuch Nr.3. der Führungsabteilung (Ia) des Gen. Kdo. (mot.) XXXX. Pz.Korps vom 31.05.1941–26.12.1941' BA-MA RH 24–40/18 (11 October 1941). The diary has no folio stamped page numbers so references must be located using the date.

6 Lucas, *Das Reich*, p. 213.

7 '20.Pz.Div. KTB vom 15.8.41 bis 20.10.41 Band Ia.' BA-MA RH 27–20/25, fol. 133 (16 October 1941).

8 Underlining in the original.

9 'Kriegstagebuch Nr.1 (Band Oktober 1941) des Oberkommandos der Heeresgruppe Mitte' BA-MA RH 19-II/411, fol. 611 (14 October 1941).

10 Landon and Leitner (eds.), *Diary of a German Soldier*, p. 113 (13 October 1941).

11 Bücheler, *Hoepner*, p. 153. For tactical details of the fighting for Gzhatsk, see Lucas, *Das Reich*, p. 72.

12 'Kriegstagebuch Nr.3. des XXXXVI.Pz.Korps vom 24.08.41–31.12.41' BA-MA RH 24–46/21, fol. 83 (15 October 1941).

13 '11.Pz.Div. KTB Abt. Ia vom 1.5.41–21.10.41' BA-MA RH 27–11/16, fol. 161 (15 October 1941).

14 'Kriegstagebuch Nr.3. des XXXXVI.Pz.Korps vom 24.08.41–31.12.41' BA-MA RH 24–46/21, fol. 82 (14 October 1941).

15 *Ibid.*, fol. 83 (15 October 1941).

16 '11.Pz.Div. KTB Abt. Ia vom 1.5.41–21.10.41' BA-MA RH 27–11/16, fol. 163 (16 October 1941). The German *Kampfgruppe* was an ad hoc, combined arms formation that was typically organised for a specific purpose.

17 'Kriegstagebuch Nr.3. des XXXXVI.Pz.Korps vom 24.08.41–31.12.41' BA-MA RH 24–46/21, fol. 82 (14 October 1941).

18 '2. Panzer Division KTB Nr.6 Teil I. Vom 15.6.41–3.4.42' BA-MA RH 27–2/21 (17 and 18 October 1941).

19 *Ibid.* (17 October 1941).

20 'Kriegstagebuch Nr.3. des XXXXVI.Pz.Korps vom 24.08.41–31.12.41' BA-MA RH 24–46/21, fols. 87–89 (17–18 October 1941).

21 'Kriegstagebuch Nr.1 (Band Oktober 1941) des Oberkommandos der Heeresgruppe Mitte' BA-MA RH 19-II/411, fol. 644 (19 October 1941).

22 Kuhnert, *Will We See Tomorrow?*, p. 105.

23 'Kriegstagebuch Nr.3. des XXXXVI.Pz.Korps vom 24.08.41–31.12.41' BA-MA RH 24–46/21, fol. 89 (18 October 1941).

24 *Ibid.*, fol. 88 (18 October 1941).

25 Michael Eickhoff, Wilhelm Pagels and Willy Reschl (eds.), *Der unvergessene Krieg. Hitler-Deutschland gegen die Sowjetunion 1941–1945* (Cologne, 1981) p. 65.

26 An SS *Obersturmführer* had the equivalent rank to an army 1st lieutenant.

27 Günther Heysing, *Sturm bis vor Moskaus Tore. Kämpfe der Panzergruppe 4 in der Schlacht um Moskau vom 14. Okt. 1941–5. Dez. 1941* (no place of publication listed, 1942) p. 7. See also Piekalkiewicz, *Moscow 1941*, p. 115.

28 An SS *Oberführer* had no direct equivalent rank in the German army, but was between a major-general and a lieutenant-general.

29 Zamoyski, *1812*, pp. 287–288.

30 As cited in Braithwaite, *Moscow 1941*, p. 210. See also Bellamy, *Absolute War*, p. 288.

31 As cited in Michael Jones, *The Retreat*, p. 59.

32 'Anlage zum KTB Pz.Gruppe 4 Meldungen von unten 15.10.41–15.11.41' BA-MA RH 21–4/39, fol. 283 (15 October 1941).

33 *Ibid.*, fol. 272 (17 October 1941).

34 As cited in Michael Jones, *The Retreat*, p. 66.

35 Nagorski, *The Greatest Battle*, p. 132. German military files also report strong Soviet resistance with numerous tank attacks against their positions: 'Anlage zum KTB Pz.Gruppe 4 Meldungen von unten 20.9.41–14.10.41' BA-MA RH 21–4/37, fol. 1 (14 October 1941).

36 Heysing, *Sturm bis vor Moskaus Tore*, p. 8. See also Piekalkiewicz, *Moscow 1941*, p. 118.

37 Lucas, *Das Reich*, p. 73.

38 Bock, *War Diary*, p. 330 (12 October 1941); Glantz, *Atlas of the Battle of Moscow*, p. 29 (12 October 1941).

39 '20.Pz.Div. KTB vom 15.8.41 bis 20.10.41 Band Ia.' BA-MA RH 27–20/25, fol. 133 (16 October 1941).

40 'Gen.Kdo.LVII.Pz.Korps KTB Nr.1 vom 15.2.41–31.10.41' BA-MA RH 24–57–2, fol. 280 (16 October 1941).

41 'Kriegstagebuch Nr.1 (Band Oktober 1941) des Oberkommandos der Heeresgruppe Mitte' BA-MA RH 19-II/411, fol. 630 (17 October 1941).

42 Bock, *War Diary*, p. 334 (17 October 1941).

43 Martin Gareis, *Kampf und Ende der Fränkisch-Sudetendeutschen 98. Infanterie-Division* (Eggolsheim, 1956) p. 143.

44 Underlining in the original; 'Kriegstagebuch Nr.1 (Band Oktober 1941) des Oberkommandos der Heeresgruppe Mitte' BA-MA RH 19-II/411, fol. 623 (16 October 1941).

45 *Ibid.*, fol. 629 (17 October 1941).

46 Underlining in the original; *ibid.*, fol. 622–623 (16 October 1941).

47 Glantz, *Atlas of the Battle of Moscow*, p. 36 (16 October 1941).

48 As cited in Meyer, *Adolf Heusinger*, p. 160.

49 Bock, *War Diary*, p. 331 (12 October 1941).

50 'Kriegstagebuch Nr.1 (Band Oktober 1941) des Oberkommandos der Heeresgruppe Mitte' BA-MA RH 19-II/411, fol. 602 (12 October 1941). See also *KTB OKW*, Volume II, Document 103, p. 675 (3 October 1941).

51 Fröhlich (ed.), *Die Tagebücher von Joseph Goebbels Teil II Band 2*, p. 116 (15 October 1941).

52 *Ibid.*, pp. 117–118 (15 October 1941).

53 'Kriegstagebuch Nr.1 (Band Oktober 1941) des Oberkommandos der Heeresgruppe Mitte' BA-MA RH 19-II/411, fol. 641 (19 October 1941).

54 Muggeridge (ed.), *Ciano's Diary 1939–1943*, p. 386 (19 October 1941).

55 *Ibid.*, p. 386 (18 October 1941).

56 Röttiger, 'XXXXI Panzer Corps During the Battle of Moscow', p. 28.

57 Bock, *War Diary*, p. 332 (14 October 1941).

58 'Kriegstagebuch Nr.7 des Kdos. Der 1.Panzer-Div. 20.9.41–12.4.42' BA-MA 27–1/58, fol. 28 (14 October 1941).

59 Robert Kirchubel, *Hitler's Panzer's Armies on the Eastern Front* (Barnsley, 2009) p. 108; Von Hardesty, *Red Phoenix. The Rise of Soviet Air Power 1941–1945* (Washington, DC, 1982) p. 70.

60 Williamson Murray, *The Luftwaffe 1933–1945. Strategy for Defeat* (Washington, DC, 1996) p. 87.

61 'Anlagenband zum KTB XXXXI A.K. Ia 1. Durchbruch durch die Wop-Kokosch Dnjepr Stellung 2.10.41 bis 9.10.41. 2. Vorstoss auf Kalinin 15.10.41–20.10.41' BA-MA RH 24–41/14 (14 October 1941).

62 'Anlagenband zum KTB XXXXI A.K. Ia 3.Verteidigung von Kalinin 15.10.41–20.11.41' BA-MA RH 24–41/15 (17 October 1941). The diary has no folio stamped page numbers so references must be located using the date.

63 Kesselring, *The Memoirs of Field-Marshal Kesselring*, p. 97.

64 Erickson, *The Road to Stalingrad*, p. 219; Chaney, *Zhukov*, p. 167.

65 Bock, *War Diary*, p. 333 (15 October 1941).

66 *Ibid.*, p. 334 (16 October 1941).

67 'Kriegstagebuch Nr.1 (Band Oktober 1941) des Oberkommandos der Heeresgruppe Mitte' BA-MA RH 19-II/411, fol. 625 (16 October 1941).

68 Röttiger, 'XXXXI Panzer Corps During the Battle of Moscow', p. 30.

69 The aforementioned Lieutenant-General Otto Ottenbacher was replaced as the commander of the 36th Motorised Infantry Division on 15 October.

70 'Kriegstagebuch Nr.7 des Kdos. Der 1.Panzer-Div. 20.9.41–12.4.42' BA-MA 27–1/58, fol. 31 (17 October 1941).

71 'Kriegstagebuch Nr.1 (Band Oktober 1941) des Oberkommandos der Heeresgruppe Mitte' BA-MA RH 19-II/411, fol. 620 (16 October 1941).

72 'Kriegstagebuch Nr.7 des Kdos. Der 1.Panzer-Div. 20.9.41–12.4.42' BA-MA 27–1/58, fol. 31 (17 October 1941). See also 'Anlagenband zum KTB XXXXI A.K. Ia 3.Verteidigung von Kalinin 15.10.41–20.11.41' BA-MA RH 24–41/15 (18 October 1941).

73 '3rd Pz. Gr. KTB Nr.2 1.9.41–31.10.41' BA-MA Microfilm 59060 (17 October 1941).

74 'Kriegstagebuch Nr.1 (Band Oktober 1941) des Oberkommandos der Heeresgruppe Mitte' BA-MA RH 19-II/411, fol. 628 (17 October 1941).

75 Bock, *War Diary*, p. 332 (14 October 1941).

76 *Ibid.*, p. 336 (19 October 1941).

77 Wagener, *Moskau 1941*, pp. 75–76. See also Michael Jones, *The Retreat*, p. 58.

78 Chales de Beaulieu, *Generaloberst Erich Hoepner*, p. 202.

79 Hans Ulrich Rudel, *Stuka Pilot* (New York, 1979) p. 47.

80 '3rd Pz. Gr. KTB Nr.2 1.9.41–31.10.41' BA-MA Microfilm 59060 (18 October 1941).

81 According to Rudel's account there were multiple tanks: 'Our infantry comrades tell us that yesterday some tanks drove into the market square, firing at everything that showed itself. They had broken through our outposts and it took a long time to deal with them in the town' (Rudel, *Stuka Pilot*, p. 48).

82 On 14 October the war diary of Panzer Group 3 listed the division as having seventy-nine serviceable tanks: '3rd Pz. Gr. KTB Nr.2 1.9.41–31.10.41' BA-MA Microfilm 59060 (14 October 1941). For the figure from 19 October, see 'Anlagenband zum KTB XXXXI A.K. Ia 3.Verteidigung von Kalinin 15.10.41–20.11.41' BA-MA RH 24–41/15 (19 October 1941).

83 'Anlagen zum Kriegstagebuch Tagesmeldungen Bd.I 1.9–31.10.41' BA-MA RH 21–3/70, fol. 232 (20 October 1941).

84 '3rd Pz. Gr. KTB Nr.2 1.9.41–31.10.41' BA-MA Microfilm 59060 (20 October 1941).

85 'Anlagenband zum KTB XXXXI A.K. Ia 3.Verteidigung von Kalinin 15.10.41–20.11.41' BA-MA RH 24–41/15 (20 October 1941).

86 Röttiger, 'XXXXI Panzer Corps During the Battle of Moscow', p. 31.

87 'Anlagen zum Kriegstagebuch Tagesmeldungen Bd.I 1.9–31.10.41' BA-MA RH 21–3/70, fol. 171 (17 October 1941).

88 '3rd Pz. Gr. KTB Nr.2 1.9.41–31.10.41' BA-MA Microfilm 59060 (18 October 1941).

89 'Kriegstagebuch Nr.1 (Band Oktober 1941) des Oberkommandos der Heeresgruppe Mitte' BA-MA RH 19-II/411, fol. 633 (18 October 1941).

90 *Ibid.*, fol. 649 (19 October 1941).

91 Bock, *War Diary*, p. 336 (19 October 1941).

92 'Kriegstagebuch Nr.1 (Band Oktober 1941) des Oberkommandos der Heeresgruppe Mitte' BA-MA RH 19-II/411, fol. 636 (18 October 1941).

93 'Anlagenband zum KTB XXXXI A.K. Ia 3.Verteidigung von Kalinin 15.10.41–20.11.41' BA-MA RH 24–41/15 (20 October 1941).

94 Rudel, *Stuka Pilot*, p. 46.

95 '3rd Pz. Gr. KTB Nr.2 1.9.41–31.10.41' BA-MA Microfilm 59060 (20 October 1941).

96 Röttiger, 'XXXXI Panzer Corps During the Battle of Moscow', p. 31.

97 '3rd Pz. Gr. KTB Nr.2 1.9.41–31.10.41' BA-MA Microfilm 59060 (14 October 1941).

98 'Kriegstagebuch Nr.1 (Band Oktober 1941) des Oberkommandos der Heeresgruppe Mitte' BA-MA RH 19-II/411, fol. 627 (17 October 1941); Bock, *War Diary*, p. 334 (17 October 1941).

99 Wagner (ed.), *Der Generalquartiermeister*, p. 206 (12 October 1941).

100 *Ibid.*, p. 207 (20 October 1941).

101 By 20 October Schaal's LVI Panzer Corps was not yet at Kalinin, but en route and 100 kilometres from the city: Glantz, *Atlas of the Battle of Moscow*, p. 40 (20 October 1941).

102 Schäufler and his men were not living in caves, but rather a basement to protect themselves from the heavy bombardments of Soviet artillery.

103 *Teller* mines were a common German anti-tank mine fitted with a pressure-actuated fuse which detonated at about 90 kilograms of pressure. Owing to the circular metal casing of the mines they earned the name '*Teller*', which is German for plate or dish.

104 Schäufler (ed.), *Knight's Cross Panzers*, p. 142.

105 'Kriegstagebuch 4.Panzer-Division Führungsabtl. 26.5.41–31.3.42' BA-MA RH 27–4/10, p. 205 (11 October 1941).

106 Guderian, *Panzer Leader*, p. 235.

107 As cited in Hürter, *Hitlers Heerführer*, pp. 298–299, nn. 106 and 111.

108 'Kriegstagebuch 4.Panzer-Division Führungsabtl. 26.5.41–31.3.42' BA-MA RH 27–4/10, pp. 205–206 (11 and 12 October 1941).

109 'Kriegstagebuch Nr.1 (Band Oktober 1941) des Oberkommandos der Heeresgruppe Mitte' BA-MA RH 19-II/411, fol. 614 (15 October 1941).

110 Bock, *War Diary*, p. 334 (14 October 1941).

111 'Kriegstagebuch 4.Panzer-Division Führungsabtl. 26.5.41–31.3.42' BA-MA RH 27–4/10, pp. 213–214 (20 October 1941).

112 '9.Pz.Div. KTB Ia vom 19.5.1941 bis 22.1.1942' BA-MA RH 27–9/4, p. 141 (16 October 1941).

113 'Kriegstagebuch XXXXVIII.Pz.Kps. Abt.Ia October 1941' BA-MA RH 24–48/30, fol. 10 (17 October 1941).

114 '9.Pz.Div. KTB Ia vom 19.5.1941 bis 22.1.1942' BA-MA RH 27–9/4, p. 145 (20 October 1941).

115 'Kriegstagebuch Nr.1 (Band Oktober 1941) des Oberkommandos der Heeresgruppe Mitte' BA-MA RH 19-II/411, fol. 637 (18 October 1941).

116 'Armeeoberkommando 2. I.a KTB Teil.2 19.9.41–16.12.41' BA-MA RH 20–2/207, p. 70 (18 October 1941).

117 *Ibid.* (18 October 1941).

118 'Gen.Kdo.LVII.Pz.Korps KTB Nr.1 vom 15.2.41–31.10.41' BA-MA RH 24–57–2, fol. 250 (6 October 1941).

119 Bernhard R. Kroener, 'The Winter Crisis of 1941–1942: The Distribution of Scarcity or Steps Towards a More Rational Management of Personnel' in Militärgeschichtliches Forschungsamt (ed.), *Germany and the Second World War. Volume V/I*, p. 1014.

120 *True to Type*, p. 10 (10 October 1941).

121 Bähr and Bähr (eds.), *Kriegsbriefe Gefallener Studenten, 1939–1945*, pp. 81–82 (18 October 1941).

122 Hürter (ed.), *Ein deutscher General an der Ostfront*, p. 94 (16 October 1941).

123 Kleindienst (ed.), *Sei tausendmal gegrüßt*, CD-ROM (17 October 1941).

124 Humburg, *Das Gesicht des Krieges*, p. 226 (15 October 1941).

125 Wagener, *Moskau 1941*, p. 81.

126 Lammers (ed.), '*Fahrtberichte*' aus der Zeit des deutsch-sowjetischen Krieges 1941, p. 122.

127 Richard L. DiNardo, *Mechanized Juggernaut or Military Anachronism? Horses and the German Army in World War II* (London, 1991) p. 46.

128 'Armeeoberkommando 2. I.a KTB Teil.2 19.9.41–16.12.41' BA-MA RH 20–2/207, p. 36 (5 October 1941).

129 Lange, *Tagebücher aus dem Zweiten Weltkrieg*, p. 76 (22 October 1941).

130 Pabst, *The Outermost Frontier*, p. 35.

131 Hans Meier-Welcker, *Aufzeichnungen eines Generalstabsoffiziers 1939–1942* (Freiburg, 1982) p. 134 (20 October 1941).

132 Gareis, *Kampf und Ende der Fränkisch-Sudetendeutschen 98. Infanterie Division*, p. 130.

133 Kuhnert, *Will We See Tomorrow?*, p. 106.

134 Lange, *Tagebücher aus dem Zweiten Weltkrieg*, p. 64 (10 October 1941).

135 Geyer, *Das IX. Armeekorps im Ostfeldzug 1941*, p. 143.

136 DiNardo, *Mechanized Juggernaut or Military Anachronism?*, p. 47. Klaus Reinhardt suggests the figures for horse losses within *Ostheer* as of 10 November 1941 were 102,910 dead and 33,314 sick. See Klaus Reinhardt, *Moscow*, p. 149.

137 Underlining in the original; 'Kriegstagebuch Nr.1 (Band Oktober 1941) des Oberkommandos der Heeresgruppe Mitte' BA-MA RH 19-II/411, fol. 644 (19 October 1941).

138 'Kriegstagebuch der O.Qu.-Abt. Pz. A.O.K.2 von 21.6.41 bis 31.3.42' BA-MA RH 21–2/819, fol. 166 (19 October 1941).

139 'Kriegstagebuch Nr.1 (Band Oktober 1941) des Oberkommandos der Heeresgruppe Mitte' BA-MA RH 19-II/411, fol. 642 (19 October 1941).

140 As cited in Hürter, *Hitlers Heerführer*, p. 300, n. 114.

141 'KTB 3rd Pz. Div. I.b 19.5.41–6.2.42' BA-MA RH 27–3/218 (13 October 1941).

142 'KTB 3rd Pz. Div. vom 19.9.41 bis 6.2.42' BA-MA RH 27–3/15, p. 289 (19 October 1941).

143 'Kriegstagebuch 4.Panzer-Division Führungsabtl. 26.5.41–31.3.42' BA-MA RH 27–4/10, p. 213 (20 October 1941).

144 '9.Pz.Div. KTB Ia vom 19.5.1941 bis 22.1.1942' BA-MA RH 27–9/4, p. 137 (12 October 1941).

145 Guderian, *Panzer Leader*, p. 237.

146 'Kriegstagebuch Nr.2 XXXXVII.Pz.Korps. Ia 23.9.1941–31.12.1941' BA-MA RH 24–47/258, fol. 62 (20 October 1941).

147 As cited in Robert Kershaw, *War Without Garlands*, p. 187.

148 *Ibid.*

149 '18.Panzer Division, Abt.Ia KTB Teil III vom 30.9.–19.10.41' BA-MA RH 27–18/22, p. 55 (16 October 1941).

150 *Ibid.*, p. 57 (17 October 1941).

151 'Kriegstagebuch Nr.2 XXXXVII.Pz.Korps. Ia 23.9.1941–31.12.1941' BA-MA RH 24–47/258, fol. 55 (20 October 1941).

152 'Kriegstagebuch XXXXVIII.Pz.Kps. Abt.Ia October 1941' BA-MA RH 24–48/30, fol. 11 (20 October 1941).

153 Bock, *War Diary*, p. 336 (19 October 1941).

154 Wagner (ed.), *Der Generalquartiermeister*, p. 206 (17 October 1941).

155 *KTB OKW*, Volume II, p. 693 (11 October 1941); Günther Blumentritt, *Von Rundstedt. The Soldier and the Man* (London, 1952) p. 111.

156 Axworthy, Scafes and Craciunoiu, *Third Axis Fourth Ally*, pp. 49–56; Glantz, *Barbarossa*, pp. 134–135. For more on the Battle of Odessa, see Friedrich Forstmeier, *Odessa 1941. Der Kampf um Stadt und Hafen und die Räumung der Seefestung 15. August bis 16. Oktober 1941* (Freiburg, 1967); Mihai Tone

Filipescu, *Reluctant Axis. The Romanian Army in Russia 1941–1944* (Chapultepeq, 2006) ch. 2, 'The Battle for Odessa'. For a Soviet-era perspective, see N. Krylov, *Glory Eternal. Defence of Odessa 1941* (Moscow, 1972). For the air battle over Odessa, see Dénes Bernád, Dmitriy Karlenko and Jean-Louis Roba, *From Barbarossa to Odessa. The Luftwaffe and Axis Allies Strike South-East. June–October 1941* (Hinckley, 2008).

157 Fröhlich (ed.), *Die Tagebücher von Joseph Goebbels Teil II Band* 2, p. 128 (17 October 1941).

158 Mark Axworthy, 'Peasant Scapegoat to Industrial Slaughter: The Romanian Soldier at the Siege of Odessa' in Paul Addison and Angus Calder (eds.), *A Time to Kill. The Soldier's Experience of War in the West 1939–1945* (London, 1997) p. 227.

159 Trevor-Roper (ed.), *Hitler's Table Talk, 1941–1944*, p. 32 (17–18 September 1941).

160 Peter Gosztony, *Hitlers Fremde Heere. Das Schicksal der nichtdeutschen Armeen im Ostfeldzug* (Vienna, 1976) p. 152.

161 Muggeridge (ed.), *Ciano's Diary 1939–1943*, p. 386 (20 October 1941).

162 Boberach (ed.), *Meldungen aus dem Reich*, Band 8, p. 2870, Document 229 (16 October 1941).

163 Fröhlich (ed.), *Die Tagebücher von Joseph Goebbels Teil II Band* 2, p. 125 (16 October 1941).

164 Howard K. Smith, *Last Train from Berlin*, p. 110.

165 Fröhlich (ed.), *Die Tagebücher von Joseph Goebbels Teil II Band* 2, p. 154 (22 October 1941).

166 Ochsenknecht, *'Als ob der Schnee alles zudeckte'*, p. 87.

167 Gilbert, *The Second World War*, pp. 242–243.

168 Professor Pat Blackett estimated in early 1942 that throughout 1941 Bomber Command had only succeeded in killing roughly the same number of German civilians as German air defences had killed of the (highly trained) British aircrew: Max Hastings, *Bomber Command* (London, 1993) p. 111.

169 Kuhnert, *Will We See Tomorrow?*, p. 108.

170 Württembergische Landesbiblothek Stuttgart (hereafter cited as WLS), Flugblattpropaganda im 2. Weltkrieg (1941), Mappe 92–26.

171 WLS, Flugblattpropaganda im 2. Weltkrieg (1941), Mappe 92–22.

172 WLS, Flugblattpropaganda im 2. Weltkrieg (1941), Mappe 92–32 and Mappe 92–36. Harry Hopkins was one of President Roosevelt's closest confidants and the former administrator of US Lend-Lease aid.

173 WLS, Flugblattpropaganda im 2. Weltkrieg (1941), Mappe 92–38 and Mappe 92–40.

174 WLS Flugblattpropaganda im 2. Weltkrieg (1941), Mappe 92a–5.

175 WLS, Flugblattpropaganda im 2. Weltkrieg (1941), Mappe 92a–6.

176 WLS, Flugblattpropaganda im 2. Weltkrieg (1941), Mappe 92a–8.

177 Hellmuth H., MPT, 3.2002.7139 (23 October 1941). Soviet propaganda leaflets included sections which stated that the leaflet was also a pass and that the bearer was entitled to surrender and would receive good treatment.

178 Blandford (ed.), *Under Hitler's Banner*, p. 33.

179 Garden and Andrew (eds.), *The War Diaries of a Panzer Soldier*, p. 54 (20 October 1941).

180 Landon and Leitner (eds.), *Diary of a German Soldier*, pp. 115–116 (20 October 1941).

181 Bob Carruthers (ed.), *The Wehrmacht. Last Witnesses. First-Hand Accounts from the Survivors of Hitler's Armed Forces* (London, 2010) p. 56.

182 Trevor-Roper (ed.), *Hitler's Table Talk, 1941–1944*, p. 40 (25 September 1941).

183 'Kriegstagebuch Nr.1 (Band Oktober 1941) des Oberkommandos der Heeresgruppe Mitte' BA-MA RH 19-II/411, fol. 615 (15 October 1941).

184 Ulrich von Hassell, *Vom Andern Deutschland* (Freiburg, 1946) p. 229 (4 October 1941). For the English translation, see Ulrich von Hassell, *The von Hassell Diaries 1938–1944* (London, 1948) p. 199 (4 October 1941).

185 Hassell, *Vom Andern Deutschland*, pp. 229–230 (4 October 1941); Hassell, *The von Hassell Diaries 1938–1944*, pp. 199–200 (4 October 1941).

186 Humburg, *Das Gesicht des Krieges*, pp. 170–171.

187 Pabst, *The Outermost Frontier*, p. 35.

188 Bähr and Bähr (eds.), *Kriegsbriefe Gefallener Studenten, 1939–1945*, p. 83 (20 October 1941); Bähr and Bähr (eds.), *Die Stimme des Menschen*, p. 115 (20 October 1941).

189 Kleindienst (ed.), *Sei tausendmal gegrüßt*, CD-ROM (19 October 1941).

190 Günther, *Hot Motors, Cold Feet*, p. 175. Brest-Litovsk is in fact the city's former name. In June 1941 the Germans took the city of Brest.

191 Kuhnert, *Will We See Tomorrow?*, pp. 106–107.

192 Günther, *Hot Motors, Cold Feet*, p. 175.

193 Bock, *War Diary*, p. 330 (11 October 1941).

194 James S. Corum, *Wolfram von Richthofen. Master of the German Air War* (Lawrence, 2008) p. 276.

195 This case was made by Lemelsen's XXXXVII Panzer Corps, opposing the transfer of Feldt's division: 'Kriegstagebuch Nr.2 XXXXVII.Pz.Korps. Ia 23.9.1941–31.12.1941' BA-MA RH 24-47/258, fol. 66 (24 October 1941).

196 Lange, *Tagebücher aus dem Zweiten Weltkrieg*, p. 78 (25 October 1941).

197 Pabst, *The Outermost Frontier*, pp. 29–30.

198 Degrelle, *Campaign in Russia*, p. 13.

199 'Pak' is an acronym for *Panzerabwehrkanone* or anti-tank gun.

200 Bidermann, *In Deadly Combat*, p. 57.

201 *Ibid.*, pp. 58–59.

202 Humburg, *Das Gesicht des Krieges*, p. 211 (18 October 1941).

7 Weathering the storm

1 For a translation of Stalin's evacuation decree, see Hill, *The Great Patriotic War of the Soviet Union, 1941–1945*, pp. 70–71, Document 50.

2 Glantz, *Barbarossa*, p. 154.

3 In fact only twice during the war, in October 1941 and August 1942, did Stalin make any attempt to visit front-line positions. See Dmitrij A. Volkogonov, 'Stalin as Supreme Commander' in Wegner (ed.), *From Peace to War*, pp. 476–477.

4 Porter and Jones, *Moscow in World War II*, p. 119.

5 As cited in Mikhail M. Gorinov, 'Muscovites' Moods, 22 June 1941 to May 1942' in Robert Thurston and Bernd Bonwetsch (eds.), *The People's War. Responses to World War II in the Soviet Union* (Chicago, 2000) pp. 124–125.

6 *Ibid.*, p. 124.

7 Werth, *Russia at War 1941–1945*, p. 233.

8 *Ibid.*

9 As cited in Braithwaite, *Moscow 1941*, p. 202.

10 Werth, *Russia at War 1941–1945*, p. 233.

11 *Ibid.*, p. 234.

12 As cited in Porter and Jones, *Moscow in World War II*, p. 114.

13 As cited in Michael Jones, *The Retreat*, p. 62.

14 Braithwaite, *Moscow 1941*, p. 221.

15 *Ibid.*, p. 223.

16 Barber and Harrison, *The Soviet Home Front 1941–1945*, p. 66.

17 Braithwaite, *Moscow 1941*, pp. 225 and 228.

18 See Bellamy, *Absolute War*, p. 295.

19 Salisbury (ed.), *Marshal Zhukov's Greatest Battles*, p. 52.

20 As John Erickson noted: 'Too much was often heaped on the populace: civilians were to man the militia, yet keep production going; train in reserve formations, run the administration, yet fulfil a host of paramilitary duties. The women, the youth and the aged had by their extreme exertions to plug gaps left by the failure to plan and failure to forecast. "Popular response" thus became one of the highest priorities of the regime; its counterpart was a direct, and often dramatic relationship between the populace and the "the authorities", when the latter failed to do their job. The Moscow panic was a prime example of this; the contract of obedience was broken when "the authorities" failed to provide [a] minimum assurance of security' (Erickson, *The Road to Stalingrad*, p. 231).

21 Roger R. Reese, *Why Stalin's Soldiers Fought*, pp. 115–118.

22 Geoffrey Roberts, *Stalin's Wars. From World War to Cold War, 1939–1953* (New Haven, 2006) p. 108.

23 Gorinov, 'Muscovites' Moods, 22 June 1941 to May 1942', p. 125.

24 For an example of the latter see Nagorski, *The Greatest Battle*, ch. 7, 'Panic in Moscow'.

25 Braithwaite, *Moscow 1941*, p. 229.

26 As cited in Porter and Jones, *Moscow in World War II*, p. 117.

27 Bellamy, *Absolute War*, p. 290.

28 Braithwaite, *Moscow 1941*, p. 229.

29 Nagorski, *The Greatest Battle*, pp. 175–176.

30 As cited in Merridale, *Ivan's War*, pp. 127–128.

31 For a translation of Stalin's decree, see Hill, *The Great Patriotic War of the Soviet Union, 1941–45*, p. 71, Document 51.

32 For an account of the meeting at which the 'state of siege' decree was decided, see Bialer (ed.), *Stalin and His Generals*, pp. 304–305.

33 Bellamy, *Absolute War*, pp. 294–295.

34 Nagorski, *The Greatest Battle*, pp. 119–121.

35 Alexander Statiev, 'Blocking Units in the Red Army', *Journal of Military History* 76, 2 (April 2012) p. 484.

36 Anfilov, 'Zhukov', p. 353.

37 Gilbert, *The Second World War*, p. 246.

38 Salisbury (ed.), *Marshal Zhukov's Greatest Battles*, p. 60.

39 Erickson, *The Road to Stalingrad*, pp. 218–219.

40 Braithwaite, *Moscow 1941*, p. 205.

41 Nagorski, *The Greatest Battle*, p. 186.

42 Werth, *Russia at War 1941–1945*, p. 234.

43 A 'hedgehog' was a static anti-tank obstacle usually made of thick angled iron.

44 Porter and Jones, *Moscow in World War II*, p. 107.

45 As cited in Nagorski, *The Greatest Battle*, p. 186.

46 For a first-rate perspective on the problems of city fighting in Operation Barbarossa, see Adrian Wettstein, 'Operation "Barbarossa" und Stadtkampf', *Militärgeschichtliche Zeitschrift* 66 (2007) pp. 21–44; Adrian Wettstein, 'Urban Warfare Doctrine on the Eastern Front' in Kay, Rutherford and Stahel (eds.), *Nazi Policy on the Eastern Front, 1941*, pp. 45–72.

47 Nagorski, *The Greatest Battle*, pp. 195 and 207.

48 Bellamy, *Absolute War*, p. 286.

49 Erickson, *The Road to Stalingrad*, p. 227; Gilbert, *The Second World War*, p. 245.

50 Braithwaite, *Moscow 1941*, p. 217.

51 Nagorski, *The Greatest Battle*, pp. 196–197.

52 A number of these resettlements were of Moscow's small ethnic German population. By 20 September 1941 some 1,142 ethnic Germans had been

arrested and another 8,449 resettled. Only 1,620 were permitted to remain in the capital. See Bellamy, *Absolute War*, p. 286.

53 Nagorski, *The Greatest Battle*, p. 168; Broekmeyer, *Stalin, the Russians, and Their War 1941–1945*, p. 60. Mark Harrison had suggested that as many as 1.4 million people were evacuated from Moscow during the course of the autumn of 1941. See Mark Harrison, *Soviet Planning in Peace and War 1938–1945* (Cambridge, 2002) p. 69.

54 Roger R. Reese, *Why Stalin's Soldiers Fought*, p. 118.

55 Destruction formations were paramilitary organisations operated by the NKVD from the summer of 1941 and typically used to organise resistance to the Germans in cities, towns and occupied areas. They are not to be confused with 'destroyer' formations which were first formed in April 1942. Thanks to David Glantz for his assistance on this matter.

56 Braithwaite, *Moscow 1941*, p. 205.

57 Salisbury (ed.), *Marshal Zhukov's Greatest Battles*, p. 59.

58 *Ibid.*, pp. 59–60.

59 For contrasting results from two of Moscow's *opolchenie* divisions, see Roger R. Reese, *Why Stalin's Soldiers Fought*, p. 240.

60 Joachim Hoffmann, 'The Conduct of the War Through Soviet Eyes' in Militärgeschichtliches Forschungsamt (ed.), *Germany and the Second World War. Volume IV*, pp. 890–891.

61 By the end of the battle for Moscow more than 100 Soviet divisions had been transferred to the central front, including nine from the Far East: Roberts, *Stalin's Wars*, p. 108.

62 Hoffmann, 'The Conduct of the War Through Soviet Eyes', p. 893. For a differing (higher) set of figures, see Forczyk, *Moscow 1941*, p. 67.

63 Glantz, *Barbarossa*, p. 155.

64 Salisbury (ed.), *Marshal Zhukov's Greatest Battles*, p. 55.

65 Roger R. Reese, *Why Stalin's Soldiers Fought*, p. 117.

66 See Ronald Smelser and Edward J. Davies II, *The Myth of the Eastern Front. The Nazi–Soviet War in American Popular Culture* (Cambridge, 2008) chs. 4–6.

67 Bellamy, *Absolute War*, p. 476.

68 For an introduction to the systems at work transforming 'a horde of riflemen' into 'a superior fighting machine', see John Erickson, 'Red Army Battlefield Performance, 1941–1945: The System and the Soldier' in Addison and Calder (eds.), *A Time to Kill*, pp. 237–248.

69 Roger R. Reese, *Why Stalin's Soldiers Fought*, ch. 6, 'Mobilizing the Nonvolunteers'.

70 Gennadi Bordiugov, 'The Popular Mood in the Unoccupied Soviet Union: Continuity and Change During the War' in Thurston and Bonwetsch (eds.), *The People's War*, p. 58; Roger R. Reese, *Why Stalin's Soldiers Fought*, p. 184.

71 As cited in Alan Clark, *Barbarossa. The Russian–German Conflict 1941–1945* (London, 1996) p. 162.

72 This was the international English title; the Russian was *Razgrom nemetskikh voisk pod Moskvoi* ('The rout of the German forces near Moscow').

73 Barber and Harrison, *The Soviet Home Front 1941–1945*, pp. 106–107. For more on the many cultural aspects of the Soviet Union during the war, see Richard Stites (ed.), *Culture and Entertainment in Wartime Russia* (Bloomington and Indianapolis, 1995).

74 Werth, *Russia at War 1941–1945*, pp. 273–274.

75 G. F. Krivosheev (ed.), *Soviet Casualties and Combat Losses in the Twentieth Century* (London, 1997) p. 93.

76 Simonov originally wrote it to his wife, but the poem's real strength was its generic appeal: Porter and Jones, *Moscow in World War II*, p. 110. There was also a wartime film based on the poem: Peter Kenez, 'Black and White: The War on Film' in Stites (ed.), *Culture and Entertainment in Wartime Russia*, p. 169.

77 Werth, *Russia at War 1941–1945*, pp. 272–273.

78 Muller, *The German Air War in Russia*, p. 51.

79 Walter Warlimont, *Im Hauptquartier der deutschen Wehrmacht 1939 bis 1945. Band 1: September 1939–November 1942* (Koblenz, 1990) pp. 198–199, n. 74 (English translation: Walter Warlimont, *Inside Hitler's Headquarters, 1939–1945* (New York, 1964)). See also *KTB OKW*, Volume II, pp. 1021–1022, Document 69 (8 July 1941) and Document 71 (14 July 1941); Halder, *KTB III*, p. 73 (13 July 1941).

80 Boog, 'The Luftwaffe', pp. 809–810.

81 Braithwaite, *Moscow 1941*, p. 176.

82 Nagorski, *The Greatest Battle*, p. 188.

83 Kesselring, *The Memoirs of Field-Marshal Kesselring*, p. 89.

84 Braithwaite, *Moscow 1941*, p. 186.

85 Rudel, *Stuka Pilot*, p. 45.

86 Murray, *The Luftwaffe 1933–45*, pp. 88–89 and 95.

87 Braithwaite, *Moscow 1941*, pp. 169 and 186.

88 Bergström, *Barbarossa*, p. 51.

89 Nagorski, *The Greatest Battle*, p. 189.

90 Cassidy, *Moscow Dateline, 1941–1943*, p. 71.

91 Kesselring, *The Memoirs of Field-Marshal Kesselring*, p. 94.

92 For figures of those delivered, see Hill, *The Great Patriotic War of the Soviet Union, 1941–1945*, p. 171, Document 118.

93 Axell, *Russia's Heroes 1941–1945*, pp. 125–126.

94 For a useful insight into Soviet preparations to deal with a German bombing campaign against Moscow, see Bellamy, *Absolute War*, pp. 280–282.

95 Nagorski, *The Greatest Battle*, pp. 187–188.

96 Gorinov, 'Muscovites' Moods, 22 June 1941 to May 1942', p. 114.

97 Nagorski, *The Greatest Battle*, p. 182.

98 Porter and Jones, *Moscow in World War II*, pp. 93–94.

99 *Ibid.*, p. 91.

100 Irving, *The Rise and Fall of the Luftwaffe*, p. 131.

101 Klaus Reinhardt, *Moscow*, p. 144.

102 As cited in Gilbert, *The Second World War*, p. 245.

103 Corum, *Wolfram von Richthofen*, p. 275.

104 Kurt Braatz, *Werner Mölders. Die Biographie* (Moosburg, 2008) p. 338. Mölders's private correspondence reveals that by October he was also gravely concerned about the Luftwaffe's ability to maintain itself in the east, and he particularly feared for the strain that the fighter wing was under. See Klaus Schmider, 'German Military Tradition and the Expert Opinion on Werner Mölders: Opening a Dialogue Among Scholars', *Global War Studies* 7, 1 (2010) p. 27.

105 Braatz, *Werner Mölders*, p. 338.

106 Bergström, *Barbarossa*, p. 53.

107 As cited in Axell, *Russia's Heroes 1941–1945*, pp. 60–62 and 70; Axell, *Stalin's War*, pp. 151–152. For more specific literature on Soviet airwomen in World War II, see Reina Pennington, *Wings, Women, and War. Soviet Airwomen in World War II Combat* (Lawrence, 2001); Kazimiera J. Cottam, *Women in Air War. The Eastern Front of World War II* (Newburyport, 1998); Anne Noggle, *A Dance with Death. Soviet Airwomen in World War II* (College Station, TX, 1994). For more general surveys of Soviet women fighting in World War II, see Anna Krylova, *Soviet Women in Combat. A History of Violence on the Eastern Front* (Cambridge, 2010); Reina Pennington, 'Women' in Stone (ed.) *The Soviet Union at War 1941–1945*, pp. 93–120; Reina Pennington, 'Offensive Women: Women in Combat in the Red Army in the Second World War', *Journal of Military History* 74, 3 (July 2010) pp. 775–820; Roger R. Reese, *Why Stalin's Soldiers Fought*, Part V, 'Russia's Female Soldiers'.

108 Dunn, *Stalin's Keys to Victory*, p. 39.

109 Harrison, *Soviet Planning in Peace and War 1938–1945*, p. 251.

110 Alexander Hill, 'British Lend-Lease Tanks and the Battle for Moscow, November–December 1941: Revisited', *Journal of Slavic Military Studies* 22, 4 (November 2009) p. 582.

111 Below, *Als Hitlers Adjutant 1937–1945*, p. 294.

112 Hermann Hoss related his unit's improvised tactics to deal with T-34s: 'To combat the T-34s, an 8.8 centimetre Flak and 10 centimetre cannon accompanied us in tactics we had developed. They were the only weapons capable of effectively engaging the thick armour of the T-34s. Whenever we

encountered them, the tanks would halt and pull back a bit. The Russian T-34s immediately pursued, only to be knocked out by the 8.8 centimetre Flak and the 10 centimetre cannon that had gone into position in the meantime. But it took the 8.8 ten minutes to set up; the 10 centimetre even longer. Nevertheless, the T-34s were so eager to do battle, that they always fell for the trick and suffered losses' (Schäufler (ed.), *Knight's Cross Panzers*, p. 147).

113 As cited in Steiger, *Armour Tactics in the Second World War*, p. 82.

114 As cited in Schröder, 'German Soldiers' Experiences During the Initial Phase of the Russian Campaign', p. 315.

115 Kesselring, *The Memoirs of Field-Marshal Kesselring*, p. 97.

116 As cited in Clark, *Barbarossa*, p. 164.

117 Even before the advent of Soviet power, the Russian army had traditionally fought with a higher ratio of artillery to infantry than was the case in other European armies: Lieven, *Russia Against Napoleon*, p. 250.

118 Dunn, *Stalin's Keys to Victory*, p. 32.

119 Alexander and Kunze (eds.), *Eastern Inferno*, p. 115 (30 September 1941).

120 Carruthers (ed.), *The Wehrmacht*, p. 49.

121 Braithwaite, *Moscow 1941*, p. 214.

122 Bidermann, *In Deadly Combat*, p. 54.

123 For studies dealing with the fighting prowess of the Wehrmacht in World War II, see Kevin W. Farrell, '"Culture of Confidence": The Tactical Excellence of the German Army of the Second World War' in Christopher Kolenda (ed.), *Leadership. The Warrior's Art* (Carlisle, PA, 2001) pp. 177–203; John F. Antal, 'The Wehrmacht Approach to Maneuver Warfare Command and Control' in Richard D. Hooker Jr. (ed.), *Maneuver Warfare. An Anthology* (Novato, 1993) pp. 347–359; Martin van Creveld, *Fighting Power. German and US Army Performance, 1939–1945* (Westport, 1982). For an interesting assessment of the complex interplay between representing the German army as a fighting force without sidelining its criminal role, see Kevin W. Farrell, 'Recent Approaches to the German Army of World War II: Is the Topic More Accessible After 65 Years?', *Global War Studies* 7, 2 (2010) pp. 131–156.

124 Walter Neuser, MPT, 3.2002.0947 (15 October 1941). For the many uses of Soviet mines, see Meier-Welcker, *Aufzeichnungen eines Generalstabsoffiziers 1939–1942*, p. 133 (11 October 1941).

125 Walter Neuser, MPT, 3.2002.0947 (15 October 1941).

126 Bidermann, *In Deadly Combat*, p. 62.

127 An SS *Brigadeführer* had the equivalent rank to an army major-general.

128 Pichler, *Truppenarzt und Zeitzeuge*, p. 106 (14 October 1941).

129 Walter Kempowski (ed.), *Das Echolot Barbarossa '41. Ein kollektives Tagebuch* (Munich, 2004) p. 152 (29 June 1941); Manstein, *Lost Victories*, pp. 180–181; Manstein, *Verlorene Siege*, pp. 178–179.

130 As cited in Omer Bartov, *Hitler's Army. Soldiers, Nazis, and War in the Third Reich* (Oxford, 1992) p. 93.

131 *True to Type*, p. 107 (date and month not recorded, 1941).

132 Hannes Heer, 'How Amorality Became Normality: Reflections on the Mentality of German Soldiers on the Eastern Front' in Hannes Heer and Klaus Naumann (eds.), *War of Extermination. The German Military in World War II 1941–1944* (New York and Oxford, 2006) pp. 329–344.

133 Alexander and Kunze (eds.), *Eastern Inferno*, p. 113 (29 September 1941).

134 For the best work on the planning for the war of annihilation and economic exploitation of the Soviet Union, see Alex J. Kay, *Exploitation, Resettlement, Mass Murder. Political and Economic Planning for German Occupation Policy in the Soviet Union, 1940–1941* (Oxford, 2006). For the results of such policies in the occupied areas, see Jörn Hasenclever, *Wehrmacht und Besatzungspolitik. Die Befehlshaber der rückwärtigen Heeresgebiete 1941–1943* (Paderborn, 2010); Theo Schulte, *The German Army and Nazi Policies in Occupied Russia* (Oxford, 1989); Dieter Pohl, *Die Herrschaft der Wehrmacht. Deutsche Militärbesatzung und einheimische Bevölkerung in der Sowjetunion 1941–1944* (Munich, 2008); Alexander Dallin, *German Rule in Russia 1941–1945. A Study of Occupation Policies* (London, 1957); Omer Bartov, *The Eastern Front, 1941–1945. German Troops and the Barbarisation of Warfare* (London, 1985); Bernhard Chiari, *Alltag hinter der Front. Besatzung, Kollaboration und Widerstand in Weißrußland 1941–1944* (Düsseldorf, 1998); Gerlach, *Kalkulierte Morde*; Wendy Lower, *Nazi Empire-Building and the Holocaust in Ukraine* (Chapel Hill, 2005); Ray Brandon and Wendy Lower (eds.), *The Shoah in Ukraine. History, Testimony, Memorialization* (Bloomington, 2008); Karel C. Berkhoff, *Harvest of Despair. Life and Death in Ukraine Under Nazi Rule* (Cambridge, MA, 2004); Antonio Munoz and Oleg V. Romanko, *Hitler's White Russians. Collaboration, Extermination and Anti-Partisan Warfare in Byelorussia 1941–1944. A Study of White Russian Collaboration and German Occupation Policies* (New York, 2003); Geoffrey P. Megargee, *War of Annihilation. Combat and Genocide on the Eastern Front 1941* (Lanham, 2006).

135 As cited in Goldensohn, *Nuremberg Interviews*, p. 344 (26 June 1946).

136 Reddemann (ed.), *Zwischen Front und Heimat*, p. 288 (20 August 1941).

137 Trevor-Roper (ed.), *Hitler's Table Talk, 1941–1944*, p. 71 (17–18 October 1941).

138 *Ibid.*, pp. 68–69 (17 October 1941).

139 For the best works on the criminal orders, see Felix Römer, 'The Wehrmacht in the War of Ideologies: The Army and Hitler's Criminal Orders on the Eastern Front' in Kay, Rutherford and Stahel (eds.), *Nazi Policy on the Eastern Front, 1941*, pp. 73–100; Felix Römer, '"Kein Problem für die Truppe"', *Die Zeit*

Geschichte – Hitlers Krieg im Osten 2 (2011) pp. 42–45; Felix Römer, *Der Kommissarbefehl. Wehrmacht und NS-Verbrechen an der Ostfront 1941/42* (Paderborn, 2008). The full text of the orders is reproduced in Erhard Moritz (ed.), *Fall Barbarossa. Dokumente zur Vorbereitung der faschistischen Wehrmacht auf die Aggression gegen die Sowjetunion (1940/41)* (Berlin, 1970), Documents 97 and 100, pp. 316–318 and 321–323; Gerd R. Ueberschär and Wolfram Wette (eds.), '*Unternehmen Barbarossa*', pp. 313–314.

140 As cited in Jürgen Förster, 'Operation Barbarossa as a War of Conquest and Annihilation' in Militärgeschichtliches Forschungsamt (ed.), *Germany and the Second World War. Volume IV*, p. 485. See also Jürgen Förster, 'The German Army and the Ideological War Against the Soviet Union' in Gerhard Hirschfeld (ed.), *The Policies of Genocide. Jews and Soviet Prisoners of War in Nazi Germany* (London, 1986) pp. 15–29.

141 *True to Type*, p. 11 (27 June 1941).

142 For a good study showcasing soldiers who refused to follow Nazi precepts, see Wolfram Wette, *Retter in Uniform. Handlungsspielräume im Vernichtungskreig der Wehrmacht* (Frankfurt am Main, 2003).

143 Bähr and Bähr (eds.), *Kriegsbriefe Gefallener Studenten, 1939–1945*, p. 179 (18 October 1941).

144 Humburg, *Das Gesicht des Krieges*, p. 219 (12 October 1941).

145 Wolfram Wette, *The Wehrmacht. History, Myth, Reality* (Cambridge, 2006), ch. 1, 'Perception of Russia, the Soviet Union, and Bolshevism as Enemies'.

146 Jürgen Förster, 'Motivation and Indoctrination in the Wehrmacht, 1933–1945' in Addison and Calder (eds.), *A Time to Kill*, pp. 263–273.

147 Kleindienst (ed.), *Sei tausendmal gegrüßt*, CD-ROM (8 October 1941).

148 For a detailed list of supplies, see Gilbert, *The Second World War*, p. 240.

149 As cited in Robert Huhn Jones, *The Roads to Russia. United States Lend-Lease to the Soviet Union* (Norman, 1969) p. 62.

150 Ministry of Foreign Affairs of the USSR (ed.), *Stalin's Correspondence with Churchill, Attlee, Roosevelt and Truman 1941–1945* (New York, 1958) p. 29, Document 16 (3 October 1941).

151 *Ibid.*, p. 30, Document 17 (6 October 1941).

152 Richard Woodman, *Arctic Convoys 1941–1945* (Barnsley, 2007) p. 39.

153 'PQ' did not have a special meaning; they were simply the initials of an officer in the Operations Division of the Admiralty, Commander P. Q. Roberts (Paul Kemp, *Convoy! Drama in Arctic Waters* (London, 1993) p. 23).

154 Woodman, *Arctic Convoys 1941–1945*, p. 42.

155 Known also as the Bren Gun Carrier, these were armoured tracked vehicles used for transporting personnel and towing support weapons. They were fitted with a heavy machine gun.

156 Ministry of Foreign Affairs of the USSR (ed.), *Stalin's Correspondence*, p. 30, Document 17 (6 October 1941).

157 Gorodetsky (ed.), *Stafford Cripps in Moscow 1940–1942*, p. 176 (2 October 1941).

158 Kemp, *Convoy!*, pp. 23–24.

159 Hill, 'British Lend-Lease Tanks and the Battle for Moscow, November–December 1941 – Revisited', pp. 581–583 and 587. See also Alexander Hill, 'British "Lend-Lease" Tanks and the Battle for Moscow, November–December 1941: A Research Note', *Journal of Slavic Military Studies* 19, 2 (June 2006) pp. 289–294. Only a handful of American tanks were delivered to the Soviet Union in 1941: Hubert P. van Tuyll, *Feeding the Bear. American Aid to the Soviet Union, 1941–1945* (Westport, 1989) pp. 53 and 167, Table 22.

160 Hill, *The Great Patriotic War of the Soviet Union, 1941–1945*, pp. 172–173, Document 118 and Table 8.2.

161 Bergström, *Barbarossa*, pp. 79–80; John Erickson and Ljubica Erickson, *Hitler Versus Stalin. The Second World War on the Eastern Front in Photographs* (London, 2004) p. 54.

162 George Mellinger, *Soviet Lend-Lease Fighter Aces of World War 2* (Oxford, 2006) pp. 9–12.

163 *Ibid.*, pp. 23–27.

164 Ministry of Foreign Affairs of the USSR (ed.), *Stalin's Correspondence*, p. 31, Document 18 (12 October 1941).

165 Gorodetsky (ed.), *Stafford Cripps in Moscow 1940–1942*, p. 191 (26 October 1941).

166 Ivan Maisky, *Memoirs of a Soviet Ambassador. The War 1939–1943* (London, 1967) p. 199.

167 David Carlton, *Churchill and the Soviet Union* (New York, 2000) pp. 87–88.

168 Ministry of Foreign Affairs of the USSR (ed.), *Stalin's Correspondence*, p. 31. Document 18 (12 October 1941).

169 Gorodetsky (ed.), *Stafford Cripps in Moscow 1940–1942*, p. 192 (26 October 1941).

170 *Ibid.*, p. 193 (28 October 1941). See also Churchill, *The Second World War*, p. 468.

171 As cited in Carlton, *Churchill and the Soviet Union*, p. 89.

172 As Churchill explained to General Claude Auchinleck: 'It is impossible to explain to Parliament and the nation how it is our Middle East armies had to stand for four and a half months without engaging the enemy while all the time Russia is being battered to pieces' (Martin Kitchen, *A World in Flames. A Short History of the Second World War in Europe and Asia 1939–1945* (London, 1990) p. 94).

173 Martin Kitchen, *British Policy Towards the Soviet Union During the Second World War* (London, 1986) p. 83.

174 Ian Kershaw, *Fateful Choices. Ten Decisions that Changed the World, 1940– 1941* (New York, 2007) p. 326.

175 'Kriegstagebuch Nr.1 (Band Oktober 1941) des Oberkommandos der Heeresgruppe Mitte' BA-MA RH 19-II/411, fols. 591–592 (10 October 1941).

8   Running on empty

1 Gareis, *Kampf und Ende der Fränkisch-Sudetendeutschen 98. Infanterie-Division*, p. 147.

2 Piekalkiewicz, *Moscow 1941*, p. 159.

3 Bock, *War Diary*, p. 338 (21 October 1941).

4 'Kriegstagebuch Nr.1 (Band Oktober 1941) des Oberkommandos der Heeresgruppe Mitte' BA-MA RH 19-II/411, fol. 661 (22 October 1941).

5 Blumentritt, 'Moscow', pp. 55–56.

6 Fröhlich (ed.), *Die Tagebücher von Joseph Goebbels Teil II Band 2*, p. 152 (21 October 1941).

7 'Kriegstagebuch Nr.1 (Band Oktober 1941) des Oberkommandos der Heeresgruppe Mitte' BA-MA RH 19-II/411, fol. 658 (21 October 1941).

8 Bock, *War Diary*, pp. 337–338 (21 October 1941).

9 *Ibid.*, p. 338 (22 October 1941).

10 As cited in Bücheler, *Hoepner*, p. 153.

11 'Kriegstagebuch Nr.3. des XXXXVI.Pz.Korps vom 24.08.41–31.12.41' BA-MA RH 24–46/21, fols. 90–91 (19 October 1941).

12 *Ibid.*, fol. 93 (21 October 1941).

13 Bock, *War Diary*, p. 340 (24 October 1941).

14 On 20 October Scheller replaced the aforementioned Major-General Hans-Karl Freiherr von Esebeck.

15 'Kriegstagebuch Nr.3. des XXXXVI.Pz.Korps vom 24.08.41–31.12.41' BA-MA RH 24–46/21, fol. 94 (22 October 1941).

16 '2. Panzer Division KTB Nr.6 Teil I. Vom 15.6.41–3.4.42' BA-MA RH 27–2/21 (25 October 1941).

17 'Kriegstagebuch Nr.3. des XXXXVI.Pz.Korps vom 24.08.41–31.12.41' BA-MA RH 24–46/21, fol. 99 (26 October 1941).

18 'Anlage zum KTB Pz.Gruppe 4 Meldungen von unten 15.10.41–15.11.41' BA-MA RH 21–4/39, fol. 234 (24 October 1941).

19 '5. Panzer Division KTB Nur.8 vom 11.9.41–11.12.41' BA-MA RH 27–5/29, fol. 51 (19 October 1941).

20 'Kriegstagebuch Nr.3. des XXXXVI.Pz.Korps vom 24.08.41–31.12.41' BA-MA RH 24–46/21, fol. 99 (26 October 1941).

21 Forczyk, *Moscow 1941*, p. 57.

22 'Kriegstagebuch Nr.3. der Führungsabteilung (Ia) des Gen. Kdo. (mot.) XXXX. Pz.Korps vom 31.05.1941–26.12.1941' BA-MA RH 24–40/18 (19 October 1941).

23 Heysing, *Sturm bis vor Moskaus Tore*, p. 11. See also Piekalkiewicz, *Moscow 1941*, pp. 146–147.

24 'Kriegstagebuch Nr.3. der Führungsabteilung (Ia) des Gen. Kdo. (mot.) XXXX. Pz.Korps vom 31.05.1941–26.12.1941' BA-MA RH 24–40/18 (23 October 1941).

25 As cited in Michael Jones, *The Retreat*, p. 67.

26 As cited in Carell, *Hitler's War on Russia*, p. 151.

27 Forczyk, *Moscow 1941*, p. 57.

28 '20.Pz.Div. KTB vom 15.8.41 bis 20.10.41 Band Ia.' BA-MA RH 27–20/25, fol. 133 (16 October 1941); Glantz, *Atlas of the Battle of Moscow*, p. 42 (24 October 1941).

29 '20.Pz.Div. KTB vom 21.10.41 bis 30.12.41 Band Ia2.' BA-MA RH 27–20/26, fol. 7 (23 October 1941).

30 'Gen.Kdo.LVII.Pz.Korps KTB Nr.1 vom 15.2.41–31.10.41' BA-MA RH 24–57–2, fol. 295 (21 October 1941).

31 Bock, *War Diary*, p. 340 (25 October 1941).

32 'Kriegstagebuch Nr.1 (Band Oktober 1941) des Oberkommandos der Heeresgruppe Mitte' BA-MA RH 19-II/411, fol. 686 (25 October 1941).

33 *Ibid.*, fol. 690 (26 October 1941).

34 Bock, *War Diary*, p. 341 (26 October 1941).

35 'Kriegstagebuch Nr.1 (Band Oktober 1941) des Oberkommandos der Heeresgruppe Mitte' BA-MA RH 19-II/411, fols. 692–693 (26 October 1941).

36 Albert Seaton, *The Battle for Moscow* (New York, 1971) pp. 108–109.

37 Gareis, *Kampf und Ende der Fränkisch-Sudetendeutschen 98. Infanterie-Division*, pp. 153–154 and 157.

38 Wagner (ed.), *Der Generalquartiermeister*, p. 211 (24 October 1941).

39 Martin van Creveld, *Supplying War. Logistics from Wallenstein to Patton* (Cambridge, 1984) p. 171.

40 Klaus Schüler, 'The Eastern Campaign as a Transportation and Supply Problem' in Wegner (ed.), *From Peace to War*, pp. 214–216 and nn. 9 and 10; Wagener, *Moskau 1941*, p. 79.

41 'Kriegstagebuch der Abt. Ib 15.Inf. Div. für die Zeit von 25.6.41–3.5.42' BA-MA RH 26–15/54 (24–25 October 1941). The diary has no folio stamped page numbers so references must be located using the date.

42 Gareis, *Kampf und Ende der Fränkisch-Sudetendeutschen 98. Infanteric-Division*, p. 150.

43 Lucas, *War of the Eastern Front 1941–1945*, pp. 107–108.

44 Heysing, *Sturm bis vor Moskaus Tore*, p. 10. Catherine Merridale's popular book *Ivan's War* cites a number of almost identical quotations, including this one, purportedly written in letters by Hoepner and later captured by the Russians in December 1941. Her quotations, however, are almost certainly from Heysing's *Sturm bis vor Moskaus Tore* and not attributable to Hoepner. See Merridale, *Ivan's War*, pp. 117–118.

45 Fröhlich (ed.), *Die Tagebücher von Joseph Goebbels Teil II Band* 2, p. 178 (26 October 1941).

46 'Anlage zum KTB Panzer Gruppe 4: 15.10.41–10.11.41' BA-MA RH 21–4/35, fol. 176 (20 October 1941).

47 Gerhard Kunde, MPT, 3.2002.1941 (19 October 1941).

48 Carruthers (ed.), *The Wehrmacht*, p. 40.

49 Klaus K., MPT, 3.2002.0817 (17 October 1941).

50 Bidermann, *In Deadly Combat*, p. 46.

51 Klink, 'The Military Concept of the War Against the Soviet Union', p. 318.

52 Klaus Reinhardt, *Moscow*, p. 148; Richard Overy, *Why the Allies Won* (New York, 1996) pp. 215–216.

53 'Anlage zum KTB Panzer Gruppe 4: 15.10.41–10.11.41' BA-MA RH 21–4/35, fol. 172 (20 October 1941).

54 See my discussion in Stahel, *Kiev 1941*, p. 325.

55 'Anlage zum KTB Panzer Gruppe 4: 15.10.41–10.11.41' BA-MA RH 21–4/35, fol. 172 (20 October 1941). The figures cited for the 11th Panzer Division equal a total of 199 tanks, which is much higher than my earlier estimate reported in my study cited by the previous note (where I suggested the division's strength was between 75 and 125 tanks at the start of Typhoon). There would seem to be two possibilities that account for the discrepancy. Firstly, although it is not recorded in the available figures, the 11th Panzer Division may have received a large number of the new tanks released by Hitler for Operation Typhoon. Indeed, given that the division started the war with only 175 tanks, this would appear to be the most likely answer. Secondly, the figures could simply have been miscalculated or based on incorrect information, which is not at all unlikely given that when figures for a panzer division can occasionally be cross-referenced from separate files it is not uncommon to find differing totals.

56 '20.Pz.Div. KTB vom 21.10.41 bis 30.12.41 Band Ia2.' BA-MA RH 27–20/26, fol. 10 (25 October 1941).

57 As cited in Piekalkiewicz, *Moscow 1941*, p. 140.

58 Landon and Leitner (eds.), *Diary of a German Soldier*, p. 116 (24 October 1941).

59 Reddemann (ed.), *Zwischen Front und Heimat*, p. 335 (27 October 1941).

60 'Anlagen zum Kriegstagebuch Tagesmeldungen Bd.I 1.9–31.10.41' BA-MA RH 21–3/70, fol. 246 (26 October 1941).

61 As cited in Michael Jones, *The Retreat*, p. 71.

62 Raus, *Panzer Operations*, p. 88.

63 'Kriegstagebuch Nr.3 der 7.Panzer-Division Führungsabteilung 1.6.1941–9.5.1942' BA-MA RH 27-7/46, fol. 161 (28 October 1941).

64 Fuchs Richardson (ed.), *Sieg Heil!*, p. 147 (26 October 1941).

65 '3rd Pz. Gr. KTB Nr.2 1.9.41–31.10.41' BA-MA Microfilm 59060 (27 October 1941).

66 'Anlagen zum Kriegstagebuch Tagesmeldungen Bd.I 1.9–31.10.41' BA-MA RH 21-3/70, fol. 190 (20 October 1941).

67 'Kriegstagebuch Nr.7 des Kdos. Der 1.Panzer-Div. 20.9.41–12.4.42' BA-MA 27-1/58, fol. 34 (21 October 1941).

68 '3rd Pz. Gr. KTB Nr.2 1.9.41–31.10.41' BA-MA Microfilm 59060 (14 October 1941).

69 *Ibid.* (21 October 1941).

70 *Ibid.* (23 October 1941).

71 'Anlagenband zum KTB XXXXI A.K. Ia 3.Verteidigung von Kalinin 15.10.41–20.11.41' BA-MA RH 24-41/15 (22 October 1941); 'Anlagen zum Kriegstagebuch Tagesmeldungen Bd.I 1.9–31.10.41' BA-MA RH 21-3/70, fol. 214 (22 October 1941).

72 'Anlagenband zum KTB XXXXI A.K. Ia 3.Verteidigung von Kalinin 15.10.41–20.11.41' BA-MA RH 24-41/15 (24 October 1941); 'Anlagen zum Kriegstagebuch Tagesmeldungen Bd.I 1.9–31.10.41' BA-MA RH 21-3/70, fol. 232 (24 October 1941).

73 Röttiger, 'XXXXI Panzer Corps During the Battle of Moscow in 1941', p. 30.

74 Pabst, *The Outermost Frontier*, p. 36.

75 Röttiger, 'XXXXI Panzer Corps During the Battle of Moscow in 1941', p. 31.

76 '3rd Pz. Gr. KTB Nr.2 1.9.41–31.10.41' BA-MA Microfilm 59060 (24 October 1941).

77 'Kriegstagebuch Nr.1 (Band Oktober 1941) des Oberkommandos der Heeresgruppe Mitte' BA-MA RH 19-II/411, fol. 661 (22 October 1941).

78 *Ibid.*, fol. 653 (21 October 1941).

79 Bock, *War Diary*, p. 339 (23 October 1941).

80 *Ibid.*, p. 340 (24 October 1941).

81 'Kriegstagebuch Nr.1 (Band Oktober 1941) des Oberkommandos der Heeresgruppe Mitte' BA-MA RH 19-II/411, fol. 693 (26 October 1941).

82 *Ibid.*, fol. 691 (26 October 1941).

83 Bock, *War Diary*, p. 341 (26 October 1941).

84 *Ibid.*, pp. 341–342 (26 October 1941).

85 '3rd Pz. Gr. KTB Nr.2 1.9.41–31.10.41' BA-MA Microfilm 59060 (21 October 1941); 'Anlagen zum Kriegstagebuch Tagesmeldungen Bd.I 1.9–31.10.41' BA-MA RH 21-3/70, fol. 205 (21 October 1941).

86 Fröhlich (ed.), *Die Tagebücher von Joseph Goebbels Teil II Band 2*, p. 178 (26 October 1941).

87 Hans Reinhardt, 'Panzer-Gruppe 3 in der Schlacht von Moskau und ihre Erfahrungen im Rückzug', p. 1.

88 '3rd Pz. Gr. KTB Nr.2 1.9.41–31.10.41' BA-MA Microfilm 59060 (21 October 1941).

89 Boberach (ed.), *Meldungen aus dem Reich*, Band 8, p. 2902, Document 231 (26 October 1941). Samara was the former name for Kuibyshev, which the Soviets renamed in 1935.

90 Buchbender and Sterz (eds.), *Das andere Gesicht des Krieges*, p. 85 (25 October 1941).

91 Hürter, *Ein deutscher General an der Ostfront*, p. 96 (23 October 1941).

92 'KTB 3rd Pz. Div. vom 19.9.41 bis 6.2.42' BA-MA RH 27–3/15, p. 295 (23 October 1941).

93 Schäufler (ed.), *Knight's Cross Panzers*, pp. 146–147.

94 Bock, *War Diary*, p. 340 (25 October 1941).

95 Guderian, *Panzer Leader*, pp. 242–244.

96 Carell, *Hitler's War on Russia*, p. 153.

97 'Kriegstagebuch der O.Qu.-Abt. Pz. A.O.K.2 von 21.6.41 bis 31.3.42' BA-MA RH 21–2/819, fol. 158 (27 October 1941).

98 Bock, *War Diary*, p. 345 (29 October 1941).

99 Guderian, *Panzer Leader*, p. 244.

100 See the damning comments of Oskar Munzel, the commander of the 6th Panzer Regiment, in Oskar Munzel, *Panzer-Taktik. Raids gepanzerter Verbände im Ostfeldzug 1941/42* (Neckargemünd, 1959) p. 109.

101 'KTB 3rd Pz. Div. vom 19.9.41 bis 6.2.42' BA-MA RH 27–3/15, p. 313 (30 October 1941).

102 Carell, *Hitler's War on Russia*, p. 157.

103 Seaton, *The Battle for Moscow*, pp. 105–106.

104 Eremenko, *The Arduous Beginning*, pp. 259–260.

105 Forczyk, *Moscow 1941*, p. 59.

106 'Kriegstagebuch Nr.1 (Band Oktober 1941) des Oberkommandos der Heeresgruppe Mitte' BA-MA RH 19-II/411, fol. 666 (23 October 1941).

107 'Armeeoberkommando 2. I.a KTB Teil.2 19.9.41–16.12.41' BA-MA RH 20–2/207, p. 78 (24 October 1941).

108 Bock, *War Diary*, p. 338 (22 October 1941).

109 *Ibid.*, p. 339 (24 October 1941).

110 Trevor-Roper (ed.), *Hitler's Table Talk, 1941–1944*, p. 82 (21–22 October 1941).

111 'Kriegstagebuch Nr.1 (Band Oktober 1941) des Oberkommandos der Heeresgruppe Mitte' BA-MA RH 19-II/411, fol. 679 (24 October 1941).

112 Bock, *War Diary*, p. 340 (25 October 1941).

113 'Kriegstagebuch Nr.1 (Band Oktober 1941) des Oberkommandos der Heeresgruppe Mitte' BA-MA RH 19-II/411, fol. 690 (26 October 1941).

114 Bock, *War Diary*, p. 341 (26 October 1941).

115 *Ibid.*, pp. 342–343 (27 October 1941).

116 *Ibid.*, p. 343 (27 October 1941).

117 *Ibid.* Army Group Centre's war diary makes clear that there were frequent discussions on 27 October between Bock's headquarters and Second Panzer Army, indicating that Guderian knew full well what was being ordered, but supported Bock in not following the order. See 'Kriegstagebuch Nr.1 (Band Oktober 1941) des Oberkommandos der Heeresgruppe Mitte' BA-MA RH 19-II/411, fol. 699 (27 October 1941).

118 Bock, *War Diary*, p. 344 (28 October 1941).

119 Overmans, *Deutsche militärische Verluste im Zweiten Weltkrieg*, p. 278.

120 Halder, *KTB III*, p. 286 (10 November 1941).

121 Overmans, *Deutsche militärische Verluste im Zweiten Weltkrieg*, p. 279.

122 Görlitz, *Paulus and Stalingrad*, p. 140.

123 Ernst Kern, *War Diary 1941–1945*, p. 14.

124 Günther, *Hot Motors, Cold Feet*, p. 178.

125 Gareis, *Kampf und Ende der Fränkisch-Sudetendeutschen 98. Infanterie-Division*, p. 148.

126 Guido Knopp, *Der Verdammte Krieg. 'Unternehmen Barbarossa'* (Munich, 1998) p. 187.

127 Bock, *War Diary*, p. 347 (30 October 1941).

128 Lange, *Tagebücher aus dem Zweiten Weltkrieg*, p. 64 (7 October 1941).

129 Kurt Miethke, MPT, 3.2002.0912 (24 October 1941).

130 Stader (ed.), *Ihr daheim und wir hier draußen*, p. 46 (29 October 1941).

131 Ochsenknecht, *'Als ob der Schnee alles zudeckte'*, p. 90.

132 Norman Davies, *No Simple Victory. World War II in Europe, 1939–1945* (London, 2006) p. 261.

133 Kuhnert, *Will We See Tomorrow?*, p. 112.

134 Paul Carell [Paul Karl Schmidt], *Unternehmen Barbarossa im Bild. Der Russlandkrieg fotografiert von Soldaten* (Frankfurt am Main, 1991) p. 322.

135 Haape with Henshaw, *Moscow Tram Stop*, pp. 195–196.

136 Ochsenknecht, *'Als ob der Schnee alles zudeckte'*, p. 90.

137 Rudolf Stützel, *Feldpost. Briefe und Aufzeichnungen eines 17-Jährigen 1940–1945* (Hamburg, 2005) p. 60 (8 August 1941).

138 On the Aktion T4 programme, see Evans, *The Third Reich at War*, pp. 524–530.

139 Blandford (ed.), *Under Hitler's Banner*, p. 89.

140 Kroener, 'The Winter Crisis of 1941–1942', p. 1014.

141 Davies, *No Simple Victory*, p. 260.

142 Kroener, 'The Winter Crisis of 1941–1942', p. 1014.

143 Humburg, *Das Gesicht des Krieges*, p. 158 (5 October 1941).

144 Lucas, *War of the Eastern Front 1941–1945*, p. 108.

145 Kroener, 'The Winter Crisis of 1941–1942', pp. 1014–1015.

146 *Ibid.*, p. 1012.

147 As cited in Bartov, *Hitler's Army*, p. 18.

148 Bähr and Bähr (eds.), *Kriegsbriefe Gefallener Studenten, 1939–1945*, p. 83 (20 October 1941); Bähr and Bähr (eds.), *Die Stimme des Menschen*, p. 115 (20 October 1941).

149 Gareis, *Kampf und Ende der Fränkisch-Sudetendeutschen 98. Infanterie-Division*, p. 139.

150 Kuhnert, *Will We See Tomorrow?*, p. 106.

151 See descriptions in Metelmann, *Through Hell for Hitler*, pp. 35–36; and Alexander and Kunze (eds.), *Eastern Inferno*, pp. 120 and 122 (27 October 1941).

152 Fuchs Richardson (ed.), *Sieg Heil!*, p. 147 (20 October 1941).

153 Landon and Leitner (eds.), *Diary of a German Soldier*, p. 105 (12 September 1941).

154 Pabst, *The Outermost Frontier*, p. 36.

155 Beevor and Vinogradova (eds.), *A Writer at War*, p. 38.

156 Günther, *Hot Motors, Cold Feet*, p. 184.

157 Wagener, *Moskau 1941*, p. 59.

158 Pabst, *The Outermost Frontier*, pp. 35.

159 Garden and Andrew (eds.), *The War Diaries of a Panzer Soldier*, p. 54 (15 October 1941).

160 Pabst, *The Outermost Frontier*, p. 37.

161 My thanks to Dr Vincent S. Smith, Cybertaxonomist at the Natural History Museum in London.

162 Haape with Henshaw, *Moscow Tram Stop*, p. 138. Haape was under the mistaken impression the lice caused spotted fever, but as indicated they do not. Epidemic typhus, which is spread by lice, causes a spotted rash that could be confused with spotted fever. See Hans Zinsser, *Rats, Lice and History* (Boston, 1963) pp. 161–164 and 220–221.

163 Department of the US Army (ed.), *Effects of Climate on Combat in European Russia*, p. 42.

164 Ernst Kern, *War Diary 1941–1945*, p. 21.

165 Humburg, *Das Gesicht des Krieges*, p. 153 (24 October 1941).

166 Robert W. Stephan, *Stalin's Secret War. Soviet Counterintelligence Against the Nazis, 1941–1945* (Lawrence, 2004) p. 122.

167 As cited in Barry Leach, *German Strategy Against Russia 1939–1941* (Oxford, 1973) p. 91.

168 Stephan, *Stalin's Secret War*, p. 127.

169 Leach, *German Strategy Against Russia 1939–1941*, p. 91.

170 Stephan, *Stalin's Secret War*, pp. 128–129.

171 Geoffrey P. Megargee, *Inside Hitler's High Command* (Lawrence, 2000) pp. 107 and 111.

172 Albert Seaton, *The Russo-German War 1941–45* (Novato, 1971) pp. 43–45.

173 Glantz and House, *When Titans Clashed*, pp. 67–70.

174 Osten-Sacken, *Vier Jahre Barbarossa*, p. 39.

175 David Thomas, 'Foreign Armies East and German Military Intelligence in Russia 1941–1945', *Journal of Contemporary History* 22 (1987) pp. 274–275. See also Andreas Hillgruber, 'The German Military Leaders' View of Russia Prior to the Attack on the Soviet Union' in Wegner (ed.), *From Peace to War*, pp. 169–185; Olaf Groehler, 'Goals and Reason: Hitler and the German Military' in Joseph Wieczynski (ed.), *Operation Barbarossa. The German Attack on the Soviet Union June, 1941* (Salt Lake City, 1993) pp. 48–61. Germany's academic experts on the east (*Ostforscher*) were profoundly influenced by entrenched anti-Slavic and anti-Bolshevik beliefs and stereotypes: Michael Burleigh, *Germany Turns Eastwards. A Study of 'Ostforschung' in the Third Reich* (Cambridge, 1988).

176 Robert Gibbons, 'Opposition gegen "Barbarossa" im Herbst 1940 – Eine Denkschrift aus der deutschen Botschaft in Moskau', *Vierteljahrshefte für Zeitgeschichte* 23 (1975) pp. 337–340.

177 Franz Halder, *Kriegstagebuch: Tägliche Aufzeichnungen des Chefs des Generalstabes des Heeres 1939–1942. Band II*, p. 86 (4 September 1940).

178 Seaton, *The Russo-German War 1941–1945*, p. 45; Stahel, *Operation Barbarossa and Germany's Defeat in the East*, pp. 46–47.

179 Geoffrey P. Megargee, 'Questions and Answers: Geoffrey P. Megargee', *Global War Studies* 7, 2, (2010) p. 201.

180 Thomas, 'Foreign Armies East and German Military Intelligence in Russia 1941–1945', p. 273.

181 Steiger, *Armour Tactics in the Second World War*, p. 120.

182 Bradley F. Smith, *Sharing Secrets with Stalin. How the Allies Traded Intelligence, 1941–1945* (Lawrence, 1996) pp. 82–83. On Soviet–British co-operation during the war, see Donal O'Sullivan, *Dealing with the Devil. Anglo-Soviet Intelligence Cooperation During the Second World War* (New York, 2010).

183 See Nagorski, *The Greatest Battle*, pp. 214–218.

184 Ian Kershaw, *Fateful Choices*, p. 283.

185 Bellamy, *Absolute War*, pp. 308–310.

186 Gerhard Krebs, 'Japan and the German–Soviet War, 1941' in Wegner (ed.), *From Peace to War*, p. 557.

187 Anne Nelson, *Red Orchestra. The Story of the Berlin Underground and the Circle of Friends Who Resisted Hitler* (New York, 2009).

188 Clark, *Barbarossa*, pp. 150–151.

9 The eye of the storm

1 Chris Bishop, *Hitler's Foreign Divisions. Foreign Volunteers in the Waffen-SS 1940–1945* (London, 2005) p. 60.

2 Bock, *War Diary*, p. 303 (3 September 1941).

3 Kleinfeld and Tambs, *Hitler's Spanish Legion*, pp. 55–56.

4 Bishop, *Hitler's Foreign Divisions*, p. 60.

5 Kleinfeld and Tambs, *Hitler's Spanish Legion*, p. 63.

6 Ulrich de Maizière, *In der Pflicht. Lebensbericht eines deutschen Soldaten im 20. Jahrhundert* (Bielefeld, 1989) p. 71.

7 Fröhlich (ed.), *Die Tagebücher von Joseph Goebbels Teil II Band 2*, pp. 112–113 (14 October 1941).

8 *Ibid.*, p. 85 (10 October 1941).

9 *Ibid.*, p. 198 (29 October 1941).

10 Förster, 'Volunteers for the European Crusade Against Bolshevism', pp. 1058–1063.

11 A reorganised French force was used in anti-partisan warfare; later in the war a French volunteer regiment of the Waffen-SS was formed and, with better training and leadership, performed much more effectively than the LVF. See Bishop, *Hitler's Foreign Divisions*, pp. 40–41.

12 The memoir of the Belgian nationalist leader Léon Degrelle who fought in the Légion Wallonie is one of the few published accounts from this formation. It should, however, be noted that Degrelle propagates extreme anti-Soviet and pro-Nazi ideals. See Degrelle, *Campaign in Russia*.

13 For an authoritative history of the regiment, see Amir Obhodaš and Jason D. Mark, *Croatian Legion. The 369th (Croatian) Infantry Regiment on the Eastern Front 1941–1943* (Pymble, 2011).

14 Bishop, *Hitler's Foreign Divisions*, pp. 33, 100–101 and 116.

15 DiNardo, *Germany and the Axis Powers*, p. 117.

16 Trevor-Roper (ed.), *Hitler's Table Talk, 1941–1944*, p. 66 (17 October 1941).

17 Sebastian, *Journal, 1935–1944*, pp. 427 and 428 (14 and 17 October 1941).

18 Forstmeier, *Odessa 1941*, pp. 107 and 111.

19 Axworthy, Scafes and Craciunoiu, *Third Axis Fourth Ally*, p. 67.

20 Alexander Dallin, *Odessa, 1941–1944. A Case Study of Soviet Territory Under Foreign Rule* (Oxford, 1998) p. 74.

21 Dennis Deletant, *Hitler's Forgotten Ally. Ion Antonescu and His Regime, Romania 1940–1944* (London, 2006) p. 127. See also Wendy Lower, 'Axis

Collaboration, Operation Barbarossa, and the Holocaust in Ukraine' in Kay, Rutherford and Stahel (eds.), *Nazi Policy on the Eastern Front, 1941*, pp. 186–219.

22 Muggeridge (ed.), *Ciano's Diary 1939–1943*, p. 385 (17 October 1941).

23 The CSIR was only semi-motorised to begin with and included a multiplicity of different vehicle types that included seventeen variants of light and thirty variants of heavy trucks. This made the acquisition of spare parts extremely complicated, which compounded the problem of mobility in October because the Italian war ministry had failed to provide low-temperature lubricants for vehicles and weapons. See MacGregor Knox, *Hitler's Italian Allies. Royal Armed Forces, Fascist Regime, and the War of 1940–1943* (Cambridge, 2009) p. 128.

24 Gosztony, *Hitlers Fremde Heere*, pp. 172–173.

25 The city has a number of former names – Yuzovka, Staline and Stalino – but today it is Donetsk. For more on the CSIR's military campaign in October, see Patrick Cloutier, *Regio Esercito. The Italian Royal Army in Mussolini's Wars 1935–1943* (Lexington, 2010) pp. 94–96.

26 Muggeridge (ed.), *Ciano's Diary 1939–1943*, p. 387 (22 October 1941).

27 Förster, 'The Decisions of the Tripartite Pact States', p. 1031.

28 *Ibid*. Franz von Adonyi-Naredy, *Ungarns Armee im Zweiten Weltkrieg. Deutschlands letzter Verbündeter* (Neckargemünd, 1971) pp. 59–60.

29 Gosztony, *Hitlers Fremde Heere*, p. 161.

30 Förster, 'The Decisions of the Tripartite Pact States', pp. 1031–1032.

31 *Ibid.*, p. 1032; Gosztony, *Hitlers Fremde Heere*, p. 161; Deborah S. Cornelius, *Hungary in World War II. Caught in the Cauldron* (New York, 2011) pp. 177–178.

32 Axworthy, *Axis Slovakia*, pp. 109 and 112.

33 Förster, 'The Decisions of the Tripartite Pact States', pp. 1034–1036.

34 Vehviläinen, *Finland in the Second World War*, p. 91.

35 Menger, 'Germany and the Finnish "Separate War" Against the Soviet Union', p. 535.

36 Vehviläinen, *Finland in the Second World War*, pp. 91–92 and 99–101.

37 Müller, *An der Seite der Wehrmacht*, p. 32; Jürgen Förster, 'Strategy and Policy in Northern Europe' in Militärgeschichtliches Forschungsamt (ed.), *Germany and the Second World War. Volume IV*, p. 982.

38 '20.Pz.Div. KTB vom 21.10.41 bis 30.12.41 Band Ia2.' BA-MA RH 27–20/26, fol. 12 (26 October 1941).

39 Bock, *War Diary*, p. 342 (27 October 1941).

40 *Ibid.*, p. 342 (27 October 1941).

41 'Kriegstagebuch Nr.3. des XXXXVI.Pz.Korps vom 24.08.41–31.12.41' BA-MA RH 24–46/21, fol. 101 (28 October 1941).

42 'Anlage zum KTB Panzer Gruppe 4: 15.10.41–10.11.41' BA-MA RH 21-4/35, fol. 167 (30 October 1941).

43 Bock, *War Diary*, p. 344 (28 October 1941).

44 *Ibid.*, p. 347 (31 October 1941).

45 Trevor-Roper (ed.), *Hitler's Table Talk, 1941–1944*, p. 94 (29 October 1941).

46 Richard Lamb, 'Kluge' in Barnett (ed.), *Hitler's Generals*, pp. 402 and 404.

47 Stahel, *Operation Barbarossa and Germany's Defeat in the East*, p. 340.

48 Fröhlich (ed.), *Die Tagebücher von Joseph Goebbels Teil II Band 2*, p. 197 (28 October 1941).

49 *Ibid.*, pp. 208–209 (31 October 1941).

50 *Ibid.*, p. 207 (30 October 1941).

51 Boberach (ed.), *Meldungen aus dem Reich*, Band 8, p. 2927, Document 233 (30 October 1941).

52 Gareis, *Kampf und Ende der Fränkisch-Sudetendeutschen 98. Infanterie-Division*, p. 160.

53 As cited in Michael Jones, *The Retreat*, p. 72.

54 *Ibid.*

55 As cited in Porter and Jones, *Moscow in World War II*, p. 126.

56 As cited in Bücheler, *Hoepner*, p. 155.

57 Bock, *War Diary*, p. 342 (27 October 1941).

58 'Anlagen zum Kriegstagebuch Tagesmeldungen Bd.I 1.9–31.10.41' BA-MA RH 21-3/70, fol. 291 (29 October 1941).

59 'Anlagenband zum KTB XXXXI A.K. Ia 3.Verteidigung von Kalinin 15.10.41–20.11.41' BA-MA RH 24-41/15 (29 October 1941).

60 'Kriegstagebuch Nr.7 des Kdos. Der 1.Panzer-Div. 20.9.41–12.4.42' BA-MA 27-1/58, fols. 38–39 (30 October 1941).

61 Raus, *Panzer Operations*, p. 88.

62 Bock, *War Diary*, p. 343 (28 October 1941).

63 '3rd Pz. Gr. KTB Nr.2 1.9.41–31.10.41' BA-MA Microfilm 59060 (28 October 1941).

64 Bock, *War Diary*, pp. 344–345 (29 October 1941).

65 '3rd Pz. Gr. KTB Nr.2 1.9.41–31.10.41' BA-MA Microfilm 59060 (29 October 1941).

66 *Ibid.* (30 October 1941).

67 Bock, *War Diary*, p. 345 (29 October 1941).

68 *Ibid.*, pp. 346–347 (31 October 1941).

69 '3rd Pz. Gr. KTB Nr.2 1.9.41–31.10.41' BA-MA Microfilm 59060 (28 and 31 October 1941).

70 Bock, *War Diary*, pp. 347–348 (1 November 1941).

71 Stader (ed.), *Ihr daheim und wir hier draußen*, p. 44 (letter states only 'end of October' 1941).

72 Fuchs Richardson (ed.), *Sieg Heil!*, p. 150 (4 November 1941).

73 Buchbender and Sterz (eds.), *Das andere Gesicht des Krieges*, p. 85 (29 October 1941).

74 Gareis, *Kampf und Ende der Fränkisch-Sudetendeutschen 98. Infanterie-Division*, p. 159.

75 Alexander and Kunze (eds.), *Eastern Inferno*, p. 119 (27 October 1941).

76 Klaus Becker, MPT, 3.2002.0224 (21 October 1941).

77 Haape with Henshaw, *Moscow Tram Stop*, p. 133.

78 Clark, *Barbarossa*, p. 163.

79 'Armeeoberkommando 2. I.a KTB Teil.2 19.9.41–16.12.41' BA-MA RH 20–2/207, pp. 84 and 90 (28 and 31 October 1941).

80 See the graphic description in Ingrid Hammer and Susanne zur Nieden (eds.), *Sehr selten habe ich geweint. Briefe und Tagebücher aus dem Zweiten Weltkrieg von Menschen aus Berlin* (Zürich, 1992) pp. 255–257 (27 October 1941). See also Buchbender and Sterz (eds.), *Das andere Gesicht des Krieges*, pp. 84–85 (23 October 1941).

81 'Kriegstagebuch Nr.3. der Führungsabteilung (Ia) des Gen. Kdo. (mot.) XXXX. Pz.Korps vom 31.05.1941–26.12.1941' BA-MA RH 24–40/18 (28 October 1941).

82 Haape with Henshaw, *Moscow Tram Stop*, p. 133.

83 Dunn, *Stalin's Keys to Victory*, p. 44.

84 Carruthers (ed.), *The Wehrmacht*, p. 58.

85 Hammer and Nieden (eds.), *Sehr selten habe ich geweint*, p. 254 (14 October 1941).

86 'Kriegstagebuch Nr.3. des XXXXVI.Pz.Korps vom 24.08.41–31.12.41' BA-MA RH 24–46/21, fol. 100 (27 October 1941).

87 *Ibid.*, fol. 102 (29 October 1941); '2. Panzer Division KTB Nr.6 Teil I. Vom 15.6.41–3.4.42' BA-MA RH 27–2/21 (29 October 1941).

88 'Anlage zum KTB Pz.Gruppe 4 Meldungen von unten 15.10.41–15.11.41' BA-MA RH 21–4/39, fol. 193 (29 October 1941).

89 Bernhard von Lossberg, *Im Wehrmachtführungsstab. Bericht eines Generalstabsoffiziers* (Hamburg, 1950) p. 136.

90 See the first-rate study by Robert M. Citino, *The German Way of War. From the Thirty Years' War to the Third Reich* (Lawrence, 2005).

91 Munzel, *Panzer-Taktik*, p. 109.

Conclusion

1 Even as late as 1991 R. H. S. Stolfi published his thesis, relatively unchallenged at the time, that Hitler's war in the east represented a credible war-winning opportunity for Hitler. As the book's cover claimed: 'But for one fateful decision

Hitler could have won World War II in the summer of 1941.' See R. H. S. Stolfi, *Hitler's Panzers East. World War II Reinterpreted* (Norman, 1993). More recently, Heinz Magenheimer has suggested: 'All things being equal, an attack date between 20 and 24 September would have offered the possibility not only of destroying the Soviet forces confronting Army Group Centre, but also of taking Moscow before the onset of the autumn rains and the arrival of reinforcements from the Far East. This brings us back to the assessment already made that a time-span of between seven and ten days was wanting for a victorious conclusion of the campaign in the east' (Heinz Magenheimer, *Hitler's War. Germany's Key Strategic Decisions 1940–1945* (London, 1999) pp. 115–116). The first volume of Brian Taylor's two-volume history of the eastern front suggested that by the late summer of 1941 Germany had brought the Soviet Union to the 'very edge of destruction' (p. 33). He later portrayed the battle of Moscow as 'the last battle before final victory' in which the German army suffered defeat, 'at the very moment victory was within reach' (Brian Taylor, *Barbarossa to Berlin. A Chronology of the Campaigns on the Eastern Front 1941 to 1945. Volume 1 The Long Drive East 22 June 1941 to 18 November 1942* (Staplehurst, 2003) p. 133).

2 For Russian figures as well as an excellent discussion of the reasons behind the Soviet debacle in October 1941, see Mawdsley, *Thunder in the East*, p. 97. For a discussion of German figures for Army Group Centre in October 1941, see Stahel, *Kiev 1941*, p. 339, plus p. 429 n. 30.

3 Mawdsley, *Thunder in the East*, p. 99.

4 As cited in Porter and Jones, *Moscow in World War II*, p. 126.

5 In addition to numerous army commands between June 1944 and April 1945, Tippelskirch was the acting commander of Army Group Vistula during the final days of the war.

6 As cited in Ihno Krumpelt, *Das Material und die Kriegführung* (Frankfurt am Main, 1968) p. 178.

7 Kesselring, *The Memoirs of Field-Marshal Kesselring*, p. 99.

8 Ian Kershaw, *Hitler 1936–1945*, p. 419.

9 Zhukov, *The Memoirs of Marshal Zhukov*, p. 334.

10 Blumentritt, 'Moscow', p. 53.

11 As cited in Mark Mazower, *Hitler's Empire. Nazi Rule in Occupied Europe* (London, 2009) p. 323.

12 This was the thesis of my first book, *Operation Barbarossa and Germany's Defeat in the East*.

13 Mawdsley, *Thunder in the East*, p. 95.

14 Citino, *Death of the Wehrmacht*, p. 45. See also Citino, *The German Way of War*.

15 As cited in Megargee, *Inside Hitler's High Command*, p. 181.

16 *Ibid.*, p. 286. The letter was dated 6 August 1951.

17 Timothy Snyder, *Bloodlands. Europe Between Hitler and Stalin* (New York, 2010) p. 408. See also David Stahel, '*Bloodlands: Europe Between Hitler and Stalin*', *Journal of Military History* 75, 1 (January 2011) pp. 320–322.

18 Krivosheev (ed.), *Soviet Casualties and Combat Losses in the Twentieth Century*, p. 83.

19 Willy Peter Reese, *A Stranger to Myself. The Inhumanity of War. Russia, 1941–1944* (New York, 2005) pp. 137–138.

20 *Ibid.*, p. 18.

BIBLIOGRAPHY

Archival references

I.   Bundesarchiv-Militärarchiv, Freiburg im Breisgau (BA-MA)

Army Group South

BA-MA RH 19-I/73 'Heeresgruppe Süd Kriegstagebuch II.Teil Band 4, 16 Sept.–5 Okt. 1941'

Army Group Centre

BA-MA RH 19II/386 'Kriegstagebuch Nr.1 (Band August 1941) des Oberkommandos der Heeresgruppe Mitte'

BA-MA RH 19-II/411 'Kriegstagebuch Nr.1 (Band Oktober 1941) des Oberkommandos der Heeresgruppe Mitte'

BA-MA RH 19 II/128 'Tagesmeldungen der Heeresgruppe Mitte vom 22.6.41 bis 15.7.41'

BA-MA RH 19 II/129 'Tagesmeldungen der Heeresgruppe Mitte vom 16.7.41 bis 5.8.41'

Panzer Group 2

BA-MA RH 21-2/928 'KTB Nr.1 Panzergruppe 2 Bd.II vom 22.7.1941 bis 20.8.41'

BA-MA RH 21-2/931 'Kriegstagebuch Nr.1 Panzergruppe 2 Band II vom 21.8.1941 bis 31.10.41'

BA-MA RH 21-2/819 'Kriegstagebuch der O.Qu.-Abt. Pz. A.O.K.2 von 21.6.41 bis 31.3.42'

BA-MA RH 24-47/258 'Kriegstagebuch Nr.2 XXXXVII.Pz.Korps. Ia 23.9.1941–31.12.1941'

BA-MA RH 24-48/30 'Kriegstagebuch XXXXVIII.Pz.Kps. Abt.Ia Oktober 1941'

BA-MA RH 27-3/15 'KTB 3rd Pz. Div. vom 19.9.41 bis 6.2.42'

BA-MA RH 27-3/218 'KTB 3rd Pz. Div. I.b 19.5.41–6.2.42'

BA-MA RH 27-4/10 'Kriegstagebuch 4.Panzer-Division Führungsabtl. 26.5.41–31.3.42'

BA-MA RH 27-9/4 '9.Pz.Div. KTB Ia vom 19.5.1941 bis 22.1.1942'

BA-MA RH 27-18/22 '18.Panzer Division, Abt.Ia KTB Teil III vom 30.9.–19.10.41'

BA-MA RH 21-2/757 'Verlustmeldungen 5.7.1941–25.3.1942'

Panzer Group 3

BA-MA Microfilm 59054 '3rd Pz. Gr. KTB 25.5.41–31.8.41'

BA-MA Microfilm 59060 '3rd Pz. Gr. KTB Nr.2 1.9.41–31.10.41'

BA-MA RH 21-3/70 'Anlagen zum Kriegstagebuch Tagesmeldungen Bd.I 1.9–31.10.41'

BA-MA RH 24-41/14 'Anlagenband zum KTB XXXXI A.K. Ia 1. Durchbruch durch die Wop-Kokosch Dnjepr Stellung 2.10.41 bis 9.10.41. 2. Vorstoss auf Kalinin 15.10.41–20.10.41'

BA-MA RH 24-41/15 'Anlagenband zum KTB XXXXI A.K. Ia 3.Verteidigung von Kalinin 15.10.41–20.11.41'

BA-MA 27-1/58 'Kriegstagebuch Nr.7 des Kdos. Der 1.Panzer-Div. 20.9.41–12.4.42'

BA-MA RH 27-7/46 'Kriegstagebuch Nr.3 der 7. Panzer-Division Führungsabteilung 1.6.1941–9.5.1942'

Panzer Group 4

BA-MA RH 21-4/34 'Anlage zum KTB Panzer Gruppe 4: 20.9.41–14.10.41'

BA-MA RH 21-4/35 'Anlage zum KTB Panzer Gruppe 4: 15.10.41–10.11.41'

BA-MA RH 21-4/37 'Anlage zum KTB Pz.Gruppe 4 Meldungen von unten 20.9.41–14.10.41'

BA-MA RH 21-4/39 'Anlage zum KTB Pz.Gruppe 4 Meldungen von unten 15.10.41–15.11.41'

BA-MA RH 24-46/21 'Kriegstagebuch Nr.3. des XXXXVI.Pz.Korps vom 24.08.41–31.12.41'

BA-MA RH 24-40/18 'Kriegstagebuch Nr.3. der Führungsabteilung (Ia) des Gen. Kdo. (mot.) XXXX.Pz.Korps vom 31.05.1941–26.12.1941'

BA-MA RH 24-57-2 'Gen.Kdo.LVII.Pz.Korps KTB Nr.1 vom 15.2.41–31.10.41'

BA-MA RH 27-2/21 '2. Panzer Division KTB Nr.6 Teil I. Vom 15.6.41–3.4.42'

BA-MA RH 27-5/29 '5. Panzer Division KTB Nur.8 vom 11.9.41–11.12.41'

BA-MA RH 27-11/16 '11.Pz.Div. KTB Abt. Ia vom 1.5.41–21.10.41'
BA-MA RH 27-20/25 '20.Pz.Div. KTB vom 15.8.41 bis 20.10.41 Band Ia.'
BA-MA RH 27-20/26 '20.Pz.Div. KTB vom 21.10.41 bis 30.12.41 Band Ia2.'

Second Army
BA-MA RH 20-2/207 'Armeeoberkommando 2. I.a KTB Teil.2 19.9.41–16.12.41'

Fourth Army
BA-MA RH 26-15/54 'Kriegstagebuch der Abt. Ib 15.Inf. Div. für die Zeit von 25.6.41–3.5.42'

Personal Files
BA-MA Pers. 6/38 'Personalakten für Hoth, Hermann'
BA-MA PERS/6/50 'Personalakten für Reinhardt, Hans'
BA-MA Pers. 6/56 'Personalakten für Strauss, Adolf'

II.   Liddell Hart Centre for Military Archives (LH)
LH 15/4/40 'The Germans in Russia'

III.   Museumsstiftung Post und Telekommunikation (MPT) Berlin

3.2002.0985 – Heinz Rahe (26 September 1941)
3.2002.7139 – Hellmuth H. (30 September and 23 October 1941)
3.2002.0947 – Walter Neuser (15 October 1941)
3.2002.1941 – Gerhard Kunde (19 October 1941)
3.2002.0817 – Klaus K. (17 October 1941)
3.2002.0912 – Kurt Miethke (24 October 1941)
3.2002.0224 – Klaus Becker (21 October 1941)

IV.   Württembergische Landesbibliothek Stuttgart (WLS)

Flugblattpropaganda im 2. Weltkrieg (1941); Mappe 92–26
Flugblattpropaganda im 2. Weltkrieg (1941); Mappe 92–22
Flugblattpropaganda im 2. Weltkrieg (1941); Mappe 92–32
Flugblattpropaganda im 2. Weltkrieg (1941); Mappe 92–36
Flugblattpropaganda im 2. Weltkrieg (1941); Mappe 92–38
Flugblattpropaganda im 2. Weltkrieg (1941); Mappe 92–40
Flugblattpropaganda im 2. Weltkrieg (1941), Mappe 92a–5
Flugblattpropaganda im 2. Weltkrieg (1941), Mappe 92a–6
Flugblattpropaganda im 2. Weltkrieg (1941), Mappe 92a–8

Primary and secondary sources

Addison, Paul and Angus Calder (eds.), *A Time to Kill. The Soldier's Experience of War in the West, 1939–1945* (London, 1997).

Adonyi-Naredy, Franz von, *Ungarns Armee im Zweiten Weltkrieg. Deutschlands letzter Verbündeter* (Neckargemünd, 1971).

Alexander, Christine and Mark Kunze (eds.), *Eastern Inferno. The Journals of a German Panzerjäger on the Eastern Front, 1941–1943* (Philadelphia and Newbury, 2010).

Anfilov, Viktor, 'Zhukov' in Harold Shukman (ed.), *Stalin's Generals* (London, 1993) pp. 343–360.

Antal, John F., 'The Wehrmacht Approach to Maneuver Warfare Command and Control' in Richard D. Hooker Jr (ed.), *Maneuver Warfare. An Anthology* (Novato, 1993) pp. 347–359.

Arnold, Klaus J., *Die Wehrmacht und die Besatzungspolitik in den besetzten Gebieten der Sowjetunion. Kriegführung und Radikalisierung im 'Unternehmen Barbarossa'* (Berlin, 2005).

Arnold, Klaus Jochen and Gerd C. Lübbers, 'The Meeting of the Staatssekretäre on 2 May 1941 and the Wehrmacht: A Document up for Discussion', *Journal of Contemporary History* 42, 4 (October 2007) pp. 613–626.

Axell, Albert, *Russia's Heroes 1941–1945* (New York, 2001).

Stalin's War. Through the Eyes of His Commanders (London, 1997).

Axworthy, Mark, *Axis Slovakia. Hitler's Slavic Wedge 1938–1945* (New York, 2002).

'Peasant Scapegoat to Industrial Slaughter: The Romanian Soldier at the Siege of Odessa' in Addison and Calder (eds.), *A Time to Kill*, pp. 221–232.

Axworthy, Mark, Cornel Scafes and Cristian Craciunoiu, *Third Axis Fourth Ally. Romanian Armed Forces in the European War, 1941–1945* (London, 1995).

Baberowski, Jörg, 'Kriege in staatsfernen Räumen: Rußland und die Sowjetunion 1905–1950' in Dietrich Beyrau, Michael Hochgeschwender and Dieter Langewiesche (eds.), *Formen des Krieges. Von der Antike bis zur Gegenwart* (Paderborn, 2007) pp. 291–309.

Bähr, Walter and Hans Bähr (eds.), *Kriegsbriefe Gefallener Studenten, 1939–1945* (Tübingen and Stuttgart, 1952).

(eds.), *Die Stimme des Menschen. Briefe und Aufzeichnungen aus der ganzen Welt. 1939–1945* (Munich, 1961).

Barber, John and Mark Harrison, *The Soviet Home Front 1941–1945. A Social and Economic History of the USSR in World War II* (London, 1991).

Bartov, Omer, *The Eastern Front, 1941–1945. German Troops and the Barbarisation of Warfare* (London, 1985).

Hitler's Army. Soldiers, Nazis, and War in the Third Reich (Oxford, 1992).

Becker, Hans, *Devil on My Shoulder* (London, 1957).

Beevor, Antony and Luba Vinogradova (eds.), *A Writer at War. Vasily Grossman with the Red Army 1941–1945* (New York, 2005).

Bellamy, Chris, *Absolute War. Soviet Russia in the Second World War* (New York, 2007).

Below, Nicolaus von, *Als Hitlers Adjutant 1937–1945* (Mainz, 1999).

Benz, Wigbert, *Der Hungerplan im 'Unternehmen Barbarossa' 1941* (Berlin, 2011).

Bergström, Christer, *Barbarossa. The Air Battle. July–December 1941* (Hersham, 2007).

Berkhoff, Karel C., *Harvest of Despair. Life and Death in Ukraine Under Nazi Rule* (Cambridge, MA, 2004).

Bernád, Dénes, Dmitriy Karlenko and Jean-Louis Roba, *From Barbarossa to Odessa. The Luftwaffe and Axis Allies Strike South-East. June–October 1941* (Hinckley, 2008).

Bialer, Seweryn (ed.), *Stalin and His Generals. Soviet Military Memoirs of World War II* (New York, 1969).

Bidermann, Gottlob Herbert, *In Deadly Combat. A German Solder's Memoir of the Eastern Front* (Lawrence, 2000).

Bishop, Chris, *Hitler's Foreign Divisions. Foreign Volunteers in the Waffen-SS 1940–1945* (London, 2005).

Blandford, Edmund (ed.), *Under Hitler's Banner. Serving the Third Reich* (Edison, 2001).

Blumentritt, Günther, 'Moscow' in William Richardson and Seymour Freidin (eds.), *The Fatal Decisions* (London, 1956) pp. 29–75.

Von Rundstedt. The Soldier and the Man (London, 1952).

Boberach, Heinz (ed.), *Meldungen aus dem Reich. Die geheimen Lageberichte des Sicherheitsdienstes der SS 1938–1945. Band 8* (Berlin, 1984).

Bock, Fedor von, *Generalfeldmarschall Fedor von Bock. The War Diary 1939–1945*, Klaus Gerbet (ed.) (Munich, 1996).

Bomba, Ty, 'Proud Monster: The Barbarossa Campaign Considered' in Command Magazine (ed.), *Hitler's Army. The Evolution and Structure of the German Forces, 1933–1945* (Cambridge, MA, 2003) pp. 119–135.

Boog, Horst, 'The Luftwaffe' in Militärgeschichtliches Forschungsamt (ed.), *Germany and the Second World War. Volume IV*, pp. 763–832.

Bordiugov, Gennadi, 'The Popular Mood in the Unoccupied Soviet Union: Continuity and Change During the War' in Robert Thurston and Bernd Bonwetsch (eds.), *The People's War. Responses to World War II in the Soviet Union* (Chicago, 2000) pp. 54–70.

Braatz, Kurt, *Werner Mölders. Die Biographie* (Moosburg, 2008).

Braithwaite, Rodric, *Moscow 1941. A City and Its People at War* (New York, 2006).

Brandon, Ray and Wendy Lower (eds.), *The Shoah in Ukraine. History, Testimony, Memorialization* (Bloomington, 2008).

Broekmeyer, Marius, *Stalin, the Russians, and Their War 1941–1945* (London, 2004).

Buchbender, Ortwin and Reinhold Sterz (eds.), *Das andere Gesicht des Krieges. Deutsche Feldpostbriefe 1939–1945* (Munich, 1982).

Bücheler, Heinrich, *Carl-Heinrich von Stülpnagel. Soldat – Philosoph – Verschwörer* (Berlin, 1989).

  Hoepner. Ein deutsches Soldatenschicksal des 20. Jahrhunderts (Herford, 1980).

Burleigh, Michael, *Germany Turns Eastwards. A Study of 'Ostforschung' in the Third Reich* (Cambridge, 1988).

  The Third Reich. A New History (London, 2001).

Bushkovitch, Paul, 'The Romanov Transformation 1613–1725' in Kagan and Higham (eds.), *The Military History of Tsarist Russia*, pp. 31–45.

Carell, Paul [Paul Karl Schmidt], *Hitler's War on Russia. The Story of the German Defeat in the East* (London, 1964).

  Unternehmen Barbarossa im Bild. Der Russlandkrieg fotografiert von Soldaten (Frankfurt am Main, 1991).

Carlton, David, *Churchill and the Soviet Union* (New York, 2000).

Carruthers, Bob (ed.), *The Wehrmacht. Last Witnesses. First-Hand Accounts from the Survivors of Hitler's Armed Forces* (London, 2010).

Cassidy, Henry, *Moscow Dateline, 1941–1943* (London, 1943).

de Caulaincourt, Armand, *At Napoleon's Side in Russia* (New York, 2008).

Cecil, Robert, *Hitler's Decision to Invade Russia 1941* (London, 1975).

Chales de Beaulieu, Walter, *Generaloberst Erich Hoepner. Militärisches Porträt eines Panzer-Führers* (Neckargemünd, 1969).

Chaney, Otto Preston, *Zhukov* (Norman, 1996).

Chiari, Bernhard, *Alltag hinter der Front. Besatzung, Kollaboration und Widerstand in Weißrußland 1941–1944* (Düsseldorf, 1998).

Churchill, Winston S., *The Second World War. Abridged Edition* (London, 1959).

Citino, Robert M., *Death of the Wehrmacht. The German Campaigns of 1942* (Lawrence, 2007).

  The German Way of War. From the Thirty Years' War to the Third Reich (Lawrence, 2005).

Clark, Alan, *Barbarossa. The Russian–German Conflict 1941–1945* (London, 1996).

von Clausewitz, Carl *On War*, Howard, Michael and Peter Paret (eds.) (New York, 1993).

Cloutier, Patrick, *Regio Esercito. The Italian Royal Army in Mussolini's Wars 1935–1943* (Lexington, 2010).

Cornelius, Deborah S., *Hungary in World War II. Caught in the Cauldron* (New York, 2011).

Corum, James S., *Wolfram von Richthofen. Master of the German Air War* (Lawrence, 2008).

Cottam, Kazimiera J., *Women in Air War. The Eastern Front of World War II* (Newburyport, 1998).

Creveld, Martin van, *Fighting Power. German and US Army Performance, 1939–1945* (Westport, 1982).

   Supplying War. Logistics from Wallenstein to Patton (Cambridge, 1984).

Cumins, Keith, *Cataclysm. The War on the Eastern Front 1941–1945* (Solihull, 2011).

Dallin, Alexander, *German Rule in Russia 1941–1945. A Study of Occupation Policies* (London, 1957).

   Odessa, 1941–1944. A Case Study of Soviet Territory Under Foreign Rule (Oxford, 1998).

Davies, Norman, *No Simple Victory. World War II in Europe, 1939–1945* (London, 2006).

Degrelle, Léon, *Campaign in Russia. The Waffen SS on the Eastern Front* (Torrance, 1985).

Deletant, Dennis, *Hitler's Forgotten Ally. Ion Antonescu and His Regime, Romania 1940–1944* (London, 2006).

Department of the US Army (ed.), *Effects of Climate on Combat in European Russia* (Washington, DC, 1952).

   Small Unit Actions During the German Campaign in Russia (Washington, DC, 1953).

DeWitt, Kurt and Wilhelm Koll, 'The Bryansk Area' in John A. Armstrong (ed.), *Soviet Partisans in World War II* (Madison, 1964) pp. 458–516.

Dietrich, Otto, *The Hitler I Knew. Memoirs of the Third Reich's Press Chief* (New York, 2010).

DiNardo, Richard L., *Germany and the Axis Powers. From Coalition to Collapse* (Lawrence, 2005).

   Mechanized Juggernaut or Military Anachronism? Horses and the German Army in World War II (London, 1991).

Domarus, Max, *Hitler. Speeches and Proclamations 1932–1945. The Chronicle of a Dictatorship. Volume IV. The Years 1941 to 1945* (Wauconda, 2004).

Dunn, Walter S. Jr, *Hitler's Nemesis. The Red Army, 1930–1945* (Mechanicsburg, 2009).

Stalin's Keys to Victory. The Rebirth of the Red Army in WWII (Mechanicsburg, 2006).

Eickhoff, Michael, Wilhelm Pagels and Willy Reschl (eds.), *Der unvergessene Krieg. Hitler-Deutschland gegen die Sowjetunion 1941–1945* (Cologne, 1981).

Elmshäuser, Konrad and Jan Lokers (eds.), *'Man muß hier nur hart sein'. Kriegsbriefe und Bilder einer Familie (1934–1945)* (Bremen, 1999).

Englund, Peter, *The Battle that Shook Europe. Poltava and the Birth of the Russian Empire* (New York, 2003).

Eremenko, A., *The Arduous Beginning* (Honolulu, 2004).

Erickson, John, 'Red Army Battlefield Performance, 1941–1945: The System and the Soldier' in Addison and Calder (eds.), *A Time to Kill*, pp. 233–248.

The Road to Stalingrad. Stalin's War with Germany. Volume One (London, 1975).

Erickson, John and Ljubica Erickson, *Hitler Versus Stalin. The Second World War on the Eastern Front in Photographs* (London, 2004).

Evans, Richard J., *The Third Reich at War. How the Nazis Led Germany from Conquest to Disaster* (London, 2009).

Farrell, Kevin W., '"Culture of Confidence": The Tactical Excellence of the German Army of the Second World War' in Christopher Kolenda (ed.), *Leadership. The Warrior's Art* (Carlisle, PA, 2001) pp. 177–203.

'Recent Approaches to the German Army of World War II: Is the Topic More Accessible After 65 Years?', *Global War Studies* 7, 2 (2010) pp. 131–156.

Filipescu, Mihai Tone, *Reluctant Axis. The Romanian Army in Russia 1941–1944* (Chapultepeq, 2006).

Fonzi, Paolo, 'The Exploitation of Foreign Territories and the Discussion of *Ostland*'s Currency in 1941' in Kay, Rutherford and Stahel (eds.), *Nazi Policy on the Eastern Front, 1941*, pp. 155–185.

Forczyk, Robert, *Moscow 1941. Hitler's First Defeat* (Oxford, 2006).

Förster, Jürgen, 'The Decisions of the Tripartite Pact States' in Militärgeschichtliches Forschungsamt (ed.), *Germany and the Second World War. Volume IV*, pp. 1021–1048.

'The German Army and the Ideological War Against the Soviet Union' in Gerhard Hirschfeld (ed.), *The Policies of Genocide. Jews and Soviet Prisoners of War in Nazi Germany* (London, 1986) pp. 15–29.

'Motivation and Indoctrination in the Wehrmacht, 1933–1945' in Addison and Calder (eds.), *A Time to Kill*, pp. 263–273.

'Operation Barbarossa as a War of Conquest and Annihilation' in Militärgeschichtliches Forschungsamt (ed.), *Germany and the Second World War. Volume IV*, pp. 481–521.

'Securing "Living-space"' in Militärgeschichtliches Forschungsamt (ed.), *Germany and the Second World War. Volume IV*, pp. 1189–1244.

'Strategy and Policy in Northern Europe' in Militärgeschichtliches Forschungsamt (ed.), *Germany and the Second World War. Volume IV*, pp. 941–1020.

'Volunteers for the European Crusade Against Bolshevism' in Militärgeschichtliches Forschungsamt (ed.), *Germany and the Second World War. Volume IV*, pp. 1049–1080.

Forstmeier, Friedrich, *Odessa 1941. Der Kampf um Stadt und Hafen und die Räumung der Seefestung 15. August bis 16. Oktober 1941* (Freiburg, 1967).

Frieser, Karl-Heinz, *The Blitzkrieg Legend. The 1940 Campaign in the West* (Annapolis, 2005).

Frisch, Franz A. P. in association with Wilbur D. Jones Jr, *Condemned to Live. A Panzer Artilleryman's Five-Front War* (Shippensburg, 2000).

Fröhlich, Elke (ed.), *Die Tagebücher von Joseph Goebbels Teil II Diktate 1941–1945 Band 1 Juli–September 1941* (Munich, 1996).

Die Tagebücher von Joseph Goebbels Teil II Diktate 1941–1945 Band 2 Oktober–Dezember 1941 (Munich, 1996).

Fuchs Richardson, Horst (ed.), *Sieg Heil! War Letters of Tank Gunner Karl Fuchs 1937–1941* (Hamden, 1987).

Fugate, Bryan I., *Operation Barbarossa. Strategy and Tactics on the Eastern Front, 1941* (Novato, 1984).

Fuller, William C. Jr, *Strategy and Power in Russia 1600–1914* (New York, 1992).

Garden, David and Kenneth Andrew (eds.), *The War Diaries of a Panzer Soldier. Erich Hager with the 17th Panzer Division on the Russian Front 1941–1945* (Atglen, 2010).

Gareis, Martin, *Kampf und Ende der Fränkisch-Sudetendeutschen 98. Infanterie-Division* (Eggolsheim, 1956).

Gerlach, Christian, *Kalkulierte Morde. Die deutsche Wirtschafts- und Vernichtungspolitik in Weißrussland 1941 bis 1944* (Hamburg, 2000).

Geyer, Hermann, *Das IX. Armeekorps im Ostfeldzug 1941* (Neckargemünd, 1969).

Geyer, Michael, 'German Strategy in the Age of Machine Warfare, 1914–1945' in Peter Paret (ed.), *Makers of Modern Strategy. From Machiavelli to the Nuclear Age* (Oxford, 1999) pp. 527–597.

Gibbons, Robert, 'Opposition gegen "Barbarossa" im Herbst 1940 – Eine Denkschrift aus der deutschen Botschaft in Moskau', *Vierteljahrshefte für Zeitgeschichte* 23 (1975) pp. 332–340.

Gilbert, Martin, *The Second World War. A Complete History* (London, 2009).

Glantz, David M., *Atlas and Operational Summary of the Border Battles 22 June–1 July 1941* (privately published by David M. Glantz, 2003).

Atlas of the Battle for Kiev Part I. Penetrating the Stalin Line and the Uman' Encirclement 2 July–9 August 1941 (privately published by David M. Glantz, 2005).

Atlas of the Battle for Kiev Part II. The German Advance to the Dnepr River, 9–26 August 1941 (privately published by David M. Glantz, 2005).

Atlas of the Battle for Kiev Part III. The Encirclement and Destruction of the Southwestern Front, 25 August–26 September 1941 (privately published by David M. Glantz, 2005).

Atlas of the Battle of Moscow. The Defensive Phase. 1 October–5 December 1941 (privately published by David M. Glantz, 1997).

Atlas of the Battle of Smolensk 7 July–10 September 1941 (privately published by David M. Glantz, 2001).

Barbarossa Derailed. The Battle for Smolensk 10 July–10 September 1941. Volume 1. The German Advance, the Encirclement Battle, and the First and Second Soviet Counteroffensives, 10 July–24 August 1941 (Solihull, 2010).

Barbarossa Derailed. The Battle for Smolensk 10 July–10 September 1941. Volume 2. The German Offensives on the Flanks and the Third Soviet Counteroffensive, 25 August–10 September 1941 (Solihull, 2012).

Barbarossa. Hitler's Invasion of Russia 1941 (Stroud, 2001).

'The Border Battles on the Bialystok–Minsk Axis: 22–28 June 1941' in Glantz (ed.), *The Initial Period of War on the Eastern Front 22 June–August 1941*, pp. 184–225.

Colossus Reborn. The Red Army at War, 1941–1943 (Lawrence, 2005).

(ed.), *The Initial Period of War on the Eastern Front 22 June–August 1941* (London, 1997).

'Vatutin' in Harold Shukman (ed.), *Stalin's Generals* (London, 1993) pp. 287–298.

Glantz, David M. and Jonathan House, *When Titans Clashed. How the Red Army Stopped Hitler* (Lawrence, 1995).

Goldensohn, Leon, *Nuremberg Interviews. An American Psychiatrist's Conversations with the Defendants and Witnesses*, Robert Gellately (ed.) (New York, 2004).

Gorinov, Mikhail M., 'Muscovites' Moods, 22 June 1941 to May 1942' in Robert Thurston and Bernd Bonwetsch (eds.), *The People's War. Responses to World War II in the Soviet Union* (Chicago, 2000) pp. 108–134.

Gorlitz [Görlitz], Walter (ed.), *The Memoirs of Field-Marshal Keitel. Chief of the German High Command, 1938–1945* (New York, 1966).

Görlitz, Walter, *Paulus and Stalingrad* (London, 1963).

'Reichenau' in Correlli Barnett (ed.), *Hitler's Generals* (London, 1989) pp. 209–219.

Gorodetsky, Gabriel (ed.), *Stafford Cripps in Moscow 1940–1942. Diaries and Papers* (London, 2007).

Gosztony, Peter, *Hitlers Fremde Heere. Das Schicksal der nichtdeutschen Armeen im Ostfeldzug* (Vienna, 1976)

Groehler, Olaf, 'Goals and Reason: Hitler and the German Military' in Joseph Wieczynski (ed.), *Operation Barbarossa. The German Attack on the Soviet Union, June, 1941* (Salt Lake City, 1993) pp. 48–61.

Guderian, Heinz, *Panzer Leader* (New York, 1996).

Günther, Helmut, *Hot Motors, Cold Feet. A Memoir of Service with the Motorcycle Battalion of SS-Division 'Reich' 1940–1941* (Winnipeg, 2004).

Haape, Heinrich with Dennis Henshaw, *Moscow Tram Stop. A Doctor's Experiences with the German Spearhead in Russia* (London, 1957).

Halder, Franz, *Hitler als Feldherr* (Munich, 1949).

Kriegstagebuch. Tägliche Aufzeichnungen des Chefs des Generalstabes des Heeres 1939–1942. Band II Von der geplanten Landung in England bis zum Beginn des Ostfeldzuges (1.7.1940–21.6.1941), Hans-Adolf Jacobsen (ed.) (Stuttgart, 1963).

Kriegstagebuch. Tägliche Aufzeichnungen des Chefs des Generalstabes des Heeres 1939–1942. Band III Der Russlandfeldzug bis zum Marsch auf Stalingrad (22.6.1941–24.9.1942), Hans-Adolf Jacobsen and Alfred Philippi (eds.) (Stuttgart, 1964).

Hammer, Ingrid and Susanne zur Nieden (eds.), *Sehr selten habe ich geweint. Briefe und Tagebücher aus dem Zweiten Weltkrieg von Menschen aus Berlin* (Zürich, 1992).

Hardesty, Von, *Red Phoenix. The Rise of Soviet Air Power 1941–1945* (Washington, DC, 1982).

Harrison, Mark, *Soviet Planning in Peace and War 1938–1945* (Cambridge, 2002).

Hartmann, Christian, *Wehrmacht im Ostkrieg. Front und militärisches Hinterland 1941/42* (Munich, 2010).

Hasenclever, Jörn, *Wehrmacht und Besatzungspolitik. Die Befehlshaber der rückwärtigen Heeresgebiete 1941–1943* (Paderborn, 2010).

Hassell, Ulrich von, *Vom Andern Deutschland* (Freiburg, 1946).

The von Hassell Diaries 1938–1944 (London, 1948).

Hastings, Max, *Bomber Command* (London, 1993).

Hayward, Joel, *Stopped at Stalingrad. The Luftwaffe and Hitler's Defeat in the East, 1942–1943* (Lawrence, 1998).

Heer, Hannes, 'How Amorality Became Normality: Reflections on the Mentality of German Soldiers on the Eastern Front' in Hannes Heer and Klaus Naumann (eds.), *War of Extermination. The German Military in World War II 1941–1944* (New York and Oxford, 2006) pp. 329–344.

Heysing, Günther, *Sturm bis vor Moskaus Tore. Kämpfe der Panzergruppe 4 in der Schlacht um Moskau vom 14. Okt. 1941–5. Dez. 1941* (no place of publication listed, 1942).

Hill, Alexander, 'British "Lend-Lease" Tanks and the Battle for Moscow, November–December 1941: A Research Note', *Journal of Slavic Military Studies* **19**, 2 (June 2006) pp. 289–294.

'British Lend-Lease Tanks and the Battle for Moscow, November–December 1941: Revisited', *Journal of Slavic Military Studies* **22**, 4 (November 2009) pp. 574–587.

The Great Patriotic War of the Soviet Union, 1941–1945. A Documentary Reader (Abingdon and New York, 2010).

The War Behind the Eastern Front. The Soviet Partisan Movement in North-West Russia 1941–1944 (Abingdon and New York, 2006).

Hillgruber, Andreas, 'The German Military Leaders' View of Russia Prior to the Attack on the Soviet Union' in Wegner (ed.), *From Peace to War*, pp. 169–185.

Hoffmann, Joachim, 'The Conduct of the War Through Soviet Eyes' in Militärgeschichtliches Forschungsamt (ed.), *Germany and the Second World War. Volume IV*, pp. 833–941.

Howell, Edgar M., *The Soviet Partisan Movement 1941–1944* (Washington, DC, 1956).

Humburg, Martin, *Das Gesicht des Krieges. Feldpostbriefe von Wehrmachtssoldaten aus der Sowjetunion 1941–1944* (Wiesbaden, 1998).

Hürter, Johannes (ed.), *Ein deutscher General an der Ostfront. Die Briefe und Tagebücher des Gotthard Heinrici 1941/42* (Erfurt, 2001).

Hitlers Heerführer. Die deutschen Oberbefehlshaber im Krieg gegen die Sowjetunion 1941/42 (Munich, 2006).

Irving, David, *Hitler's War. Volume I* (New York, 1977).

The Rise and Fall of the Luftwaffe. The Life of Erhard Milch (London, 1973).

Jacobsen, Hans-Adolf (ed.), *Kriegstagebuch des Oberkommandos der Wehrmacht (Wehrmachtfürungsstab). Band I/2. 1. August 1940–31. Dezember 1941* (Munich, 1982).

Jarausch, Konrad H., *Reluctant Accomplice. A Wehrmacht Soldier's Letters from the Eastern Front* (Princeton, 2011).

Jones, Michael, *The Retreat. Hitler's First Defeat* (London, 2009).

Jones, Robert Huhn, *The Roads to Russia. United States Lend-Lease to the Soviet Union* (Norman, 1969).

Joseph, Frank, *The Axis Air Forces. Flying in Support of the German Luftwaffe* (Santa Barbara, 2011).

Juliá, Xavier Moreno. *La División Azul. Sangre española en Rusia, 1941–1945* (Barcelona, 2005).

Kagan, Frederick W., 'Russia's Wars with Napoleon, 1805–1815' in Kagan and Higham (eds.), *The Military History of Tsarist Russia*, pp. 107–122.

Kagan, Frederick W. and Robin Higham (eds.), *The Military History of Tsarist Russia* (New York, 2002).

Kay, Alex J., *Exploitation, Resettlement, Mass Murder. Political and Economic Planning for German Occupation Policy in the Soviet Union, 1940–1941* (Oxford, 2006).

'Germany's Staatssekretäre, Mass Starvation and the Meeting of 2 May 1941', *Journal of Contemporary History* 41, 4 (October 2006) pp. 685–700.

'"The Purpose of the Russian Campaign Is the Decimation of the Slavic Population by Thirty Million": The Radicalization of German Food Policy in Early 1941' in Kay, Rutherford and Stahel (eds.), *Nazi Policy on the Eastern Front, 1941*, pp. 101–129.

'Revisiting the Meeting of the Staatssekretäre on 2 May 1941: A Response to Klaus Jochen Arnold and Gert C. Lübbers', *Journal of Contemporary History* 43, 1 (January 2008) pp. 93–104.

'A War in a Region Beyond State Control? The German–Soviet War, 1941–1944', *War in History*, 18, 1 (January 2011) pp. 109–122.

Kay, Alex J., Jeff Rutherford and David Stahel (eds.), *Nazi Policy on the Eastern Front, 1941. Total War, Genocide and Radicalization* (Rochester, 2012).

Kemp, Paul, *Convoy! Drama in Arctic Waters* (London, 1993).

Kempowski, Walter (ed.), *Das Echolot Barbarossa '41. Ein kollektives Tagebuch* (Munich, 2004).

Kenez, Peter, 'Black and White: The War on Film' in Stites (ed.), *Culture and Entertainment in Wartime Russia*, pp. 157–175.

Kern, Erich, *Dance of Death* (New York, 1951).

Kern, Ernst, *War Diary 1941–1945. A Report* (New York, 1993).

Kershaw, Ian, *Fateful Choices. Ten Decisions that Changed the World, 1940–1941* (New York, 2007).

Hitler 1936–1945. Nemesis (London, 2001).

Kershaw, Robert, *War Without Garlands. Operation Barbarossa 1941/42* (New York, 2000).

Kesselring, Albrecht, *The Memoirs of Field-Marshal Kesselring* (London, 1988).

Kirchubel, Robert, *Hitler's Panzer's Armies on the Eastern Front* (Barnsley, 2009).

Operation Barbarossa 1941 (3). Army Group Centre (Oxford, 2007).

Kitchen, Martin, *British Policy Towards the Soviet Union During the Second World War* (London, 1986).

A World in Flames. A Short History of the Second World War in Europe and Asia 1939–1945 (London, 1990).

Kleindienst, Jürgen (ed.), *Sei tausendmal gegrüßt. Briefwechsel Irene und Ernst Guicking 1937–1945* (Berlin, 2001; includes CD-ROM).

Kleinfeld, Gerald R. and Lewis A. Tambs, *Hitler's Spanish Legion. The Blue Division in Russia* (St Petersburg, FL, 2005).

Klink, Ernst, 'The Conduct of Operations' in Militärgeschichtliches Forschungsamt (ed.), *Germany and the Second World War. Volume IV*, pp. 525–763.

'The Military Concept of the War Against the Soviet Union' in Militärgeschichtliches Forschungsamt (ed.), *Germany and the Second World War. Volume IV*, pp. 225–325.

Knappe, Siegfried with Ted Brusaw, *Soldat. Reflections of a German Soldier, 1936–1949* (New York, 1992).

Knopp, Guido, *Der Verdammte Krieg. 'Unternehmen Barbarossa'* (Munich, 1998).

Knox, MacGregor, *Hitler's Italian Allies. Royal Armed Forces, Fascist Regime, and the War of 1940–1943* (Cambridge, 2009).

Koch-Erpach, R., '4th Panzer Division's Crossing of the Dnepr River and the Advance to Roslavl' in Glantz (ed.), *The Initial Period of War on the Eastern Front 22 June–August 1941*, pp. 403–404.

Koschorrek, Günter K., *Blood Red Snow. The Memoirs of a German Soldier on the Eastern Front* (London, 2002).

Krebs, Gerhard, 'Japan and the German–Soviet War, 1941' in Wegner (ed.), *From Peace to War*, pp. 541–560.

Krivosheev, G. F. (ed.), *Soviet Casualties and Combat Losses in the Twentieth Century* (London, 1997).

Kroener, Bernhard R., 'The Winter Crisis of 1941–1942: The Distribution of Scarcity or Steps Towards a More Rational Management of Personnel' in Militärgeschichtliches Forschungsamt (ed.), *Germany and the Second World War. Volume V/I*, pp. 1001–1127.

Krumpelt, Ihno, *Das Material und die Kriegführung* (Frankfurt am Main, 1968).

Krylov, N., *Glory Eternal. Defence of Odessa 1941* (Moscow, 1972).

Krylova, Anna, *Soviet Women in Combat. A History of Violence on the Eastern Front* (Cambridge, 2010).

Kubik, Willi, *Erinnerungen eines Panzerschützen 1941–1945. Tagebuchaufzeichnung eines Panzerschützen der Pz.Aufkl.Abt. 13 im Russlandfeldzug* (Würzburg, 2004).

Kuhnert, Max, *Will We See Tomorrow? A German Cavalryman at War, 1939–1942* (London, 1993).

Kunz, Norbert, 'Das Beispiel Charkow: Eine Stadtbevölkerung als Opfer der deutschen Hungerstrategie 1941/42' in Christian Hartmann, Johannes Hürter and Ulrike Jureit (eds.), *Verbrechen der Wehrmacht. Bilanz einer Debatte* (Munich, 2005) pp. 136–144.

Kursietis, Andris J., *The Wehrmacht at War 1939–1945. The Units and Commanders of the German Ground Forces During World War II* (Soesterberg, 1999).

Lamb, Richard, 'Kluge' in Correlli Barnett (ed.), *Hitler's Generals* (London, 1989) pp. 395–409.

Lammers, Walther (ed.), *'Fahrtberichte' aus der Zeit des deutsch-sowjetischen Krieges 1941. Protokolle des Begleitoffiziers des Kommandierenden Generals LIII. Armeekorps* (Boppard am Rhein, 1988).

Landon, H. C. Robbins and Sebastian Leitner (eds.), *Diary of a German Soldier* (London, 1963).

Lange, Horst, *Tagebücher aus dem Zweiten Weltkrieg* (Mainz, 1979).

Leach, Barry, *German Strategy Against Russia 1939–1941* (Oxford, 1973).

LeDonne, John P., *The Grand Strategy of the Russian Empire, 1650–1831* (Oxford, 2004).

Lehnstaedt, Stephan, 'The Minsk Experience: German Occupiers and Everyday Life in the Capital of Belarus' in Kay, Rutherford and Stahel (eds.), *Nazi Policy on the Eastern Front, 1941*, pp. 240–266.

Lévesque, Jean, 'A Peasant Ordeal: The Soviet Countryside' in Stone (ed.) *The Soviet Union at War 1941–1945*, pp. 182–214.

Leyen, Ferdinand Prinz von der, *Rückblick zum Mauerwald. Vier Kriegsjahre im OKH* (Munich, 1965).

Liddell Hart, Basil, *The Other Side of the Hill* (London, 1999).

Lieven, Dominic, *Russia Against Napoleon. The Battle for Europe, 1807 to 1814* (London, 2010).

Lossberg, Bernhard von, *Im Wehrmachtführungsstab. Bericht eines Generalstabsoffiziers* (Hamburg, 1950).

Loud, Graham A., *The Crusade of Frederick Barbarossa. The History of the Expedition of the Emperor Frederick and Related Texts* (Farnham, 2010).

Lower, Wendy, 'Axis Collaboration, Operation Barbarossa, and the Holocaust in Ukraine' in Kay, Rutherford and Stahel (eds.), *Nazi Policy on the Eastern Front, 1941*, pp. 186–219.

Nazi Empire-Building and the Holocaust in Ukraine (Chapel Hill, 2005).

Lubbeck, William with David B. Hurt, *At Leningrad's Gates. The Story of a Soldier with Army Group North* (Philadelphia, 2006).

Lubrich, Oliver (ed.), *Travels in the Reich. Foreign Authors Report from Germany* (Chicago, 2010).

Lucas, James, *Das Reich. The Military Role of the 2nd SS Division* (London, 1991).

War of the Eastern Front 1941–1945. The German Soldier in Russia (London, 1980).

Luck, Hans von, *Panzer Commander. The Memoirs of Colonel Hans von Luck* (New York, 1989).

Macksey, Kenneth, *Guderian. Panzer General* (London, 1975).

Magenheimer, Heinz, *Hitler's War. Germany's Key Strategic Decisions 1940–1945* (London, 1999).

Maisky, Ivan, *Memoirs of a Soviet Ambassador. The War 1939–1943* (London, 1967).

de Maizière, Ulrich, *In der Pflicht. Lebensbericht eines deutschen Soldaten im 20. Jahrhundert* (Bielefeld, 1989).

Manstein, Erich von, *Lost Victories* (Novato, 1994).

Verlorene Siege. Erinnerungen 1939–1944 (Bonn, 1991).

Mark-Alan, Roy, *White Coats Under Fire. With the Italian Expedition Corps in Russia – 1941* (New York, 1972).

Mawdsley, Evan, *Thunder in the East. The Nazi–Soviet War 1941–1945* (London, 2005).

Mazower, Mark, *Hitler's Empire. Nazi Rule in Occupied Europe* (London, 2009).

Megargee, Geoffrey P., *Inside Hitler's High Command* (Lawrence, 2000).

'Questions and Answers: Geoffrey P. Megargee', *Global War Studies* 7, 2, (2010) pp. 193–202.

'Vernichtungskrieg: Strategy, Operations, and Genocide in the German Invasion of the Soviet Union, 1941' in *Acta of the International Commission on Military History's XXXIV Annual Congress* (Commissione Italiana di Storia Militare, 2009) pp. 459–464.

War of Annihilation. Combat and Genocide on the Eastern Front 1941 (Lanham, 2006).

Meier-Welcker, Hans, *Aufzeichnungen eines Generalstabsoffiziers 1939–1942* (Freiburg, 1982).

Mellinger, George, *Soviet Lend-Lease Fighter Aces of World War 2* (Oxford, 2006).

Menger, Manfred, 'Germany and the Finnish "Separate War" Against the Soviet Union' in Wegner (ed.), *From Peace to War*, pp. 525–539.

Menning, Bruce W., 'The Imperial Russian Army 1725-1796' in Kagan and Higham (eds.), *The Military History of Tsarist Russia*, pp. 48–75.

Merridale, Catherine, *Ivan's War. Life and Death in the Red Army, 1939–1945* (New York, 2006).

Metelmann, Henry, *Through Hell for Hitler* (Havertown, 2005).

Meyer, Georg, *Adolf Heusinger. Dienst eines deutschen Soldaten 1915 bis 1964* (Berlin, 2001).

Militärgeschichtliches Forschungsamt (ed.), *Das Deutsche Reich und der Zweite Weltkrieg. Band 4. Der Angriff auf die Sowjetunion* (Stuttgart, 1983).

(ed.), *Germany and the Second World War. Volume IV. The Attack on the Soviet Union* (Oxford, 1998).

(ed.), *Germany and the Second World War. Volume V/I. Organization and Mobilization of the German Sphere of Power* (Oxford, 2000).

Ministry of Foreign Affairs of the USSR (ed.), *Stalin's Correspondence with Churchill, Attlee, Roosevelt and Truman 1941–1945* (New York, 1958).

Mitcham, Samuel W. Jr, *The Men of Barbarossa. Commanders of the German Invasion of Russia, 1941* (Newbury, 2009).

Moritz, Erhard (ed.), *Fall Barbarossa. Dokumente zur Vorbereitung der faschistischen Wehrmacht auf die Aggression gegen die Sowjetunion (1940/41)* (Berlin, 1970).

Muggeridge, Malcolm (ed.), *Ciano's Diary 1939–1943* (Kingswood, 1947).

Muller, Richard, *The German Air War in Russia* (Baltimore, 1992).

Müller, Rolf-Dieter, *An der Seite der Wehrmacht. Hitlers ausländische Helfer beim 'Kreuzzug gegen den Bolschewismus' 1941–1945* (Berlin, 2007).

'Beginnings of a Reorganization of the War Economy at the Turn of 1941/1942' in Militärgeschichtliches Forschungsamt (ed.), *Germany and the Second World War. Volume V/I*, pp. 722–786.

'The Failure of the Economic "Blitzkrieg Strategy"' in Militärgeschichtliches Forschungsamt (ed.), *Germany and the Second World War. Volume IV*, pp. 1081–1188.

'The Victor's Hubris: Germany Loses Its Lead in Armaments After the French Campaign' in Militärgeschichtliches Forschungsamt (ed.), *Germany and the Second World War. Volume V/I*, pp. 564–721.

Müller, Rolf-Dieter and Gerd R. Ueberschär, *Hitler's War in the East 1941–1945. A Critical Assessment* (Oxford, 2009).

Müller-Hillebrand, Burkhart, *Das Heer 1933–1945. Band III. Der Zweifrontenkrieg. Das Heer vom Beginn des Feldzuges gegen die Sowjetunion bis zum Kriegsende* (Frankfurt am Main, 1969).

Munoz, Antonio and Oleg V. Romanko, *Hitler's White Russians. Collaboration, Extermination and Anti-Partisan Warfare in Byelorussia 1941–1944. A Study of White Russian Collaboration and German Occupation Policies* (New York, 2003).

Munzel, Oskar, *Panzer-Taktik. Raids gepanzerter Verbände im Ostfeldzug 1941/42* (Neckargemünd, 1959).

Murray, Williamson, *The Luftwaffe 1933–1945. Strategy for Defeat* (Washington, DC, 1996).

Nagorski, Andrew, *The Greatest Battle. Stalin, Hitler, and the Desperate Struggle for Moscow that Changed the Course of World War II* (New York, 2007).

Neitzel, Sönke, *Tapping Hitler's Generals. Transcripts of Secret Conversations, 1942–1945* (St Paul, 2007).

Nelson, Anne, *Red Orchestra. The Story of the Berlin Underground and the Circle of Friends Who Resisted Hitler* (New York, 2009).

Neulen, Hans Werner, *In the Skies of Europe. Air Forces Allied to the Luftwaffe 1939–1945* (Ramsbury, 2000).

Newton, Steven H., *Hitler's Commander. Field Marshal Walter Model – Hitler's Favorite General* (Cambridge, MA, 2006).

Noggle, Anne, *A Dance with Death. Soviet Airwomen in World War II* (College Station, TX, 1994).

Obhodaš, Amir and Jason D. Mark, *Croatian Legion. The 369th (Croatian) Infantry Regiment on the Eastern Front 1941–1943* (Pymble, 2011).

Obryn'ba, Nikolai I., *Red Partisan. The Memoir of a Soviet Resistance Fighter on the Eastern Front* (Washington, DC, 2007).

Ochsenknecht, Ingeborg, *'Als ob der Schnee alles zudeckte'. Eine Krankenschwester erinnert sich an ihren Kriegseinsatz an der Ostfront* (Berlin, 2005).

Osten-Sacken, Peter von der, *Vier Jahre Barbarossa. Authentische Berichte aus dem Russlandfeldzug 1941 bis 1945* (Frankfurt am Main, 2005).

O'Sullivan, Donal, *Dealing with the Devil. Anglo-Soviet Intelligence Cooperation During the Second World War* (New York, 2010).

Overmans, Rüdiger, *Deutsche militärische Verluste im Zweiten Weltkrieg* (Munich, 2000).

Overy, Richard, *Russia's War* (London, 1997).

  'Statistics' in I. C. B. Dear and M. R. D. Foot (eds.), *The Oxford Companion to the Second World War* (Oxford, 1995).

  Why the Allies Won (New York, 1996).

Pabst, Helmut, *The Outermost Frontier. A German Soldier in the Russian Campaign* (London, 1957).

Paoletti, Ciro, *A Military History of Italy* (Westport, 2008).

Pennington, Reina, 'Offensive Women: Women in Combat in the Red Army in the Second World War', *Journal of Military History* **74**, 3 (July 2010) pp. 775–820.

  Wings, Women, and War. Soviet Airwomen in World War II Combat (Lawrence, 2001).

  'Women' in Stone (ed.), *The Soviet Union at War 1941–1945*, pp. 93–120.

Pichler, Hans, *Truppenarzt und Zeitzeuge. Mit der 4. SS-Polizei-Division an vorderster Front* (Dresden, 2006).

Piekalkiewicz, Janusz, *Moscow 1941. The Frozen Offensive* (London, 1981).

Pleshakov, Constantine, *Stalin's Folly. The Tragic First Ten Days of World War II on the Eastern Front* (New York, 2005).

Plocher, Hermann, *The German Air Force Versus Russia, 1941* (New York, 1965).

Pohl, Dieter, *Die Herrschaft der Wehrmacht. Deutsche Militärbesatzung und einheimische Bevölkerung in der Sowjetunion 1941–1944* (Munich, 2008).

Porter, Cathy and Mark Jones, *Moscow in World War II* (London, 1987).

Raus, Erhard, *Panzer Operations. The Eastern Front Memoir of General Raus, 1941–1945*, Steven H. Newton (ed.) (Cambridge, MA, 2005).

Rauss [Raus], Erhard, 'Effects of Climate on Combat in European Russia' in Tsouras (ed.) *Fighting in Hell*, pp. 167–258.

'Russian Combat Methods in World War II' in Tsouras (ed.), *Fighting in Hell*, pp. 13–153.

Reddemann, Karl (ed.), *Zwischen Front und Heimat. Der Briefwechsel des münsterischen Ehepaares Agnes und Albert Neuhaus 1940-1944* (Münster, 1996).

Rees, Laurence, *War of the Century. When Hitler Fought Stalin* (London, 1999).

Reese, Roger R., *Why Stalin's Soldiers Fought. The Red Army's Military Effectiveness in World War II* (Lawrence, 2011).

Reese, Willy Peter, *A Stranger to Myself. The Inhumanity of War. Russia, 1941–1944* (New York, 2005).

Reinhardt, Hans, 'Panzer-Gruppe 3 in der Schlacht von Moskau und ihre Erfahrungen im Rückzug', *Wehrkunde* Heft 9 (September 1953).

Reinhardt, Klaus, *Moscow: The Turning Point. The Failure of Hitler's Strategy in the Winter of 1941–1942* (Oxford, 1992).

Roberts, Geoffrey, *Stalin's Wars. From World War to Cold War, 1939–1953* (New Haven, 2006).

Römer, Felix, '"Kein Problem für die Truppe"', *Die Zeit Geschichte – Hitlers Krieg im Osten* 2 (2011) pp. 42–45.

Der Kommissarbefehl. Wehrmacht und NS-Verbrechen an der Ostfront 1941/42 (Paderborn, 2008).

'The Wehrmacht in the War of Ideologies: The Army and Hitler's Criminal Orders on the Eastern Front' in Kay, Rutherford and Stahel (eds.), *Nazi Policy on the Eastern Front, 1941*, pp. 73–100.

Röttiger, Hans, 'XXXXI Panzer Corps During the Battle of Moscow in 1941 as a Component of Panzer Group 3' in Steven H. Newton (ed.), *German Battle Tactics in the Russian Front 1941–1945* (Atglen, 1994) pp. 13–54.

Rudel, Hans Ulrich, *Stuka Pilot* (New York, 1979).

Rutherford, Jeffrey, 'The Radicalization of German Occupation Policies: *Wirtschaftsstab Ost* and the 121st Infantry Division in Pavlovsk, 1941' in Kay, Rutherford and Stahel (eds.), *Nazi Policy on the Eastern Front, 1941*, pp. 130–154.

Salisbury, Harrison E. (ed.), *Marshal Zhukov's Greatest Battles* (London, 1971).

The Unknown War (London, 1978).

Schäufler, Hans (ed.), *Knight's Cross Panzers. The German 35th Panzer Regiment in WWII* (Mechanicsburg, 2010).

Scheuer, Alois, *Briefe aus Russland. Feldpostbriefe des Gefreiten Alois Scheuer 1941–1942* (St Ingbert, 2000).

Schmider, Klaus, 'German Military Tradition and the Expert Opinion on Werner Mölders: Opening a Dialogue Among Scholars', *Global War Studies* 7, 1 (2010) pp. 6–29.

Schröder, Hans Joachim, 'German Soldiers' Experiences During the Initial Phase of the Russian Campaign' in Wegner (ed.), *From Peace to War*, pp. 309–324.

Schüler, Klaus, 'The Eastern Campaign as a Transportation and Supply Problem' in Wegner (ed.), *From Peace to War*, pp. 205–222.

Schulte, Theo, *The German Army and Nazi Policies in Occupied Russia* (Oxford, 1989).

'Die Wehrmacht und die nationalsozialistische Besatzungspolitik in der Sowjetunion' in Roland G. Foerster (ed.), *'Unternehmen Barbarossa'. Zum historischen Ort der deutsch-sowjetischen Beziehungen von 1933 bis Herbst 1941* (Munich, 1993) pp. 163–176.

Seaton, Albert, *The Battle for Moscow* (New York, 1971).

The Russo-German War 1941–1945 (Novato, 1971).

Sebastian, Mihail, *Journal, 1935–1944* (London, 2003).

Shepherd, Ben, *War in the Wild East. The German Army and Soviet Partisans* (Cambridge, 2004).

Showalter, Dennis, *The Wars of Frederick the Great* (London, 1996).

Shtemenko, Sergei M., *The Soviet General Staff at War 1941–1945* (Moscow, 1975).

Simms, Brendan, 'Walther von Reichenau: der politische General' in Ronald Smelser and Enrico Syring (eds.), *Die Militärelite des Dritten Reiches. 27 biographische Skizzen* (Berlin, 1995) pp. 423–445.

Slepyan, Kenneth, 'The People's Avengers: The Partisan Movement' in Stone (ed.), *The Soviet Union at War 1941–1945*, pp. 154–181.

Stalin's Guerrillas. Soviet Partisans in World War II (Lawrence, 2006).

Smelser, Ronald and Edward J. Davies II, *The Myth of the Eastern Front. The Nazi–Soviet War in American Popular Culture* (Cambridge, 2008).

Smith, Bradley F., *Sharing Secrets with Stalin. How the Allies Traded Intelligence, 1941–1945* (Lawrence, 1996).

Smith, Howard K., *Last Train from Berlin* (New York, 1943).

Snyder, Timothy, *Bloodlands. Europe Between Hitler and Stalin* (New York, 2010).

Stader, Ingo (ed.), *Ihr daheim und wir hier draußen. Ein Briefwechsel zwischen Ostfront und Heimat Juni 1941–März 1943* (Cologne, 2006).

Stahel, David, '*Bloodlands: Europe Between Hitler and Stalin*', *Journal of Military History* 75, 1 (January 2011) pp. 320–322.

  Kiev 1941. Hitler's Battle for Supremacy in the East (Cambridge, 2012).

  Operation Barbarossa and Germany's Defeat in the East (Cambridge, 2009).

  'Radicalizing Warfare: The German Command and the Failure of Operation Barbarossa' in Kay, Rutherford and Stahel (eds.), *Nazi Policy on the Eastern Front, 1941*, pp. 19–44.

Stahlberg, Alexander, *Bounden Duty. The Memoirs of a German Officer 1932–1945* (London, 1990).

Statiev, Alexander, 'Blocking Units in the Red Army', *Journal of Military History* 76, 2 (April 2012) pp. 475–495.

Steiger, Rudolf, *Armour Tactics in the Second World War. Panzer Army Campaigns of 1939–1941 in German War Diaries* (Oxford, 1991).

Stein, George H., *The Waffen SS. Hitler's Elite Guard at War 1939–1945* (New York, 1984).

Stein, Marcel, *A Flawed Genius. Field Marshal Walter Model. A Critical Biography* (Solihull, 2010).

Steinert, Marlis, *Hitlers Krieg und die Deutschen. Stimmung und Haltung der deutschen Bevölkerung im Zweiten Weltkrieg* (Düsseldorf and Vienna, 1970).

Stephan, Robert W., *Stalin's Secret War. Soviet Counterintelligence Against the Nazis, 1941–1945* (Lawrence, 2004).

Stern, J. P., *Hitler. The Führer and the People* (Berkeley, 1992).

Stites, Richard (ed.), *Culture and Entertainment in Wartime Russia* (Bloomington and Indianapolis, 1995).

Stolfi, R. H. S., *Hitler's Panzers East. World War II Reinterpreted* (Norman, 1993).

Stone, David R., *A Military History of Russia. From Ivan the Terrible to the War in Chechnya* (Westport, 2006).

  (ed.), *The Soviet Union at War 1941–1945* (Barnsley, 2010).

Strauss, Franz Josef, *Friedens- und Kriegserlebnisse einer Generation. Ein Kapitel Weltgeschichte aus der Sicht der Panzerjäger-Abteilung 38 (SF) in der ehemaligen 2. (Wiener) Panzerdivision* (Neckergemünd, 1977).

Streit, Christian, *Keine Kameraden. Die Wehrmacht und die sowjetischen Kriegsgefangenen 1941–1945* (Bonn, 1997).

'Soviet Prisoners of War in the Hands of the Wehrmacht' in Hannes Heer and Klaus Naumann (eds.), *War of Extermination. The German Military in World War II 1941–1944* (Oxford, 2006) pp. 80–91.

'Die sowjetischen Kriegsgefangenen in der Hand der Wehrmacht' in Walter Manoschek (ed.), *Die Wehrmacht im Rassenkrieg. Der Vernichtungskrieg hinter der Front* (Vienna, 1996) pp. 74–89.

Stützel, Rudolf, *Feldpost. Briefe und Aufzeichnungen eines 17-Jährigen 1940–1945* (Hamburg, 2005).

Sweeting, C. G., *Blood and Iron. The German Conquest of Sevastopol* (Washington, DC, 2004).

Taylor, Brian, *Barbarossa to Berlin. A Chronology of the Campaigns on the Eastern Front 1941 to 1945. Volume 1 The Long Drive East 22 June 1941 to 18 November 1942* (Staplehurst, 2003).

Tewes, Ernst, *Seelsorger bei den Soldaten. Erinnerungen an die Zeit von 1940 bis 1945* (Munich, 1995).

Thomas, David, 'Foreign Armies East and German Military Intelligence in Russia 1941–1945', *Journal of Contemporary History* 22 (1987) pp. 261–301.

Thomas, Georg, *Geschichte der deutsch Wehr- und Rüstungswirtschaft (1918–1943/45)*, Wolfgang Birkenfeld (ed.) (Boppard am Rhein, 1966).

Tooze, Adam, *The Wages of Destruction. The Making and Breaking of the Nazi Economy* (London, 2006).

Trevor-Roper, Hugh R. (ed.), *Hitler's Table Talk, 1941–1944. His Private Conversations* (London, 2000).

(ed.), *Hitler's War Directives 1939–1945* (London, 1964).

True to Type. A Selection from Letters and Diaries of German Soldiers and Civilians Collected on the Soviet–German Front (London, undated).

Tsouras, Peter G. (ed.), *Fighting in Hell. The German Ordeal on the Eastern Front* (New York, 1998).

'Introduction' in Tsouras (ed.), *Fighting in Hell*, pp. 1–9.

(ed.), *Panzers on the Eastern Front. General Erhard Raus and His Panzer Divisions in Russia 1941–1945* (London, 2002).

Turney, Alfred W., *Disaster at Moscow. Von Bock's Campaigns 1941–1942* (Albuquerque, 1970).

Tuyll, Hubert P. van, *Feeding the Bear. American Aid to the Soviet Union, 1941–1945* (Westport, 1989).

Ueberschär, Gerd R. (ed.), 'Armeebefehl des Oberbefehlshabers der 6. Armee, Generalfeldmarschall von Reichenau, vom 10.10.1941' in Ueberschär and Wette (eds.), 'Unternehmen Barbarossa', pp. 339–340.

(ed.), 'Befehl des Oberbefehlshabers der Heeresgruppe Süd, Generalfeldmarschall von Rundstedt, vom 12.10.1941' in Ueberschär and Wette (eds.), 'Unternehmen Barbarossa', p. 340.

'Das Scheitern des Unternehmens "Barbarossa": Der deutsch-sowjetische Krieg vom Überfall bis zur Wende vor Moskau im Winter 1941/42' in Ueberschär and Wette (eds.), 'Unternehmen Barbarossa', pp. 141–172.

Ueberschär, Gerd R. and Wolfram Wette (eds.), 'Unternehmen Barbarossa'. Der deutsche Überfall auf die Sowjetunion 1941 (Paderborn, 1984).

Vehviläinen, Olli, Finland in the Second World War. Between Germany and Russia (New York, 2002).

Volkogonov, Dmitrij A., 'Stalin as Supreme Commander' in Wegner (ed.), From Peace to War, pp. 463–478.

Wagener, Carl, Moskau 1941. Der Angriff auf die russische Hauptstadt (Dorheim, 1985).

Wagner, Elisabeth (ed.), Der Generalquartiermeister. Briefe und Tagebuchaufzeichnungen des Generalquartiermeisters des Heeres General der Artillerie Eduard Wagner (Munich, 1963).

Warlimont, Walter, Im Hauptquartier der deutschen Wehrmacht 1939 bis 1945. Band 1: September 1939–November 1942 (Koblenz, 1990). English translation: Warlimont, Walter, Inside Hitler's Headquarters, 1939–1945 (New York, 1964).

Weal, John, More Bf 109 Aces of the Russian Front (Oxford, 2007).

Wegner, Bernd (ed.), From Peace to War. Germany, Soviet Russia and the World, 1939–1941 (Oxford, 1997).

Weinberg, Gerhard L., 'The Yelnya–Dorogobuzh Area of Smolensk Oblast' in John A. Armstrong (ed.), Soviet Partisans in World War II (Madison, 1964) pp. 389–457.

Werth, Alexander, Russia at War 1941–1945 (New York, 1964).

Wette, Wolfram, Retter in Uniform. Handlungsspielräume im Vernichtungskreig der Wehrmacht (Frankfurt am Main, 2003).

The Wehrmacht. History, Myth, Reality (Cambridge, 2006).

Wettstein, Adrian, 'Operation "Barbarossa" und Stadtkampf', Militärgeschichtliche Zeitschrift 66 (2007) pp. 21–44.

'Urban Warfare Doctrine on the Eastern Front' in Kay, Rutherford and Stahel (eds.), Nazi Policy on the Eastern Front, 1941, pp. 45–72.

Woodman, Richard, Arctic Convoys 1941–1945 (Barnsley, 2007).

Zamoyski, Adam, 1812. Napoleon's Fatal March on Moscow (London, 2004).

Zhukov, G. K., The Memoirs of Marshal Zhukov (London, 1971).

Ziemke, Earl F., The German Northern Theater of Operations 1940–1945 (Washington, DC, 1959).

Ziemke, Earl F. and Magna E. Bauer, Moscow to Stalingrad. Decision in the East (New York, 1988).

Zinsser, Hans, Rats, Lice and History (Boston, 1963).

Zobel, Horst, '3rd Panzer Division Operations' in Glantz (ed.), *The Initial Period of War on the Eastern Front 22 June–August 1941*, pp. 238–247.
'3rd Panzer Division's Advance to Mogilev' in Glantz (ed.), *The Initial Period of War on the Eastern Front 22 June–August 1941*, pp. 393–397.

INDEX

BASEMENT

SEP. 2013